ISBN 978-1-330-40053-1
PIBN 10052274

1 MONTH OF
FREE
READING

at

www.ForgottenBooks.com

By purchasing this book you are eligible for one month membership to ForgottenBooks.com, giving you unlimited access to our entire collection of over 700,000 titles via our web site and mobile apps.

To claim your free month visit:

www.forgottenbooks.com/free52274

Similar Books Are Available from
www.forgottenbooks.com

CONTENTS OF VOLUME II.

CONTENTS

LIST OF ILLUSTRATIONS TO VOLUME II.

LIST OF ILLUSTRATIONS

ACROSS WIDEST AFRICA

———•———

CHAPTER I.

No accusation of wasting time upon the road could be brought against me, nor of sparing myself. If halts were made anywhere it was because of my animals. At Dem Zebir, having given my poor donkeys a short rest, I was, by May 4th, quite ready to start again with my caravan and the faithful Somali.

During the three days I stayed at Dem Zebir I greatly enjoyed the company of Bimbashi Percival, a fully-awake and able officer, who knew his work well. I experienced two terrific tornadoes while at that post, and one evening, while dining with the Bimbashi, we actually had to eat in our mackintoshes inside the house, with servants holding umbrellas over our heads and over the dishes. Rain came down in torrents through the roof, and at one moment the howling wind broke through a barricaded window, blowing tablecloth and most things off the table. As it was, our food was floating or sunken in water according to its specific weight.

The frontier between the Bahr-el-Ghazal province and the High-Ubanghi in the French Congo had not been properly defined. The watershed between the Nile Valley and the Ubanghi should, of course, be the natural boundary line, but there is so little difference in the elevation that an accurate survey will be necessary before the exact geographical limit of the two countries is established, and before it can be settled which tribes are actually under British protection and which under French.

To the west of Dem Zebir the country at once becomes slightly more hilly, and a few marches are sufficient to take us to streams flowing towards the south or the south-west instead of northwards into the Nile basin.

I obtained a few Banda and Kresh carriers, who were to help at the beginning of the journey. One Banda, particularly, was a valuable addition to the party—a stout little fellow with a big paunch and a comical face, as flat as if somebody had sat on it ; he was the first black native I had met in Africa who had really a hearty laugh. True enough, he always laughed about nothing ; but at any rate he did laugh. Central Africa has a depressing effect. One never sees nor hears anybody enjoy life thoroughly. All moan, sulk, and look or feel nasty about everything. So the jolly merriment of this fellow was a great moral boon to me.

When we started, as is generally the case with jocular people, his companions made him carry the heaviest load. As he struggled to lift the package upon his head and discovered the heavy weight, he roared loudly at the trick that had been played upon him, and kept on roaring while they deposited the load upon him, nearly smothering him under it. His already short neck was almost telescoped under the load, his body was bent in two, and he just managed to keep up by supporting himself with his hands upon his knees When he stopped laughing, he marched along all right. Every now and then, however, he burst out again into uproarious hilarity and collapsed with the load on the top of him. We all laughed at the comical scene. Personally I was glad to move on once more, although I felt that we had hard times to face. I well knew that we had before us a troublesome journey down to the Mbomu river in the French Congo, as no trail existed, and we should have to cross the dense forest as best we could.

There was a trail from Dem Zebir by making a détour as far as Kossinga, and then down to the Babodo River as far as Rafay. That trail was beaten a good deal by natives carrying rubber and ivory into the French Congo, but from Dem Zebir direct—the way I travelled—no communication existed with the French. Therefore, even the trail that was supposed to have been there at the time of Zebir Pasha was now smothered in vegetation and could not be traced.

We were travelling over undulating country, mostly descending through scantily-wooded regions, with a great deal of shrub and comparatively young trees with a good space between them. Only an hour after leaving Dem Zebir we had descended by a depression of volcanic iron rock to 240 feet lower than Dem Zebir (1,750 feet).

We first travelled due west, then made a great détour towards the west-south-west. One or two abandoned villages were passed, and we followed a channel made by the water on the slope of a hill, where boulders of iron-stone were sometimes exposed. Towards noon we had risen again to 2,150 feet, and at 1.35 p.m. we stopped higher up in an open space, where we found two or three large pools of stagnant water in the flat volcanic rock (2,290 feet).

Although this place was fairly high, the air was heavy and saturated with miasma. It gave me, there and then, a severe attack of fever, although this was in the middle of the day and no mosquitoes were about— the mosquitoes of Central Africa being most obliging and never putting in an appearance before sunset.

Negakombu was, as far as I could ascertain, the name of this delightful spot, some eleven miles from Dem Zebir. One of the characteristics of malarial fever is the rapidity with which it can take every atom of strength away from you. When you are attacked by it you become in a few minutes as limp as a rag and hardly have the strength to stand. In my experience it is always fatal on these occasions to give in. I found that a powerful dose of castor oil taken at once almost invariably effected a cure. It certainly did on my men and myself, where quinine, which I had tried on other occasions, made my men irritable, almost drove them to lunacy, and whilst temporarily suspending the fever would not drive it away altogether like a good purge.

On May 5th we continued rising gently among a lot of stunted trees and some magnificent *cudjera* trees of immense size. The *endayii* of the Kresh, or *layük*, as it was called in the impure Arabic spoken at Dem Zebir, was also to be found here, a gum tree, which when cut into small pieces and placed in cold water overnight turned the whole into a glutinous substance. The *boggu* cactus was also found here.

Three hours after starting from camp we found a *khor* which flowed at that point towards the south-west,

Two wild dogs and a Kresh Sultan.

but which eventually turned northwards into the Biri. By noon we had arrived at the Biri river (1,910 feet), also flowing south-west in this portion, but eventually, as we have already seen, flowing northwards into the Chel and thence into the Bahr-el-Ghazal. We found quantities of volcanic rock in patches as we went along.

My Somali and I had a good deal of trouble with our donkeys, as we had to look after all the animals, neither the Kresh nor the Banda showing any inclination to go within a reasonable distance of them. In such rough country the animals would often collide with trees, and the loads were constantly tumbling off. The carriers I had were not sufficient to take the animals along un-laden. In fact, with the extra provisions of grain which I had purchased at Dem Zebir, all the beasts were heavily laden.

The next day we went over rolling country, sometimes with open grassy patches with merely a few trees upon them. We crossed two or three small *khors* and the usual flat tables of volcanic rock. We saw many elephants that day and several buck; also some wild dogs, with large upstanding ears and short hair. They were not unlike a cross between a dog and a hyena; they were fierce and had long, pointed teeth.

Stunted vegetation was again on each side, with big *cudjera* trees similar to those of the previous day. We arrived at the Bibi river, about four yards wide and one foot deep. We had done fairly good marching at the rate of about three miles an hour, the highest elevation on our way having been 2,150 feet. The elevation of the Bibi river itself was 2,140 feet, and it flowed north.

This was most unhealthy country and I got another bad attack of fever, which made marching painful until I could unpack the loads. The heat was intense, and I think fever was brought on again by the great exertion of loading the animals some forty or fifty times a day. Each load, weighing fifty to sixty pounds, had to be lifted up to the pack-saddle ; in addition we had the tiring work of chasing the animals about in the high grass, among shrubs and over broken ground, which was indeed trying. The thermometer registered as much as 42° to 44° Centigrade (107$\frac{3}{4}$° to 111$\frac{1}{5}$° Fahrenheit), and this extra exertion was more than most Europeans could stand.

At times I marched ahead so as to get the donkeys to follow. The animals had a way of always following me, as I generally gave them barley when we arrived in camp. Unfortunately that day, while I was half stupefied by the intense fever, some of my animals behind were lost, and when I arrived at a place suitable to make a camp at six in the evening, I had to start back with my Somali in order to try and find the missing animals. I became so exhausted—as we had already marched from seven o'clock in the morning, nearly eleven hours—that I had to entrust the Somali with the job of finding the animals again, while I remained on the way lying on a few vines and some grass, making an improvised bed. Myriads of flies and mosquitoes, ants and beetles, moths and insects of all kinds buzzed round, and bit me and stung me all over.

Far from believing that mosquitoes give fever, I always noticed that mosquitoes rather took away fever from you. In fact, when I was in good health, although many mosquitoes buzzed round me, few of them actually stung, whereas the moment I was attacked by fever hundreds of them would settle on me and sting me for all they were worth.

Tornadoes having been frequent of late, the lower vegetation was beginning to putrefy and the air in this region was most noxious. On May 7th I had another strong attack of fever, as during the night the air was so pestilential that I felt all the time it was poisoning me. My strength had given way to such an extent that I was unable to make a start until late in the afternoon.

We gradually rose to 2,350 feet, forcing our way through fairly dense vegetation with no trail at all, except that here and there we found elephant trails which helped us sometimes for some hundreds of yards when they proceeded in the direction we wanted. We came across an extensive dome of volcanic and surface iron-red rock, and we crossed two small *khors* about one hour's distance apart. When we came to the third *khor* (2,110 feet) an hour later—this one flowing south—I had to halt, having marched only eight miles that day. I was too exhausted to go on.

On the next morning, May 8th, we passed three small streamlets, with red-barked, yellow-leaved *congo* trees. More domes of granite were encountered. Three hours after leaving camp we reached the summit (2,620 feet) of a group of three hillocks of volcanic ironstone, after which we found ourselves on a big flat table-land quite open and grassy for several hundred yards.

We began to descend on the west side into a lovely forest of immense trees with innumerable vines. These trees were much of the same kind as those we had seen so far, only of greater age and healthier in condition, instead of being stunted in growth, owing to constant fires, like those we had so far seen. Every now and then there were big patches of grass in the forest, the trees having evidently been cleared by fire.

At noon we crossed a little crystal-like rivulet flowing southward, and at 12.35 we reached the edge of the plateau (2,800 feet) by a steep ascent on rock which gave us no end of trouble in pushing donkeys and loads to the summit This was the highest point on our route between Dem Zebir and the Mbomu River. When we reached the summit I observed nothing higher or as high to the south-west or south. I think that this is the highest point of the watershed, and possibly the point where the frontier line should be. On a fine clear day one should obtain a beautiful panorama from this point, but, unfortunately, at the time of my visit the stifling moisture was such that there was a thick mist hanging over the earth's surface, and one could only see things that projected above this layer of mist.

This portion was extremely rocky, and large patches of volcanic rock were again encountered. Fortunately for my animals, we came across open stretches of country with excellent grazing. We came to one *khor*, and soon after, at 1.45, to another, the latter flowing south-south-east at an elevation of 2,500 feet. On this one we encamped, as I was still weak from the attack of fever the previous day.

On May 9th we left at 7.25 in the morning, and we had before us flat, fairly open country, upon which grew a few *lulu* trees, with their long oval leaves— very prominently ribbed—of a deep green and slightly fluted. When cut, these emit a white milky substance. There were fairly tall *kavva* and some small *andje* trees, with large two-pointed leaves. Then *bagara* trees were plentiful, with their greyish leaves ; and *jadjera*. The *mara*, a rustic-looking plant with small leaves of a deep waxy green, and the *dondo*, producing a granulated spherical fruit, one and a half inches in diameter, also grew here, as well as the *dafa*, which possessed elongated leaves radiating in a bunch from the end of each branch.

It was beautiful country all along on this side of the watershed, quite different from that of the eastern side. We now had stretches of verdant country, prettily dotted with fine healthy trees of immense size, and here and there the usual patches of red volcanic rock.

We rose or descended nearly all the time, finding water only twice that day : once early in the march, the other on arrival in camp about seven hours later. Uncertain as to whether we should find more water at a reasonable distance, we encamped at this place, notwithstanding that the water was bad, of a dark greenish colour, stagnant and muddy.

Wild game was plentiful in this region, and we saw some large buck, two wart-hogs (the *phacochærus*) and several giraffes. In fact, I was nearly knocked down by a giraffe in flight as I was trying to photograph it only five or six yards away. One of my men had gone with an old matchlock in order to kill it, and the giraffe came towards me unexpectedly. Had it not been for the stupidity of my Somali, who, seeing the giraffe coming, dropped the camera as he was handing it to me, I could have taken a beautiful picture of the animal. Giraffes were as tame here as those we had seen on the Sobat—in fact, tamer. I always endeavoured to stop my men from going after them, but sometimes they got out of hand.

We heard the trumpeting of elephants during the night, and we saw some in the afternoon crashing a passage through the forest. They were frightened of something and were stampeding. I do not know that I have ever seen such an impressive sight. A dozen or so of these brutes forced their way through the forest. The disturbance they made, bellowing and smashing everything along their passage, was deafening. They passed only a short distance from us.

At this camp (2,450 feet) we found a refreshing little wild fruit, quite sweet, with a thin yellow skin, called by the natives the *yago*.

The Kresh and Banda people were wonderful at improvising small domed huts of grass thatch over a frame of wood, so strongly built that they stood in the strongest gale of wind and let in no water in the most torrential rain. They call them " *mommo*."

We found on our next day's march more immense smooth white-barked *djera*, a kind of acacia, and while going over a beautiful grassy valley we saw *dafa* trees, with elongated leaves somewhat resembling those of the *lulu* and growing in tufts radiating from a longish stem.

The country was really beautiful in this part. We came to another open plain—in fact, most of the country we were crossing now was fairly well open and neat-looking, the stems of the trees being clean and strong, with healthy, deep-coloured foliage. Hardly a decayed tree was to be seen anywhere, or a yellow or a brown leaf. Everything was of the richest green— the richest, indeed, that vegetation of any kind could supply.

Creepers and parasitic plants were not so common

in this particular forest. Even vines were only to be noticed near *khors*, where the vegetation was over-crowded, unduly luxuriant and diabolically entangled. In fact, when the soil was moist near these *khors* it was quite dark under these galleries through the forest, no light ever penetrating through the dense foliage even in the middle of the day.

After four hours' marching—these marches were trying to my Somali and myself, owing to the trouble we had to keep the loads upon our donkeys' backs and the terrific exertion in which we had to indulge every minute of the day—we came to a small *khor* of stagnant water, which gave us endless trouble to cross owing to the soft, sticky mud in which the first donkeys of my caravan, which we had driven in, not only gradually sank but absolutely disappeared. We had the greatest trouble in getting them out again with their loads, as we sank into the mud too.

So much time was wasted in fording this little *khor* (2,150 feet), flowing towards the north-west, that, late in the afternoon, we were still pulling things across by means of ropes. Men and beasts got to the other side in the filthiest condition, smothered all over with black mud.

Animals, I am sure, even donkeys, possess a keen sense of the ridiculous. When we got to the other side I could not help laughing in observing one of my donkeys, a splendid little animal called "Chuk-Chuk," owing to his inveterate habit of trotting all the time and shaking off his load every few minutes. With eyes full of humour he was examining all the other donkeys so black with mud in huge lumps all over their bodies that it was difficult to tell what animals they were ; then he looked at us, also unrecognizable. Seized by a fit of uncontrollable hilarity, he brayed and brayed to his heart's content, and each time he turned round to look at us, again and again fell into other fits of braying. Certainly the comical sight amused him more than it did us.

CHAPTER II.

I HAD quite a narrow escape. As we were crossing an open patch of grassy land somewhat on a slope, I saw in the highest part under some trees two enormous elephants, a male and a female, the male with magnificent tusks. My Somali happened to be quite close to me. As I never carried weapons upon me, I snatched his rifle, a small .303 carbine, and asked him for two cartridges, which he at once handed me.

Creeping along in the rather short grass, I stalked the elephants and got quite close. One of my Kresh, who had a useless matchlock of his own, followed me. My Somali had carried the cartridges in his pocket. They were in a filthy condition, so that when I came to insert one in the rifle I had to force it in, and only with difficulty could I close the bolt.

I got up to within ten yards of the male elephant, who was first lifting up one ear and then the other like huge fans, in order better to hear the approaching danger, stretching out his trunk as if he were scenting us, and looking my way with his short-sighted eyes. The sight of elephants is generally poor. Having got quite close, I stood up before him, as he squeezed his eyes to perceive what I was. Having taken careful aim, I pulled the trigger.

The cartridge never went off, but unfortunately my Kresh, who relied on the effectiveness of my weapon, fired the same moment with his matchlock. We were such a short distance from the animal that he actually hit him in the head. I never shall forget my surprise when the elephant lifted his trunk skyward, and in his fury roared like thunder. Then encircling with his proboscis a good-sized tree near by, he snapped it in two as easily as I should break a lucifer match. My Kresh gave a piercing yell and bolted, his face, as I caught sight of him, quite disfigured with terror. Shrieking at the top of his voice, he dashed past me as I was endeavouring to open the bolt of my rifle, hopelessly jammed.

A moment later the elephant with his trunk extended dashed after us, I, too, with my useless rifle in my hand having by that time acquired a high speed in my flight, and making sharp angles in order to gain time. Fortunately the elephant ran after the Kresh first, whom he could hear owing to the piercing yells. But the Kresh was too smart, and made in haste for some bushes. On getting near them the black man turned a sharp angle and quickly hid himself in a heap in the black shadow of some shrubs. The elephant lost him, and, having bellowed like thunder for a moment or two in his angry despair, caught sight of me, all dressed up in white that day—for a change—and soon caught me up with his gigantic strides. The ground on which I was running was, as I have said, sloping, and I was going down hill, making for some high grass at the bottom, where I intended to hide.

Had I been running a race for the world's record I am sure I should have won the prize. It was amazing to me how fast I could run, as I confess my blood turned perfectly cold when I could feel the hoarse blowing trunk of the elephant only a few yards behind me, and I expected every minute to be crushed into a jelly. The strength in my legs seemed to have increased a hundredfold in the desperate effort to get away.

When I got to the bottom of the slope, the reason the grass was higher there was, of course, because of the moisture which is generally found in these depressions. In that particular part of the country these marshy plains were extraordinarily sticky and slushy, so the moment I dashed into the grass, at the record-breaking speed at which I was travelling, my feet stuck in the soft and slushy mud, and I was precipitated with my face and hands flat into the slush, my rifle sinking deep. This was a moment of apprehension. I said good-bye to the world and imagined myself dead. No one could have been more surprised than I was when, a reasonable time to be killed in having elapsed, I got up again and perceived the elephant a few yards off cantering away in the opposite direction. His back view was a great relief to me. He had come to within two or three yards of where I had fallen, and, having himself sunk in the soft mud, had turned round and struggled away, leaving big circular footmarks—regular holes—four or five feet deep in the mud. Elephants are very diffident, in fact, quite frightened, of these swampy places, where they experience great difficulty in getting out again if once they begin to sink deep.

For my part, I should not care to have the thrill of another three hundred yards' race like that. My heart beat for some time after I got up, and tried to shake off the slush with which I was covered. The exertion had been somewhat too great in such terrific heat, although

I believe that excitements like that are not unwholesome in malarial countries, as they stir up one's blood and help to keep one in good condition.

Since leaving Dem Zebir we had experienced heavy thunderstorms nearly every other night. We generally had fine weather in the morning, and it invariably got cloudy towards the east in the afternoon about two o'clock. These tornadoes began with black clouds near the horizon-line, and then got larger and larger, developing into huge white globular clouds higher up in the sky vault. Gradually these masses covered the entire eastern portion of the sky, and by evening had extended right across as far as the west. Storms invariably came from the east. Towards the evening cloud effects were sometimes picturesque. Soft yellow, green, blue, pink and violet tints in the sky were to be observed. The sun was always piercingly hot after heavy storms. Rain came down in torrents in the heavy gale at the beginning of the tornado, and became generally intermittent during the cooler hours of the night until 4 or 5 a.m. It was usually clear again at sunrise.

On May 11th we went over hilly country charmingly beautiful, and passed a hill-range to the south of us. Two hours after leaving the *khor* we skirted a wooded hill of volcanic rock and red earth (2,350 feet), from which I got an extensive view with an almost absolutely flat horizon-line towards the south and west, with no interruptions of any kind, and only trees, trees, trees— uninterrupted forest as far as the eye could perceive.

From this point we descended into lovely country, with open grassy spaces so beautifully clean that they reminded one strongly of European meadows, particularly the unsurpassable ones of old England.

In the forest we found quantities of honey in hollowed trees. As the honey was generally at the summit of the tree, the way my men got it was by knocking down the tree, and then smoking the bees out of their lodgings with burning grass. The honey was then quickly collected and brought triumphantly back to camp.

Near a *khor*, my donkeys had got swamped in the deep elephants' holes in the mud of the stream, and badly entangled in the twisted roots of trees under the slush. It took us the best part of two hours to take animals and baggage across, and we halted for some hours among a lot of fine *lulu* trees as the heat was unbearable that day.

My men as usual went about for honey, and presently they returned with quantities of it, in the combs, of course. We were gaily enjoying it, I with a plateful before me and all my men squatting round me, their teeth biting off huge chunks from the honeycombs. Suddenly an alarm was raised. The men jumped to their feet and threw the combs away. A significant buzz was fast approaching, and behold an army of bees had descended quickly upon us and surrounded my camp, stinging the naked men all over. My men held their hands upon their faces and stampeded in all directions—a most fatal thing to do—each one with a large contingent of bees after him.

My poor Somali, who, being a strict Mussulman, never would touch anything that had been fingered by unbelievers, was the only one in camp who had not partaken of the honey. As, however, he had a perfect horror of bees, he was the first one to dash away when he first heard them. The result was that he who had not touched the honey at all had the greatest number of bees after him. At one time the whole army seemed to have concentrated round him. Piercing were his yells and high the leaps he made in the air. His legs, body and head were simply riddled with stings.

Curiously enough, I, who had still the plate of honey upon my knees, and remained motionless like a statue, did not receive a single sting, although myriads of bees kept buzzing around me in a most alarming manner.

All my men suffered agony for some hours, and the poor Somali was so badly stung that I really feared he might die. His head became swollen in a dangerous way. His eyelids were simply covered with stings. I counted as many as eight stings on the upper eyelids and eight big lumps, which caused him intense pain, on the back of his head. Upon his body I quite gave up counting the innumerable big lumps which had grown on it since the invasion.

As soon as the bees had gradually cleared away from the place where I was, leaving me quite untouched, the first thing I did was to collect a lot of dry grass and light up three or four big fires, piling damp grass on them so as to make as much smoke as possible. Having done this, I called again for my men, telling them that they could come back safely, and eventually all of them returned, quite unrecognizable, so much had they suffered in the encounter.

The poor Somali was seized with shivers and shudders and fever at 104°. For an hour or so he was quite delirious, the pain being so intense.

Notwithstanding that all were feeling bad, late in the afternoon we deemed it wise to abandon that place and go on further, in case the bees might take it into their heads to pay us another visit. The sick Somali was treated to a donkey ride, and we left again over undulating country, partly wooded with thick forest and fine open patches here and there.

By eight o'clock in the evening, owing to the dark clouds which made it impossible for us to see where we were going, and unable to find water, we had to make camp, having travelled that day altogether some twenty-two miles, owing to the fair condition of the country we were traversing. We were then at the bottom of an extensive grassy basin, with only a few small *lulu* and *dafa* trees. Myriads of mushroom-shaped anthills studded the landscape. These ants were a great nuisance, as they ate up all our things when we laid them upon the ground. Care had to be taken to raise all the loads upon stone supports or upon pieces of wood, so as to lift them above the ground. I found that sole-leather trunks, soaked in grease and varnished over were not attacked so much as wooden packages. In fact, nearly all my packages of leather suffered little from white ants, whereas wooden boxes fell to pieces.

In one single night white ants could eat up the entire bottom of a box, and in one night they actually ate up all the cloth, stuffing, and sewing of an English saddle I had with me. On another occasion, also in one night, they devoured the greater part of a pair of serge trousers which had dropped upon the ground. The destructiveness of this pest of Africa was really remarkable.

We left again at 7 a.m. on May 12th, over open, undulating country. We descended to another swampy *khor*, which fortunately was negotiated in an easier way than we expected, as we were getting a deal of experience in dealing with mud and swamps. The entire plain during the height of the rainy season must be a marsh extremely difficult to cross, owing to the many elephants' trails and footmarks leaving deep holes all over the ground, thousands of them.

From this swampy plain, which was now comparatively dry, we rose on a hill-range. On the side of it we came to a flat terrace of volcanic rock, from which we obtained a pretty view of the deep valley below us, and hills beyond forming a flat horizon-line. There was no trail at all, as usual, and we travelled over hard, difficult country, most troublesome for men and animals.

On descending from the hill we got among tufts of bamboo, of which there was an extensive growth in patches. It was difficult to extricate ourselves from them, as many of the bamboo canes, when rotted at the base, fell down and formed a regular matting, barring the way. We had constantly to cut down these barriers, or else crawl under in order to get through. The leaves of the bamboo were as sharp as razors, and we were constantly getting cut.

In the open patches we saw many large *antelope caama*, commonly called *hartebeest*, and numerous smaller antelopes of the *madoqua* and *leucotis* kinds.

It was not till 11.30 that we came to the stagnant water of a *khor*, where we halted for lunch, having found no drinkable water since the day before, at 3 a m.

The natives were wonderful at finding water in the most unlikely places. As far as they were concerned, quality mattered little. By the colour of foliage, or the greenness of grass, as well as by the formation of the land, we could always tell where water could be obtained by digging a few feet in the ground.

In the afternoon we went over an open plain. Then over rolling country, and after that, on the flat again, we came across an extensive growth of bamboos of inferior quality and no great diameter. The largest I saw was about three inches in circumference.

We were now once more among short, stunted trees, some of them dwarf mimosas, but principally *lecco*, or *leocco*, with fat, greyish-green, wax-like leaves, about four inches long, having hardly distinguishable ribs on the back of the leaf. The face of the leaf was quite smooth and much darker in colour than the back. *Averh*, or *averla*, was also plentiful, and produced a small greenish-black berry quite good to eat. The leaf of this plant had an indented edge, and a few ribs placed alternately along the central ridge of the leaf, showing prominently at the back. The berries grew in bunches hanging from a long stem, and were shaped somewhat like olives, with many dots upon them in the lower portion, and an additional cap on the upper portion. They were only fit to eat when the lower section turned black. They tasted something like the cassia bean. The tree produced excellent hard wood.

A charming small-leaved tree of the mimosa type was the *kakkeri*, with tiny light green leaves, perfectly oval in shape and deliciously soft under one's fingers, almost velvety in feeling, and with no spikes along the stems.

In all this region we were much troubled by the *ngai*, an old friend, the tiny little fly which had a great fondness for dashing into one's eyes and ears. Millions of them followed us everywhere and gave us quite sore eyes, as it was impossible to open one's eyes even for a moment without their finding their way in. We also had to stop our ears with cotton so as to prevent them getting in. This was an additional trial, because in the great heat we were experiencing one wished to have one's body as free as possible. Horse-flies—one more kind which is credited with being of the tze-tze family were also abundant and troublesome here.

CHAPTER III.

WE saw any number of elephants and we had good sport. Antelopes were plentiful, too, and wart-hogs were met in large numbers. I had quite an amusing time that afternoon. I saw some one hundred and fifty wild hogs, and some forty or fifty of the larger wart-hogs enjoying the green grass of a meadow. The latter creatures reached a height of about four feet and had fangs of a most vicious curl. Creeping along behind low bushes I got within thirty yards of these animals peacefully grazing, and, while screened by a bush, shot one. All the others, hearing the report, pricked up their ears and looked my way, two big brutes moving towards me in a most determined manner. I fired a second shot into them, and, to my amazement, instead of seeing the lot stampede, they all charged at once.

I only had two more cartridges in my pocket, and by the time I had reloaded, the largest beasts were only a few yards on the other side of the bush, all the others behind them. They stopped in a long row like a regiment of soldiers. For some minutes I was undecided whether to fire or await my luck. The cries from my anxious men some hundred yards behind attracted the attention of the animals, and, much to my comfort, they were suddenly seized by a panic. Instead of seeing a row of pointed teeth displayed before me in a long line, I next perceived an equally long row of curly tails, according to the truest rules of perspective, gradually diminishing in size as they drew further from me.

We made camp at sunset that afternoon near a *khor* (2,050 feet), but no water was to be obtained. We had made another good march that day of over twenty-one miles.

On May 12th we again traversed beautiful undulating country and more fine open grassy stretches. We passed two troublesome *khors* where my donkeys were simply swamped in the soft mud. We now found nearly all the lower valleys marshy and swampy from the drainage of the hills on either side. The numberless tangled roots of trees just below the surface made these marshes all the more troublesome, as the animals caught their legs in them and got involved.

Four hours after we had left camp we passed over a high, flat plateau, between two hills some two hundred yards apart, and about one hundred and fifty feet higher than the plateau. We were marching mostly south and south-west, keeping a general direction of south-south-west.

There were high *shishi* trees, another kind of mimosa, with tiny leaves and minute white flowers; the *verver* plant, with elongated leaves and a small spherical berry of light green colour; the *baggarah* and the *kierela*, producing a fruit like a small light-green ball within a hard shell containing a yellowish soft substance, quite good to eat. The *badfango* was not unlike a diminutive grape-vine, the shoots of which were of a reddish colour and were edible. The *mbishi* was another kind of small thorny mimosa.

Quantities of game were met with that day: innumerable wild boars and huge wart-hogs playing in a fine open valley and later some hundreds grazing. Shortly after we came upon a herd of red buck.

The country was undulating. At 5.10 in the afternoon we descended among a lot of creepers to the Ngawa stream flowing south. On the west bank of this stream I made camp, having marched eighteen miles.

Water in the hypsometrical apparatus boiled at this point at a temperature of 208–4°. The temperature of the atmosphere was 75° Fahrenheit, which gave an elevation of 2,049 feet.

I had a suspicion that we were being watched. In fact, I found footmarks quite close to my camp the next morning, and following these footmarks in the soft ground I discovered several natives with their spears hiding behind bushes. They were upset and frightened, and confessed that they had been sent by Sultan Dakako, whose village was not very distant now, to watch our movements. They had been spying us unseen for several days.

There is nothing like taking advantage of one's opportunities, and as I had got to a point where I did not know exactly where I was, and had not of late been able to take accurate astronomical observations, I gave these men a good shaking and told them that they must take us at once to the sultan's village.

We went through thick forest with no trail whatever, with innumerable *nduku*, or rubber-vines, which seemed extraordinarily plentiful in that region.

Two hours after leaving camp we crossed the river Daraui, and at ten we arrived at the river Bissi, near which stood Sultan Dakako's village (2,150 feet).

The sultan himself was a little boy, while a power-fully-built brute, a man called Mabu, acted as regent.

There was a commotion when we arrived. The sultan came to pay his respects, accompanied by Mabu, and a fellow in ample crimson trousers, long coat, and an Egyptian *tarbouche*. The latter was the commander of the sultan's soldiers. Many of the men possessed good Gras rifles, with stocks ornamented with brass nails.

Syrian and Arab traders, I was told, had come to this place a year before, smuggling small calibre fire-arms for the natives. One of them had eventually been arrested some two hundred kilometres further south by the French officer in charge of the military post.

When I arrived these people were not certain whether I was an Arab trader too. They cross-examined me at length and with a great deal of shrewdness, asking me whether I would sell them rifles. I at once gave them to understand that I was not a trader and would sell nothing whatever to them, but I gave them presents of cloth, beads, salt and brass wire—all articles they valued much—in return for the gifts of *dhura*, bread, meat stew, chickens and eggs, which the sultan sent me, on making sure that I was not a smuggler.

The sultan himself was a gentlemanly little fellow with *aplomb* quite remarkable for a young savage in the forest. He was mystified when I asked him his age. Neither he nor his prime minister, nor his general-in-chief could, to save their lives, calculate the number of years the child had lived.

Later in the day the sultan came back to my camp beaming all over with joy, his hair decorated with large multi-coloured beads I had given him and with several necklaces round his neck. Behind him came many armed men, some—about ten or twelve—with Gras rifles, the others armed with old muzzle-loaders.

The population of this village consisted mostly of Kresh and Gabu in two large *zeribas*. The huts had mud walls, with outer posts supporting a conical roof, an interstice of several inches being left between it and the wall. The doors were low, quite backbreaking as you stooped low to enter. The floor inside the hut had been scooped out several inches lower than the level of the ground outside. I was amazed at the coolness and perfect ventilation of these huts.

There were numerous *uaua* palms with their broad leaves, and *baua*, also a palm with long, narrow, sharp-edged leaves. Both these palms were common in the undergrowth in the forest, particularly in the moist, dark galleries where trees were growing thickly in marshy valleys.

I continued my journey in the afternoon until sunset, when I halted by a stream four yards wide, flowing towards the south-west into the Biri river (1,950 feet). We had here high grass through which we had to force our way, and during the afternoon I lost five of my donkeys with their loads, as it was impossible to see more than a yard or so ahead. They had strayed somewhere and I only discovered that they were missing when we arrived in camp.

Adem (the Somali), who was really an amazing tracker, started in the middle of the night while a terrific thunderstorm was raging in order to find the animals, and, in fact, towards two o'clock in the morning, he returned to camp having tracked and found all of them. On numerous occasions I availed myself of Adem's marvellous ability in tracking, and I, too, got to be quite an expert at that work. It is a useful accomplishment for any one going exploring who wishes to be independent of local tribes. We could always trace our way to villages and discover people in the most unlikely places ; we could find our way to places where water could be obtained ; besides tracking animals, which, of course, are very easy to track. The main points in tracking are to know the customs and ways of the people or animals one wishes to search for, and to apply as much as possible one's gift of observation.

On one or two occasions we evaded pits with spikes, which had been placed where natives imagined we should pass unawares, and into which we should have certainly fallen had we not noticed suspicious signs of disturbed vegetation before we got to them. Some of the tribes in the forest had curious ways of hiding in trees and dropping spears upon one's head as one went by, or else had spears so balanced that when you passed a string gave way and the spear dropped automatically.

On May 14th young Sultan Dakako with his soldiers joined me, professing that I had been so kind that he would accompany me as far as Djema, the first large settlement in the French Congo. I left about 7.15 by way of fairly open country, and after passing several swampy *khors*, in which my donkeys got absolutely swamped and all the baggage soaked, we rose upon a hill (2,170 feet), from which we got a beautiful view of a hill-range in front of us to the west and fine open country below us towards the south. On descending we came to another stream flowing southwards. Here was a cactus I had not yet seen, the *djendu*, straight-stemmed and much spiked, five to six feet high, with soft umbrella-like leaves at the summit.

We arrived at the Djema *zeriba* at noon. The chief had got into trouble with the French authorities, as he had purchased a .303 Lee-Metford from a Syrian trader. He had paid for it several hundred pounds of ivory. He was summoned before the French officer at Zemio.

Near the *zeriba* was a row of outer huts for the workmen of the *Société des Sultanats du Haut Ubanghi*, who had here the most north-easterly *factorerie* of their concession. In fact, a quarter of an hour later I arrived at the society's buildings, some large drying-sheds for the rubber and warehouses for the ivory. Here again I was at first mistaken for an Arab trader, as I drove my caravan into the enclosure. Hostile expressions were visible on the faces of the two Frenchmen in charge of the place, but the moment my identity was made known a hearty and most cordial reception awaited me.

No Englishman had travelled this way, and partly owing to my sunburnt face and my town attire and straw hat, which are not usual with people in the heart of Africa, I was greatly amused to see how perplexed the Frenchmen were when I approached.

Monsieur Brachiel, *chef de zone* of the *Société des Sultanats*, was suffering from fever. He was very kind and hospitable, and explained at great length how several Greek and Syrian merchants came over to smuggle modern rifles and ammunition to the chiefs. They carried on a slave trade at a considerable profit. The French Government, as well as the society, intended to put a stop to this irregular state of affairs. He told me—amidst our mutual merriment—how he was already about to despatch a message to Zemio in order to have a trap laid to capture me, as the natives had been spying me for several days. I had been suspected of being a slave merchant, the suspicion having arisen because I spoke politely to the natives I met! That is what comes of being polite to natives!

There is no more unsatisfactory work in Central Africa than surveying. Not only have villages a way of changing their name every time a chief dies (the village always going by the name of the chief), but also the villages are constantly changing their positions, being sometimes built on one river, sometimes on another, sometimes upon a hill, and at other times in a low valley, according to superstitions, agricultural necessities, the needs of war, or the fear of neighbouring tribes. Thus I found Djema in a different place altogether from where I expected it to be and where it was marked on Marchand's map. Marchand himself had never been to this place, his route being about one hundred and sixty kilometres further south. The distance between the Djema visited by me and the Djema on the maps was, if I remember right, some fourteen or sixteen kilometres. The latter position had been established by a member of the Marchand expedition, who had deviated in that direction for surveying and exploring purposes.

The place where I found it had been selected by the Société des Sultanats as a more suitable locality for the collection of rubber. It was discovered, nevertheless, that the difficulty of transport of the goods from and to the river was too great and the quarters were to be shifted back once more to the site of the old Djema.

A beautiful garden had been made at the quarters of the society, with good vegetables and a rich growth of flowers. Experiments had been made on various kinds of rubber plants. The *manihot ceara glazioti*, imported from Brazil, had not yielded the satisfactory results expected, as it was brittle and delicate when young and not suited to the climate of Central Africa. The *ire*, which we shall find later spread all over French and Belgian Congo, was the quality most adapted for the locality and gave excellent results. A large nursery of these plants was kept at the *factorerie*. When I was there these plants were gradually being transported to the new quarters of the society at a spot where the Mabiso stream meets the Goangua, the latter being quite an important river navigable at all times even for large canoes.

On May 16th I went over to old and now-revived Djema, where Monsieur Brachiel was busy constructing new quarters.

I left Djema at 8.30 by an undulating trail, with bridges over the five *khors* met on the way. The undulating country was in some of the lower portions liable to inundation during the rainy season. Patches of the familiar volcanic rock showed through, particularly on heights or hill-tops.

We arrived at new Djema (the old Djema of the maps) at 2.30 p.m., having been caught in a heavy tornado which drenched us to the marrow of our bones and soaked the loads once more.

All kinds of antelopes were to be found in this country. Buffaloes, hippopotami, rhinoceri, the large red " antilope cheval " of the French, and elephants of great size were plentiful.

New Djema certainly seemed a better-situated place than the old *factorerie* as far as the transport of the goods down the stream was concerned, but it seemed an extraordinarily moist place, the damp saturating everything at night. In the morning a dense fog enveloped everything, and although white instead of black it quite paralleled in thickness our worst experiences of the winter months in London.

The remains of the kitchen and mud prison house of Marchand's days were still to be seen at the new Djema.

CHAPTER IV.

AFTER leaving new-old Djema (1,880 feet) a series of troubles came upon us. My Somali had such a violent attack of fever that it looked to me as if he would die. A huge dose of castor oil, however, which would have killed most men, cured him in a few hours.

The Kresh and Banda had abandoned me, and I was now absolutely at the mercy of men I could pick up on the road. The question of carriers in this region was a serious one, so grave that the *Société des Sultanats* had experienced considerable difficulty in obtaining sufficient men to do the work.

All my poor animals, half dead with fatigue, had to be loaded again. We forded the Goangua river, about thirty yards wide and three feet deep, soon after leaving Djema. This river when in flood rose several yards, and inundated a considerable portion of the neighbouring country.

We left the Goangua at 9.30 a.m. and by 11.10 we passed Tickima village, with two half-abandoned *zeribas* and a few scattered huts with mud walls and low thatched roofs.

The natives—the Biri—were short, and, indeed, resembled the neighbouring Niam-Niam, to whom they were closely allied.   The women did their hair into little tresses in three separate tufts.   The chief here, too, was a mere child, with expressive eyes.   The Biri possessed a short nose and prominent lips.   The women were well formed, short in stature, with finely-cut cicatrices of the double-angle pattern, crosses, and an angular waved pattern upon the chest.   There were four large round marks upon the fore-arm, and also lines and angles combined reaching up to the shoulder.

From this village we first climbed, and then descended a good deal over undulating country, occasionally finding flat stretches of volcanic iron rock and fine grassy open spaces.   We crossed two or three small but very deed streamlets of good water, over which rickety bridges had been constructed, that, however, were constantly being devoured by white ants or rotted away by the intense moisture in the air, so that they needed constant renewing. These bridges were merely intended for foot passengers, and did not bear the weight of loaded animals, almost unknown in this region.   The result was that whenever we went over these structures the animals sank through and occasionally disappeared.   The trouble my Somali and I had in taking the animals across these places was more than I care to tell.   The donkeys became so nervous of these bridges that it took no end of persuasion to make them go over.   The patience of Job, of Bible fame, was nothing as compared to the good temper we had to exercise on these occasions.   It took us sometimes a couple of hours or longer of pushing and tugging to persuade the donkeys to go over bridges two or three yards long.

We reached the first portion of Sanango village, on the top of a hill, at four o'clock in the afternoon, having started at 9.30 in the morning ; and a quarter of an hour later we had descended to the chief's *zeriba* (1,810 feet) lower down on the Ualla (or Wella) river, which after being joined by the Goangua and other tributaries became the Ouarra river, discharging its waters into the Mbomu river at a place called Ali.

I had obtained a few carriers from Djema, but by the time I had reached Sanango half of them had run away. Taking our donkeys through the high grass was trying for the Somali and myself. The heat was suffocating, and marching along through the high, wet grass we were drenched all the time, and our hands and faces constantly getting cut by the blades of grass, as sharp as knives.

On May 18th we crossed the Wella (1,780 feet), flowing south-west and twenty yards wide. Chief Sanango, to whom I had given a present of cloth, helped us a good deal in crossing the swift stream, but it took us more than an hour to take animals and loads to the other side. The trail was then fairly good, with many villages all along.

We went among stunted vegetation, much stunted, owing perhaps to the ferruginous rock which underlies the soil a little below the surface. Grassy inclines were met with, and two hours later we obtained a beautiful view of distant blue hills on the horizon-line, with high palm-trees in the immediate foreground of the scene.

Three hours and a half's march took us to Amenago village, where we received lavish gifts of *vünde*, a sort of native bread; *agghu*, a purée of winged ants, was served to us ; also *gaddia*, a green vegetable with a seven-pointed leaf, which, boiled, tastes like spinach.

My Somali, who, owing to his strict religious notions,

never touched meat prepared by non-Mussulmans, mistook the purée of ants for a vegetable, and dipping his fingers in the pot, licked his hands, saying it was the most delicious thing he had ever tasted. I told him that he could take it all, and he proceeded to scoop out handful after handful, when I asked him whether he knew what he was eating. He said it was a mixture of honey and vegetables. When I informed him that he was devouring squashed ants, and actually took out of the pot some fine specimens of the *termix voratrix* and the *dophira-alata*, he became so disgusted that he placed his fingers down his throat and ejected all he had eaten.

The natives themselves consider these ants a great delicacy and eat them ravenously.

Amenago village (2,100 feet) was enclosed in a small *zeriba*.

After a copious luncheon we left by an undulating trail, obtaining extensive views from the highest points, generally consisting of exposed patches of ferruginous rock with the usual swampy *khors* between. We reached a place called Basungo (1,670 feet) at sunset, a hamlet of four huts and a couple of storehouses. We met with a hearty reception and lavish offerings of food were brought to us.

On May 19th, by nine o'clock, we had climbed up to Bilallih (1,700 feet). At the bottom of each valley we invariably found dark galleries under stifling vegetation along the *khors* and in the marshy drainages of surrounding hills. Creepers were abundant, and long-bladed cutting grass; the ground soft and swampy underfoot. In this particular region there were luxuriant groves of palm-trees producing a red date, the *nghiro*, technically

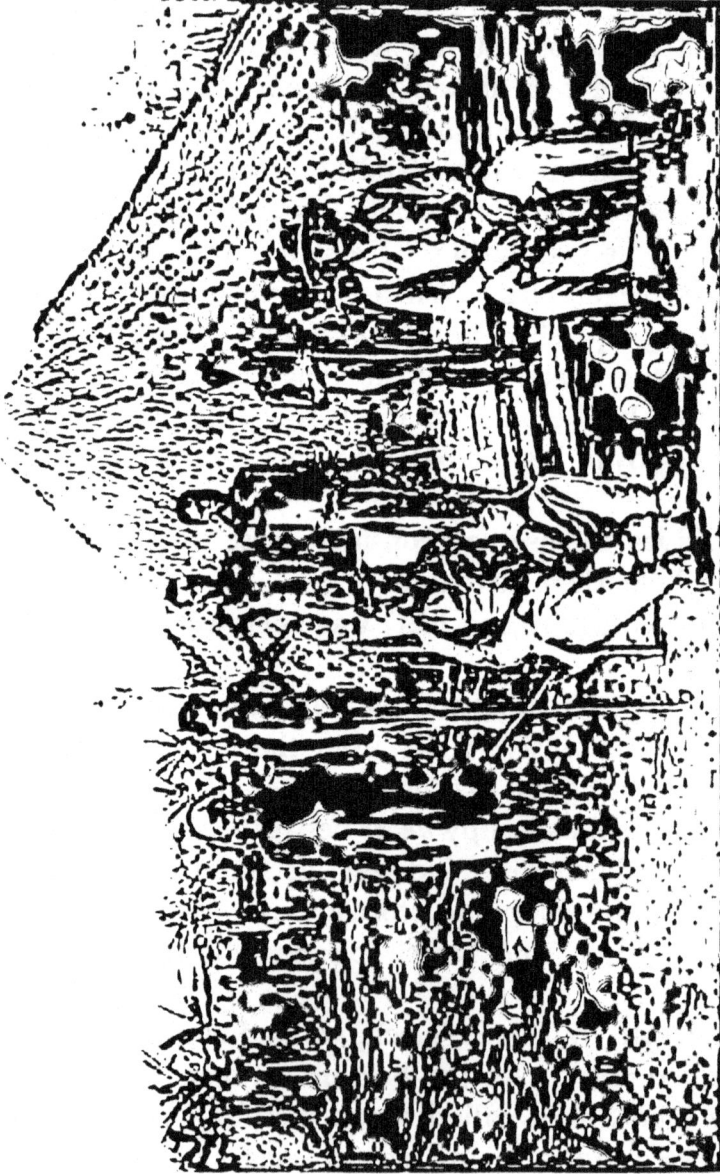

Tambura.   Gimbara.

The Sub-chiefs of Buddia,

called the *phœnix*, the parent stock perhaps of date palms. The fruit was fibrous and had a large stone inside, so that there was but little to eat, but it had quite a refreshing, nourishing, oily taste. The natives extracted oil from these dates.

We went up and down over finely-gravelled country and across beautiful meadows, reminding one of England. On nearing Beduch or Buddia, we rose to 1,800 feet on a flat plateau, green and grassy, with gravelly soil.

Buddia (1,580 feet) was a large village of several *zeribas*. The people were particularly interesting for the peculiar plaited hats of all shapes which they themselves manufactured, and for the cheap felt hats, and fancy naval caps with gold braiding imported from France, which formed their chief pride. One of the principal points about these naval caps was that they always wore them with the price ticket attached to them, and great care was taken that it should not drop off.

The sub-chiefs Gubbera and Tambura were sent by Buddia, the chief of the village, to receive me. The first arrived in a garb of large blue check mattress-covering, while Tambura walked under a much discoloured nautical cap several sizes too big for him. We were gazed at by a lot of open-mouthed men who surrounded us. These receptions were dreary in the extreme, as they lasted several hours, the natives and their chiefs squatting down like idiots, taking themselves so seriously all the time that it was not possible to draw a grin from their uncomely countenances. This was to kill time while presents of native polenta, various soups, stews, concoctions of vegetables and squashed winged ants were in course of preparation for us, which were eventually brought and placed before me in black pots neatly covered over with palm-leaves.

In the French Congo it was the habit of the natives to bring these gifts of food to a passing stranger. Personally, I never touched any of the stuff that was conveyed to me, and the people who brought it generally ate it themselves. It was a nuisance, as each time one had to reward them for their good intentions, and it meant giving back a present of a roll of cloth worth at least one hundred times more than value received.

Buddia was the largest village we met between the Anglo-Egyptian Sudan and the Mbomu river. It was charmingly situated on a sloping plain, quite open, and surrounded by distant hills to the west-north-west, the Gangara, a flattened plateau, rising considerably higher than other hills. The inhabitants of this village had only arrived here lately from Zemio, and the village therefore, had quite a new appearance.

Buddia, eldest son of the sultan of Zemio, was the highest chief in the place. He was laid up with a terrific attack of the worst imaginable blood complaint, which had eaten up his nose and palate, and various other parts of his anatomy. He and Tambura, his sub-chief, were unscrupulous scoundrels, absolute degenerates. From my very arrival they began pestering me for whisky and brandy, or fire-water of any kind, which, of course, I could not supply. They seemed to have enough intoxicants of their own. They were incapable from drink all the time. At eight o'clock the next morning Tambura, who came to see me, was in such a drunken condition that two men had to hold him up on his legs. He was a depraved, fat, putrid-looking, slippery devil, who gave evasive answers to everything I asked him.

Chief Gubbera, the second son of the sultan of Zemio, a youth of eighteen or twenty, who displayed two large felt hats one above the other on his head, had rather a pleasant although weak face.

The sultan of Zemio had ten sons, viz.: Buddia, Gubbera, Djema, Badunga, Dakako, Kakko, Kajima, Zemio, Kirekire and Ephon.

Gubbera had been summoned up to Buddia as that chief was too ill to live long. He—Gubbera—was the chief of Tambura village, further east on the Mbomu river.

The village of Buddia was on the stream Bakkari, which flowed southward into the Mbomu. The population consisted of Golo, Biri, Kare and Gabu, although, of course, the chief and the more important people were of the ruling Zandes tribe. These Zandes were a finer people, taller and more intelligent-looking, than the tribes they had conquered. Their faces were frequently bearded. In many ways these Zandes reminded one strongly of the Abyssinians. They were, in fact, much lighter in colour than either the Basiri, the Kare, the Biri or the Gabu.

The women went about quite naked and had ugly countenances. Some wore the usual tufts of verdure in front and behind. The breasts were extraordinarily pendent. The hair was worn in a tuft upon the head, or in a series of smaller tufts along the top of the skull.

The people of Buddia were mostly smooth-skinned and of a dark chocolate colour; their eyes elongated, and their noses extraordinarily wide at the nostrils, with flattened tips. The eyelids were so heavy that they were swollen-looking and prominent. In fact, the inferior classes had many characteristics in common with the A-sandeh or Niam-Niam, whom we have already met.

Whether Biri, Kare, or Gabu, all these people possessed short, under-developed legs and a long, curved body, usually with a much enlarged paunch.

The upper part of the profile was concave, the lower part highly convex, owing to the extremely prominent lips.

Unlike most tribes, who walk with the feet perfectly straight, these people kept the feet turned outward while walking.

They had no strength to speak of. The strongest of them was hardly able to carry a load of more than 40 or 50 lbs. for some twenty miles a day, whereas I have had carriers in China and in Northern India who could carry 80 and 100 lbs. easily for a longer distance and not be any the worse for it.

The squeezing power of the fingers of these people when measured with the dynamometer was shown to be poor, some of them sending the register slightly higher than 60 lbs., but the majority of them between 40 and 50 lbs. The Kresh and the Banda had slightly stronger fingers, the strongest among sixteen specimens registering 76 lbs.; the average, about 60 lbs. The Banda were weaker, between 58 and 60 lbs. being the average; whereas the strongest people I found in the region near the boundary between English and French possessions were the Yango, who sent the dynamometer up to 78 lbs.

The palms of the hands and the soles of the feet of these people were light pink in colour.

When sitting down they kept their legs raised wide apart. The elbows rested on the knees, the arms were folded, and the hands joined in front of the forehead.

None of these people had a religion to speak of, but they believed in a deity called *iberi*, to whom they sometimes made offerings of food placed in conical wooden baskets ornamented with feathers, and stuck upon stone cairns upon roads or at river fords. This devotion was a precaution taken in the hope of escaping death when crossing the streams, or because of fear during storms, the *iberi* being more or less of an evil spirit, who when not properly treated caused accidents and trouble to people. There was no benevolence about this deity.

In the High Ubanghi I again found the custom of placing stones upon forked trees, but here it was done more as a " toss-up," in order to see whether something one wished would turn out right or not. If the stone remained on the tree until the man who placed it passed the spot a second time the wish would be fulfilled ; if not, bad luck might be expected.

As far as I could understand, there was no marriage ceremony gone through among these people, marriages taking place in a promiscuous fashion ; nor was the custom prevalent of giving gifts of cattle, etc., among the people. The girl merely went to live with her future husband. The richer people had two or three wives. The bigger chiefs recognized all their children as their own. The sultan of Zemio, for instance, provided a living for them by giving them a village each, of which they became chiefs. All seemed extremely immoral, and conjugal faithfulness appeared almost unknown to them. The umbilical cord of newly-born children was tied by the mother herself.

I had many interviews with Zandes chiefs and the better people, and every time I was more and more impressed with the strong resemblance between this bearded class of warriors and conquerors and the darker type of Abyssinians. Not only in their physical appearance, but also in their demeanour, in the way of moving and walking, etc., was the likeness marked.

In all tribes of this region power was generally exerted rather from than towards the body, as in tightening ropes, straps, etc. Weights and burdens were carried upon the head. When pointing, they always employed the extended arm and open hand, and not the index finger as we do. They frequently used their foot for holding ropes or sticks between the big toe and the next. Feet were also constantly employed for raising light objects from the ground without stooping. They could use their toes almost as easily as we do our thumb and first finger in seizing objects and holding them firmly between them. The big toe was quite supple, and they could raise it well above, almost vertical to, the plane of the foot ; or lower it equally well below its normal extended position.

The mental qualities of all these tribes, whether they be Zandes, Biri, Kare or Gabu, were of the lowest type. Whether because of the climate, of unrestrained immorality, or for other reasons, their intellect was practically non-existent. Their memory seemed only keen in remembering names of trees and plants, for which they had an extensive vocabulary, but they seemed to possess no memory whatever for anything else.

They had no idea of how to measure distances. When you were told, by pointing at the sun, that you were only

Karc.

half an hour away from a place, you might easily march on steadily for a day, or even two, and not arrive there. Or when the sun was on the meridian and they pointed towards the west to say that you would arrive there when the sun touched the horizon—some six hours' march—you often reached the place in less than a quarter of an hour. So the information one got direct from the people was of little use, and one did better without it. Occasionally, of course, in the case of distances, they intended to deceive, but frequently they really knew no better.

In rough map drawing, at which some tribes of Asia are marvellously clever, these people were absolutely no good ; but they were certainly wonderful in their power of guiding themselves by the mere look of a country and by remembering the appearance of certain trees in the forest, or certain rocks or patches of grass. For the features of trees their memory is particularly amazing, and in that solitary respect, perhaps, vastly superior to the memory of English people for the faces of individuals, for instance.

I noticed this particular quality especially with the Banda and the Kresh when we lost our way in the forest. They went about in all directions until they came to some particular tree they had seen some years before—"two handsful, ten rainy seasons," ago—and remembered quite well. They then were all right again.

It was impossible to make these people take an honest interest, as Asiatics for instance do, in things new to them, no matter how wonderful. They seldom were astonished at anything. They showed no intelligent inquisitiveness, no matter what strange objects one showed them.

They had no sequence of ideas, and while conversing they would, for no obvious reason, jump inconsistently from one topic to another of quite a different kind.

Anything in connection with personal looks appealed to them a little more. A looking-glass, or, rather, their own reflection in the mirror, would keep their attention for hours.

Suspicious to an incredible degree, deceitful beyond words, their meekest question had some ulterior motive ; so that, what with their wilful lying and their national idiocy, little was to be learnt from them in conversation. They seemed to possess no affection, no courage, no gratitude, no knowledge of time, no art, no literature, no will-power and no imagination. In their conversation, in their rough ornamentations upon the gourds and pottery, and in their cicatrices—the only way in which their artistic merit displays itself—a constant repetition of most elementary ideas is to be noticed.

Their cooking-pots were of a black unglazed clay, either almost spherical, with a small rim at the aperture, or else shaped like three-quarters of a sphere, with a cone upside down forming the mouth, the smaller circle of the cone meeting the spherical part. These pots were roughly ornamented with three circular horizontal lines of consecutive angles near the top, the lower portion being divided into square vertical sections filled with dots, separated by other rows of angles, each of these angles with an additional line on its right side. The bottom of these spherical pots was roughened by lines and dots, so that the pot would stand up in any position in which it was placed.

I saw one or two pots glazed with a black varnish, but the majority were merely half-baked, and chipped easily ; one could cut deep grooves with one's nails in the composition which was easily powdered.

Curious spindle-wheels, of a piece of wood with a heavy square of hide, were noticeable among these people. They used them for twisting thread and rope from a vegetable fibre. A long vine was considerably used in the construction of their homes, both in tying the rafters together, and in making a circular framework between the pillars that form the main support of the wall in their huts.

They plaited a palm-leaf—it resembled the Spanish palm—and made it into *tarbouches* and all kinds of fancy hats, sometimes altogether white, occasionally white with black lines.

Art, in the higher sense, did not exist among these people ; no representation of human figures or animals or imitations of leaves were to be found, their only ornamentations consisting of combinations of triangles and black and white squares or lozenges, which one saw burnt black upon their gourd vessels or cooking-pots. Their wine vessels were made of the greater portion of a gourd, the neck of the gourd being ingeniously left as a handle ; while a gourd split in two, and including half the longitudinal section of the neck, was used as a drinking bowl for water.

These, like most other Central African races, seemed exhausted. They appeared quite beyond showing, or even feeling, not only strong emotions, but any emotions at all, if funk were excepted. Even that took more the form of dumb paralysis than of a hysterical display.

The language of these particular tribes—with variations—was dry and unmusical, with ugly sounds in it. No poetic expressions could, of course, be expected from these people. One never found anyone who knew his own age, nor did I find among them a recognized tribal system of recording time beyond days and moons, or by the rainy and dry seasons.

Illusions played a great part in their daily life and misery. With their intensely suspicious nature, they were always labouring under some illusion or other. Thus a mere look or an unusual movement would cause a whole crowd to bolt. The omen which they derived from the song of a passing bird, or the scratching or some other movement of some animal close by, was often looked upon by them as a warning that something was going to happen.

CHAPTER V.

I HAD endless trouble in this village, as Chief Buddia actually kept me a prisoner for three or four days within a *zeriba*. I was not allowed to go out, the *zeriba* being guarded all round by men with guns and spears.

He had frightened away the few porters I had with me, and I suspected him of poisoning my animals. Critical was my plight, as it was impossible for me to convey all my loads with the much-reduced means of transport I then possessed.

To get out of this dilemma a ruse was necessary. Only patience and a constant smile might get me out where force would be of little avail, perhaps disastrous.

Tambura endeavoured to drive even my Somali away from me. When he did not succeed, various methods were adopted to decoy Adem away, but I was keeping a strict watch on events, and I baffled them on every occasion. Had Adem left the *zeriba* I doubt whether he would have ever returned, as these Buddia people were unbounded blackguards.

I thought I would make the best of my captivity by pretending that I was extremely happy and was charmed with the place. In fact, I led them to believe that I intended to remain there for the rest of my life, which rather amazed my friend Buddia and his aide-de-camp,

Tambura. They then said I could not stay, but must go.

My demands for carriers from the chief to enable me to continue my journey to the Mbomu river had so far been left uncomplied with. Tambura was getting threatening in his drunken visits to me, and I fancied that he was inclined to blackmail me, trying to extort my rifles, my ammunition, and all that I possessed before he would let me go. This I gathered from conversations which he had with my Somali, by whom Tambura could make himself understood in Arabic.

One day Tambura came with many soldiers. I treated him with unusual politeness, and asked him to sit down on my folding-chair, as I said I wanted to have a serious talk with him. I said I must have thirty men within two hours, and with my hand described an arc of a circle in the sky to make him well understand that when the sun had reached that particular point in its declination the men must be in my camp.

We had experienced torrential rains all the time I was in this village, so much so that the hut in the *zeriba* collapsed altogether one day. For three days my camp bed was pitched in a lake of water a foot deep, which flooded the entire *zeriba*. I had to lie on my bed the whole day under a thick mosquito net, the heat being quite unbearable, or else be with my feet in the water with swarms of flies making life miserable. When the water was gradually absorbed, heaps of filth emerged around us in the enclosure. I was somewhat tired of the situation. I had another bad attack of fever at this place, and the Somali also became very ill. Evidently Buddia and Tambura were taking advantage of this. In fact, in the case of my boy I suspected that poison had been placed in the food which Tambura had brought over one day as a present.

Tambura was impudent that day, and openly said that I was at their mercy and should not be allowed to leave the place. He would not supply me with men. Pretending not to be upset by his words I repeated my demand, and asked him not to make me angry, because I had the power to do many things which might frighten him and his men. I had no intention of doing them harm, I said, but just to show what I could do I would push my left eye right out of its socket; I would pass it from one hand to the other, put it in my pocket and then re-place it without feeling the slightest inconvenience. On saying these words I forced my eye until it bulged out, they thought. " I can see into your head and I can read your ideas," I exclaimed, pulling the eye out alto-gether in my hand, and with outstretched arm I made a glass duplicate eye which I was holding instead of my own describe circles around Tambura's head. Tam-bura fell off his chair with fright and his soldiers dashed away in confusion.

I asked Tambura, sprawling on the ground, whether he wished to have further exhibitions of what I could do, or whether he would supply the men at once. Tambura swore by all he held most sacred that the men should be forthcoming immediately.

On May 22nd, at 9.30 in the morning, Tambura, who would not come too near me, brought with him the number of men I required. Most of them were old, quite decrepit-looking or fever-stricken, and I foresaw great trouble with them.

Notwithstanding the infamous way in which these people had treated me, I had given the chief lavish presents of tobacco, handkerchiefs, rolls of cloth, salt, and brass wire to the value of some four or five pounds sterling, as I did not wish to be under an obligation for the poisonous food sent me. But no gratitude existed among these people. All was contemptible lying; their untruthfulness, their drunken habits, indeed every possible bad quality that man can possess—if " men " these fellows can be called—made it impossible to do anything with these rascals.

Arab demoralization and falseness had evidently crept in, principally by means of slave-traders, through Wadai and Darfur, but also from the neighbouring land of Sinoussi.

The ruling class of Zandes seemed to have little faith in the people under them, whom they ill-treated in a most infamous manner, sometimes cutting the arms or hands of men, women and children, or mutilating them in various ways.

Even when the chief sent a pot or two of food by some of his slaves, they always had to be accompanied by two or three soldiers armed with rifles, or else they would escape.

Incredible greediness was their chief characteristic. The better classes were simply rotten with disgusting venereal diseases, their blood being in no way improved by feeding on any putrid animal they could lay their hands upon.

I was indeed glad when I made a start from this place.

My favourite and faithful donkey, Chuk-Chuk, was poisoned during the night. His legs were half eaten up by leeches, ants, centipedes and swarms of flies of all kinds. I left the poor animal dying, as I had not the courage to shoot him. The reproachful expression in his eyes as I patted him for the last time and he saw the caravan move out made my heart quite sore.

Where the village stood, the damp was such that a heavy mist hung all over the low and swampy valley, and many natives suffered from fever. The day I started I had another bad attack. All my donkeys had been more or less poisoned in this deadly place, and were struggling on in a pitiful manner.

From the *zeriba* of our captivity we descended to the stream (1,520 feet), some ten yards wide, with water reaching up to our chests. We had a miserable march through swampy, damp, suffocating vegetation extremely tangled and half-putrid.

There were many large *bima* trees in the neighbourhood of Buddia, with dark green foliage, and also *bavra*, with metallic green bark overcrowded with spikes. The latter were large trees, from each smaller bough of which eight much-elongated leaves radiated, as many as ten boughs shooting out of the main stem, and producing an overcrowding of foliage. The *bavra* seemed almost a botanical deformity, as its huge trunk was crooked to begin with, then it suddenly contracted into a small stem, from which sprang branches quite out of proportion with the size of the trunk.

A great number of *nghiro* palms were to be seen in the damper places where they seemed to flourish—in fact, there were regular groves of them. Only now and then we came to some open bits of country. Otherwise, we found only stunted vegetation growing on volcanic rock, which was here slightly padded with surface soil, or else innumerable creepers and musty foliage. Occasionally, we saw a fine tree half smothered in creepers. We ate many dates of a brilliant red, with a dark violent tip, that grew on the *nghiro*. From these oily dates a buttery substance is extracted by the natives.

Many mysterious things happened. A soldier from Buddia who accompanied us met another excited soldier on the road, who was hidden by the trail, and who on cross-examination professed to come from the sultan of Zemio in order to meet me. Undoubtedly, my visit was causing a sensation in that part of the country.

We had not gone many miles when five of my carriers escaped into the tall grass, making things diffi-cult for me as my donkeys were half dead and unable to carry even small loads.

A violent storm broke, worse than the one we had had the evening before leaving the flooded *zeriba* at Buddia. We got dreadfully chilled in the afternoon by the drenching rain and wind, and partly owing, no doubt, to the fever from which I was suffering. I do not think I have ever felt the cold so much as I did that day. My teeth were chattering and I was shivering all over.

I marched on foot until 6.30 p.m., when I had to make for a hamlet called Bettini, or Badini (1,600 feet), a place about half a mile off on the right of the trail. Chief Rehan, taken by surprise, was as polite as he could be, but he had nothing to give in the way of food for my men.

This was, indeed, a day of misfortunes. Just before going to sleep, I discovered that the most valuable box I possessed, with all my note-books, sketches, photo-graphic plates and a considerable sum of solid gold had been lost or stolen upon the trail during the day by one of the carriers who had vanished. When unwell one feels things much more keenly than when in good health. To find myself in the most central point of Africa, with all I most valued gone, very likely for ever, was a blow to me.

The rain came down in such torrents during the night that I could not send out a search party ; besides, I had to look after the carriers, who were most troublesome, and tried several times to escape. In fact, although I placed all the men inside a hut, and put faithful Adem on guard with a rifle at the door, the poor Somali was so ill and worn that he fell asleep. The men inside took advantage of the rumbling thunder going on all the time and made an aperture on the other side of the hut. Six more of them escaped.

" Araignée le matin malheur et chagrin," says a French proverb for the superstitious. For two consecutive mornings, on waking up, the very first living things I had seen on opening my eyes were two huge spiders, one close to my face upon my pillow, the other enjoying the warmth of the soft camel-hair blanket over my body. The previous morning two spiders were on my pillow.

Chief Rehan played excruciating music the whole night upon a one-stringed instrument, a rod to which was attached a harmonic case made of a gourd, in the lower portion of which an opening had been cut so as to allow the vibrating sound to escape. At the end of the rod a string rested on three pieces of wood which marked the notes on which the musician harped, either alternately or repeating the single note endless times with the second finger of his right hand, while the instrument was being held horizontally in front of his face.

From Badini the next day I could only march a short distance to Yangah (1,600 feet), loading the donkeys once more as I had not sufficient carriers to get along. We crossed two streams and travelled mostly over flat country as far as the Yangah *zeriba*, which was situated in an extensive picturesque grove of *nghiro* palms. There were only a few huts inside the *zeriba*. The chief seemed a pleasant old fellow, with a highly-strung temperament.

Superstitious people say that if you touch a hump-back upon his hump good luck is sure to come. The first human being I met at Yangah was a deformed boy with a huge hump on his back and a smaller one in front, not unlike Mr. Punch. I immediately tapped him hard, first on the back and then in front, so as to make sure that my lost box would be recovered. The poor fellow's legs were atrophied, and he was dragging himself along the ground upon his knees, merely the skin and bones of his legs remaining, the knee-joints enlarged and stiffened. Curvature of the spine seemed to be his complaint. His huge head was entirely shaved, barring a tuft of small knots left on the top of his skull.

The people of this village, who were Zandes, were bearded and possessed a fairly heavy moustache. They had large lascivious lips, but the nose extraordinarily small for negroes. Most of these people did not shave the head, but tied the hair into little tresses.

We still found here the primitive fashion of lighting fires by friction of two pieces of wood. One piece of soft wood in which dents had been cut was set horizontally and firmly upon the ground. After placing sand over these dents, a vertical rod of hard wood with a pointed end was made to revolve by quickly rotating it between both palms. Spitting copiously upon the heated hands in order to facilitate matters was indulged in, while volunteers came gaily forth to take up the rotation of the vertical rod when the preceding man was exhausted. It generally took two or three men to revolve the rod consecutively as hard as they could before smoke began to rise, a couple of minutes or so after. A bit of flax, or some easily inflammable stuff—grass, as a rule—was then placed under the rod until ignited by blowing upon it as hard as their lungs permitted. From this a flame was obtained. This method of lighting a fire was not always required, as the natives never let fires go out, and all they had to do was to go from one hut to the other to get a piece of lighted wood when necessary.

The chiefs, who are great smokers, always had a slave in attendance, or sometimes several, carrying pieces of lighted wood.

Small caps of plaited grass with a tuft of feathers in them were worn jauntily on one side of the head, generally the left side, in the style rendered familiar to us by " Tommy Atkins."

In nearly all villages we found, generally in the middle of the *zeriba*, or directly outside in an open space, a big drum made of a tree-trunk hollowed out. Upon its upper side was a rectangular slit, while the drum itself stood upon two wooden rests in order to allow the full vibration of sound waves. These drums could produce a loud rumbling noise even when tapped gently with a finger.

By giving many presents to the chief of Yangah I got him to despatch a search party to look for the valuable missing baggage. I feared, even if the load had not been stolen, the carrier would have flung it, according to habit, off the trail, and in the high grass it would be difficult to trace it.

To show how simple-minded the poor Somali was, when I asked the chief to recover the box for me I was not anxious to particularize the contents. I thought that would be the surest way never to find it again. To my amazement, I found that the Somali, who could converse with this fellow in Arabic, in a fit of devotion, had gone to the chief's hut and begged him to find the box again for me, as it contained "handfuls of gold, magnificent beads of all kinds, lovely silks and velvets," and all the most valuable things he could think of. This, he believed, would encourage the natives to find it. I thought so, too—but to find it and to return it were two different questions.

You can imagine my anger when he repeated his conversation with the chief. Adem was at once despatched with four men with strict orders not to return to camp until the box had been found again.

Two entire days elapsed, during which I began to fear that not only had I lost the box for ever, but my only faithful servant too. What a prospect! All my notes, which I had so carefully collected, gone, together with lots of negatives, not to speak of other valuable property. At sunset of the second day I heard peculiar cries in the distance, and I recognized Adem's voice calling out with great glee, in his broken and genderless French · "*Monsieur, le boîte il a trouvé!*" My heart bounded with joy. Some minutes later Adem triumphantly returned with two men carrying the heavy box. They had discovered it by a mere miracle some two hundred yards from the trail, where the escaping carrier had hidden it under some bushes. The box had not been opened. Adem, with his exceptional tracking ability, had been able to find it.

I was unable to get fresh carriers at this place, and, much as they seemed to have the inclination, I was resolved that no more should escape. It was generally during the night they managed to get away, so, to make sure of things, I tied each man by the neck with a long rope, leaving, of course, plenty of room for him to breathe freely, but not enough to take his head out of the noose. They greatly rebelled against this, but I would stand no nonsense. Having tied endless knots, so that they should not undo them, I deposited the two ends of the rope in faithful Adem's hands and made him sleep with his rifle at the entrance of the hut, having taken care to remove all knives, etc. Nobody escaped.

I was feeding the men well and paid them amply in cloth and beads, but I would not endure any of their tricks, and, certainly, after all the trouble I had experienced, I was not going to abandon my baggage in the heart of Africa.

On the march, Adem walked in front, holding one end of the string, and I walked at the tail of the procession holding the other end. The carriers dropped their loads constantly, taking special delight in getting me to pick them up and put them back upon their heads, as they said that with a rope round the neck they could not do so themselves. The first time or two I was patient, and put the loads back gently upon their skulls ; but, seeing they were taking advantage of my good nature, next time a man dropped one of the heavy wooden packages I did put it back on his head, but with such a bump that the affair never occurred again.

Humour of this kind is the humour which appeals to blacks.

A fine Egyptian riding donkey which I possessed, and which had so far kept in excellent health, dropped dead that day after drinking water from a stream. He seemed in terrific internal agony during the last minutes of his life.

What with fever, the moral shocks I had received of late, the fearful weather, the marshy condition of the country, and the death of my favourite animals, to which I was much attached, I was almost beginning to be depressed. My poor Somali, too, was suffering, so that I feared he might break down at any moment and pass away. I felt this all the more, as he was brave right through everything, and I never heard a word of complaint from him. My strength was fast vanishing ; I had practically none left, and I was dragging on as best I could, hardly able to carry a rifle to keep the carriers in order. Poor Adem was unable to keep watch on the men at night, and I had to tie the ends of the rope to my bedstead to prevent them escaping unnoticed.

The entire march from Yangah was over undulating open country with plenty of water ; this district could, I think, be cultivated to advantage, except where the patches of red ferruginous rock occurred. Round us were charming hills.

Before reaching Tissoloh we had endless trouble in crossing three streams, my surviving donkeys getting swamped, and then we came to a fourth stream, extremely boggy, and we wasted an infinity of time in getting the whole caravan over.

In the absence of the chief, I was received by an

Arab, a certain Moussa, evidently a former slave-dealer, who had found his way to these regions, and having gained the chief's confidence had established himself as a sort of factotum. He was under the influence of drink, like all the better people of this region. He had plenty to say for himself. His eyes were shifty in the extreme. Upon his face lines indicating cruelty, almost ferocity, were but half-disguised under an assumed air of intoxicated benevolence.

Nothing was harder upon me after long and troublesome marches than to have to entertain these drunken idiots for several uninterrupted hours. One had to be patient with them. I did not want to put more obstacles in my way than I had already. None of these men were intelligent or humorous, like the natives of Asia, with whom it is always a pleasure to converse. Either purposely or naturally, they were so intensely ignorant that they could not disclose even the name of the smallest stream in the immediate neighbourhood, nor were they able to tell you in which direction the stream eventually flowed. They knew, or pretended to know, absolutely nothing.

A trifle more honest than the Arab was Samaka, a Zandes, the second chief. The sultan had gone on a shooting expedition.

The inhabitants of this village were Kare, people like the Niam-Niam, their neighbours ; short in stature, with deformed, elongated skulls, flat, ugly countenances, and a skin of a deep chocolate colour. The lower jaw was abnormally long, the ears placed far back upon the skull. The bizygomatic breadth was exaggerated, the cheek-bones abnormally prominent ; in fact, they were the most notable and projecting parts of the entire head.

When seen full face, they gave the appearance to the cheek-bones of swellings at the side of the face. The forehead was low and narrow. The chin tapered down almost to a point. The distance from the lower lip to the chin was extraordinarily short, the lips only fairly prominent and tightly closed in a perfectly straight line. The lobes of their ears were attached. The Kare had deep hollows below the cheek-bones, due, I think, to the much elongated " V " shape of their palates and upper jaws. The eyes were far apart and close under the eyebrows, bloodshot in most instances, and sinister-looking. They possessed a slight beard on the chin and a moustache.

Unlike many other tribes of this region, who sat on the ground, the Kare squatted down upon their heels, very much in the manner of Mongolian and Malay people. When sleeping, they doubled up their legs and slept in a heap, and never extended themselves at full length like the negroes of other tribes that I had encountered. Even when lying on the back, the legs were always folded and sticking up in the air.

The Kare went about naked. The men had curious customs, especially with their genital organs, which they pulled up in front as high as the waist, where they were fastened with a string.

After three hours more of travelling along a fairly good trail my troubles had ended. With only five remaining donkeys out of my original caravan of some thirty animals, and the row of carriers tied by the neck, I arrived at Zemio, the French military post upon the Mbomu river, a most delightful little place, with plantations of bananas, mangoes and pineapples. Well-shaded avenues had been made round the drilling ground. I was received with open arms by Lieutenant Charlemagne, who, with a non-commissioned officer and six Senegalese soldiers, was in charge of the post.

The astonishment of this officer when I arrived was intense, and his kindness to me during the two days I stayed with him could not possibly have a parallel.

Perhaps the following incident will show the incredible stupidity of the Kare. I spread all my carriers in a row and asked what they preferred by way of payment. They all said they wished for blue cloth. I asked them how much blue cloth, and they declared the length of two arms well spread out was the measure they required. So great was my delight at having conveyed all my loads so far, that, instead of two arms'-lengths I gave them double. Each received the gift with evident expressions of delight except one man, who, for no reason whatever, and before the gift was handed to him, suddenly bolted away and disappeared in the forest, absolutely refusing to be paid. Men were sent to catch him, but he would not return, nor would he take money, cloth, beads, salt or wire, all of which were sent out to him.

While I was staying in one of the houses in the post, I one night received a strange message from an Arab, who came into my camp saying a British colonel was a prisoner in this military post and wished me to help him to get away. I sent my Somali to inquire into the matter, as it seemed most astonishing to me that a British colonel should be here ; and, in fact, my servant returned, having ascertained that the British colonel was a mere Syrian trader who did not know a single word of English, a smuggler of firearms of precision for the natives, and who had been seized by a French officer *in flagrante delicto,* having sold a Lee-Enfield rifle of the latest pattern to the sultan of Djema.

I would have nothing to do with this man, and I sent back a message that if he chose to smuggle firearms into other people's countries he had better bear the consequences himself; that French justice was as good as English, and certainly quite as good as Syrian justice; and as he had got himself into trouble he had better get out of it as best he could.

One of these smugglers had, by a strange coincidence and unwittingly, nearly caused my death the day an elephant chased me. Two days before the occurrence, in halting at a place where grass had been cut and made into a sort of bed, I had rested on it, and feeling something hard under my back, I proceeded to remove it. I came upon a quantity of ammunition—.303 cartridges. These cartridges were in bad condition, as they had been there during the rainy weather, but my Somali, who was of a saving disposition, took them, and unfortunately got them mixed with my good cartridges of the same calibre. When I went after the elephants, he handed me two of the bad ones, with the result which I have already described in Chapter II. of this volume.

Zemio was perhaps the most central point of Africa, as it was almost equidistant from the Cape of Good Hope, from Cape Verde, from the Mediterranean and the Red Sea. To me, after the trouble I had experienced in conveying my whole caravan, practically with only one man, the Somali, in safety to this place, it seemed when I arrived that I had dropped into a small heaven on earth—my idea of Heaven being a modest one, you will notice. First of all, delicious fruit and vegetables upon Lieutenant Charlemagne's table; then a giant talking machine scraping familiar airs on warped records, and kept going from 9.30 that morning till 2.30 the next morning, something like eighty-four records being enjoyed, with encores.

I here paid duty upon and obtained licences to carry my rifles, with a permission to shoot big game.

The graveyard at this place, where French officers who had succumbed to the climate were buried, was a pathetic sight; and a strange sight were the graves of the Annamite prisoners, who had been sent up the Mbomu river by the French Government as an experiment, when local native labour was not obtainable.

At a distant date, perhaps, not only will anthropologists be puzzled at finding Annamite skulls in this region, but as these strangers intermarried with native women and were most prolific, their strong racial characteristics are bound to leave an indelible mark upon their descendants. Many children can be seen near Zemio with strong Annamite characteristics about them, which would certainly come as a great surprise to any student in Central Africa who did not know exactly how they happened to be there.

After two days I proceeded by a most beautiful road which had been cut from the military post to the *factorerie* of the *Société des Sultanats du Haut Ubanghi* on the right bank of the Mbomu river, two and a half hours distant and directly in front of the Npiri hill, where stands the residence and *zeriba* of the sultan of Zemio, one of the great sultans of Central Africa.

CHAPTER VI.

THE Mbomu river formed the boundary between the Congo Free State and the French Protectorate of the High Ubanghi. Although most of the land of the sultan of Zemio was on French territory, the sultan preferred to maintain his residence in the Congo Free State. When the question arose whether the Mbomu river or the river Welle, south of it, was to define the boundary between the Congo Free State and French territory, the portion of the country which lies between the two rivers now belonging to the Congo Free State ought really to have been handed over to the French, as the main river is undoubtedly the Welle, which is infinitely longer and carries a larger body of water than the Mbomu.

The sultan of Zemio sent me various presents— two beautiful bandoliers of leather, native shoes, a great number of chickens, eggs and vegetables—to take along on my journey.

I called on him one day in the company of Lieutenant Charlemagne. He sent mules to take us up the steep hill on which stood his *zeriba*. The sultan of Zemio, Ik Piri Tikima, was unmistakably the most gentlemanly and best man all round of the three great sultans of Central Africa—the sultans of Zemio, Rafay, and

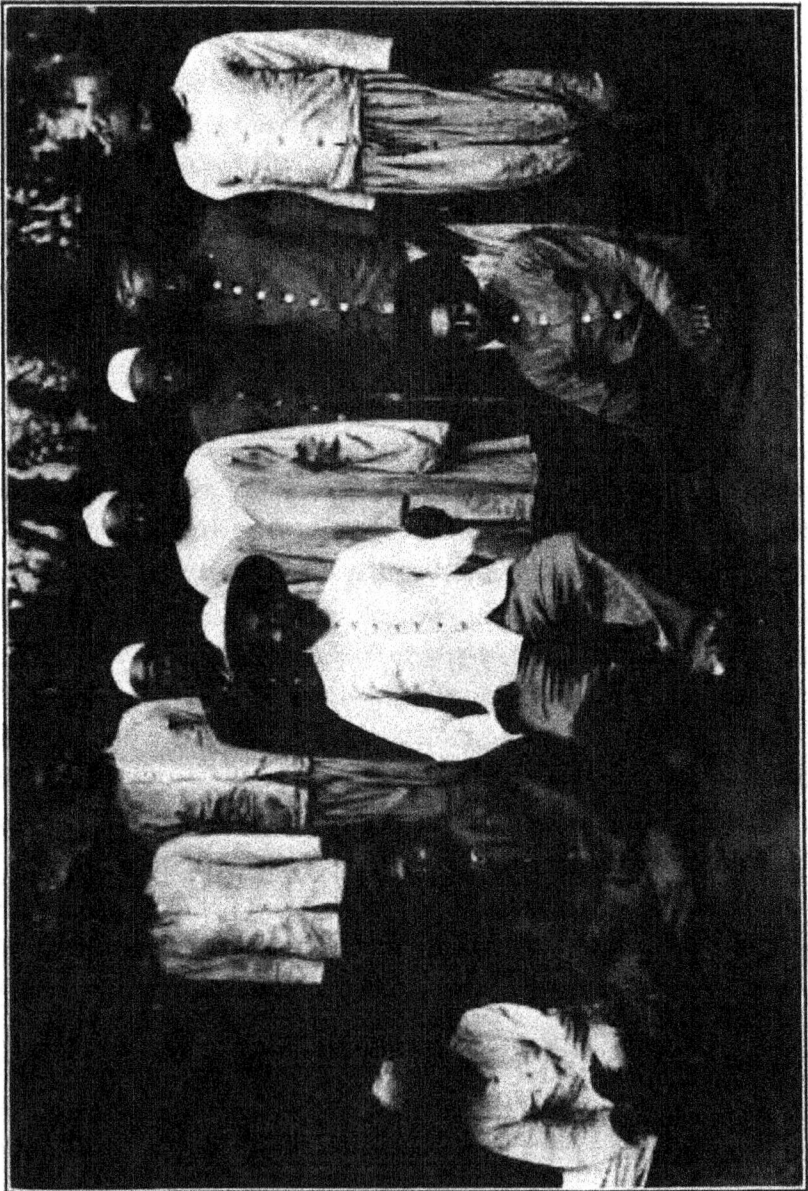

Bongasso. He possessed a magnificent head, and although much better-looking and finer built altogether, he bore a striking resemblance in his face and manner to Emperor Menelik of Abyssinia. A Zandes by birth, he had wonderful power over the country under him. He seemed a sensible ruler, strong-willed, business-like, and at the same time generous enough for a black king.

The country of Zemio was immensely rich in rubber and ivory—I should think, perhaps, the richest part of Central Africa in those two products.

The sultan entertained us to native wine and refreshing lemonade made from the small juicy lemons found in the country. We had a long and pleasant talk with him on the verandah of his large house, which was of no great artistic beauty, but quite comfortable-looking. His place was enclosed in a massive stockade, well guarded by armed men ; none of these sultans, I think, trust anybody. It is difficult to eradicate from their minds a certain suspicion that their power will not last much longer. Perhaps they are right.

I was quite amazed when the sultan informed me of the smallest incidents which had happened to me right across the forest since I had entered his country. He told me how his men, unseen by us, had kept a watch all the time I was in the forest, and messengers had been sent continually to report on everything that had taken place. Indeed, the natives had a perfect and astounding system of espionage and signalling.

I was impressed with the dignity of this particular sultan, a dignity which I must say was not to be dis-covered in the other two sultans of Rafay and Bongasso. The sultan of Zemio was on amicable terms with the French authorities and with the officials of the *Société des Sultanats,* which had obtained a concession for exploiting ivory and rubber in the three Sultanates; but, notwithstanding all this, he preferred to remain on the other side of the river outside French territory.

The entire transport arrangements on the River Mbomu were absolutely in the hands of the *Société des Sultanats.* The goods were conveyed by canoe. Owing to the many dangerous rapids on the Mbomu and the Ubanghi, constant transhipments were necessary, some of the rapids being quite impassable.

I was much indebted, first of all, to M. Pierre, director of the company, and to Messieurs Brachiel and De Villelume, the agents of the society at Zemio—where a fine *factorerie* had been erected—for their kindness in arranging for canoes to take me downstream.

Having received charming hospitality from these French gentlemen, I was able to depart down the Mbomu on June 1st. On the Belgian side, soon after leaving Zemio, I travelled between banks eighty to one hundred feet high, with innumerable monkeys playing among the trees of the thick forest; whereas on the French side the country was flat and the banks only about ten feet above the level of the water. The incline was so insignificant in this part that the river, fifty yards wide, was almost stagnant. The water was at that time just beginning to rise.

We went over two small rapids. The Yacoma oarsmen, who did all the navigating of the rivers for the society, were experts at the work and we had no difficulty. We sped along at a good rate, and, having travelled from six to seven hours, we made camp by a small and limpid stream.

These camps along the stream were rather uncomfortable, generally among high grass. The air was stifling, and there were swarms of mosquitoes. I possessed a mosquito net of thick cotton material, but it was so hot inside that I had to cut a large window in it. I preferred to be stung by mosquitoes rather than be suffocated altogether. It was impossible to breathe inside until this ventilating hole had been made.

During the night a chief came with presents of food. In fact, down the river it was the practice of chiefs to bring presents to white men—generally officers, or agents of the society—who happened to be passing. Of course, it was also the custom to give these chiefs a present in return, generally half a roll or a roll of cloth, according to the presents they had brought. Money was absolutely no use.

I had been able to purchase from the *Société des Sultanats* a quantity of salt, beads and cloth, which came in useful to me, as my stock had practically become exhausted by the time I had arrived at the Mbomu river.

Early the next morning a messenger arrived in a canoe, conveying a basketful of delicious lemons from the sultan of Zemio.

On June 2nd we were between thickly-wooded banks, with magnificent trees spreading their branches over the water; here and there groups of *manga* trees grew right out of the stream, and elephants roared close to the water-side where they had come to drink. Sometimes numbers of these lumbering creatures crossed the stream, while innumerable hippopotami snorted all over the surface of the water, dipping their heads as we approached. Crocodiles lined the banks. It was really

an interesting spectacle of tropical nature almost un-
spoiled.

The Yacoma in my long narrow canoe—scooped out
of the trunk of a tree—sang a gay chorus with a peculiar
rhythm. They did not sing in unison, but formed a
curious and not unpleasant combination of bass notes
in accompaniment to shrill sounds, usually ending
abruptly in a loud cry, made now by one, then by
another of the men ; this cry, after a short pause, was
followed by the repetition of a deep note held for some
time. The chorus was occasionally interrupted to give
place to woeful solos, but more frequently to indulge
in lively improvised songs always harping on one subject—love. These caused more or less merriment,
according to the wit of the singer—always ready, but
more or less coarse. While they sang, the Yacoma got
excited and paddled faster, and we went along at a good
pace.

On descending rapids or going through difficult
passages among rocks, two men stood on the prow of
the canoe, with long poles in order to avoid striking
rocks, six men paddling astern. The paddles used were
about two and a half feet long, the blade being half
this length. A good leverage was obtained, the paddle
being shoved almost vertically along the side of the
canoe.

From the high hill on the Belgian side, where the
river took a sharp turn, we began to see a few rocks on
the French bank of the river.

Two streams were passed on the Belgian side, the
larger one south of Baiemba village. A thickly-wooded
hill-range was to the west of us. Between Ossumo and
Baiemba, at Bentchi, were difficult rapids to go over.

The Yacoma get nervous when strangers are in the boat, and in endeavouring to take too much care they generally capsize. So all the baggage was landed and for some five hundred yards or so conveyed overland. The canoe thus lightened, and with only three or four men in it, shot down safely through the rapids, although there were many dangerous rocks slightly under the surface.

To the north of us from this place we had a high hill. We reached the Bouri river late in the afternoon, west of which we encamped for the night.

The village of Baiemba itself was about half a mile from the main stream and about five hundred yards from the Bouri, a tributary, ten yards wide, on the north side of the Mbomu. The chief of Baiemba had constructed an elaborate bridge on the small tributary for the overland trail between Rafay and Zemio.

Severe critics might find that many of the villages on Marchand's map are not marked exactly where they are now. Baiemba is one of them; but it must be remembered, as I have already stated, that villages in Central Africa have a way of constantly changing their position. The present village of Baiemba had only just been put up, in a different position altogether to where it was some years ago when Marchand's expedition passed through. Marchand's map is excellent as far as stationary points are concerned, such as rivers, tributaries, mountains and rapids.

In the new village, the chief of Baiemba had two *zeribas*. In one stood his dwelling, a mud-walled house, with an outer colonnade supporting a conical thatched roof. This colonnade, which we have already noticed in other parts, was to allow a ventilating space between the roof and the top of the wall. The furniture consisted of a bedstead of wooden logs and a mat or two.

In the other *zeriba* was a large shed, under which two wooden drums of the usual hollowed trunks were to be seen, and several small conical drums with tight skins stretched upon them both on the top and bottom. A couple of abandoned huts stood in this *zeriba*, where the natives congregated at night to dance to the sound of their drums. Outside in an open space was a high post, and near it a trophy of skulls. Evidently this was a spot where festivals and feasts took place.

We shall find these posts all down the river, especially further west among the N'Sakkara, in the sultan of Bongasso's territory. These posts—sometimes trees are used for the same purpose—are called the *basina*, and are erected in a place dedicated to the spirits of the dead, of whom these people are in mortal terror. Further in the interior it is not uncommon to find near these *basina* human skulls, as all these tribes go in for cannibalism. The lower jaw of an elephant is frequently placed round the bottom of the *basina*. Beads—always of a kind which has fallen into disuse and out of fashion—are thrown as offerings to the spirits of the ancestors.

The spirits are generally invoked by the chief, surrounded by his men, when the new moon appears. At the beginning of the hunting season offerings are placed at the foot of the *basina*. The natives believe that the spirits of the dead are jealous of all enjoyments and happiness of the living, and to propitiate their anger many sacrifices have to be endured. The living, therefore, abstain from food and drink for given periods, following the advice of sorcerers, of whom one or more are found near each village. During these sacrifices they have no intercourse with their wives.

Before starting upon an elephant hunt, good or evil fortune is predicted this way. Small pieces of wood are placed across cricket holes in the ground so as to close the apertures. These holes are watched by the sorcerers. If the sticks are not disturbed after a given number of days, the answer is that good luck will await the hunters ; but if the sticks have been disturbed by the cricket coming through them to the surface, it means, according to the position in which the little sticks have been disturbed, that the men will be killed in the hunt, or that a complete disaster is to be expected.

When a chief dies, certain parts of a goat are amputated, and the animal is fed and fattened in the village. When it dies, another one undergoes the same operation, and is fattened at the expense of the villagers in memory of the deceased chief. The poorer people who cannot afford a goat use a cock for this purpose.

At Baiemba I noticed again one of the baskets in which offerings were placed for their deity, but the contents of which the natives generally ate themselves afterwards.

The chief of Baiemba, like all chiefs of these villages, was a Zandes, and possessed, like all other chiefs of his race, a nervous, jerky temperament, quite typical of the Zandes. His shifty eyes were never steady for one moment and never looked straight into one's face when he was spoken to.

The slaves and menials in this village were Kare, who lived in conical sheds on wooden frames reaching down to the ground. They possessed no furniture, except a raised bed of wooden logs supported on four

forked pillars.   Two square mud houses, copied evidently
from French buildings, were also built in this place,
and here, for the first time since leaving the east coast
at Djibuti, I saw attempts at art.   Figures drawn in a
child-like fashion, much caricatured and exaggerated,
yet showing some accurate observation, represented
one a French officer, with characteristic long flat feet,
and another a French bugler with a trumpet of gigantic
proportions.   Other military pictures showed soldiers
saluting and also a man on horseback, the impression of
the movement of the galloping horse being wonderfully
rendered.   These were, of course, mere line drawings of
the crudest description, but it was interesting to see how
the artist had grasped the salient points of his subjects,
which he had faithfully represented so far as his rudimentary knowledge of art allowed him.

The Zandes had an extraordinary talent for mimicking
everything and everybody, not unlike monkeys and
parrots combined.   One night I heard a fellow, quite
drunk, imitating the sounds of French military posts in
a manner that at a short distance was most amazing.
Although he did not know a single word of French, the
sound of commands was perfectly imitated.   After the
commands came the bugle calls, which he reproduced
quite accurately with his mouth ; then the clattering of
a galloping horse was equally well rendered.   Next came
the noise of the soldiers on foot keeping step, which he
imitated with such faithfulness that at a distance the
illusion was perfect.

After my experiences with the Kresh, the Niam
Niam, the Gabu, the Biri and the Kare, a gloomy lot
at best, the Yacoma who paddled my canoe seemed angels
by comparison.   They were a happy-go-lucky, jolly

lot, always laughing and joking among themselves. They worked well during the day, and were anxious to help, the moment we made camp at night somewhere along the banks of the stream. Above all things, no matter what they did, they always had smiling faces, and when one had not seen smiling faces for five or six months this was a great relief. There is nothing that I detest more to see around me than ugly or dissatisfied people.

Some of my paddlers had the lobes of their ears so extended by heavy rings and decorations forced through them that one could easily pass one's thumb through the aperture in the lobe, the skin hanging down almost as far as the shoulder.

The moisture one absorbed in camping along the river was incredible. Everything was reeking wet, so heavy was the dew, and a dense mist rose in curious pointed drifts over the tepid stream when the sun appeared. As we went further down the mist became thicker, and we could not see even the length of the canoe, but after an hour or so the heat of the sun cleared it all away.

There were high hills on the Belgian side and vertical banks of alluvial formation, twenty feet high, on the French side. The scenery was occasionally beautiful, with numerous *imzera* trees, which grew at the level or in the water itself, projecting their whitish branches thirty or forty feet over the water. One of the characteristics of this tree when upon the higher banks was that it grew horizontally instead of vertically.

Numerous monkeys and occasional birds were to be noticed. Below Baiemba we had more rapids to get over, and again it was necessary to convey the baggage overland, in order to avoid the risk of the canoe turning over. One of the peculiarities of going down the Mbomu river was that no matter where you found yourself you saw before you a small range of hills. We passed on our right the mouth of the Ouarra river, here about twenty-five yards wide, which under the name of Wella we had crossed nearer its source on May 18th, at the village of Sanango in our march across the forest.

The village of Ali was situated at the mouth of this tributary, but I proceeded still further to Cari, where I was met by a tall *capitan*, a sort of sub-chief, a Zandes, too, with hundreds of cuts upon his forehead. As with most Zandes chiefs, these vertical incisions were just above the eyebrows and extended right over the temples and forehead. The operation was quite dangerous, I was told, unless skilfully performed.

The Cari village stood upon a hillside cleared from the forest, and consisted merely of three or four miserable huts. The sub-chief, however, produced a chicken, twelve eggs, and a delicious bunch of bananas. More than these gifts, I enjoyed the view from the top of the hill, from which one obtained a wonderful bird's-eye view of the Mbomu river, here describing a well-defined horseshoe, as it came from the north-north-east and turned sharply to the south-east.

The Belgian side was quite flat here, but with hills in the near distance; whereas on the French side the country was mostly undulating, with well-rounded hills, from fifty to eighty feet high.

There was a small Zandes village with conical huts, the roofs reaching to the ground. In the interior was a shelf over the fireplace in the centre, two bamboo bedsteads, a pot or two, a couple of spears; that was all.

The sheds under which these people spent most of their time during the day were open all round, and were more interesting than the huts in which the people only slept. Flat, polished granite stones were used by the natives, after they had ground *manioc* into fine flour, for compressing it into a paste with water. By the side were shelters over broken conical mounds, the graves of some of their people.

The usual presents of *merissa*, the native liquor, *manioc*, stewed vegetables and purée of winged ants were brought.

CHAPTER VII.

I WENT after several elephants on the Belgian side that day. There were dozens of them about. The popular idea is that elephants are clumsy, slow-moving beasts, but such is not at all the impression of those who have come in close contact with them. I had already experienced how fast an elephant—not to speak of myself —could run. Here I was amazed, in chasing two elephants up the hillside, to see with what ease they could climb up the steepest gradients over the most slippery clay soil; their facility was such as no other animal—not even the proverbial goat—could possibly emulate. I myself, who have considerable experience in climbing could not manage to get up in the tracks of these animals. In fact, in one or two places the clay was so sticky that neither my Somali nor I could extricate ourselves for some minutes.

On getting higher up on the hill I found large grottoes, some forming an angle inside the mountain, which had been bored by elephants with their tusks. With some reluctance the Somali and I went in, as we did not wish to find ourselves face to face with these brutes inside such narrow dark caves. We lighted matches and examined how the walls had been gradually worn down by their powerful tusks. Some of these grottoes were as much as fifteen yards deep. Elephants, as you know, use the right tusk—which is generally more rounded at the point than the left, and frequently chipped—as a work-tool. With it they dig these holes in the mountain side for the protection of their young and to keep cool during the hot hours of the day when they go and rest. Also, I am told, they dig these holes in the earth where saltpetre is to be found, which they relish. It is with the right tusk that they generally break down trees and force their passage through the forest ; whereas the left tusk, more sharply pointed, is used as a weapon of defence and offence.

At Cari during the whole night we heard numerous elephants snorting near camp. The natives kept fires alight and beat drums for protection.

On June 4th, having left Cari at seven o'clock in the morning, we heard many elephants on both sides of the stream, and later fired at two on the steep hill on the Belgian side. Again I was surprised to see how these big brutes could climb up the slippery slopes of the hill. While going after them I came across many other caves dug in the *tufa*, some as much as thirty to forty feet long and quite tortuous, and at an elevation of over one hundred feet above the river.

Our next excitement that day was when we were chased by a young hippopotamus, snorting angrily as he approached quickly with his head half out of the water. We put on as much speed as we could, as these animals occasionally think it great fun to get under your canoe and turn it over. To take no risks, I also put a bullet into his head, when he disappeared and never came to the surface again.

Further down stream we came across another herd of elephants. By noon we came to a tributary on the

this barrier of rock we passed yet another smaller one, also two streams on our left side and a number of smaller ones, mere springs, on the right. In the afternoon we went down a series of bad rapids with an interval of about three hours between. When we were going down the last rapid there was a fierce storm raging, with rain in torrents, and for a moment or two things were difficult. The canoe came near turning over once or twice as we struck on rocks, but the Yacoma were skilful, and in a moment all were overboard and, swimming along, righted the canoe again. It was with trouble that we eventually reached a sheltered place up on the Mpamo river.

Some three-quarters of an hour later we saw two men, spear in hand, rushing, or rather stumbling, towards the water. They were dead drunk, and had come to greet us and help us to bring the baggage into a hut.

The Yacoma were, like all other people of this region, cannibals by nature. They would eat any fetid thing that came their way, whether human or not. My men, for instance, who were simply bursting with lavish good food all the time, saw that day a big rodent, a *nduta*, about as big as a cat in its normal condition, but in this case, owing to its decomposed state, swollen to the size of a small pig. They immediately swerved the canoe towards it. When the floating animal came alongside the stench was such that it made me quite ill. I was nearly choked. Unable to speak or breathe, I was trying to signal to my men not to touch it and to get away, but in a moment the putrid beast was hauled on board and, in less time than it takes to write about it, it was eaten. The odour when they dug their knives into it was enough to kill the strongest of men.

When I recovered, my admiration for the digestive powers of these people was intense. They were smacking their lips and they said the *nduta* had provided most excellent eating.

From the mouth of the Mpamo river the navigation of the Mbomu became impossible, as there were rapids over which no canoe could proceed, among a lot of islets with intricate channels. From a picturesque point of view the panorama of the delta was lovely. Between Baguessi and Kombu the rapids were bad. So, having gone up the little tributary, we walked from Baguessi to the *factorerie* of the society at Kombu, where I was most hospitably received by Monsieur Piquet, *chef de zone* of Rafay. Another *factorerie* was on the Mbomu river, from which we had come the previous evening.

I left Kombu in the afternoon in order to proceed to the sultan of Rafay's place. Travelling overland we rose on an elevated plateau upon which I found an extensive series of villages called Sandu. They belonged to the sultan's uncle, who bears that name. Although the present sultan's name is actually Hetman, he still continues to go by the name of Sultan of Rafay, his father having rendered that name famous.

The Sandu villages were enclosed in a huge *zeriba* of grass and reeds on wooden posts. Only in some parts was the wall made of high, thick matting. The ground inside the *zeribas* was extraordinarily clean. The houses of the better people possessed conical roofs and mud walls occasionally painted white.

The settlement of Rafay, only a few months before I arrived, had shifted its position to a high place on the left bank of the Chinko river, an important navigable tributary of the Mbomu. The former place was deemed too unhealthy, several officers having died there. In fact, only a short time before I arrived, the officer in charge had to leave the place in a dying condition, and a military doctor, Dr. Fulconis, was now in charge of the new post, which he was gradually building in a most practical as well as decorative manner. He had already put up two or three dwellings, raised a considerable height above the ground, using red bricks locally baked, and lime locally extracted from shells found in the river.

When I arrived the doctor was busy marking down avenues of pineapples in the garden. When I approached in my straw hat and London clothes, his surprise was evident. My face was sunburnt, and when I addressed him—the last news he had heard from the east being that Arab and Syrian merchants had tried to smuggle firearms into the country—he at once mistook me for an Arab smuggler, and, speaking bluntly, almost harshly, inquired who I was and what I wanted. I produced my official letters, and watched his face intently. From the austere, evil-disposed expression when he snatched the papers out of my fingers —he would not even shake hands with me when I proffered mine to him—the nervous strain upon his frowning brow gave place first to a more placid smile, then, having forcibly struck his forehead with the palm of his hand, he burst into profuse apologies, laughing to his heart's content about the mistake he had made, and insisted on my accepting his hospitality.

The doctor was an extremely charming host. He had made important studies of the diseases prevalent in that region—malarial fever, the sleeping sickness, complaints of the blood, etc.—and the conversations with him were both highly instructive and interesting. Unfortunately, the poor man was suffering from a severe attack of malarial fever. Constant powerful doses of quinine, phenacetine, and all other remedies at hand were unable to effectively stop it, and his general health had been appreciably affected.

After my long walk and the climb up the hill where the post had been established (2,070 feet), I was ravenously hungry, and my appetite was further increased when the doctor told me he had an excellent cook.

I always endeavoured to stay as little as possible in these posts, as the lonely officers, who for months at a time never saw a white man, possessed no luxuries. Their goodness of heart always impelled them to give away to a passing stranger whatever they possessed. So, in order not to impose upon them, I always moved on, or else insisted on their accepting some of my provisions in exchange. But the doctor would not hear of anything that evening. He only had two or three tins left, and, much to my sorrow, he insisted on opening them for dinner. My grief was even greater when he opened the first tin. What was it ? . . . . " *Escargots.*" Snails in the best Parisian fashion ! Now, if there are three things in the world that I never touch, one is certainly *escargots*, whether in Parisian or any other style. Tin No. 2 was produced. Unluckily the label had disappeared. What was it ? Ham—the best French ham. Ham of any nationality happened to be the second of the three things I detest.

The poor doctor was distressed. So as not to offend him I professed not to be at all hungry and told him I had eaten just before arriving there, which was indeed a bad story. I stopped the doctor just in time as he was about to open the third tin—a tin of butter, which he said all English people were fond of, but which happened to be exactly the third thing that I perfectly loathe in warm climates.

I was seized at this place with another violent attack of fever, when I really thought my end had come. In trying to get up from my camp bed I collapsed altogether, and although the temperature of the atmosphere was well above 100° I shivered with cold. I had not sufficient strength in my arms to lift up even a glass of water, and I felt that something radically wrong was happening. Adem was summoned, and an extra strong dose of castor oil was produced. The result ? The next morning I was perfectly well again.

While the fever lasted Dr. Fulconis and Monsieur Pierre, the director of the *Société des Sultanats*, whom I had the great pleasure of meeting here, showed most thoughtful anxiety about me. In fact, M. Pierre, to whom I told my plan of crossing the African continent by way of Lake Tchad, dissuaded me from undertaking the task and advised me to make my way home as soon as possible, for he said I was in no condition to travel further.

I never shall forget his astonishment the next day when I walked three miles in the middle of the day in the hot sun to go and call on him at a place close to the stream, where the society was putting up new buildings for a most extensive *factorerie* in charge of Monsieur Levassort.

One day I went to call on the sultan—quite young. He was a man who thought himself quite *à la française*, and who wore a helmet upon his head, and a captain's

Ietman he Su tan of Rafay, and his attendants.

coat upon his back, his lower limbs being clad in ample trousers and top-boots. At one time he had been acting as valet to a French officer, and he had mastered the French language.

He did not possess the dignity of the sultan of Zemio, nor anything approaching it. He appeared to me to have a somewhat inflated opinion of himself. He was civil enough, but vainglorious and magniloquent. I asked him if he had ever visited France.

"*Les Français seraient très heureux de me voir*" (The French would be very happy to see me), he replied with a self-satisfied air. "*Ils me connaissent bien et ils m'aiment beaucoup*" (They know me well and love me much).

Like all these chiefs, Hetman knew little about his own people. One could get from him no historical data and no information of any use from an ethnological point of view ; any question asked him about his ancestors, his religion, the manners and customs of his tribes, he considered extraordinarily ludicrous. To anything one asked him he replied : "*La même chose comme les Français,*" which was not a bit the case.

He could stand a deal of drink, and seemed upset when I did not join him in a glass of absinthe. He had heard that the English people had a strong liquor called " viski," of which they consumed great quantities. I told him I had heard of it too ; in fact, I believed it to be true, but that I never drank it if I could help it. He seemed very much astonished.

Hetman and the sultans of Bongasso and Jabir were three Banja sultans. Jabir had removed himself altogether, possibly across the boundary into the Congo Free State.

Sandu, whose village we have already visited, was a brother of the old sultan of Rafay, a man at one time extraordinarily powerful.

There were seventeen Senegalese soldiers at the post of Rafay under Dr. Fulconis, who fulfilled the following functions : architect, teacher in the agricultural school, foreman of the village, cattle breeder, surveyor of roads, and justice of the peace, with a far-reaching jurisdiction. He had, in addition, to attend to his duties as a doctor, hospital warder and chemist. He was about to write a work on the sleeping sickness and malaria, which ought to be of great interest, as he had unusual opportunities of studying both in the region where he was stationed.

A lovely site had been selected for the post at Rafay, some two hundred feet above and east of the Chinko stream. An extensive green grassy plain on the other side of the water was intersected only by the long straight line of the trail leading to Bongasso. Herds of antelopes were frequently to be seen playing in this valley. On the horizon-line a wooded hill-range stood to the southwest. Below the post, along the river bank and upon the slope of the hill-range on which the post was situated, was a forest of ancient trees of great picturesqueness.

The most practical houses for colonial purposes that I saw in my entire journey across Africa were at this place. They were raised four feet above the level of the ground. The balustrade of the outer balcony was perforated all along so as to let the air circulate freely. Doors in double sets in opposite walls always supplied a cool draught, and there was an ample space between the raised roof and the top of the wall where the air could circulate freely.

The happiness of officers in Central Africa depends a great deal upon their habitations. It is undeniable that unduly hot climates are not intended by nature for white people, who, with few exceptions, suffer intensely unless conditions are studied carefully and the best is made of opportunities. Average Europeans —not able to indulge in abdominal breathing, and un- accustomed to breathe through the nose instead of through the mouth—experience difficulty in breathing freely in damp tropical climates. As white men spend most of their time indoors I think no care is too excessive that is given to constructing dwellings so that they may not eventually turn into regular death-traps, like many I saw in various parts of Africa.

Insects of all kinds collect in all houses, no matter how well they are kept. Far from keeping the sun out of the rooms, as is generally done in the tropics, I think people who want to keep in good health should let the sun's rays enter the rooms—perhaps not when the sun is too strong in the middle of the day, but in the morning and afternoon when the sun is lower in the sky. The more I travel, the more I am convinced that no better disinfectant can be found than sunshine. In my own personal experience I know that I owe my vitality and my comparative freedom from illness, where other people die by the score, to the fact that I spend most of my time in the sun and not in the shade. I march in the sun where other people march at night, and, except when absolutely necessary, I never get up before the sun. I camp in the sun, generally without pitching a tent, and, far from protecting every part of my body from its rays, I absolutely get sun-roasted.

I have always looked upon the sun as my best friend, and so far I have not been sorry for it.

At the post of Rafay a splendid shed for cattle was being built, as many animals were owned by the military.

On the bank of the Chinko river down below, a luxuriant vegetable and fruit garden had been made, with all kinds of tropical and European products. Mangoes in profusion, pineapples, bananas, papayas, tomatoes, lettuces, cabbages, carrots, *aubergines* (egg plant), onions, etc. In the post, two avenues of pineapples bordered the paths in graceful designs. Male and female papayas seemed to flourish at Rafay. The fruit was delicious. For the first time I saw in this place a curious specimen of a hermaphrodite papaya plant.

Thanks to the unbounded politeness of Monsieur Pierre, of the *Société des Sultanats*, arrangements were made enabling me to continue my journey in one of the company's canoes down the Chinko and then down the Mbomu river.

CHAPTER VIII.

On June 14th, having stayed one night at the *factorerie*, where I was treated to a most elaborate dinner, I was taken to the canoe, in which I found among my baggage a large box which I did not recognize as one of my own. M. Pierre insisted that the box must come down with the canoe, and that I must not open it until I had reached my next camp. After a great deal of arguing I had to accept the box. Another large package was also deposited in the boat, M. Pierre saying that it would provide me with a better lunch than I could get for myself, and would save the trouble of stopping on the road to cook whatever I possessed.

It is impossible to describe the exquisite politeness and tact of these Frenchmen or to express their goodness of heart. I could not possibly persuade them to accept anything in payment or in exchange for what they gave me. They would deprive themselves of anything in order to show their hospitality to a passing stranger.

A curious incident happened. I started at 8.15 down the Chinko, a handsome stream with thickly-wooded banks, one hundred to one hundred and twenty yards wide, with a gentle current and small rapids as we descended. Towards 10.30 we went over a great barrier of rocks and between wooded islets. Further down we passed a picturesque island with huge palm-trees towering above the rest of the vegetation. At 2 p.m. we had reached the mouth of the Chinko and entered the Mbomu, which was divided here into two arms embracing a long, good-sized island.

At this spot I unpacked Monsieur Pierre's package and found two huge *pâtés*, which, on being dissected, showed inside expensive truffles galore. I must confess that when I saw the size of the two *pâtés*—they were each about a foot and a half long and six inches in height—I felt sorry. My appetite is always good, true enough, but there is a limit even to my capacity. I knew that I could not eat them both within a reasonable time before they would be spoilt by the intense heat. I ate *pâté* for breakfast, lunch and dinner for three days. At the end of the third day there was still a *pâté* and a quarter left, unfortunately gone bad.

A year after this lunch, on passing through Paris, I again met M. Pierre, who had also returned to Europe. " You are a bad man," said he, after greeting me; " you took away my *pâté de truffes* on the Chinko ! " He further explained what had happened. He himself was to have started the same morning on an expedition to visit a new station the society had established further north on the Chinko river. He had ordered his cook to make two *pâtés*, one for me and one for himself. The cook had put both in the same package and sent them down to my canoe. M. Pierre, who was then in bad health, having waited until three or four o'clock in the afternoon in order to get a good appetite for his *pâté*, and having by then become ravenously hungry, ordered his " boy " to produce the relished dish, when, much to his amazement, he discovered that both *pâtés* had gone down the river in my canoe, and he had nothing

Monsieur C. Pierre.   onsieur Levassort.

whatever for lunch himself, I by that time being some forty or fifty miles away from where he was.

Where we entered the Mbomu, there were small rapids every little while—the rapids of Goui, Bedoua, and the rapids of Bekoua. At three o'clock the river was about three hundred yards wide, of indescribable beauty, with luxuriant vegetation on either side and upon the islands. Shortly after we got among rocks again. Beyond the rapids of Bekoua, long barriers were found across the river, which was here quite shallow, owing to its great width. Rapid after rapid had to be tackled, some not easy to be got over.

We stopped at sunset at a small village. The *capitan* of the village was civil, and, as usual, gave us music on a peculiar instrument, not unlike one I had noticed further up the river, made with half a gourd, to which a wooden rod with three projecting keys was attached. Only this instrument had two strings instead of one lying directly upon the keyboard on which the violin notes were played, the middle note being sounded once to every twice of the two others combined. One string rested on a bridge, the second lay flat upon the wooden bar and was twanged with the thumb of the left hand, while the first string was twanged with the second finger of the right hand.

We left this village at sunrise the next morning, and half an hour later came to a good-sized tributary, the Moi river, on the right of the Mbomu. There was a thick fog upon the water owing to the lower temperature of the atmosphere above the almost tepid water of the stream. We soon found ourselves going over the numerous rapids of Ganapia. There were impassable rapids at this place, especially the rapids of Mongunbo, where it was necessary to abandon the canoe altogether and proceed overland.

The Moi river formed the boundary between the sultanates of Rafay and Bongasso. Ganapia was one of the transit stations of the *Société des Sultanats*, and all the ivory and rubber had to be transhipped here. There was a fine *factorerie* in charge of Monsieur Boursier. The buildings were kept in excellent condition, and a beautiful rubber plantation had been made by the company, as well as a most productive fruit and vegetable garden.

We were soon getting out of the " ivory " country. In this region the principal product was rubber.

The rocks in the river were beautiful. In the centre of the Mbomu rose an island several miles long, full of game. There had been a great discussion between the French and the Congo Free State regarding the possession of this island. The Congo Free State had appropriated it, and in order to establish their priority of claim they had made extensive rubber plantations on it.

At Ganapia the *Société des Sultanats* kept a large fleet of canoes. I saw at this place a canoe nineteen yards long, scooped out of a solid block of wood ; this was specially constructed by the natives in exchange for one match-lock.

The Belgians had a small post a short distance off on their side of the stream.

After leaving Ganapia in a fresh canoe on June 16th, at the lower terminus of the big rapids we successfully negotiated smaller rapids. Beyond these, the river became two hundred and fifty yards wide and fairly free from rocks. Trees grew right down to the water.

Yacoma crew in Author's canoe on the River Mbomu.'

Further down again we came to a great number of
rapids, the Bagouangu. On the French side stood
pretty hills ; on the Belgian side was a high hill-range.
The river was getting wider all along with the many
tributaries it received on its course.

We made camp at sunset at a place where two sheds
had been erected by the *Société des Sultanats* for the use
of their agents. At sunrise the next morning we again
left, the *pagayeurs* paddling splendidly as usual. We
spun through the water at the rate of six or seven
miles an hour in a swift canoe about a foot and a half
wide and some thirty-six feet long.

The Mbomu by now was three hundred and fifty yards
wide. On both sides, close to the banks, creepers and
trees hung over the water, so that it would almost be
impossible to land anywhere except in places where
the natives or hippopotami had cut passages.

Three or four hours before reaching Bongasso we
suddenly saw facing us down-stream three high grassy
table-lands, all exactly alike in shape, and to the left
of them a mountain with a pointed peak. On the
Belgian side in front of Bongasso were high hills.

We arrived at this place, the principal seat of the
society, and at 3.30 I landed among a large fleet of
canoes moored to long poles stuck in the mud.

There were many villages on the French side and a
large one on the Belgian side of the stream. Here
again I was mistaken for an Arab trader by Monsieur
Raulic, *chef de zone* of the *factorerie*, and until the
mistake was discovered it gave me a good deal of
amusement. He and Monsieur Chanu were, however,
extremely kind afterwards.

I went to call on the sultan, an old cannibal, extremely sly and not particularly trustworthy, I should think, by the look of him.

This man possessed not only an imposing harem for himself, but he was the chief supplier of his daughters as wives to the few white men within a radius of some hundreds of miles round. He sent me two of his daughters as a present, also a little lamb and four chickens. I appreciated the compliment, but as I. was not on marriage bent I took the chickens and the lamb and returned the wives with thanks. To see them was quite sufficient. Quite, indeed.

The sultan of Bongasso seemed proud of his harem, and I photographed him one day amidst his entire contingent of local feminine beauty. There was no mistake about this old cannibal chief going in more for numbers and size than quality. He had wives of all ages, of all sizes, of all shapes, and all colours, except natural white.

His favourite lady was a plump creature who had smeared herself all over with terra-cotta paint. Her hair was adorned with beads innumerable. Her first youth had long gone by, but she was not aware of it evidently. She seated herself by the sultan's side in a most coquettish fashion, with no clothes of any kind upon her body, in order to preserve intact the coat of red paint. You can imagine my surprise when she and the sultan asked me if I had not mistaken her for a white woman. I said, " No, most certainly not ; but she might have passed for a terra-cotta woman to all but the colour-blind."

Some of the other ladies in the sultan's harem were chiefly remarkable for the ways in which they had done their hair—some in a sort of helmet, plaited most care-

The Cult of Bonrasso and his wives

fully, especially at the back of the head ; others in many concentric arcs from the ear right up to the top of the head.

There was nothing impressive about this great chief. In his *zeriba* there were merely a lot of tumble-down huts with a somewhat more elaborate hut for the chief—a crooked two-storied building of bricks with a heavy colonnade round it, no two columns being abso-lutely vertical. In fact, most of them were at a danger-ous angle. The leaning tower of Pisa was not in it with the sultan's residence.

Giving this building a wide berth when the sultan pointed it out to me, we wound our way among conical huts, quite humble, with high platforms of bamboo out-side them, upon which elephant meat was placed to dry. Under a big tree the old sultan seated himself upon a high wooden stool, and a crowd of picturesque natives encircled him.

Bongasso had a long black stick in his hand, and he harangued a most attentive audience. Let us look at them. There was a giant among them with flabby arms and sunken chest, and a most brutal face ; next to him an old warrior with a hemispherical headgear of blue and white beads. Then there were soldiers, with raised circular cicatrices in a line from the top of the forehead to the tip of the nose. Others had only three cicatrices on the forehead. Several unfortunate mortals were to be seen with huge goitre-like swellings in front and at the side of the neck, some even at the back. Then a rabble of rascals clad in rags and carrying Gras, Albini or old Remington rifles. These were Bongasso's warriors. Some wore large straw hats locally plaited ; others a crown of feathers, North American Indian style, whereas others, more humble, contented themselves with a single feather stuck on one side of the head, in a tuft of kinky hair left for this special purpose upon their otherwise clean-shaven skulls. A few wore five or six little tresses sticking up straight just over the forehead, while others preferred these little tresses at the back of the head.

The ears of these people were in most cases elongated to an unusual extent, studs of black wood or big discs of ivory being inserted into the large opening of the lobe.

The warriors carried high shields of plaited Spanish reed some three feet in length. Inside these shields were several throwing knives of the boomerang type, with a number of blades in each, not unlike those we have already seen among the Niam-Niam. Some of these knives had as many as three or four blades, some even more, and they could be hurled through the air at a terrific speed. The wounds from these weapons were ghastly. Unlike the boomerang, however, they did not possess the quality of returning to their point of departure if the target were not hit—or, at any rate, the natives did not know the art of making them do so.

A photograph of these cannibals is reproduced in this book, so it is not necessary for me to describe their countenances ; but by glancing at the illustration it will be noticed how brutal were the expressions of these men-eaters. Their mouths were prominent and re-pulsive, their noses flattened and extremely broad at the base, and their foreheads low and slanting, with little room in the braincase of the cranium, the back part of the head generally forming a straight line with the

Group of cannibals (a number of throwing knives can be seen attached to each shield).

nape of the neck. What is with us the white of the eye was so dark in these cannibals that their deep brown iris hardly made a contrast at all, and as the eyes were frequently bloodshot, especially at the corners, their expressions were quite vicious. The upper part of the iris was much discoloured, and the transparent cornea abnormally raised beyond the spherical surface of the eyeball.

Unlike the sultan of Zemio, who had a gentlemanly manner, old Bongasso was one of the most vulgar, ill-bred savages I met in Central Africa. All sorts of curious noises came from his mouth, perhaps the result of a bad digestion, and every few minutes or so he yawned in the loudest fashion and stretched his arms skyward, opening his mouth in a most alarming way. And what a huge mouth! with a palate as black as watered ink, and a thickly-furred tongue green from something he had been eating.

"I am very tired," said the old man; "I did not sleep the whole night. I drank too much *togo* and too much 'shempin' [by which he meant champagne] and 'bodo'" (Bordeaux).

In fact, the previous evening a most genial dinner had been given at the *factorerie* when I had arrived, and I sat next to the sultan. The old savage, who only a few years ago went about naked and ate with his fingers, was now garbed in a French khaki uniform —in which he was sweating—and handled a knife and fork in fair imitation of civilized table manners.

It is true that occasionally, while excited in conversation, he brandished his fork about in such a reckless manner that he nearly stuck it into my eye; and again, when he had finished with the plate, and some sauce remained, he first licked the plate himself by twirling it round, and then he passed it to his grandson, a favourite of his, who sat under the table and who licked what little had remained on the plate.

The little child was only three years old. To my amazement old Bongasso every now and then stooped to call him, as one would a dog, and then gave the child brandy to drink and a few drops of champagne. At the end of dinner, the sultan, having had a big cigar handed to him, smoked about two-thirds of it, puffing so hard that the weed was fast being consumed, and then gave the end to the child to smoke under the table.

This little boy was the son of M'bari, the sultan's eldest son.

The sultan emptied glass after glass of wine and absinthe with marvellous celerity, but seemed none the worse for it.

To return to our visit to his *zeriba*, when he had finished yawning and stretching himself, which lasted for some time, he began to pay clumsy compliments, telling me that he loved all the white people—French, English or German—all were the same to him. As long as he lived they would be safe in his country. He was trying to impress equal love for the whites upon his sons and upon all his people. The Belgians, too, on the other side, he said, were very good. In fact, all white people were good. He had never known any bad ones.

This is what he said, and I suppose he meant it, as he had nothing to complain of in regard to the considerate way in which he was treated by the French.

The sultan, although unscrupulous, had rather a

clever head, well formed, with a spacious forehead marked by many cicatrices in parallel angles. His expression was sly and did not inspire excessive trust. His lack of self-respect was remarkable even for a cannibal, and a man who could hand over any of his daughters as concubines to the first-comer in order to ingratiate himself seemed to me a person not to be admired. Neither the sultan of Zemio nor the one of Rafay, I think, would ever descend so low.

His *zeriba* and villages simply swarmed with women. As one prowled about one saw naked females lying about in bunches everywhere, either squatting down in the shade of trees, or reclining lazily, and more or less gracefully, upon cane beds, or more often squatting down in a most unbecoming manner upon little four-legged stools adorned with brass nails. Only a few were at work pounding *mànioc*, but most of the others spent their life in absolute laziness. Two or three were garbed in robes of broad red and blue stripes. Many had pendants of beads from the hair on each side at the temples and at the back of the head.

I found a deep chocolate-coloured skin prevalent among these people instead of the coal-black of some of the tribes of a lower type.

Taking things all round, these people, the N'Sakkara, were slightly better looking and better formed than other tribes we had met along the Mbomu. The women when young had fairly graceful figures, with small, statuesque busts ; but when older their breasts became repulsively pendent, with badly enlarged nipples, and, as usual, great, ugly paunches were to be seen in most women over twenty years of age.

There is no accounting for people's tastes. The

local fashions for the smarter ladies of the lower order were peculiar. At certain times of the month they would wear palm-leaves passed between the legs and tied up at the waist behind. Otherwise they generally went about absolutely naked. Some of them, however, took a large, long banana-leaf, and, having tied it in front at the waist, they would pass it and hold it firmly between the legs, leaving it to stick straight out behind for a foot or so, just like a small square green railway signal-flag. They paraded about with these and thought themselves beautiful. I fear they looked upon me as a lunatic because I could not always repress hearty shrieks of laughter when I saw them.

The N'Sakkara women showed elaborate cicatrices upon the chest as well as on the back, with attempts at the leaf pattern and coil, which were frequently and successfully rendered in highly-raised cicatrices. Squares and angles, either superposed or inverted, also parallel lines, were often noticeable in designs upon their bodies.

Morality practically does not exist among the N'Sakkara, particularly among unmarried women, not even among the chief's daughters or the sultan's, as we have seen. Any one of them will go and live with a white man and be proud of it, and in order to accumulate a dowry she will leave her home and cohabit for a time with any stranger—of any colour—and get all she can out of him. When sufficiently wealthy she will return to her paternal home and get honourably married to one of her own tribe, when she becomes a faithful wife, they say.

Unfaithfulness on the part of a woman is punished with throat-cutting, or such other radical punishment, which, no doubt, keeps women faithful to their husbands, but the husbands are never faithful to their wives.

The sultan, garbed in skins of animals, gave wonderful war-dances before his people. Although not young, he could perform difficult evolutions with great agility, while hundreds of women of his harem, trained in a most amazing manner—a regular *corps de ballet* of black coryphées—described figures and cross-figures around him with the utmost precision. The music consisted of the tam-tam and a five-stringed harp, the sounding-board of the latter covered with a tight skin perforated in two places.

A curious habit among these people was that when the sultan sat down they clapped their hands for some time.

The sultan himself was a Banja by birth. The sultan of Rafay was comparatively young, but the other two sultans of Zemio and Bongasso were quite old, and it will be interesting to watch events when they die. The sultan of Zemio and old Bongasso were men of abnormal will-power, who had been able to hold their position by sheer force, but their sons and heirs were insignificant creatures.

We have met the loathsome, drunken, degenerate Buddia, the eldest son of Zemio, and here at Bongasso we had Gambu, the heir to the sultanate, also a worthless drunkard, half-witted, and he, too, eaten up with a bad complaint of the blood—a fellow who hung on to white people merely to see what he could squeeze out of them. Gambu was the sultan's third son, selected by him as his successor. The first son was called Labassu, and was afflicted by paralysis, while his second son was Bai or Ganapia.

At Bosegui we shall find Bongasso's brother, Wanzarengu, with his two sons, Kunda and Yinga.

Another taller and older son, who had been discarded from the succession by the sultan, seemed little or no better than the above and others of his sons, such as one I met later at Baguessi, who was a mere beggar of the lowest and most importunate kind.

Bongasso, the old cannibal chief, was not ashamed to tell you that until quite lately he had indulged in human meals. He cared little what happened after his death ; as we have seen, he did not mind what became of his daughters, and he had made his sons a contemptible lot. This old cannibal chief, I am informed, has lately died.

Rubber xein   h   n a   the Société des Sullanats

CHAPTER IX.

THE *factorerie* of the *Société des Sultanats* was charmingly situated, perhaps a little too far from the stream, the site having been chosen in order to get on healthier and absolutely flat ground. Avenues of rubber trees had been made and also a handsome *plaza*, with a fine monkey-house in the centre.

The director had a fine brick building facing the square, and many more brick buildings stood all round, including the store, the theatre of gay scenes during bartering hours. The square became a regular market-place in the morning, with a great concourse of people. Business was particularly brisk at the store window where rubber was exchanged for beads, cloth, wire, or within reason for any article the natives fancied.

Fruit and vegetables, yellow *nghiro* dates, powdered *manioc*, were laid out in quantities upon gourd-vessels or in baskets in the square. The wealthier native traders were attired in bright colours and were a great contrast to the men and women who stood beside them absolutely naked.

Bongasso, being the central office of the *Société des Sultanats*, was a busy spot. Thousands of pounds (in weight) of rubber were drying in appropriate sheds, but I was told that ivory was fast disappearing in this region.

The military post was in charge of two non-commissioned officers, an " adjutant " and a serjeant. The post was formerly built by Captain Raymond, and was prettily situated near the stream. It had a tidy and beautifully-kept garden, with all sorts of delicious fruit, neat hedges of pineapples and *citronelle*, a fine-bladed plant which, besides being most ornamental, makes a delicately-flavoured, refreshing decoction far superior to tea in those climates, as it helped digestion and did not affect the nerves. The French used it extensively.

The concession given to the *Société des Sultanats* in the High Ubanghi was perhaps the largest and most important granted by the French Government in their Central African possessions. The work of that society was carried out in such a practical and therefore highly-successful manner that I think a few words on their methods should be of interest.

The *Société des Sultanats* began their work in December, 1900, with a first *factorerie* at Bongasso. Monsieur Charles Pierre took over the management in May, 1901, and founded twelve establishments, of which the principal three, as centres of each zone, remained at Bongasso, Rafay and Zemio, the seats of the three big sultans to whom the country belonged.

At the time of my visit there were fourteen *factoreries* belonging to the society, and all were prospering. The country was divided into three sultanates and one independent region (Yacoma), the latter producing no rubber, but supplying the society with all the paddlers for the canoes required as means of transport on the rivers of the concession. The rubber and ivory were brought to the river Mbomu and sent down the Ubanghi into the Congo, from which it was shipped to the great ivory and rubber market of Antwerp.

The European staff employed by the society in Africa consisted only of one general manager and a *chef de zone* in each of the three sultanates; in every *factorerie* was one *chef de factorerie* and sometimes one assistant. A most excellent and highly-successful plan had been adopted by the society to encourage their European staff to do good work. Each employee received a percentage on the production of both ivory and rubber. Some of the more enterprising were able to make a good thing out of it.

The *factoreries* consisted of houses for the European employees, generally built of fire- or sun-baked bricks, with thatched roofs; and of stores, shelters, and ample *séchoirs* (or drying sheds) for the rubber. The mortar and all building material was locally made, and it was astonishing what ingenuity had been used in obtaining excellent results with the poor materials at hand. Most of the houses, if not luxurious, were extremely comfortable and well adapted to the climate.

Strict orders had been given to all the *chefs des factoreries* to establish kitchen gardens in every *factorerie* and to grow all kinds of vegetables; every three months a box was despatched from France with seeds of all kinds for every *factorerie*. This was deemed an important precaution to keep Europeans in good health, the need of good fresh vegetables being felt, especially in the great heat of the summer. They made, indeed, a welcome change from the tinned goods on which the white people had to feed to a great extent, and which were undoubtedly injurious, except, perhaps, when on the march, when the constant and violent exercise worked off the effects of the poison contained in tinned provisions.

I have heard people talk a lot in England of French methods and of how badly employees are provided for. This is one of those insular prejudices which, with many others, unfortunately prevail in this country regarding anything done by people of other nationalities. On the contrary, it was a pleasure to notice how thoughtful and generous—almost motherly—the *Société des Sultanats* was towards her staff. Constant and regular supplies were sent out at much expense to every agent of the company, each receiving a ration box containing a quantity of flour, plenty of wholesome red wine, a bottle of cognac, some champagne as a medicinal comfort, butter, biscuits, mustard, tea and other articles highly welcome in Central Africa.

The development of the *Société des Sultanats* has been enormous during the last few years. Last year, 1906, the production of rubber packed and sent over to Antwerp was over three hundred tons, and this year I am told on good authority that over four hundred tons are expected.

The concession has an immense area, one hundred and forty-five thousand square kilometres, the richest in Central Africa in rubber and ivory. On the south the concession is limited by the right bank of the Ubanghi from the Koto river (a tributary of the Ubanghi) and the entire right bank of the Mbomu as far as its source. On the west the boundary is the Koto river from the source of its most easterly branch; on the north and east, a line separating the basin of the Ubanghi from those of Lake Tchad and the Nile. The society, officially called the *Société des Sultanats du Haut Ubanghi*, has the right for thirty years to carry on all commercial operations of import and export, as well as operations of a financial, industrial, mining, forestry and agricultural character within the concession ; also any transport enterprise by land or water along the many streams, works of colonization and of any other kind that may increase the value of the concession and its exploitation. Reserves have been made for the natives, and Government lands have also been deducted for military purposes.

I have seen with my own eyes the kindly way in which the natives were treated, and I was most favourably impressed by the patient, kindly, honest, even generous way in which trading was carried on by the employees of the company.

The society pays annually fifty thousand francs (£2,000) to the French Government for ten years from January 1st, 1900, and a hundred thousand francs (£4,000) yearly for the next decade. After that they are to pay one hundred and fifty thousand francs (£6,000) for each succeeding year until the expiration of the concession. Besides this, they give the Government fifteen per cent. on their net profits and pay ten per cent. duty on all imports as well as upon the exports.

It is unnecessary to say that, notwithstanding the fact that the society is only practically at the beginning of the exploitation of that immensely wealthy country, handsome dividends are being paid to the fortunate shareholders. As far as I could see, when the work is carried further into the virgin country, still larger profits must necessarily accrue. The society's capital is only nine million francs (£360,000), of which only one quarter has been paid up.

There are some rather interesting ministerial instructions regarding concessions granted in the French Congo by the French Government.

For instance, a provision is made to protect concessionaries in case of a third party intervening in the conceded territories and undertaking commercial operations. The concessionaries have no right to compel these third parties to renounce their intentions altogether, in the conceded land, nor can the concessionaries prevent them from going about freely upon the rivers and the public paths of the domain, nor entering into relations with the natives in order to sell them imported goods and buy the products of the territory reserved for these natives. But third parties have no right to establish buildings or *factoreries,* either on the ground reserved for the natives or upon land not conceded but reserved in the interior of the concession. These lands are considered as dependencies of the State, and the State alone has a right to dispose of them.

Furthermore, third parties have no right to build or make usurpations of any kind upon territories within the concession ; and either the military officer in charge of the region or the civil *administrateur* must give immediate help to repress usurpations of this kind.

In other words, the advantage which the administration engages itself to ensure to the concessionaries is that they alone shall reap whatever benefit is to be obtained from the conceded domain.

The case in which a third party might attempt to obtain products from the concession by establishing themselves on neutral ground and bribing the natives is also provided for. In this case, too, the concessionary can claim his rights through a judicial channel, and the

Administrateur, or *Chef de Poste*, must lend his hand to take note of the theft and bring the matter before a competent tribunal.

To ensure protection against the hostility of the tribes, each concessionary society can claim to have police posts established near the *factoreries* by paying all expenses. In no case are the directors of *factoreries* allowed to have directly under their authority the police force which is supposed to protect them. Moreover, the concessionaries have the right to request the establishment of police posts in any place where it is deemed necessary for the safety of the colony, and the concessionaries are only obliged to furnish free lodgings for the men, other expenses being paid by the administration.

The principal *postes* in charge of the police will be established by the colony at no expense to the concessionaries, especially in cases when the ground for the erection of barracks and buildings, as well as a sufficient area of cultivable land to make the *poste* a self-supporting ·one, has been reclaimed from the concessionaries.

The natives have a right to areas of land sufficient to produce food for their support, and also to some land fit for any further cultivation which they may desire to carry on, besides forest land sufficient for their building and heating needs. But they have no right to claim forests in order to trade at their own pleasure in the natural products of the country, and so establish a ruinous competition with the concessionaries.

Particular stress is laid on the obligation imposed upon the concessionaries concerning the planting of rubber-producing plants, as well as the preservation of the forests. Under the *Société des Sultanats* immense plantations of *ire* were being made, and from what I could see—and I saw a good deal—the country under their concession was being greatly benefited by the exploitation. The society brought up the river innumerable articles which the natives valued, and which were of much greater use to them than the latex from the rubber vines, or the ivory, which have immense value in Europe, but are absolutely of no commercial value among the natives, as far as they themselves are concerned, except in regard to foreign trade.

The *Société des Sultanats* owes most of its wonderful development to the practical methods adopted by the local director, M. Charles Pierre. With a long experience in Egypt, where he was born, half French and half English by parentage, M. Pierre first got acquainted with Central Africa in 1898, when he was making part of the *Bonnel de Mezières* expedition. During that visit he took an important journey alone across the Dar Banda country as far as the sultanate of Sinoussi, in order to go to the assistance of M. Mercuri of the Behagle expedition.

In 1900 he became one of the first directors of the society, and established, as we have seen, in most suitable sites, all the *factoreries* belonging to the society. In 1904 he took another difficult journey, crossing from the Congo basin into that of the Nile, a journey for which he received well-deserved decorations in France and in Egypt. He then returned again to Africa, but the evil climate of that region had played havoc with his health and he was compelled to return to Europe for ever. The society was so satisfied with his services that he has been elected Administrator of the society in Paris.

CHAPTER X

I LEFT Bongasso (1,690 feet) on June 19th, my canoe filled with presents of chickens, baskets of pineapples, fresh bread, vegetables of all sorts, and I do not know what else. The thoughtfulness of these Frenchmen was really immeasurable. They went to any trouble in order to make one comfortable on the journey.

I had a new set of *pagayeurs* from here, and the canoe went down stream at a great speed, the river having risen considerably during the night owing to heavy rains the last few days. Rocks which abounded in front of Bongasso were now quite covered over with water. A few rapids were successfully gone over, islands of great size dividing the river were passed, a tributary stream, the Mbari, was met, and eventually by way of a narrow arm of the river, I came at three o'clock in the afternoon to Baguessi, or Bozegui, where a Senegalese was in charge of the transhipping station.

Bongasso's nephew, in rags, came at once to beg for gunpowder, percussion caps and clothes. His father, Bongasso's brother, was even more persistent, and a greater nuisance than his son. These fellows wanted to be presented with everything one possessed.

I left overland by trail at sunrise on June 20th for Irikassa, as there were rapids here quite impossible to navigate, and I arrived at this place, further down-stream, an hour and a half later. I found waiting for me two large canoes there, which my good friend, Monsieur Pierre, had kindly placed at my disposal.

The large island which we had reached came to an end at Irikassa just in front of the landing-place. We sped on down-stream at a good pace, especially over the rapids of Sholiminghi, and at a spot where islands divided the river into long channels with lots of islands and rocks, some with palm-trees, and forming a regular maze, we went over the rapids of Mongu.

Soon after, we descended the rapids of Mayongo and Wanza, where hundreds of rocks stuck out, and I was ever more and more astonished at the skill of the Yacoma in steering their way through. One man, holding a long pole, stood on the small platform in the front of the canoe, and occasionally pointed with his open hand to the men paddling behind in which direction they had to go. Many times, in forcing the canoe to the right or left, his punting-pole would stick between rocks and we could never recover it. But we carried lots of spare ones. In one place a long pole stuck between two rocks, and while the Yacoma was trying to hold on to it and could not, the pole, which had been forcibly bent, on being released struck my poor Somali a terrific crack on the skull. He became insensible, ejecting quantities of blood from the nose and mouth.

Yes, of all the native tribes I met down the river I liked the Yacoma best. They were the most intelligent and hard-working; their faces were pleasanter to look at, although, like all cannibal tribes of that region, they possessed extraordinarily prominent lips—by far the most prominent part of their facial angle when seen in profile. The eyes were wide apart and oblong in shape,

Author's canoe going down rapids on the Mbomu river.

with heavy eyelids, their noses flattened, and somewhat curved at the end, with nostrils much raised, the opening of the nostril when seen in profile being of an angular form, not a curve. The back of the head, flattened with other tribes, is with the Yacoma well developed and spacious, only rather high up, the entire cranium having a tendency to slant unduly from back to front. In their case the general rule could not be applied, as when drawing a head in profile, of placing the ear between two parallel horizontal lines, one from the eyebrows and one from the base of the nose. I noticed that the top of the ear in Yacoma heads was on a lower horizontal plane than the lowest protuberance of the back of the skull. The ears were otherwise fairly well formed, only the lobe was abnormally large, even when in its natural state, unspoilt by artificial lengthening, and the concha with the auditory canal high up.

The Yacoma shave the head, leaving fancy patterns of hair here and there upon the skull. Their hands are well formed, with short fingers and extremely pink nails.

We were in for a succession of rapids. Later in the day we went down the rapids of Maragun. The Mbomu River, which had flowed, with some détours, practically west from Zemio as far as the Gulombri Mountains, proceeded in a south-westerly direction from that point as far as the mouth of the Welle.

My men every now and then got off the canoe to pick up big orange-like fruit, called the *pah*, which were extremely fibrous inside, and gave an acid white fluid.

All the way down the river we were troubled by large elephant flies, which hung over the canoe and stung the occupants in the most merciless manner, especially in the back of the head, over the eyes, under the knees and wherever the skin was soft. It was sufficient to shut one's eyes for a moment to receive two or three painful stings, which caused large swellings within a few minutes. I never was able to catch one of those flies, as they flew about at such quick, sharp angles that it was almost impossible to hit them.

The Yacoma, who wore no clothes, suffered terribly from these flies. At one moment, when a swarm of them attacked us, all the men jumped into the water in order to escape being stung.

In less exciting moments we sped along beautifully, with occasional solo songs, one which interested me particularly being exactly like the Neapolitan Tarantella with a Yacoma strain to it. We had two large drums in the canoe. These people never could be made to work willingly unless they had one or two drums going all the time.

After passing Gozobanghi, in a small arm of the Mbomu to our right, we eventually reached Ouango, where a small military post with a sergeant and five Senegalese soldiers stood at a point 190 feet above the river—the river at this place being at an elevation of 1,510 feet above sea-level.

There was a *factorerie* here, 120 feet above the river, the last station of the *Société des Sultanats* towards the west. From it one obtained a beautiful view of the Mbomu, with its many channels and rapids bordered by dense forest. Looking back, there were hundreds of little islands and rocks, and one could easily conceive why navigation was impossible in that section.

I had abandoned the canoe at Gozobanghi, where there was a post of the *Société des Sultanats* in charge of a Senegalese, and had walked the few kilometres which separated that place from Ouango. A good trail had been made, useful in conveying the goods which have to travel overland by carriers for transhipment, owing to the impossibility of taking them over the rapids either up or down.

Monsieur Lelièvre, the agent of the society, received me hospitably. I stayed there one night in order to get fresh men and another canoe to take me further downstream.

At this place ivory was obtainable from the country to the north, but hardly any rubber, the little which came in being brought from great distances. This was a *factorerie* of transit rather than of barter. It was the last I met of the society's stations where a European was in charge.

Upon the hill the air seemed deliciously cool, quite refreshing and invigorating—a great contrast to the stifling atmosphere on the water, the refraction from the surface of the river in the hot hours of the day being at times quite trying.

Curiously enough, although all kinds of European vegetables flourished in the beautiful vegetable garden near the water, potatoes would not grow at all at Ouango. Small Madagascar potatoes, however, did well.

I saw an immense canoe belonging to the society, the length of which I measured—twenty-four metres (about twenty-six yards).

All the white people I had met at Bongasso and in the few other posts were painfully ill with fever. At Bongasso, particularly, the people were suffering greatly, and here at Ouango the sergeant was in a critical condition—not so much from malarial fever, I think, as from the medicine he had taken to cure it. In all the military posts a chest containing various remedies was handed over to the officer in charge. It was a great temptation for these lonely people to use, one after the other, all the medicines, trying experiments in case any of them might cure whatever ailment they were suffering from. Thus, I found the sergeant at Ouango had used up all his medicines, regardless of their properties, to get rid of some ailment, inadequately diagnosed— merely a bad attack of fever. A baking hot brick upon his stomach was the latest remedy, when I called on him, as he believed his liver had gone wrong, and he thought this would cure him. I advised him to throw the case of medicine into the river where it was deepest, and to use the bricks for building purposes only, for which they were meant. Perhaps after a simple purge and a thorough sweat he might get better. The poor man, who was quite poisoned and in a dying condition, survived.

I left Ouango in a swift canoe with fifteen paddlers, and men as usual beating a drum. We spun away down-stream, here four hundred yards wide.

There were plenty of small villages on the Belgian side, but only few on the French bank, where, however, many existed further inland. Dendi was the name of the tribe inhabiting the north bank of the Mbomu, with the N'Sakkara further inland, north of them. We again saw conical thatched roofs, only these were steeper, with the point much elongated and with an ornamental tuft of grass at the summit. The walls were of mud.

Islands of various sizes were met with in the stream, and innumerable palm-trees lined the banks, particularly on the Belgian side. The water in the stream having risen to about half its flood limit, made navigation quicker and easier, as many of the rocks were now absolutely submerged and we were able to float over them.

With the constant rumbling of the tam-tam and the melodious chorus following the solos of the Yacoma, we sped along, meeting natives fishing with nets, the fish of good size, making excellent eating. The largest I saw were about three feet long, but I was told that some of great size, similar to the Nile fish, were frequently caught. Angular fishing-snares had been made across the entire width of the river, the angles facing downstream. Platforms were erected a few feet above the water for fishermen to keep watch; some had even a little thatched shelter. The point of each angle in the snare was made of fine bamboo matting, with sides from five to six yards long. A fine curtain of bamboo hung in front of these angles, and was used, they told me, for lifting the fish out of the water. These snares were built mostly upon rapids in shallow water.

On both banks was a continuous string of Yacoma villages with steep conical roofs. At the small station of Colico we were handed more tomatoes, cabbages, onions and all sorts of vegetables by the Sierra Leonese who was in charge.

Women went along near the banks of the stream with water up to the breasts, carrying elongated baskets (about three feet long and one wide) just in front of them directly under the water. When a fish was caught, they lifted the basket up and placed the captured fish in a bottle-shaped basket tied to their foreheads.

At noon of June 22nd I arrived at the junction of the Mbomu with the Welle river, forming here the river Ubanghi, 2,100 yards wide, where the rivers met. I halted at Yacoma (1,480 feet) in the Congo Free State, where Commandant Van Luppen gave me a hearty reception and showed me his splendidly-drilled native soldiers, some sixty of them. There was a beautiful farm, with one hundred and five oxen and cows, twenty-six horses, one mule and three donkeys, and innumerable sheep, pigs, fowls and ducks, all in the healthiest condition.

It was pleasant to see how ingenious this man had been in making agricultural implements for his people, such as spades, picks, and even a most elaborate iron plough locally constructed out of old pieces of iron.

The natives were picturesque, as they were receiving quantities of brass and copper wire and beads in exchange for rubber, and they used all these articles for decorating their bodies, the hair particularly being matted into most elaborate caps of beads in remarkable designs woven into the hair itself.

The natives on the Belgian side worked iron with considerable skill with a forge similar to the one we had seen among the Djur ; only these people used a set of three bellows instead of two, placed horizontally upon the ground, the upper part of the loose skin arrangement being fastened in the centre to a vertical rod which was made to pull up or press down, causing a powerful draught. The current of air from the three bellows (kept in constant alternate motion by two people) was collected in a common earthenware funnel placed in front of the three tubes and acted on a charcoal fire.

Large hammers, made of hard stone tied to a wooden handle, were used by these blacksmiths ; while similar hammers and anvils of iron locally cast, the first triangular in shape, fixed on to a split piece of wood and

Tongu with hair ornamentations of beads (Yacoma, Congo Free State).

fastened with a fine vine, were also used for more delicate work.

The natives improvised crudgels for smelting the ore in an anthill, to which they applied several bellows on the upper part in order to increase the combustion. Ignited charcoal was mixed with the ore, and an earthen vessel placed underneath, in a hollow dug for the purpose, received the molten metal.

Spearheads, all kinds of throwing knives and implements, were made by the natives. The *nza*, armlets worn by the Dendi, particularly by the children, to whom they are given as amulets to prevent disease, were also manufactured locally.

All these people were, of course, cannibals, although the Congo Free State authorities were endeavouring to put a stop to cannibalism. In fact, severe laws were in force. I do not suppose that any of the tribes along the river would kill a person in order to make a human meal, but if they found a dead body anywhere in the forest, whether that of a white or a black man, they would certainly not miss the opportunity of eating it. In battle, enemies killed were always eaten. But they would never eat a member of their own tribe or an inhabitant of the same village. Only men partook of human flesh, not the women.

The Dendi were a low type of humanity, with no definite form of religion. No totems were to be found in their huts. They had, of course, superstitions. They were great believers in the *likundu*, or evil eye, also in evil spirits which brought disease and death.

The most picturesque natives of the population at the mouth of the Welle were the Tongu, of whom a photograph is reproduced in this work. Their curious head-dress will be noticed, of brilliant red beads in bunches attached to the hair.

Raised cicatrices were made by incising the skin, and, when healed, making another incision in the same place several times, until a regular notch, sometimes half an inch high, was raised on the forehead. The Yacoma, as we have already seen, had three of these lumps on the forehead. Other tribes showed as many as seven, the four additional ones extending to the tip of the nose, and giving a repulsive appearance to the face.

Parallel cuts upon the spine from the neck to the base of the spinal column were also fashionable at this place, and also on the trunk between the midriff or diaphragm and the sexual organs.

The Yacoma removed two upper front teeth and frequently sharpened the two adjoining teeth to a fine point. I have also seen others who sharpened all the front teeth to a point. The Tongu also indulged in this fashion.

The Tongu had broad nostrils of an elongated shape, not unlike the section of a sparklet. The bridge of the nose was extraordinarily flat, the eyes far apart and lengthened into an almond shape with the outer corners slightly turned up, the eyeball quite à fleur de tête, but only one-sixth of it showing when the eyes were fully open, as the eyelids were heavy and overhanging. The forehead was narrow, the hair frizzly. The upper part of the skull protruded considerably into a point at the top of the skull beyond the vertical line of the neck at the back, and had a conspicuous slant forward, leaving the forehead extremely low.

There seemed to be little room in the cranium of the Yacoma people (not to be confounded with the Yacoma tribe further down-stream) or the Tongu, for an intelligent brain; but one noticed among these Yacoma, in comparison with other tribes, a certain development of brain power which we had not met in the Kare, the N'Sakkara, and the Kresh.

Where all these river tribes were well developed was just below the shoulder blades, owing to the punting and paddling which occupied most of their time, and which greatly developed the muscles in that region. They possessed, nevertheless, but little lifting strength, and were extraordinarily weak upon their legs. They were bad walkers, and their toes, in relation to the direction of the foot, were inclined to turn outwards, not being in a direct line with the remainder of the foot, but at a considerable angle from the normal straight line of the big toe. I do not think that this characteristic was originally natural to the race. Whether it has been acquired by contraction of the muscles owing to rheumatism, as they spend much time in the water fishing, I could not say.

Marriages among these people were again by purchase, wives going cheaper here than they did in the Yambo and the Nuer countries. A first-class wife could be purchased for a bundle of spears, a broken-down gun and some ivory, which were to be handed over to the father of the bride.

The Tongu had curious and rather graceful dances; generally one or two young girls much decorated with beads, brass bracelets and anklets danced and did suggestive posturing within a semicircle of other maidens, who sat down clapping their hands and keeping time with the step of the dancing. The dancing girls were carried about from village to village, standing on a man's shoulder. They never walked a step except when dancing. Lavish presents were given them by natives.

Just the same as we have fashions in music, in art, as well as in our wearing apparel, so have these cannibals. For some years it may be the rage in these regions to beat the tam-tam or sing and dance, and they will do nothing else the whole time. Then out goes the fashion, and for years nobody will sing or dance, and the wooden tam-tams are left to rot away. The same, only in a more marked degree, happens with the wearing of certain coloured beads or peculiar coiffures.

For the first time I had that morning at Ouango seen an albino Dendi, quite a repulsive sight, his skin of light, sickly, pinky-brown colour in patches, his hair whitish, eyes without eyelashes, half-closed and watery. His nails were discoloured and pink, and so were the palms of his hands and the soles of his feet, as light in colour as those of Europeans.

At the post of Yacoma great plantations were made of rice, wheat, Indian corn, and extensive plantations of rubber, the *Functunia elastica*, commonly called the *ire*, which was the most suitable rubber plant for that particular climate, as we have seen on the Mbomu river.

The *ire* or *Functunia elastica* is the plant chosen by the Governor of the Congo Free State as being the most productive of rubber. The vine *Landolphia Klainei* is equally planted, but not in such quantities as the *ire*. The *ire* is a vine indigenous to the Congo, and owing to the excellent quality and quantity of rubber it produces and the rapid way in which it grows, the Government has ordered immense plantations to be established all over the country. To give an idea of the size of these plantations,

The best dancer on the Lean b'... ...vil Co...o Fr

one hundred thousand acres of land have been set aside in the district of the Ubanghi alone.

There are, of course, many other latex-giving plants in the Congo besides the *ire* and the *Landolphia Klainei*. The most notable are, perhaps, the *Landolphia Owariensis* and the *Clitandra Arnoldiana*, which also produce good latex. Then we have the *Landolphia Gentilii* and the *Bendawe lemoze*, which are also two good vines, the latter growing wild in the Ubanghi region. The *Clitandra Nzunde*, which is also found in the Ubanghi, is quite good too.

One finds immense quantities of the *Landolphia florida*, which ejects a sticky matter like glue, but no one has so far succeeded in coagulating it. A huge fortune awaits the lucky chemist who succeeds in solidifying the latex of this plant.

There is also another plant closely resembling the *ire Functunia*. The two varieties can be identified by one possessing a small hump in the upper part of the leaf, while the other one shows some elongated depressions on the surface of the back part of the leaf.

The *Functunia Africana* is outwardly almost identical with the above except that the leaf is devoid of the small hump. This quality is extremely bad and quite useless for commercial purposes. The vine *Carpodinus Gentilii* is also considered valueless.

Rubber-producing plants of the *Ficus* group are to be found in the Congo Free State, but their quality is not yet sufficiently known, and the Government does not possess sufficient accurate information to advise their culture on a large scale. The *Ficus elastica* and the *Ficus negbudu*, etc., are found. Some of these plants of the *Ficus* family are parasites, and grow upon other trees like vines, encircling them in their roots.

There are various processes used by the natives in coagulating the latex into rubber. Sometimes the latex is coagulated on the bark of the vine itself and rolled round small sticks or agglomerated into small balls as it is ejected. At other times the latex is collected in a large cup made of half a gourd, and coagulated by the acid juice either of lemon or of an indigenous plant called the *Bosanga* or *Bossansanga*.

In the Ubanghi region two methods are principally used : one, coagulation by means of boiling water ; in the other (used chiefly in the High Ubanghi), coagulation is obtained by delicately rubbing the tips of the fingers on the latex, which is placed upon the chest of the operator.

As to the manner of collecting the latex in the Congo Free State, it is absolutely forbidden to cut down rubber-producing vines or trees. A special Control Organization has been established in order not only to watch that no violation of the law is committed, but also to look after the welfare of the many new plantations which the State has established.

Certain experts maintain that the method of incising the vines is not practical, because one can only make these incisions of a short length. They even say that a vine cut four and a half feet from the ground will produce young shoots rapidly growing, and, therefore, they advise the method of cutting the vine horizontally Experiments are constantly being made to ascertain the most practical method of tapping the vines.

The planting of the *ire* is extraordinarily easy. One places the seeds of *ire* in a nursery, and when the plants possess as many as six or eight leaves they can be transplanted and placed where they are afterwards to remain. Having cleared the soil in a convenient manner, to keep the plants healthy they should be disposed with a free radius of four yards from one another. This is all. In the forest, too, unnecessary trees must be cut down, leaving about ten trees per hectare (2·471 acres).

There is another kind of rubber vine in the plains of the Congo, called by the French the *Caoutchouquier des herbes*. The principal and almost only kind of this plant is the *Landolphia thollonii Dewèvre*. These plants are not unlike vines growing underground, a condition to which they have subjected themselves, seeking the coolness which they cannot find above ground in arid regions where rains are not frequent. The portions of this plant exposed to the air are not voluble. They are represented by ramified stems twenty centimetres (7·874 inches) to sixty centimetres (23·622 inches) high. Like most other rubber-producing plants, these, too, produce a spherical or a peri-form fruit. The subterranean part of the plant forms rhizomes, which are the mode of propagation of the plant, and from which a rubber of excellent quality is extracted.

The collection of latex of the *Landolphia thollonii* is effected differently from that of the vines. The rhizomes are taken and dried and then beaten.

CHAPTER XI.

On leaving Yacoma, we saw all along the Belgian side of the stream an endless succession of native houses with pointed roofs. Occasionally one saw square houses, evidently copied from Belgian buildings.

The Ubanghi river was now of great width all along, with steep, high banks for some distance on our right, and flat islands, which had been severed from the mainland by the erosion of the strong current.

We were caught in a tornado when I left Yacoma, the river getting as rough as a stormy sea. Big waves nearly upset my canoe as we were endeavouring to cross over to the French side, and we shipped so much water in a sudden violent squall that I was compelled to put into Ugombe (1,470 feet), where I remained for the night.

After paddling six hours the next day I reached Dupré, the last station of the *Société des Sultanats*, where more vegetables were showered on board and were greatly appreciated, as in those hot regions one has a perfect craving for green refreshing food. I had lived most of the time on heating tinned provisions, with a medicated taste, so salted or so smothered in borax by way of preservative that my palate and gums were getting seriously affected by a complaint frequent with those who make undue use of tinned provisions, and resembling a mild form of scurvy. Along the Mbomu, however, I had been able to get fresh food, lambs, chickens, eggs, and vegetables, and I was soon cured of the trouble.

Half an hour after leaving Dupré I reached the Koto— an important tributary on the north side of the Ubanghi a fine-looking stream over one hundred yards wide at the mouth, and navigable by canoe for hundreds of kilometres. This river formed the western boundary of the sultanate of Bongasso and also of the *Société des Sultanats*.

On the west bank at the mouth of the Koto river was the *factorerie* of the Koto concession, where a handsome farm had been made, with red-brick buildings. Cattle, horses, donkeys and pigs—herds of the latter— seemed to flourish at that place.

The concession of Koto is situated along the river of the same name, as far as the country of Sinoussi to the north. The concessionaries possess a *factorerie* at Mukka, north-west of Bria on the river Bongo, a tributary of the Koto, which first goes slightly to the west then towards the north-east.

The Koto society makes plantations of *ire*, undoubtedly the best-producing latex plant, as much as six kilos being obtainable in one single tapping of the vine *landolphia*.

The Banda Tombagu people who live in the Koto region are fairly good workers. The sultan of Sinoussi imposes a tax per man upon them of five kilos of rubber per year. Otherwise they are quite free to sell whatever they can in excess of that amount.

On the Bongo river are no less than fifty-two rapids in a distance of ninety kilometres. In one spot between two mountains there is a kind of " barrage " of rock right across the stream, which for more than a hundred yards is quite impossible to navigate.

It is well known that the sultan of Sinoussi (not to be in any way confounded with the Sinoussi people we shall find much further north—north-east of Lake Tchad) is in constant connection with the Darfur, caravans constantly coming over to N'Dele from Darfur. The sultan of Sinoussi's son, Adem, now directs all affairs of State.

This fellow is an unscrupulous scoundrel, cruel to the utmost degree. Excellent rifles are brought over to his country by traders from the north and east, and stories are told of him sitting on the roof of his palace shooting innocent people in the market square to experiment how far the bullets will carry. Prisoners are used by him as targets in revolver practice.

Punishments in the Sinoussi country are, indeed, punishments. When a man is discovered talking to one of the women of the sultan, they amputate his sexual organs and stop the bleeding by applying boiling oil. This generally causes the death of the victim.

Hussein, who was the nicest of Sinoussi's sons, having disobeyed his father, was severely reprimanded by him. He took it to heart, and believing that he had been lowered in the eyes of the fifteen councillors of State, said he would leave the country. He started. Four hours later he was brought back poisoned by his father's orders, although the people were told that he had died from a snake-bite.

The pure Tombagu people who are found in the Koto concession are faithful and honest, quite amenable to

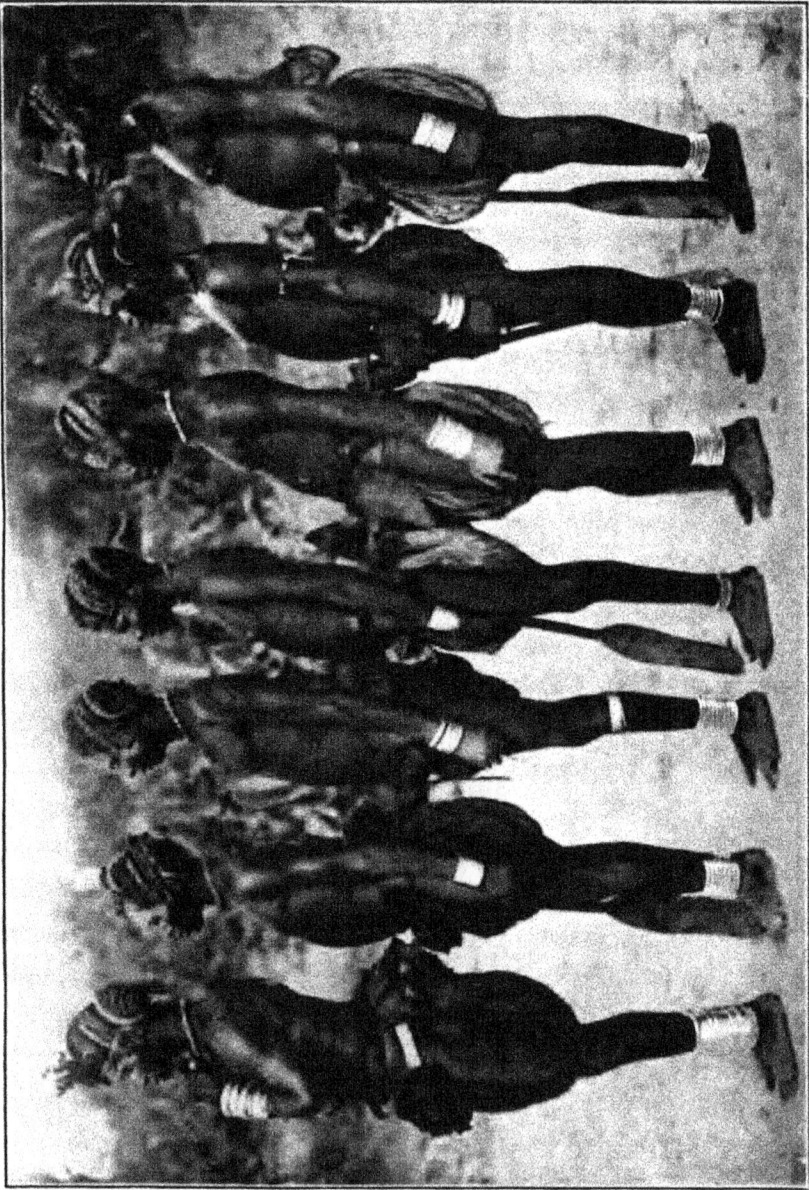

Cannibals with wonderfu bead decorations on the hair Congo Free State

reason, if, perhaps, a little lazier than the mixed Banda Tombagu. With them a European is quite safe. They do not go in for cicatrices nor tattooing of any kind. Arab civilization having come from the north, they have adopted clothing, big pantaloons generally to the knee, sometimes to the ankle. Some men also wear a short Arab shirt.

The Sinoussi in their raids have carried away most of the Tombagu women as slaves.

When a man gets married among the Tombagu he must begin by asking the chief's permission. Then the father of the girl must be consulted, and must be given a certain number of articles—clothes, beads, gunpowder and salt—as purchase money. If the woman is not faithful, however, a husband can reclaim all these goods. The chief of the village is the judge in such matters.

Polyandry exists among these people. When one man starts on a rubber-collecting expedition, he allows a friend to cohabit with his wife for an entire moon and to use his house.

The Tombagu wear long hair, and as it is frizzly they lengthen it by using grease.

Agricultural pursuits are carried on by women. Unlike the black women along the Ubanghi, they are never sold or hired to Europeans.

When a man dies he is enveloped in a cloth, and then left for two days and two nights inside his hut, during which time all the men congregate, shedding tears and dancing, moving their feet slowly backwards and forwards. Relays of dancers are supplied, so that the dancing is kept up continuously, day and night. They remain in several parallel rows outside the hut. People who stand on guard at the entrance of the dwelling fire their rifles at intervals in order to keep away evil spirits. The higher the social position of the deceased, the more frequent the firing, and the greater the number of professional weepers and dancers around his hut. The dead man is eventually buried in a straightened posture.

They believe in a good god called by them Em Zappa, who is responsible for everything good which takes place.

At Mukka there were six chiefs : Hussein, Nimu, Gombago, Gomali, Ghirigambo and Gupandeh. They have been placed there as chiefs by the sultan of Sinoussi.

On the French side of the Ubanghi the Yacoma had elaborate headgears, the hair being plaited in all directions in curves and parallel lines, making elaborate designs. Pendants of hair and white and red beads ornamented the forehead. Picturesque fellows wore semicircular flaps of interlaced hair and beads covering the ears, which produced quite an artistic effect.

Artistic feeling seemed slightly more developed among these people than among tribes further up on the Mbomu. The cicatrices upon their bodies assumed elaborate designs, with curves, spirals, coils, angles, quadrangles, lozenges, and well-rendered leaf designs. Some of the women had the chest, breasts and back literally covered with designs of most minute proportions.

The journey, on June 23rd, was continued until the village of Lindo was reached. The river was beautiful, with rocky shores on the French side and a rocky headland. Other thickly-wooded headlands stood in the background, and a fine grassy hill-range of some height

A Daoré warrior (Congo Free State).

on the Belgian side formed quite a picturesque panorama before us. A pretty little stony island, with palm-trees upon it and thick vegetation, divided the river exactly in two.

An hour or so beyond Lindo, after descending the troublesome Setema rapids, the river became fully 2,400 feet wide. On the Belgian side as we proceeded the grassy hill-range ended abruptly at the river. A flat island was separated from it by a broad channel. In the background in front of us we now had high elevations of rounded proportions, and beyond them higher mountains.

In going down the Setema rapids my canoe was nearly overturned and became filled with water, but we were just in time to take her to a place of safety, and we continued our navigation until we arrived at Mobay, the most important French military post upon the Ubanghi.

Captain Mahieu, in charge of the post, was in a dying condition, owing to a second relapse from blackwater fever, which he had contracted in going after elephant. He had to spend some hours in a marsh in order to avoid being seized by an elephant he had wounded.

The post, high up upon a hill, was in a somewhat dilapidated condition. At the foot by the river was a station of the *Compagnie de Navigation et Transport du Congo-Ubanghi*, an offshoot of the *Société des Sultanats*, under a smart, business-like Frenchman, Monsieur Moulinet. This was a great transit station, where business was brisk.

There were extensive native villages along the banks of the river, particularly flourishing-looking and numerous on the Belgian side, where stood the lovely Belgian post of Banzyville (1,450 feet). The native name of both sides of the river was really Mobaya (a rapid).

The people in the village on the French side were under a temporary belief that an infectious disease was to visit their country. As the new moon was about to appear, the women painted themselves of a brilliant terra-cotta colour, and carried, either around their arms, hung to their ears, or sticking out straight from the forehead, huge cylindrical pieces of wood—amulets to preserve them from death. All night and the greater part of next day the tam-tam was banged, and improvised prayers were rattled off fervently, to drive evil spirits away.

On the Congo Free State side, too, when I crossed over, the scare had seized the inhabitants, and the natives followed a similar custom.

Mobay on the French side was an unhealthy place, extraordinarily damp and feverish.

I spent no less than ten days in the neighbourhood of Banzyville in the Congo Free State, a province in charge of Captain Ugo Bibolini, an Italian officer in the employ of the Congo Free State. Needless to say, this officer showed me unbounded hospitality. After one had got over the delightful reception one received from the jovial Italian captain, the first thing that struck one was Captain Bibolini's canoe—the finest on the river Ubanghi—twenty-two metres (seventy-two feet) long. It was carved out of a single tree, beautifully shaped, and required no less than thirty-five men to paddle it, with a thirty-sixth to punt at the prow, where he stood on the look-out for rocks.

The post of Banzyville had been established by

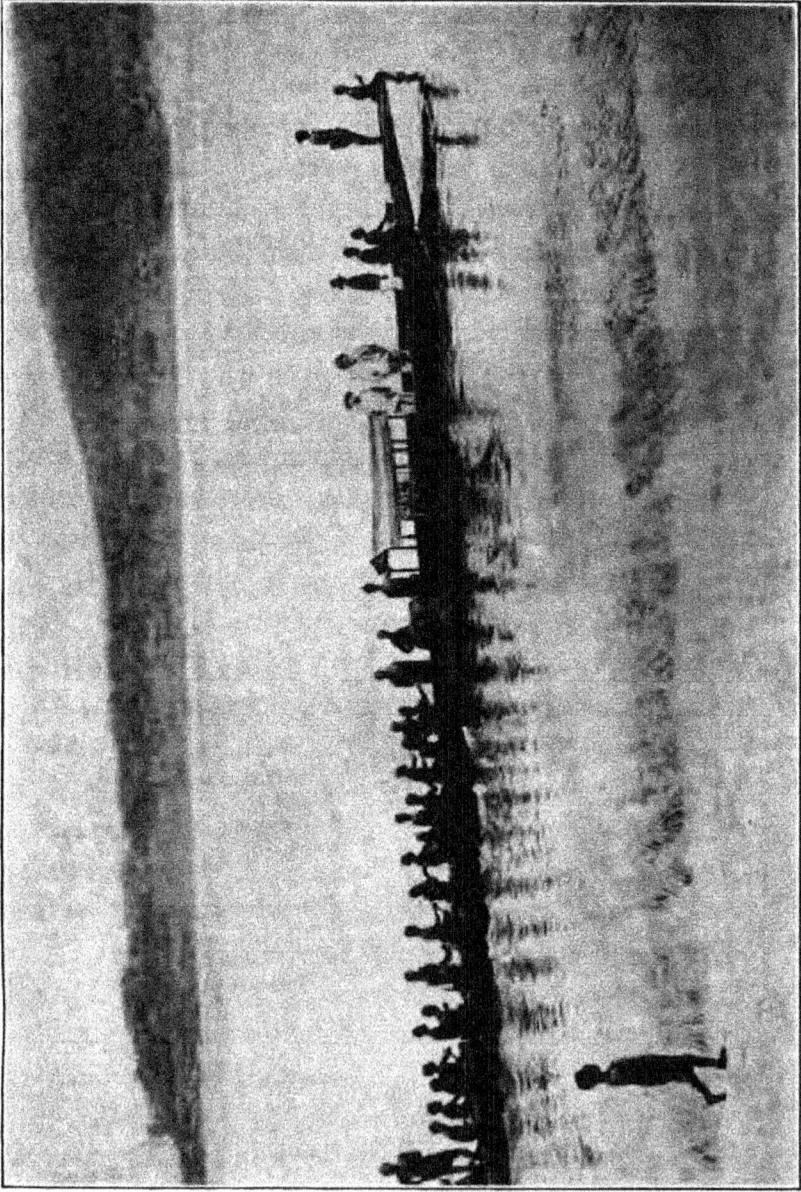

Captain Bibolini.

The longest canoe (71½ feet) on the Ubanghi.

Captain Aiuti, an Italian, but the completion of the post was due to Captain Bibolini.

It may be interesting to learn some points regarding the behaviour of officers in the Congo Free State from one who has really seen them, and had peculiar chances of observing what was going on, no obstacles of any kind having been put in the way of one's judgment.

It is well known that although the Congo Free State goes by the name of the Belgian Congo most of the officers there are not Belgian, but of various nationalities, mostly Italian and Swedish. The Italians, I think, were those who did the best work among the natives. They possessed a softer and more patient nature, and treated the natives as if they were children of their own family, a form of administration which greatly appealed to savages.

Captain Bibolini, for instance, commanded in his region a respect which many European monarchs would greatly envy in their respective countries. This was not obtained by force, but entirely by considerate kindness. Necessarily when people committed serious offences they were severely punished. For instance, one day a man came into the post carrying a small basket. Suspicions were aroused and he was searched. In the basket were found a little hand and two small feet of a child, the remains of a cannibalistic feast. On ascertaining that this man had killed the child in order to eat him, a trial took place, and he was at once strung up as an example to others.

It is impossible in those countries to deal with natives as one would with Europeans, and if severe measures were not adopted the few whites who hold that country at the present moment would soon be massacred. The people who are not criminals, however, have nothing to fear either in the French or the Belgian Congo. If anything, they have really more independence than people in Europe or America, and no comparison can be made between the taxation levied upon them and that of people in Europe and the United States.

The territory of Banzyville was enormous and thickly populated with Buwaka, Banza and Gombi. The Buwaka were an extremely bad lot, intensely opposed to the whites. In fact, these people had strongly resisted the interference of whites in their country until the reports of the fair treatment and justice which was prevalent at Banzyville had spread among them. When the Congo Free State officer visited their land he had no occasion to fire a single cartridge, but was entertained most hospitably by the natives.

I was on several occasions present at the palavers of incoming chiefs with the Italian captain, and I took special care to notice what was going on. In every case the natives seemed extremely happy and the interviews of a most jovial character. I at no time saw, either at this post or other Belgian posts, any signs of dissatisfaction.

The Italian officers employed by the Congo Free State have done remarkable work in that country. They were always much loved by the natives for their kindly treatment of them. The way in which they administered justice was always sensible and moderate, while they showed a great deal of ingenuity in improving the agricultural resources of the districts under their jurisdiction.

Rubber being brough   n, Congo Free State.

I think there could be no better proof that the natives are well treated by the Congo Free State than to see how neat and flourishing all the villages were, and how numerous was the population on the Belgian side in comparison with the other side, the French. If these people were so ill-treated as they are made out to be (only by people who have never been there), I do not believe for one moment that they would remain where they are. All they would have to do would be to cross the river and go over to the French side, where they would receive French protection at once, which would accord them equal, if not more, freedom and privileges than it does to French citizens. Nothing could be simpler. Far from it, the inclination is just the other way. The people from the French side go over to the Belgian side in far greater numbers than those of the Belgian to the French. They find they can do better business and live just as happily in the Congo Free State, where roads were constantly being cut by the Belgians, and the country was fast being improved.

One great point about Italian officers was how well they could stand the climate as compared to men of other nationalities. Their extreme sobriety, their wholesome diet, their softer, brighter, less irritable temperament, and their keen sense of the humorous, stood them in good stead in tropical regions. There is nothing worse for one's health than to lose one's temper—except perhaps repressed anger.

I well remember Captain Bibolini sitting at his desk, with a pleasant smile always upon his lips, marking carefully each basket of rubber brought into the post by natives. Each man's name was registered, so that no mistake could occur, and payment in goods was at once handed over. Money was useless, and the natives would not accept it. Hundreds of men sat down upon the ground with legs spread wide apart and crossed arms resting upon their knees. Their faces were expressionless and stupid, with a hint of cruelty in the vicious eyes. Each man had a basket of rubber before him. Every man, in the richer regions, must bring in three kilos (six pounds) of rubber a year—the only tax imposed upon them. This only means a few days' work a year for them—a work which requires no effort whatever. As they generally go *en masse* upon these rubber-collecting expeditions, they carry their entire families with them and look upon the whole thing as a great spree. Rubber has locally no value whatever among natives themselves. They have not yet risen to pneumatic motor-wheels, nor to mackintoshes, galoshes, or rubber-soled tennis shoes. No use worth referring to is made by them of this valuable latex, so that I think a good deal of fuss which is made in Europe regarding stealing the product of the country is unnecessary.

There are, of course, simple enough people who still believe that nations go and colonize savage countries merely for the sake of bringing civilization and comfort to the natives. Poor people ! they still have a lot to learn ! I have always been in favour of freedom, but with freedom everybody should work to the best of his ability. If he will not work, let others take what he himself discards as useless. I do not think that picking up an orange thrown away by a stranger constitutes a theft, nor the picking of a wild product which does not belong to anyone, and would be left to perish by the people close by, under natural circumstances.

If we compare the taxation of Europeans with that

of the natives of the Congo Free State, we shall find that we are by a long way the worse off of the two. I do not suppose that, all counted, the taxation of a native in the Free State amounts to more, in local value of rubber, than a few shillings; in value of time, merely a few pence. It should not be forgotten that if rubber has an inflated value in Europe it is because of the immense freight charges and intermediate profits which have to be added to the local African value before the rubber is placed upon the market. Common salt, for instance, which can be obtained in England at a cost of one farthing a pound, reaches a net value, with freight, of close upon four francs a kilo (three shillings and twopence halfpenny), or seventy-six and a half times its own value by the time it has reached the Upper Mbomu, so that all these things should be taken into consideration by fair critics.

Why people should storm because the natives are made to work for a few days in the year, I do not know. There are thousands—millions—of people in Europe and America who are compelled to slave, and we say nothing about it. Any well-treated servant in England, where servants are best treated, has to work harder than any of the hardest-worked natives I saw in Africa.

I will not enter here into the kindred question of slavery and the ridiculous notions Europeans and Americans entertain upon that question. If ever I have seen happy people in the world they were African slaves. They generally lived with their masters and made part of the family; they both ate identical food from the same vessels and shared the same huts. It was in the interest of their masters to keep them in good health; they went about as they pleased and did trading on their own nt: when taken away from their masters they ably returned to them. Apart from the nominal ership, the slave was just as free as his master, and none of the worries of the latter. Two-thirds of servants in Europe or America, three-quarters of our nk clerks and shop assistants are infinitely less free d more hard-worked than slaves in Africa under black asters. former slaves in America under white asters I cannot speak, as I do not know.

ith a little sobriety of reflection, let us see exactly hat happens in the Congo Free State. If a native ays his tax in rubber, his name is duly marked upon carefully-kept books and he goes home happy. If he ngs more, he is duly rewarded, or the extra quantity laced to his credit for the following year. If he brings e, and cannot give a plausible reason for it, he goes in a few days. But in America and in any pean country too, as well as in all colonies, if people ot pay their taxes they are made to suffer for it. the Congo Free State, in the various stations I saw, natives were ever treated justly. They came into st mostly singing when bringing the rubber and with happy expressions on their faces.

o show how much the natives fear Belgian er an incident I witnessed at Banzy- with his villagers, had been requested had leading to his village. He had was summoned with his men to the post. al and ordered them to go to but as the gardier was absent them to sit near the door unt when the Congo officer ar entered the crowd of blac account; when taken away from their masters they invariably returned to them. Apart from the nominal ownership, the slave was just as free as his master, and had none of the worries of the latter. Two-thirds of the servants in Europe or America, three-quarters of our bank clerks and shop assistants are infinitely less free and more hard-worked than slaves in Africa under black masters. Of former slaves in America under white masters I cannot speak, as I do not know.

With a little sobriety of reflection, let us see exactly what happens in the Congo Free State. If a native pays his tax in rubber, his name is duly marked upon specially-kept books and he goes home happy. If he brings more, he is duly rewarded, or the extra quantity is placed to his credit for the following year. If he brings none, and cannot give a plausible reason for it, he goes to prison for a few days. But in America and in any European country, too, as well as in all colonies, if people do not pay their taxes they are made to suffer for it. In the Congo Free State, in the various stations I saw, the natives were ever treated justly. They came into the post gaily singing when bringing the rubber and departed with happy expressions on their faces.

In order to show how much the natives fear Belgian prisons, let me tell of an incident I witnessed at Banzy-ville. A chief, with his villagers, had been requested to keep in order a road leading to his village. He had disobeyed. He was summoned with his men to the post. The officer reprimanded all and ordered them to go to prison for three days, but as the gaoler was absent at the moment, he told them to sit near the door until he returned. A day later, when the Congo officer and I were taking a stroll, he perceived the crowd of blacks

Bananas being conveyed by native children into the Congo Free State post of Banzyville.

at the prison door, and not recognizing them asked them what they wanted.

" We are waiting for the door to open to go to prison ! We will wait until he [the gaoler] comes," was the reply in a chorus.

The officer dismissed them with a warning to be more obedient next time, and they left, some hopping high in the air, the others quite disappointed.

Banzyville produced as much as 3,500 kilos of rubber and some six hundred kilos of ivory a month. It was a beautiful sight to see the men come in with their baskets of rubber, and a more picturesque sight still when hundreds of children, each with huge clusters of bananas, rushed in every Saturday morning, describing figures in the great square of the post, then laying down their presents in wonderful designs upon the ground.

Then came the processions of ivory tusks, for which the chiefs received old broken-down rifles, salt-cakes, fabrics, or made-up clothes, all articles of immense value in that country.

Innumerable imported pigeons were to be seen in the post of Banzyville and in all the villages.

I have absolutely no interest in the Congo Free State beyond mentioning what I actually saw in the large extent of the wildest and most cannibalistic part of that country visited by me, along the Mbomu and Ubanghi rivers, as well as what I believe to be just and fair, regardless of national, religious and political interests.

One reads a good deal about atrocities alleged to have taken place in the Congo Free State, but, frankly, when accusations of infamous crimes are brought against white men of any nation, it would be well to be certain beforehand.

Photographs have been shown of babies with hands chopped off, and of a child in a suitably-selected tropical background. "When they [Leopold's soldiers] went to kill it, the child laughed," so reads the description underneath. It would be interesting to know how the terrified native girl, whose testimony this professes to be, managed to take such an excellently-posed photograph in a country where clothes are unknown and, presumably, kodaks even more so.

One is told that women refuse to bear children, because with a baby to carry they cannot well run away from Leopold's soldiers. Rumours are spread that the rubber collectors pass days of a miserable existence. "He [the collector] has to build himself an improvised shelter which cannot possibly replace his hut ; he has not the food to which he is accustomed. They are exposed to the inclemencies of the weather and the attacks of wild beasts. . . . . Many died in the forests of hunger and exposure. The natives have been converted into beings without ambition." All this is really colossally funny. Central African blacks losing an ambition they have never been known to possess !

Perhaps the people who wrote these accusations forgot—or did not know—that the wild beasts of Africa never attack anybody unless interfered with. We shall see what the natives do when the weather is inclement. They at once take off their clothes—when they have been made to wear any ! As for the improvising of huts, no one is cleverer at work of that kind—as we have seen—than the men and women of any of the tribes in Central Africa. First of all, their very homes are merely improvised dwellings, which they put up in a few hours, and which they frequently shift here and there to suit their convenience. The most comical thing is the idea of natives starving in the tropical forest. If there is a place where a native cannot possibly starve it is in the tropical forest. The blacks know of innumerable roots and wild fruit which provide good food ; honey is to be found in quantities ; ants, locusts and insects which natives like to eat are to be found in millions; and in improvised traps and snares, which they construct in a few moments, they capture animals in profusion on land and fish in the water. Add to this fare a stray human being or two—and I really do not see how these cannibals could be happier.

We will not go into the question of black women refusing to bear children. A visit to Central Africa would soon change the mind of the author of that libel. As for the chopping off of limbs, it is easy enough in any part of Africa—whether Belgian, British, French or German—to take not half a dozen but hundreds of photographs of mutilated individuals. The natives themselves from time immemorial have inflicted, and go on inflicting, bodily punishments upon their tribesmen, and it is not easy to prevent them from doing so. A solitary European officer is in charge of a province as big as a European kingdom, and it is impossible for him to be everywhere. Leprosy and other complaints are prevalent by which individuals frequently lose their limbs. One might with equal justice put down all the cripples and blind or dumb people of London or New York, or the millions starving in India, to the infamy of the King of England or of the President of the United States.

Although no such cases have come under my observation, I do not say that perhaps some officer in the

Congo Free State may not have dealt harshly with the people. I cannot speak of people I have not known, nor of parts I have not seen. But it should not be forgotten that in those countries the provocation is strong. If there are, for instance, two white men in a post, and one day one wakes up to find that his companion is in course of being digested by the natives, it is, I think, too much to expect that the survivor should go and pat the offenders upon the back. But I cannot believe that any white man in a normal state could be found who would purposely mutilate babies by the score or singly. Then, again, it would be well to differentiate—and a good deal of allowance should be made for cases of lunacy, frequent among white people in tropical climates, where loneliness, the constant use of medicine to prevent fever, and other trials of all kinds, are severe and often affect the brain   Surely when a murder occurs in England, we do not accuse all Englishmen of being assassins.

Speaking generally from my own observation, all I can say of the Congo Free State is that the country was kept in excellent order; that the natives were happy and well cared for; and the land, far from being damaged, was greatly improved by the construction of splendid roads, by enormous plantations of rubber, rice, millet, maize, cotton; by the establishment of beautiful cattle-farms, by up-to-date schools and excellent hospital arrangements for the natives. I think that these statements are fully borne out by the last reports (1906) of the British consul in the Congo Free State, as well as by other British travellers—who have taken the trouble to go and see for themselves—in other portions of that country.

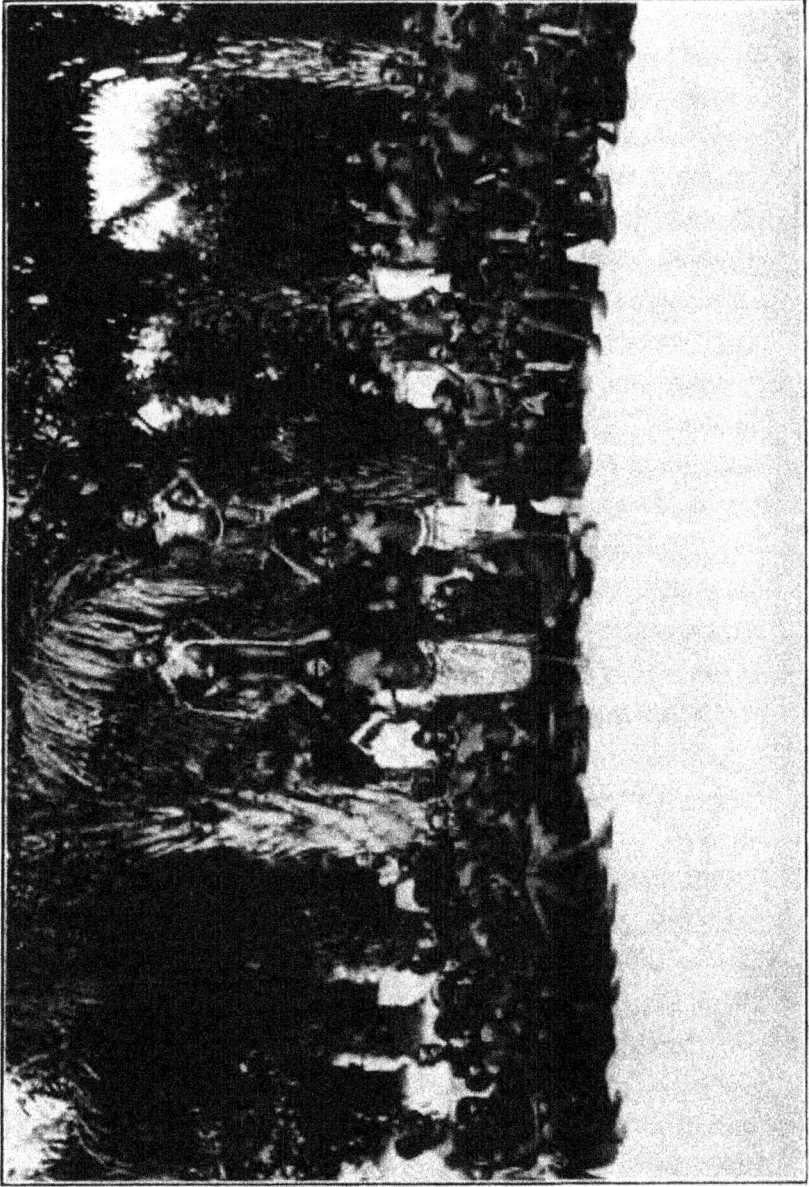

Cannibal dancers Congo Free State   The dancers are carried on men's or women's shoulders when not dancing.

CHAPTER XII.

I saw at Banzyville a typical dance of girls. Five of them took part in it. They were elaborately decorated with beads of all kinds, quantities of them upon the head, round the waist and in strings down the arms and back. A long strip of monkey-skin was attached to the right arm. Long iron bells hung from the ankles and the back of the head. A double eyebrow was painted upon the forehead.

These girls were carried on men's or women's shoulders when not dancing.

The dance itself consisted of first beating one foot, then the other, twice upon the ground, waving the head to and fro and making jerky side movements with the middle part of their body. First one girl danced, then two, then three, until all five finally took part in the performance, hastening the step as they got warmed up to it. Children and women formed a circle round, clapping their hands to keep time and urging them with cries.

When the five girls danced together in a row, terrific howling and ululations were raised on all sides.

An elaborate kind of step-dancing was then performed, each girl holding a brush in her hand and giving a peculiar rotary movement to the hand. Another dance consisted in describing a semicircle. In another dance still, they came forward moving the body first to one side, then to the other, several times with one hand raised. Then the dancer threw herself back as if collapsing, when she was caught by others before she came in contact with the ground.

Great excitement prevailed in the crowd when a little child, two or three years of age, came forward and imitated the gestures of the women.

Women with black dashes of paint on their chocolate-coloured faces and black and white feathers stuck upon one side of the head were holding their hands spread out flat over the heads of the dancers. Some of these older women were most peculiar-looking—almost witch-like. Two particularly, who seemed to have great influence on the dancers, had most magnetic eyes. They were making passes not unlike hypnotic movements.

This was interesting to me, as I had so far never come across evident proof that the natives of Central Africa used hypnotism in any way. In this case even, I think it was done unconsciously more than consciously, but it had some effect all the same.

After this the " dance of luck " took place, most women taking part in it, many of them displaying the long banana leaf, like a green flag, sticking out behind. All these naked creatures got very excited—a scene extraordinarily comical.

Old women joined as well as young in these dances and performed difficult posturing, which, though not in the most refined of taste, still showed a good deal of suppleness and skill.

The hair of the dancing girls was plastered with black paint as far as the ears. They wore bandoliers of elephant's tail hair, with brass bells and rings attached

Women dancing in the Congo Free State.

dance still, they came forward moving the body to one side, then to the other, several times with hand raised. Then the dancer threw herself back as if collapsing, when she was caught by others before she came in contact with the ground.

Great excitement prevailed in the crowd. A little child, two or three years of age, came forward and imitated the gestures of the women.

Women with black dashes of paint on their coloured faces and black and white feathers at one side of the head were holding their hands out flat over the heads of the dancers. Some of the older women were most peculiar-looking. Two particularly, who seemed to have influence on the dancers, had most magnetic were making passes not unlike hypnotic.

This was interesting to me, as I had so far across evident proof that the natives of used hypnotism in any way. In this case it was done unconsciously more than it had some effect all the same.

After this the "dance of luck" to women taking part in it, many of them long banana leaf, like a green flag sticking. All these naked creatures got very extraordinarily excited.

Old women as well as young and performed in the most natural of taste, and she suppleness and skill

The beer or palm

Black paint

orphans

The beauties of Banzyville (Congo Free State).

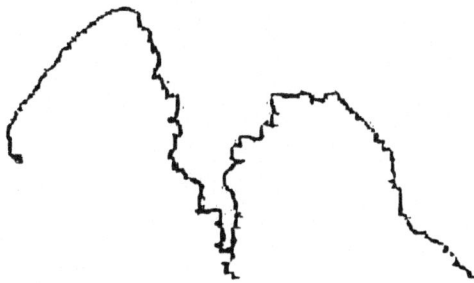

to them   The hair of the elephant tail, as thick as a wire, is believed by the natives to bring good luck. They make bracelets and rings of it.

These particular dancing girls belonged to the Sango tribe.

Then there were dances of men, who made evolutions of all kinds—extraordinarily picturesque.

Sango warriors came to the meeting as well as Daoré and N'Sakkara.   The Daoré warriors had red-beaded heads.   Their high shields of plaited Spanish reed were decorated with broad black lines in angular designs upon a light brown background.   Broad-headed spears with a short staff were carried.   Most of these warriors had pieces of wood dangling down the side, others wore two of these cylinders attached on each side of the head.

They were light upon their feet and dexterous at shifting the body quickly from one side to the other of the shield, as they would in war-time in order to avoid spears thrown at them.

Women in a circle round them sang melodiously in a chorus, somewhat too loud perhaps, while first one, then another, of the warriors came inside the ring performing a slow walk, keeping time with the singing and the drums.   This was done with a slight up-and-down movement, the knees slightly bent and the dancers proceeding along on the tips of their toes.

The dance which had most success with the natives was one of suggestive posturing by an old man and his ancient wife, a dance which does not bear describing in these pages.

The population of the district consisted mostly of Baza, Banza, Dondo, Sango and a few Kassai and Bangala.

The Baza had elongated faces of a long oval, tapering suddenly from the temple to the chin. The cheek-
bones, unlike those of the tribes on the north bank of
the Mbomu, were but slightly prominent, with deep
hollows directly under the zygomatic curve which
accentuated the prominence of the huge-sized lips.
Although large the lips were well-defined and bow-
shaped. The ears possessed detached lobes and the
width of the nostrils was quite small for negroid types.
The nostril itself was well arched, the nose as a whole
unduly flat, the facial angle in profile being practically
non-existent, and forming almost a straight line except
in cases where the chin receded.

The Banza, not to be confounded with the Baza,
were tall, powerfully built fellows, with slightly
pleasanter faces and brighter eyes than the Baza. The
nose was more finely chiselled, with a flattened tip.
They had from three to six raised cicatrices upon the
forehead, or else from eight to nine parallel horizontal
incisions. Like the Baza, some had a chocolate-coloured
skin, others bluish-black, with no oily excretion and
quite dry.

In the illustration in this volume showing "Beautiful
Ladies of Banzyville," the lady in front is a Bangala,
the others are Kassai. The Bangala are a magnificent
race of negroes whose language spreads from Boma all
up the Congo river. The Bangala tribe is located south
of Banzyville along the Congo, the Kassai in the district
of Ualaba (south of the district of Lake Leopold II.).

All the tribes in the Congo Free State around
Banzyville were polygamous, except slaves, who were
not allowed to have wives. The slaves in that region
were mostly from the French Congo. Women, too, were

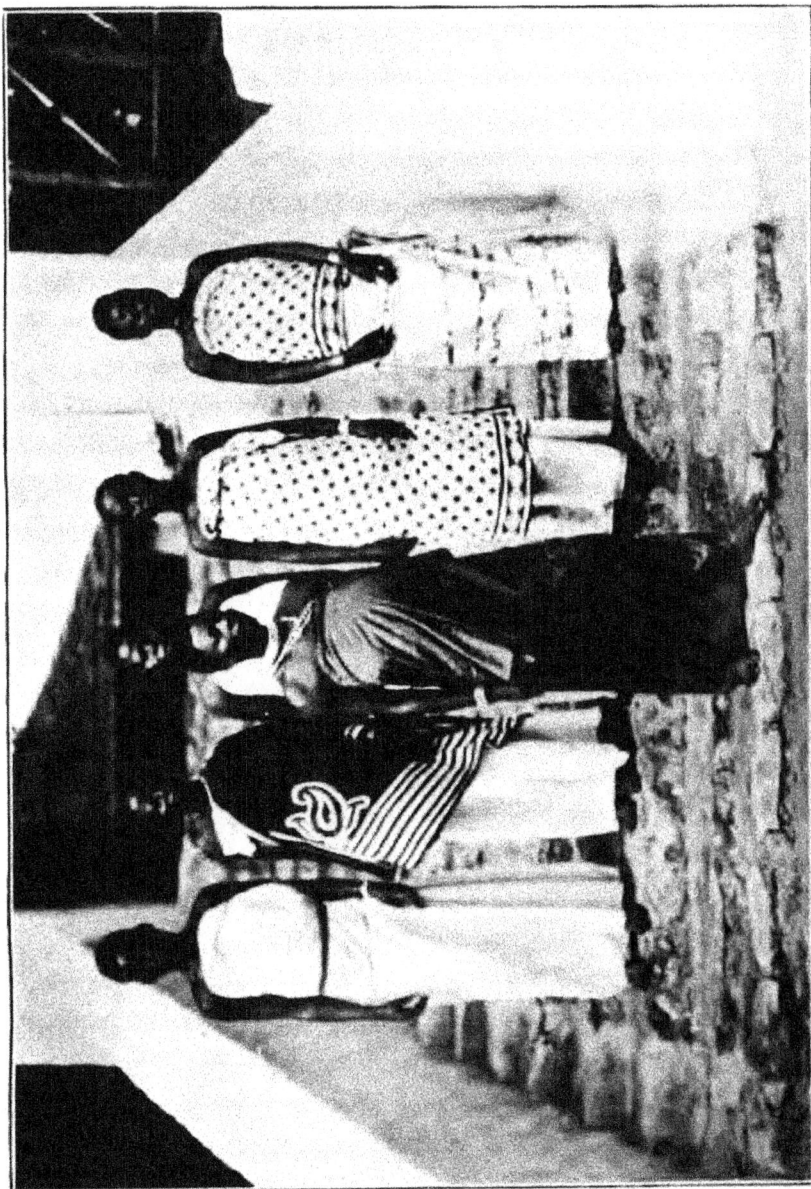

o Free Stat

kept like slaves and were mostly exchanged for dogs, the food most prized by these cannibals next to human flesh. In default of dogs, palm-oil, throwing knives or cloth were accepted.

When people die, the corpse is first placed upon a chair, all the relations forming a circle around, entreating him to think of them, as they believe his soul (life) goes to another world. They sing for two days. Formerly all the deceased's wives were buried alive near his body. Now, however, especially near Belgian posts, this is forbidden, and the widows are bequeathed like other property to the heir.

They call their deity Zapa.

The chieftainship is hereditary, either to the son or brother, according to circumstances, and the people will submit to the rule of their chief, even if he is an idiot or a physical wreck.

A native accustomed to clothes will invariably undress on being taken ill, even if he should suffer from pneumonia; also all dressed natives take off their clothes at once when it comes on to rain.

If someone dreams that by tying a piece of wood to the head they will be free from eye-soreness or any other complaint, all of his tribe tie huge pieces of wood somewhere about the body, as we have seen among people on the opposite side of the stream.

They decorate the body and arms with white patches, while on the forehead broad vertical lines are drawn. The red stuff frequently used by them for painting the body and head is the *ngula*, made from the powdered bark of a tree. It is mixed with palm-oil and made into a paste. The *ngula* is also supposed to possess medicinal qualities.

It is seldom that one finds idols in Central Africa, but in this particular section I saw several quite interesting ones, which showed a good deal of careful observation on the part of the artist. Greater care had been given to details, such as tribal marks and head-dress of beads—quite faithfully reproduced—than to general anatomical proportions. Many of these wooden idols, about one foot in height, were dyed red, but the hands, umbilicus (generally of gigantic proportions), feet and hair were black. They duly possessed the raised dots upon the forehead and some had realistic details of real hair upon the head and body. Real ear-rings, necklaces and bracelets adorned these statuettes. Pieces of looking-glass formed the eyes. One figure represented a warrior with two long feathers in his elaborate and circular headdress; other figures had merely flattened, expressionless faces.

I also saw elaborate pipes and whistles with human heads cleverly carved in wood.

The Dondo, who live in a village three and a half kilometres long by the side of an extensive Government rubber plantation, possess an idol, a male figure, carved of hard wood and standing some five feet high.

I left Banzyville and subsequently Mobay on July 3rd. The rapids were easily descended; the canoe went at a good pace down the stream, beautiful in this particular section and of immense width.

There were pretty islands as we went along. Captain Bibolini accompanied me for a few miles. The *pagayeurs* of the Congo Free State officer, laden with shiny copper bracelets and with their marvellous decorations of beads upon the head, with two huge drums going all the time, and the peculiar rhythm of their songs echoing here and there in the forest, made this quite an unforgettable experience.

Six or seven miles further down Captain Bibolini bade me good-bye. Having embarked in my canoe, I proceeded among pretty islands. In the afternoon high hills, wooded and grassy, stood before us on each side of the stream. They looked picturesque with the sun striking upon them against the jet-black sky of an approaching tornado. The water of the stream was oily and leaden, reflecting as in a mirror the tall palm-trees along the banks and the conical roofs of the many villages scattered all along, which, however, were not quite so numerous as they had been above Banzyville.

No sooner had we passed the first of two headlands than a third, seemingly a higher hill-range, stood in the gloomy tints of the background behind highly-coloured, delightful islands in the centre of the stream, on which the sun still shone.

On I went, with fourteen paddlers singing gaily, paddling somewhat spasmodically, if you like, but at a frantic rate when they did paddle at all, then leaving the current to do the rest.

At sunset I halted at a small native village and left again at sunrise the next morning (July 4th), the river in some places being over 4,500 feet wide. There were a great many islands, some quite large, and by eleven o'clock we came to a spot where the river was divided into many shallow channels, between which for a long distance stood large and small islands of sand. We did not see any more sharply-pointed conical roofs along the banks. We now had low-domed huts instead. Further, the banks of the river were flat on both sides but for a small hill on the Belgian side. Up to four o'clock it had been quite flat near both banks, except on the French side, where we had seen a long and high hill-range which was converging towards the stream, where it gradually ended in a gentle slope.

We met a convoy of canoes returning to Mobay. Near villages—now scanty and far apart—we saw many fisherwomen walking about in the water up to their chests and sometimes up to their necks, with the usual small baskets attached to the forehead and oblong nets in which they caught fish. In some places we found more enclosures of matting in the water, especially near the banks, within which women with nets were employed scooping out the imprisoned fish.

The width of the river during the last few hours of our journey varied between 2,400 feet and 4,500 feet.

We stopped for the night at a village called Ublaga (1,435 feet), with domed huts of great size. The natives, as we went further down-stream towards civilization, were getting less and less polite.

On July 5th, continuing my journey, I passed a beautiful headland on the French side, with a flat grassy summit and one solitary palm-tree standing majestically against the sky. Another high hill, also on the French side, was reached shortly after. We travelled among a number of beautiful islands until we reached Kouango, where the river was of immense width, some 6,000 feet across. Once more we were caught in a tornado, with sudden squalls of wind and high waves which nearly turned over the canoe.

The French government had given a concession here to the *Compagnie du Kouango Français*, which began

Fisherwomen on the Ubanghi Congo Free State   The fish is collected inside head-baskets.

its work in 1900. The concession extended up the entire basin of the Kouango river, an important tributary on the north bank of the Ubanghi. The company dealt chiefly in articles of exchange and to a slight extent in goods for Europeans, such as provisions, etc. They received in exchange from the natives rubber and some ivory. They were making large plantations of *functunia elastica* (*ire*). They had put up fine buildings of brick with well-fitted workshops. A handsome avenue of mango trees was a great boon to the place. The inevitable sad note in the shape of a well-kept grave-yard, with three nicely-made graves of Europeans who had lately lost their lives, was not absent at this place. Indeed, in every station up the river there were memorials of pioneers who had succumbed in endeavouring to open up that country. At least half the people who have gone out there have never come back.

I left Kouango at about nine in the morning. A violent rain obscured the view all round all day and I could see nothing.

I arrived at the troublesome Sanga rapids at about four o'clock in the afternoon. As we were descending the rapids the natives on land, who seemed greatly excited, shouted to us not to take the channel which we were about to enter, but to follow another, which, to us in the boat, seemed impracticable. However, my *pagayeurs* followed the advice from land, with the result that we struck a rock and got the boat full of water. At one moment I thought we were about to turn over altogether, which excited cries, howls, and uncontrolled laughter from the assembled crowd upon the bank. We eventually extricated ourselves from our perilous position.

When we tried to make for land we were met with a hostile demonstration from the people. They absolutely refused to let us land. The *capitan* of the village, who was in a state of angry excitement, came down to the waterside brandishing his spear and said we must get off again. Others in a chorus and with a similarly threatening manner repeated his words, and dozens of extended arms shaken forcibly at us signalled that we must go on. Some children began to throw stones and mud at us, always a bad beginning in a row.

I am not in the habit of being imposed upon by natives, no matter what happens, and, having jumped on shore with my loaded rifle in one hand and the *courbash* in the other, for one moment the angry crowd drew back. I demanded the use of a large house on the river bank, where I said I would stop for the night and for the use of which I would pay.

Adem, my faithful Somali, had followed me with another rifle. The head man of my crew endeavoured to quiet down the people. They would not listen to reason, and, after the women had flung forcible insults at us and a good deal of mud, a rush was made upon us by a great number of men with their spears. One or two spears actually passed quite close to my head, and things looked serious.

Adem, who had been scolded many times for never having the camera ready when it was needed on occasions of that kind, was quite up to the mark that day. When the men made a rush at us he handed me the camera. Notwithstanding the late hour of the day and the faint light, I chanced a snapshot of the attacking crowd, which is reproduced in the illustration on page 154. It was most tiresome. Picturesque scenes like that never took place when the sun shone brightly so that good photographic results might be obtained.

The temptation to fire on the crowd was great, but I deemed keeping cool better. The rascals would listen to nothing. A mass of them had collected and were trying to surround us, which, naturally, I prevented.

A vixen of a woman, with eyes bulging out of her head with fury and breasts dangling in a most repulsive way, came towards us, endeavouring to scratch. Pretty language she used, spitting with rage at the end of each accumulation of oaths.

Through one of my *pagayeurs* who could speak their language, I gave them to understand that if they did not quit the place at once we would fire upon them, and as I said it I ordered Adem to level his rifle at them. The half-timid, half-brave crowd stampeded some way off, but they were evidently ill-disposed, and one could hear them roaring in the high maize all round the square where they had hidden. Occasionally imbeciles brandishing their spears ran backwards and forwards. They seemed quite excited.

Fortunately, at this juncture, the chief, who had gone across the river, hastily returned. I did not like the nasty expression on his face. No sooner had he landed than we seized him, placed the muzzle of a rifle at his head, and informed the people that if a spear were hurled or the slightest trouble occurred, their chief would be shot. He would be detained as a hostage for their good behaviour.

The perplexed chief extended his hand in sign of friendship, and dropped his spear to show that he did not mean to fight. He blamed his *capitan*, who, he said, was drunk, for the row, and called for natives to bring presents of chickens and eggs at once, which, of course, I refused. Not losing sight of the muzzle of the rifle with a corner of his eye, he hastily harangued his people to return to their huts. The chief promised that nobody would annoy us any longer, but as I did not trust him I preferred to treat him as a hostage, Adem, with his loaded rifle, keeping watch on him the whole night.

The chief, having got over his apprehension, eventually fell fast asleep upon the mat which had been brought for him. Faithful Adem remained the entire night with the rifle pointed at him. At only one thing was I surprised, and that was, that the rifle never went off by mistake, as the trigger could not be set at safety, and there was no person in whose hands a loaded rifle was more dangerous than in Adem's.

Although I went to rest on my bed I remained awake, and several times came out during the night to see how things were progressing. Except on the riverside, we were absolutely surrounded by these natives, hidden in the maize field, and once or twice I had to disturb the chief's peaceful sleep that he might request his subjects to clear off at their earliest convenience.

Sitting in the canoe day after day was fatiguing to me, after having been accustomed to ride and walk long distances every day. Losing my sleep at night, too, for the foolishness of these natives was annoying. These people of Sanga, I was told afterwards, were well-known pirates upon this river. Only a short time before they had attacked and robbed a convoy of goods going up river. The Sanga people had of late got quite out of hand and the French could not control them. Possibly they were taking advantage of the severe illness of the

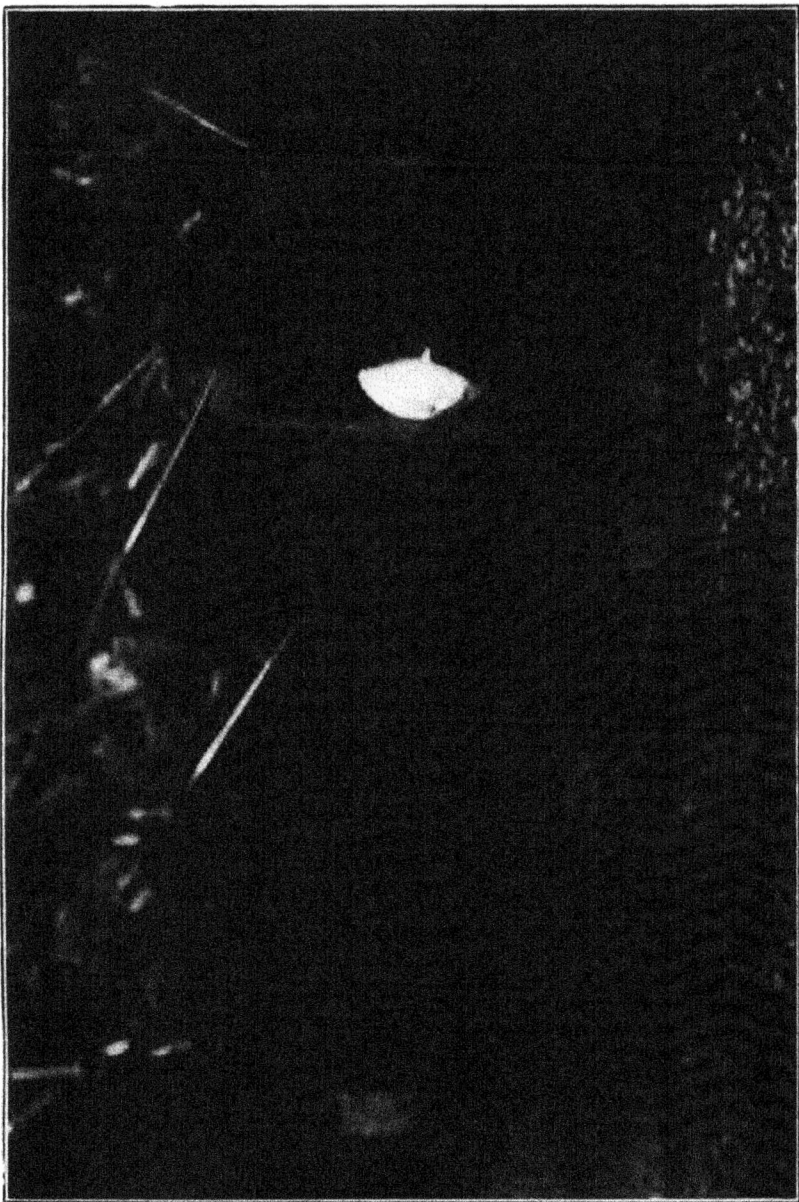

Threatening cannibals.   Photo. taken shortly before sunset,

French captain in the distant **post of** Mobay and of the dying condition of the civil *administrateur* at Fort Possel, situated at the mouth of the Kemo river a couple of days further down.

The next day, July 7th, having given presents to the chief for the loan of the house, I left, the river being here most beautiful and of immense width, with delightful islands scattered about. The Belgian side was quite open, whereas the French side was thickly wooded.

I arrived at Bessou, the first mission I had met since leaving Wau, the *Mission de la Ste. Famille des Banziris* (a mistake, as the natives at Bessou call themselves Guanziri, not Banziri). I met here that wonderful man, Father Moreau, with another Father and two Brothers. Father Moreau had been in the Congo for eleven years and had founded the mission, consisting of 350 hectares of land, with a profitable cattle farm, 104 oxen and cows, 210 sheep, 150 pigs, 20 horses and 6 donkeys. Many avenues had been cut, lined with mandarin and orange groves, mango trees and *avocatiers*—the fruit of which can be made into excellent salad. Then there were huge plantations of maize, sweet potatoes and Banda potatoes, a variety of the Madagascar potato. Wheat did not seem to flourish here, as the climate was too damp. A root called the *dazo*, a kind of bulb, growing into many points joined at the centre, was also cultivated.

There were as many as two hundred and fifty children being educated and Christianized. They have had as many as three hundred and twenty. In a charming little native village attached to the mission lived the seemingly happy population of Christian converts, in extremely tidy, square mud huts. All the buildings, including the stables, etc., had been built on sensible principles, well ventilated above all things. Notwithstanding that in that region horses were said not to live at all, the mission horses originally imported from Wadai appeared in excellent health.

The mission was only allowed to extend its influence as far as a line from Yola (in British Nigeria) to the fifth parallel of latitude N. cutting the Ubanghi at Kouango, the Khartoum mission in the Anglo-Egyptian Sudan having a right over the country east of that point.

I am sorry to say that since my return to Europe I heard that poor Father Moreau, like a few other people I met in Central Africa, had died from fever, while one of the Brothers, who had just time to return to France, had also succumbed to the sleeping sickness. Another one was left very ill.

Along the river from Kouango to Bessou one finds the Guanziri or Banziri tribe, who really extend as far as, and even further than, the Kemo river westwards up to a place called Umbella.

At Mobay itself the people were Sanga or Zanga, while between Kouango and Mobay were the Bouraka. North of Mobay, in the interior, lived the Bubu, whose country reached as far as Kouango and who were in reality Banda people. They extended as far as north of Bongasso, but remained some distance from the river as they were hunted by the N'Sakkara.

In the Koto basin one found the Languassi and Langba, two twin tribes. A small portion of the Togbo tribe inhabited north of the Sanga, and another portion

Children with atrophied limbs and the eer ' sickness.

along the Kouango, but the main part of the population of that particular tribe had settled upon the Koto river.

Along the Koto lived also the Vidri, an offshoot of the Banda race.

On the High Kouango were the Linda, and another tribe of them near Fort Crampel. Two days' distance from that place the Maruba, and south of them the Sabanga, were to be found.

Around Fort Crampel, to the north and the west, were the Ngao. Coming back towards Minciu we found the Dakua, the Ngapu, also called the Gapua. Next to them, west of the Dakua, were the Mbi.

At the mission of Bessou were also the Togba and the Kruma, while opposite on the other bank of the stream, in the Congo Free State, were the Golu, some of whom have now crossed over into French territory. Another tribe, the Monnu, whose centre was in the Belgian Congo (at Zongo), had spread in small sections all over the country along the Ubanghi river in small villages as far as Zanga.

Between the Toni and the Kemo rivers were the Baga, and behind the Baga the Ndi, who reached as far as Krebadje (Fort Sibut).

At Fort Possel, at the mouth of the Kemo river, we shall find a small group of Languassi and a larger group of Sabanga, of whom a small portion can still be found on the Kouango river. Another lot of Sabanga have gone over to the sultan of Sinoussi as auxiliaries, in order to avoid being raided by stronger tribes. The people of the Ngao tribe had also followed their example to a great extent. On the Lower Umbella river were the Wadda tribe, but on the High Umbella the

Ngao-Ngapu were to be found, a mixture of the two races. West of the Ngao-Ngapu and the Wadda were the Babba.

The Banga, one of the most powerful tribes north of the Ubanghi, extended practically from Bongasso as far as the Lobay and northwards as far as Fort Archambault on the Shari river. The Banda, called by the others—who hold them in contempt—Ndri (or savages), have been found as far as the Sanga river and even beyond Bangui.

All the tribes which I have mentioned in connection with this neighbourhood were practically Banda or of Banda extraction. They all spoke the Banda language with small variations in each dialect.

In their purer types they none of them adorn the body with cicatrices or incisions, except those who have been slaves of the sultan of Sinoussi or of Arab traders, and follow the African Mussulman fashion of cutting long incisions upon the cheeks. They most of them, however, have adopted the custom of passing a ring through a hole in the upper lip, as well as making two or three holes in the lower lip for inserting ornaments, such as long crystal cones, placed head downwards in the upper lip. The women particularly go in extensively for this habit. Sometimes the hole in the upper lip is made larger and larger by inserting pieces of wood and by constantly passing the tongue through.

The Banziri and the Bouraka, who practically belong to the same race, have small cicatrices in relief upon the forehead, but much smaller than those of the Zanga and the Yacoma. It is merely an ornament and not a tribal mark. The Banziri women tattoo themselves all over the body and legs, as they believe this increases their beauty. As far as European eyes are concerned, nothing, I think, could diminish their ugliness.

The Banda people, with their allied tribes, are perhaps the most important south of the seventh parallel of lat. N. A few of their villages remain, near Baiu, west of Kouango.

Their marriages are as usual a mere purchase, the man paying a sum to the father and occasionally also to the mother of the girl. If the father is dead, then the sum is paid to the eldest brother or the chief of the family.

Among the Banziri, at the death of a husband, his wives are divided equally among his friends.

The Banda bury their dead in a sitting posture. Mortality among these people is great, as epidemics of small-pox frequently play havoc in their country, and chest complaints are common. They seem to be affected by malaria more than other races, and when attacked by fever they quickly collapse and die.

These people never tie the umbilical cord of a child at birth, but they let it dry up in the normal course of time. This produces great lumps in the umbilical region, sometimes larger than an egg. Nearly all children have these big swellings.

They use certain roots and plants for medicinal purposes. Of the two kinds of a *cissus*, which are one square and one round in shape, both strangled at intervals of twenty centimetres, like a string of sausages, the round one is pressed and the juice is considered good for curing the whooping-cough. It is a strong emetic.

Of religion they know but little, but their god, *Tere*, is a good god, who never troubles anybody and whom

they never trouble. They never offer prayers to him.
Ngakula, on the contrary, their devil, is an individual
who produces thunder, flashes of lightning, and is responsible for all mishaps. To this spirit they offer eggs,
chickens, *manioc*, and grain, in small baskets, generally
left upon trails in the forest, as *Ngakula* waits for people
upon trails, they believe.

Rainbows have sexes in the Banda country. There
are male rainbows and female. Both of them are feared.
They say the rainbow is merely a bad beast—a serpent
emerging from the water. They leave food for it near
the streams in order to prevent misfortune. The female
rainbow is fainter in colour than the male. They believe
that rainbows bring bad luck, not only upon the people,
but also upon the sun itself, for which they have an
inexplicable reverence.

Diseases are put down to a devil, the *ngandru*, or to
an intermediate being who has entered the soul of
the sick person. This evil spirit is called the *iere*.
Even a man killed by a spear is believed to be killed,
not by the spear itself, but by this spirit entering his
life (or soul).

Women are sometimes accused of having been
entered by this evil spirit, and they are there and then
dissected alive so as to let the spirit go out again. Before
this is done, as a rule a trial poison is given to see whether
the operation is necessary or not. The demon, *ngandru*,
which causes disease, enters—according to the Banda—
the stomach of a person always during the night, in
order to feed on the " life " of the sufferer, and at dawn
he will return to his former abode, only to resume his
evil work the following night.

Certain people believe that this demon appears in

the shape of a cat. In fact, Father Moreau told me once that, having brought over some tame cats from Europe—only wild cats having been formerly known in the country—many women accused of possessing demons inside them had come to him from great distances to ask the Father to place the cat upon their chest. If the animal mewed they were reckoned guilty, and if the cat did not do anything they were considered innocent.

The *bondo* was a poisonous root used in trial cases of this sort, but the accused, since the arrival of whites in the country, generally took no chances and supplied themselves with an emetic.

The Banda never kill their children after birth. They are not prolific, and they practise abortion at all stages to an extensive degree, apparently with no fatal results to the women. They use various beverages for this purpose.

Boys and girls practise circumcision, a religious custom evidently imported here by Mussulman influence from the north. Between ten and fifteen years of age they go with an old man or woman, according to the patient's sex, into the forest, where special huts are built. Food is brought to them, but they are not allowed to speak and they are not spoken to for the several days they are kept in confinement when the operation is performed. This is done collectively, all the young people in a tribe who have to be circumcised being brought together to be operated upon. When they return to the village they garb themselves with fibres of a palm, or else with grass leaves, making a short skirt like that of our dancing girls. They walk, and sing and dance in their own villages, but never speak or laugh, and they go about with the head down, the eyes looking towards the ground, for several days.

The total length of the operation with these rites is a whole month, generally in the month of January, the middle month of the dry season.

Circumcised boys and girls go from village to village making a collection, and all natives give them food. They are smeared over with an ointment with a red powder of the *folo* (called *takoul* by the French).

The Banziri do not practise circumcision themselves, but they bring the *folo* for the other tribes from Bangui, where a lot is to be found in the forest. The Banziri, who inhabit along the Ubanghi and the northern part of the Gabon river, in fact, make quite an extensive trade of this *folo* stuff, which must be putrid to be of any saleable value, but still hard, and must not burn ; when placed near the fire it must not ignite but sweat a greasy matter. Then it is beaten in a mortar and made to dry until it becomes powdered. Lower down the river Ubanghi it is ground on a slab of wood. Sand is added to it. While being prepared it is immersed in water and made into a paste, the sand being allowed to separate again. The *folo*, pressed into a stick, is, when dry, ready for use.

The *folo* is used not only for ornament, but as a preventative against mosquitoes. The natives maintain that it makes the skin soft and keeps it in good condition.

The Banziri have no special chief and are divided mostly into families, which fight continually among themselves. In war time they join under a common chief, who is supposed by them to be invulnerable, and who leads them into battle. They are independent people. Obedience is not known among them. Children do not obey their parents, nor wives their husbands. No authority whatever is respected by them. They are therefore difficult people to deal with.

At the death of a man one or more slaves are killed, in order to keep the dead man company. If he is a wealthy man, women are also despatched and buried with him. Further into the country women are actually buried alive with the deceased.

There is a curious belief in that country that dogs come directly after men in the scale of animal life, and just as they eat human bodies the men will eat dogs with gusto ; but not the women, who believe they would have children like dogs if they indulged in canine meat. Should they not have children like dogs, the newly-born children with human features would die, or, at least, would have dogs' teeth, and so on. A husband who has eaten a dog is not allowed to cohabit with his wife during certain days. That is one of the principal reasons that the paddlers whom one employs upon the river indulge considerably in dogs' flesh while away from their better halves.

Women are not allowed to eat certain kinds of fish nor wild or tame pig.

They have curious notions about sores and wounds ; a person who has a sore not being allowed to eat meat, fish nor *arachides*, which they say make wounds worse.

Their language is extraordinarily poor. Thunder, for instance, *ivru*, of which they are in mortal terror, possesses exactly the same name as rain, clouds and mist.

They have a few musical instruments, the *püengo*, with five strings and a sounding-board of wood with a goat-skin stretched upon it.   Then they have the *lingo*, or xylophone, with wooden bars, one for each note, copied, I think, from the Portuguese on the coast.

No suicides have ever been known in their country.

Some of their words are expressive, and are common with many of the tribes along the river, such as the Sango, etc., etc.   I one day asked a man the expression for " early morning," and he said it was *kikkiriki*—the crowing of the cock, of course.   Then I asked him what was the term for " very early in the morning."   *Brrrr kikkiriki*, giving the impression of shivering with cold before the sun and the crowing cock were up.

The verbs have no declension in their language, nor are articles used ;   while the numerals are based chiefly on the hand-and-foot principle, which we have noticed among the A-sandeh and other tribes.

CHAPTER XIII.

I ARRIVED at Fort Possel, at the junction of the Kemo with the Ubanghi, towards three o'clock in the afternoon, having left the mission two hours before. There were three Europeans here, two of whom were dying from blackwater fever; in fact, Father Moreau had been summoned to this place to give extreme unction to the expiring chief of the post. The third—the postmaster of the newly-established post-office—seemed also in a pitiable condition.

Fort Possel was in a low, dull, flat, unwholesome spot, which, during the high water of the Kemo and Ubanghi rivers, became practically an island. Nothing in the way of provisions was to be obtained for love or money near this place. It was the intention of the French to make this spot the capital of the district, but I understand that the advice of those who knew better has been brought to bear, and the plan has luckily been abandoned.

From this point I proposed to leave the Ubanghi river in order to march in a north-westerly direction towards the German Cameroon and Lake Tchad.

My boiling-point thermometers registered the elevation of this place at 1,466 feet (30 feet above the river).

I will relate a curious incident. Having given an offering to the mission, Father Moreau had detained me some hours at Bussou in order to have two fat guinea-fowls roasted for me. I was delighted with the gift, as the *cuisine* of the monks was better than I could provide myself, so I kept the beautiful birds for dinner. As we were caught in a torrential shower while coming down from the mission to the Kemo, I ordered Adem on arrival to spread everything in the sun in order to dry my effects. In the meantime, for want of anything to do, I went to lie upon my camp bed, smacking my lips, and waiting for dinner-time when I expected to enjoy the plump roast guinea-fowls. What was my amazement at sunset when I rose, ready for dinner, to see the fowls in the middle of an open space, with the last rays of a dying sun giving them a beautiful golden tint. Adem was summoned in a severe tone.

" How long had the guinea-fowls been there ? "

" Since we arrived," said the astonished boy ; " you told me to put everything in the sun to dry."

In that terrific damp heat, of course, two or three hours in the sun were quite sufficient to decompose the beautiful birds, within a radius of many yards of which it was now impossible to approach.

Those are the times when murder would be excusable, but I believe that to this day Adem does not know why I severely reprimanded him.

July 9th was spent repacking the loads into weights not heavier than sixteen or eighteen kilos—about thirty-two to thirty-six pounds—as from this spot I should be marching towards Lake Tchad with carriers.

On July 10th I started with seventeen porters and one soldier towards Krebadje.

The grass was very high, the land slightly undulating, with stunted and sparse trees. Occasionally trees with

SKETCH MAP

by
A. HENRY SAVAGE LANDOR.

Showing the Relative Positions of Tribes
between the Ubanghi and the Gribanghi Rivers

Sara   Fort Archambault

Nbanga   Banyaran Riv   N'Dele

SINOUSSI SULTANATE

Bahr Sara   River Gribanghi   Bamingti Riv. River   ROUTE TO N'DELE

MANDJA

Oua River   MANDJA   Bagadu   FORT CRAMPEL

BANDA   NANA

MANDJA   Tombagu

Karin R.   Onguras   Mbri   Linda

Budigu   Mbru

Bago   Ka   Sibut Mbi   Dagapa   N'Ciapu

Mbru Di Congo   Fort   (Krebadje)   HIGH UBANGHI

Ndi

Mbru   Bago   Togbu   Languassi   Kandja

R. Umbella   Ballinga   Fort Bessou Danzizi

FRENCH   FORT POSSEL

CONGO   Baba   Kandju   R. Ubanghi

Bureue   Hada   Riv. Kuma

Mandja   Bendi   BABA   CONGO FREE STATE

Duzeri   Bangui   NDRI

fruit resembling huge sausages, which hung from long threads overhead, were seen.

The carriers were troublesome. Two of them ran away soon after we had started in a thunderstorm. I had to send back to Fort Possel for more, and several hours were wasted waiting.

We rose and descended a good deal, until we reached the Bottinga stream at six o'clock in the afternoon, where we remained for the night. We left Bottinga again the next day at sunrise, and, marching steadily through a lot of high grass, similar to the grass we had found in the South-Western Sudan on our way to Dem Zebir, and through mostly sparse and stunted vegetation, we arrived at Mbru (1,586 feet), in charge of a Senegalese sergeant. We had a hard time marching northwards, and, having changed all my carriers at Mbru, on starting next morning (July 12th) we were soon caught in a violent tornado, this being the very height of the rainy season. Result : everybody and everything drenched.

The country was slightly undulating, with streamlets flowing into the Kemo. At one time this route was used extensively for the revictualling of French military posts on the Shari river and Lake Tchad. Small bridges had been built over some of the rivulets, but since the selection of better routes for that purpose, *viâ* the Niger and the Benoue, this trail had practically been abandoned, and all the bridges were tumbling down.

We were here in a region of the elongated upper lip in women—quite a deformity—a disc being inserted in an opening in the centre of the upper lip. So far the inserted disc was only as large as a shilling, but on travelling further north we shall find this custom gradually becoming accentuated, and the disc getting larger.

The natives indulged in snuff, which they carried in small boxes of antelope horn ornamented with beads, slung with a strap over the shoulder.

Some men wore long hair in tiny oiled plaits, others in matted circles, three over the head between one ear and the other, and dozens starting from the last circle and ending on the neck. The upper lip in its normal condition, although large, was well shaped, but it did not meet the lower one. I think it is principally for the purpose of making the lips meet that this cruel fashion of inserting a disc was originally started.

The natives in that part were called the Mbru. Hardly any cicatrices were noticeable as ornaments in this tribe, except occasional ones on the shoulder-blades according to personal fancy, but not as a tribal mark.

We marched steadily till four o'clock in the afternoon, when we arrived at Yangoro (1,566 feet), a particularly neat and clean resting station, in charge of a most intelligent and obliging Senegalese sergeant. He had travelled in the British Sudan with the Marchand expedition.

I had another curious example of the suspiciousness of natives. I asked one of my men how much he wanted for some ivory bracelets he wore round his wrist. Naturally, in order to examine them, I raised his arm to look at the bracelets. He refused to sell them, and going to one side immediately covered the ivory ornaments with a red cloth. A moment later with two other friends of his, fearing the evil eye (as I had looked at them), they dashed away and deserted altogether.

The members both of the Mbru and the N'di tribes wore belts of two or three vines bent into an oval shape and going round the waist. To these they attached a small piece of cloth.

The usual distortion outwards of the toes was prevalent among them. The pulsation and respiration were fairly normal with all these people. Eighty-eight pulsations per minute was the average among the Mbru ; eighty-five among the N'di, and eighty-six among the Ingreghia, these averages being taken from a number of people of each tribe.

The N'di somewhat resembled the Zandes we had met before, and, like the Zandes, they were slightly bearded, the hairiness on the face being in patches.

I arrived at Fort Sibut (the native name being Krebadje, 1,590 feet) on the eve of July 14th, the great French holiday. It was no use attempting to get away. The Administrateur-Adjoint, Monsieur Magnant, and the three or four Frenchmen residing in the post, were preparing great festivities to commemorate that day, and would not let me go.

In fact, on July 14th I woke up to find the post decked with improvised French banners. In front of the Administrateur's house a well-greased *mât de cocagne* had been erected, as well as the game of *Pentolaccia*, in which the natives were to take part. Rifle-shooting competitions were taking place, as well as displays of spear-hurling and archery.

Without counting the amusement I got, this was an instructive show. It enabled me to see the capacity and intelligence of these natives at the different games and trials of endurance, etc.

The thread-and-scissors competition for blindfolded

women showed how stupid these ladies were at gauging the time the string to which the weight was attached would take in its oscillations, and what little control—when unaccompanied by the eyesight—the motive power of their brain had over the arm. But eventually, whether stupid or not, they all got prizes of gaudy trade mirrors, packets of salt and beads in profusion.

The resident natives of the post were dressed up in their finery, but the visitors from surrounding villages were in their natural nakedness, the ladies with the usual fresh verdure adorning back and front, only some of the wealthier ladies possessing belts with pendants of beads to replace the green grass.

There was a ladies' beauty competition, of which I took a photograph, reproduced in the illustration facing this page. The Frenchmen, with their usual tact, gave identical prizes to all who took part in it, but, for my part, I should have been much puzzled to whom to give a prize at all. All, old and young, had competed, from an old lady of at least sixty-five, with a helmet of half a calabash with a feather stuck in it, who smoked a large pipe, to middle-aged women with repulsively pendent breasts and extraordinary development behind, and to little thin-legged girls with flat faces and pulled-out lips. The more I tried the less I succeeded in discovering any beauty in any of them. Many of the women in the exhibition had the upper lip elongated, with a heavy horseshoe ring inserted ; others had both lips elongated, three holes being bored in the lower lip, in which crystal, iron or wooden cones, two and a half inches long, were inserted. In the hole in the upper lip they had a circular metal or wooden disc. When this was occasionally removed, the hole which remained

A beauty competition (Baga, Mandja and N'Di women).

there was so large that they passed the tongue right through the lip to lick the nose.

The greased climbing-pole was the next show, but the men were extraordinarily clumsy at this game, and it was only after hours of toiling that a youth succeeded in getting up.

The race of porters with heavy loads on the head was more interesting, although none of them could carry weights heavier than sixty pounds. After a two-mile walking race they arrived in a most exhausted condition.

The firing with rifles at targets by the men employed as police was also inefficient, nor was the hurling of spears and the archery any better.

The Mandja chiefs, a race of people living north of Fort Sibut, and also some south of the Umbella river, were slightly better than the Banda at spear-throwing. The Mandja threw the spear while running, while the Banda stood still, giving the shaft a vibration while holding it with the point of their fingers, the two end phalanges being kept absolutely straight.

War dances were kept up during the entire day and the greater part of the night, as well as songs and constant beating of drums. Hundreds and hundreds of people had streamed into the station and looked happy. The French behaved generously, showering valuable presents on everybody.

Monsieur Magnant, the Administrateur, entertained the few Frenchmen and myself to an elaborate and jovial lunch and dinner, when toasts were, of course, drunk to King Edward and the President of the French Republic, the *entente cordiale*, etc., etc.

There was a *factorerie* here, French in name, but

really owned by Dutchmen. Good buildings had been put up and a fine bridge spanned the stream.

Curiously enough, cheap English, and not French, goods were here exclusively sold to the natives, there being a good trade in helmets, clothes, brass buttons, corned beef (which sold extensively) and gunpowder. Unfortunately, all the goods which were sent out from England were so absurdly packed that nothing ever arrived in good condition, and the company lost a good deal by this.

We were here among more civilized natives than those we had met upon the Ubanghi and Mbomu rivers. In fact, there was a civil instead of a military government in this region. So highly civilized were these people that when they brought rubber to the *factorerie* it was generally adulterated, the rubber balls being frequently filled with all kinds of heavy rubbish instead of pure coagulated latex. Only a few days before I passed through, the *factorerie* had been robbed of some five thousand francs in silver coins, which was recovered shortly after near the river, the men who stole it being unable to open the safe in which the money was kept. Their civilization had not reached quite so far.

It was not until July 16th that I was able to leave Krebadje, going over the handsome wooden bridge constructed by the *factorerie*, and proceeding over a beautiful road four or five yards wide with side trenches. After the trailless country we had been going through, this seemed to me most luxurious, and although we went great distances every day it did not seem like marching at all on these excellent roads. The grass was over six feet high on both sides of the road, and many patches of reeds ten feet high were found along the damper places.

Up and down we journeyed, over rather rocky country, with streamlets in the depressions covered over by galleries of foliage There were high trees with winged roots. Going northwards, the forest was getting thick. The trees were larger, with creepers giving delicious shade. The light that penetrated was of a greenish tint, most restful and refreshing to the eyes. I arrived at N'poko at 2 p.m.

On July 17th, soon after sunrise, we went over hills of volcanic iron rock, with plenty of streamlets to cross again, more or less troublesome according to the amount of slush and mud in them. Some were bridged over. Over others the bridges had collapsed. There was a forest of good-sized trees all along until we arrived at the Onguras (1,920 feet). The Banda and the people who lived in the neighbourhood called this place N'gola, but on most maps it is miscalled the Onguras.

I was rather surprised to find there a negro from Sierra Leone who spoke excellent English. He being a British subject, it was quite amusing to notice his interest in King Edward's health and in the welfare of the entire Royal Family. He wanted me to give him the latest news, but I was almost as badly informed as he was, having been without letters and newspapers for seven or eight months.

From N'gola the country was hilly. We had a troublesome stream to cross, the bridges over these streams having collapsed. I had with me a horse and a donkey, and the trouble I had in taking these obstinate animals across these places was considerable. We again met on our way the granitic humps so numerous in the western portion of the British Sudan previously traversed. We were rising a good deal, until after a heavy march of eleven consecutive hours, during which numerous swampy mud streams had to be waded through, we reached Dekoa at sunset.

Bad characters of all kinds were met here, passing through on their way from Lake Tchad. Some were discharged soldiers, others camp followers, some deserters from the German Cameroon and British Nigeria.

Gunpowder can still be bartered with the natives, and is one of the chief articles of exchange, but percussion-caps have now been forbidden. Although the majority are extraordinarily stupid, one finds occasional bright-minded people among natives whose ideas are followed by everybody else. What did the natives do when the percussion-caps were prohibited ? They cut off the heads of lucifer matches and placed them under the hammer of the gun, and if the powder did not go off every time, it did so nearly as often as with percussion-caps. Many of the guns which had been sold to them did not possess even a hammer, and the explosion was caused by striking the percussion-cap (or the head of the match) with a stone.

Four hours after leaving N'gola we had entered the Mandja country. At sunrise on July 18th we were again on the trail, now much reduced in size and smothered in grass for long sections. Hills dotted the country, which resembled in its geological formation and vegetation the region between Wau and Dem Zebir in the Bahr-el-Ghazal. The water, too, from the wells was here quite white, containing calcium as in the Sudan. Again we met our enemies, the little flies, the *gnai*, who filled our eyes and ears much to our discomfort.

Wild figs, red and fat, and so round with a downy

skin that they looked almost like peaches, were found in quantities as we went along. Only they did not possess the delicious flavour of European figs, and frequently when you bit them you had the disagreeable surprise of a mouth swarming with angry ants.

We arrived at Nana by a wonderful approach, a road not less than ten yards wide but only a few hundred yards long. As I descended one hillside, directly in front of me upon another hill I saw a large house with a spacious verandah, and, as lots of other buildings stood near it, my expectations rose high. Unfortunately, when we arrived in the place the large house was shut up, and all the sheds for passengers were so filthy and damp, with walls at such dangerous angles, that I preferred to remain outside. Besides, they were so ill-ventilated that the smell of the last people who had lived in them was plainly to be detected. One could not get anything there, not even civility. A *factorerie* was to be found three kilometres away, but I did not visit it, as I intended continuing towards Lake Tchad as fast as possible.

I was detained at Nana (at an elevation by hypsometrical apparatus of 1,556 feet) the entire day, as I was unable to get carriers, and also because the rain was torrential on July 19th, the temperature being as low as 65° Fahrenheit.

The watershed between the basins of the Ubanghi and the Shari was between N'gola (Onguras) and Dekoa, which also formed the political division of the two regions of Krebadje and Fort Crampel. The river Ghifa, a stream which has always water even during the driest days of the dry season, was the first we had met on our march flowing into the Shari basin.

At the Nana river, which we had to cross before arriving at Fort Crampel (or Gribanghi), a new experience awaited us. The river was much swollen by the rains, and the suspension bridge, made of climbing plants, unfortunately gave way when my men went across with the baggage, and was actually cut in two. Luckily the baggage was saved. Only two men had got to the other side. All attempts to get over proved futile, as the current was too strong to swim across, and, besides, the river was encased in high banks with thick vegetation and thorns right down into the water, and if one had been carried away by the stream one could not have landed anywhere. A problem had to be faced which required consideration.

We had arrived at the Nana river at about eleven o'clock in the morning. The only thing to do was to endeavour to reconstruct the bridge as best we could. We set about to work in a most deliberate manner. In fact, we threw across ropes, and managed to stretch across a somewhat shaky structure, which again collapsed when the first man went over with a load on his head. We had a most exciting rescue of man and load in the swift current. Before we knew where we were, our new bridge was carried away altogether, and with it all the building material at hand. Some other device had to be discovered.

We threw another rope across two high points, and by means of a ring we slung to it one load at a time. We let them slide down to the other side, where they were received with yells of excitement by a number of natives who had assembled to help my men. Several hours of hard toil saw all the goods across, and then came the getting the men over, which was done in a similar manner. It was not till six in the afternoon, after working hard for seven steady hours, that we all got to the other side—very wet, but safe.

Just as I was pulled up by my men on the opposite side of the stream there arrived upon the scene twenty soldiers under a native sergeant, who had been hastily despatched to our rescue by the Administrateur, Monsieur Landres.

With the help of the soldiers and about an hour's march from this ugly stream we eventually arrived at the Gribanghi river, which we duly crossed, and found ourselves in a pretty little spot under a rocky mountain—Fort Crampel, established in the first instance by Monsieur Gentil, when he proceeded on his expedition against Rabah, and further embellished by Monsieur Landres. There were plantations, extending over twenty acres, of maize, four thousand banana-palms, and *arachide* producing excellent oil. Beans of all qualities, even the *haricot pistache,* so valued by the French, were grown, and *dazo,* an oblong indigenous potato quite good to eat; there was fruit, and an extensive and flourishing vegetable garden.

The following were the tribes which lived in the portions of the country I had traversed between the Ubanghi river and the Gribanghi. Near Fort Possel I had found the Sabaga, a tribe which came from near Bongasso some generations ago. In fact, the Sabaga spoke the N'Sakkara language. In 1890–91–92 they were to be found near the mouth of the M'poku, a tributary of the Ubanghi. They were formerly in the interior. In 1892–3 they began their fights against the Wadda and the Togbu, and in 1896 they established themselves on the left bank of the

Umbella, between the Umbella and the Toni. They were greatly opposed to the establishment of Fort Possel, and one portion of the tribe eventually migrated to the High Koango.

At Mbru we find two tribes, one on the right bank of the Toni, the Mbru, and one on the left bank, the Mbaga or Baga. The Mbru tribe is situated near the marshes of N'Ghie in three groups, one at Mbru, one at the confluent of the Fafa and the Fagba, and a third on the confluent of the Yambere and the Buma. They were timid people, probably the most timid in that region, although they were brave in some ways and were great hunters of elephants. There were no great agglomerations, such as villages, of these people, and they were mostly divided into families.

On the opposite side of the Toni river to the one where the Mbru lived were the Mbaga in many groups, such as the Bahr Mandja. Some Mbaga were also found east of the Kemo, forty kilometres from Krebadje, and another tribe of these people to the northeast, where they took the name of Dangba or Dagapa.

Near Mbru were also three small Bahr Mandja villages. They formed, in fact, an uninterrupted thin line between Mbru and Griko on the east of the Kemo.

The Kemo river itself was called by the natives Kuma.

At Yongoro were the Dis Aparkha, divided into two distinct families, strong, very savage, intelligent and quite serviceable people, who have quite a large centre at Yongoro.

Then came the Di Congo, who are akin to the Di Aparkha, but who have got into bad ways and are mere warlike robbers. They came from north of Fort Crampel,

Mandja women and children (showing the former's method of carrying their young

which place they abandoned after the incursions of the Sinoussi people. They have subjected all the neighbouring tribes of the Mbru and Mbaga, who are in mortal terror of them. The Di Congo were included within a huge circle made by the Toni. At Lampoku a few Di Congo were to be found, but the population was principally Banda, here called Ka, quick, enterprising, industrious people, well known for their blacksmiths' work. Their country was wealthy in rubber.

The Ongura, divided into three tribes, one at Ongura, one north of Krebadje and another fifty kilometres south of Fort Crampel on the Upper Gribanghi, were merely a Banda tribe. They were warlike and turbulent, and formerly possessed many Mandja slaves—entire villages of them.

The Mandja themselves lived due north of Ongura. It was at Dekoa we found the greatest agglomeration of Mandja, a troublesome lot, but who have now been subjected. They formerly lived near the Nana stream.

Near Nana there was a great chief, a Makuru, who was so cruel to his tribesmen that he had been abandoned by everybody.

The valley of the Kurin, a tributary of the Fafa, is entirely inhabited by the Mandja, between the trail from Dekoa to Crampel and the Fafa. On the opposite side of the Fafa stream, on the left bank, people of the Banda tribe are again to be found. Then we have another Baja tribe, the Budigri, a great cannibal race, portions of which are to be found on the rivers Fafa, Umbella and Mpoku on the limit of the basins of the Ubanghi and Tchad.

None of these tribes buy a wife, but when a man wants to get married he has to give another woman in exchange. If a man has a sister he hands her over to another man in exchange for his sister, or else hands over a slave if he has no female relations.

The Banziri sell their women as one would a goat or a chicken. Also, if a chief has many girls he uses them in order to attract young men; and if a man has no sisters to give in exchange he will let him have one as a wife on condition that the bridegroom becomes one of his own followers.

In some cases merchandise is given for a wife, but this custom is of foreign importation and not typical of the tribe. Women are scarce in that region and this is seldom practised.

Adultery is severely punished. If discovered, the man is made into a slave and obliged to pay one woman over to the chief.

Descent is reckoned through the mother, a custom which has come from the north, where it is prevalent among the Tuareg, but only on condition that she is a free woman.

Property is bequeathed to the eldest brother or to an uncle, except when these are not in their right mind. The chief of the family is obliged to provide wives for all the younger members.

There are in that country a number of medicine-men, who interfere a good deal with tribal arrangements, and help to keep up the superstitions of the people; but the arrival of the French from the south and the Arabs from the north has greatly modified the super-stitious beliefs. A good and an evil genius are believed in. The evil genius is called *gakkura*, and is supposed to be a big beast in the forest only to be met at night.

Each tribe has its own hunting territory. Poaching on each other's preserves usually ends in a tribal war. They hunt elephants and other animals, mostly by burning grass and driving the animals into traps. Antelopes are speared.

Villages constantly change their position every few years, when the ground gets sterile.

Human sacrifices are made at the death of chiefs, women being buried, as we have seen among other tribes, with the husband.

All these tribes indulge in cannibalism, the Budigri especially, who are fierce, and who have eaten no less than twenty-two traders of the society of the Ouame and the Nana.

In the eastern part of what is called the Dar-Banda country is the sultanate of Sinoussi, a protectorate of France, separated on the west side from the Bamingui. It is a great plateau, the under stratum of which is of sandstone and ferruginous conglomerate rock, as all over Central Africa, with rocky masses emerging here and there in large granitic domes.

On these rocky elevations are generally to be found the habitations of the lower and subjected races. The vegetation is mainly of the desert character, with acacias, *lophira, karité* and *daniella thurifera, parkia, baobab, deleb* palms, the rubber vine, *landolphia owarensis,* and some *landolphia heudelotii.* Cotton, sorgho, sesame, sweet potatoes and millet are the principal products of the country.

N'Dele, Sinoussi's capital, is situated on the Kaga Defile mountains, and possesses twenty-five thousand inhabitants, mostly Banda, Banga, Wadda and Tombagu.

CHAPTER XIV.

BEFORE leaving Fort Crampel on July 23rd, I could not resist the temptation of climbing up the Kaga Batundi rock, from which one obtained a good view of the surrounding country. The eye could easily follow the course of the Nana stream flowing into the Gribanghi a few hundred yards above the post. The horizon-line was formed by the line of hill-ranges we had crossed in coming to Crampel through the forest.

The Gribanghi river, which I navigated from this spot, was about twenty to thirty yards wide, with plenty of water in it. Any amount of wild game could be seen, antelopes particularly. One or two jumped into the water as we were passing along.

During the night we had another tornado, which blew down my tent. In a steel boat kindly lent me by the military authorities, and with a fine crew of Sara— tall and powerfully built, with shaved heads and an occasional comb of hair sticking up, cock-like, upon the head—we went along at a good speed and in a comfortable manner. These people did not indulge in cicatrices at all.

On July 24th we had a bank from twenty to twenty-five feet high on one side and quite a low bank on the other. Trees grew right down to the water, with creepers and vines. Plants in profusion were sub-

merged owing to the great height of the water during the rainy season.

In eleven hours' steady rowing we arrived at Finda. We had passed two fairly large tributaries on the left of the stream.

The same characteristics were visible in our twelve hours' journey to Luto on July 25th, but after leaving that place on July 26th, at 5.30 in the morning, the scenery changed, and we were between higher banks, with only short grass upon them.

Beautiful birds of a metallic blue and of glorious greens were seen that day, and strange birds, with long, hooked beaks and black plumage. All kinds of flies, including elephant flies, were abundant.

The current was strong, and we proceeded at a great rate, camping at sunset in the brush. Almost all along from Gribanghi to this place a line of trees stood along the stream, but further back were open spaces of grass; then again behind these stood patches of forest.

We performed on July 26th our usual twelve hours' steady rowing, the river here being some fifty yards wide. The following day, July 27th, the river banks got a little less monotonous, higher, and very rocky in places, where we had to descend two rapids, the first one with a swift current. There were here great sub-merged domes of volcanic rock, similar to those of the British Sudan, the tops of which showed sometimes on one side of the river, sometimes on the other. There was a substratum, also of volcanic rock of a more remote date, almost level and extending for some distance. In parts where it was visible it was padded for a depth of fifteen to twenty feet with alluvial deposits of red sand and earth. We found ourselves immediately afterwards between high banks, with a white substratum of calcareous formation on our left side, rising fully fifteen feet above the river level, and surmounted by reddish earth which extended nearly all over this plateau. One or two sandy beaches were met with. There were symptoms that we were approaching the sands of the desert. We had seen one or two of these small sandy patches during the last two days of our journey, but on July 27th we came across several extensive beaches, especially on nearing the spot at which the Gribanghi meets the Baminghi, where these patches assumed greater proportions. At this point the river changed its name and became the Shari.

The Baminghi and the Gribanghi meet at an acute angle of about twenty-five degrees, with thick vegetation on all sides, and the Shari proceeds in almost a straight line from this meeting-place, forming an almost direct continuation of the Baminghi, and running, of course, at an angle to the Gribanghi. It would be difficult to say which of the two streams carried most water, as they appeared of the same width. From this spot the main river became at once from eighty to one hundred yards wide, and the change in the appearance of the banks was remarkable, the trees here being of immense height and vigour, covered with dense, dark green foliage. There were wide sandy beaches.

After one hour's journey further down-stream we came to the post of Irena, standing on a high site, in front of a large sandbank, a neatly-kept place, with several circular huts. There was a well-built shelter, with a round hut on either side, joined together by a spacious verandah, well protected by mats and screens. Tornadoes formed terrific *tourbillons* in this particular spot,

I was unlucky enough to experience one of these whirl-winds the moment I arrived, and it scattered my belongings all over the place, the lighter things flying up in the air to a great height upon the column of wind and dust.

The Senegalese who had built this post showed an artistic turn, rudimentary, of course. He had built double-pointed and gabled roofs, and had ornamented the mud walls with primitive high reliefs. No anatomical proportion was apparent in the figures; but it was quite interesting to see how all the details of the cicatrices and ornaments had been faithfully reproduced. Ladies with fully-developed chests seemed to be the favourite subjects.

The elevation at the water level at Irena was 1,256 feet. On leaving Irena the Shari became entrancing, with high and much crevassed banks of clay, grey at the water level, and of a ferruginous red in the upper stratum, some twelve feet thick. Then we passed a few hundred yards of great lumps of granite in heaps, some almost white, others of a light-grey colour, while still others were of a reddish rust colour from contact with ferruginous soil. On our left was a high lump of rock, flat on the top, but with big projecting swellings in the lower portion. Further down a similar but smaller rock was to be seen on the right bank.

There were extensive cultivated patches, with numbers of wild guinea-fowl upon them. Numerous crocodiles slept peacefully upon rocks emerging from the water. The river was broad in places and quite narrow in others.

On the right we came to the tributary called on the maps Bangoran, and by the Sara, Shumsha. Dozens of hippopotami were basking in several pools, in one particularly, near the junction of a large stream fifty yards wide at the mouth, and coming from the south-east on our right-hand side.

There were no villages on the banks, and accumulations of sand were getting more and more numerous as we were travelling northwards, while the forest was now some distance from the river on our right, and the bank to the left of us was sparsely wooded but grassy.

The general course of the Shari was north-east. The river was tortuous and extremely marshy at the sides where there were no sandbanks. About a hundred yards of clear water were to be found all along.

Approaching Kababodo (1,240 feet above sea level), the left bank was twenty to thirty feet high, while the right bank was low, grassy and swampy. The river showed extensive sandbanks and lowlands liable to inundation. The stream was getting broad and had submerged many islets, only tufts of grass being visible now above the water. Further down were more sandbanks and a long sandy island in mid-stream.

Hastily-built villages of fishermen were to be seen on these sandbanks, especially on the right side of the stream. Numbers of naked women came in canoes to bring peanuts to my *pagayeurs*, who belonged to the Sara Baga tribe, which lived in this region.

The country further down was grassy, with sparse small trees. The river was some three hundred yards broad in many places, with low banks on either side, hardly higher anywhere than ten or fifteen feet. No rock was visible.

On nearing Fort Archambault we passed a fine plantation of maize, with ingenious scarecrows of self-agitating fascines worked by strings.

The local natives were manly and tall, with a deal of Arab blood about them. They had regular Arab beards and moustaches. The women went about absolutely naked.

The lower portion of the river banks generally showed a stratum of grey clay. Many were the fish snares close to the river banks. They were regular labyrinths of matting in complicated curves.

I arrived at Fort Archambault at a time when unrest prevailed, owing to attacks which had been made on that post by the Wadaians, who had come in great force to within a few yards of the fort. Lieutenant Tourenq, with thirty-five Senegalese *tirailleurs*, sixty-five police and twenty-five reservists, was in charge of the post, Lieutenant Cornet having been severely wounded in the ankle in another battle against the Wadaians some seventy kilometres east of the fort. He had behaved heroically against some two thousand Wadaians, who had come on a raid, on May 4th that year.

Lieutenant Tourenq and Captain Comion had also had another battle some twenty-five kilometres east of Lake Iro, where they had taken the Wadaian encampment by surprise, and had succeeded in killing many of the raiders, and had seized all the saddles and foodstuff. It was estimated that the Wadaians had as many as two thousand men, whereas the two French officers had only some seventy or eighty men all told.

Near Fort Archambault were several interesting villages of Sara and Nielim, the latter quite a small tribe. They had here a village of some sixty huts, with a hundred oxen and cows, and some five hundred storehouses with millet, which is plentiful in that region.

Archambault had been built on the site of the ancient village of Tunia.   Near it were one Banda and one Nielim village, besides the Sara.   Uedo was the chief of the Nielim village, a giant who wore typical Arab trousers. His village was half a mile from Archambault, and was reached through large plantations of long-stalked and long-leaved millet.

It was near Archambault that I found the custom of elongating the lips more exaggerated than in any other part of Africa, the women actually inserting small wooden or tin saucers in their upper lip and sometimes in both lips.   The photograph which I took, and which faces this page, will show better than a description how ghastly this fashion is.   It was most ludicrous to hear these young ladies talk, especially when they had two plates, one in the upper and one in the lower lip, as these clapped like castanets, and the voice became nasal and unmusical.

These women were otherwise well-formed anatomically and quite statuesque when young.   They adorned their ankles and arms with brass rings and wore shell ornaments round the neck.   The plates in the lips were occasionally removed, when the upper lip hung down so low in a loop as to reach lower than the chin, and left a repulsive aperture under the nose through which one could see the teeth.   As the strain of the lip being pulled hurts them considerably, when they removed the disc or plate they generally licked the lip and the nose through this unnatural aperture.

Game of all kinds is to be found near Archambault. One can go for half an hour's walk and come back with an antelope or a phacochærus or some other animal.

The Sara interested me.   As I have already said,

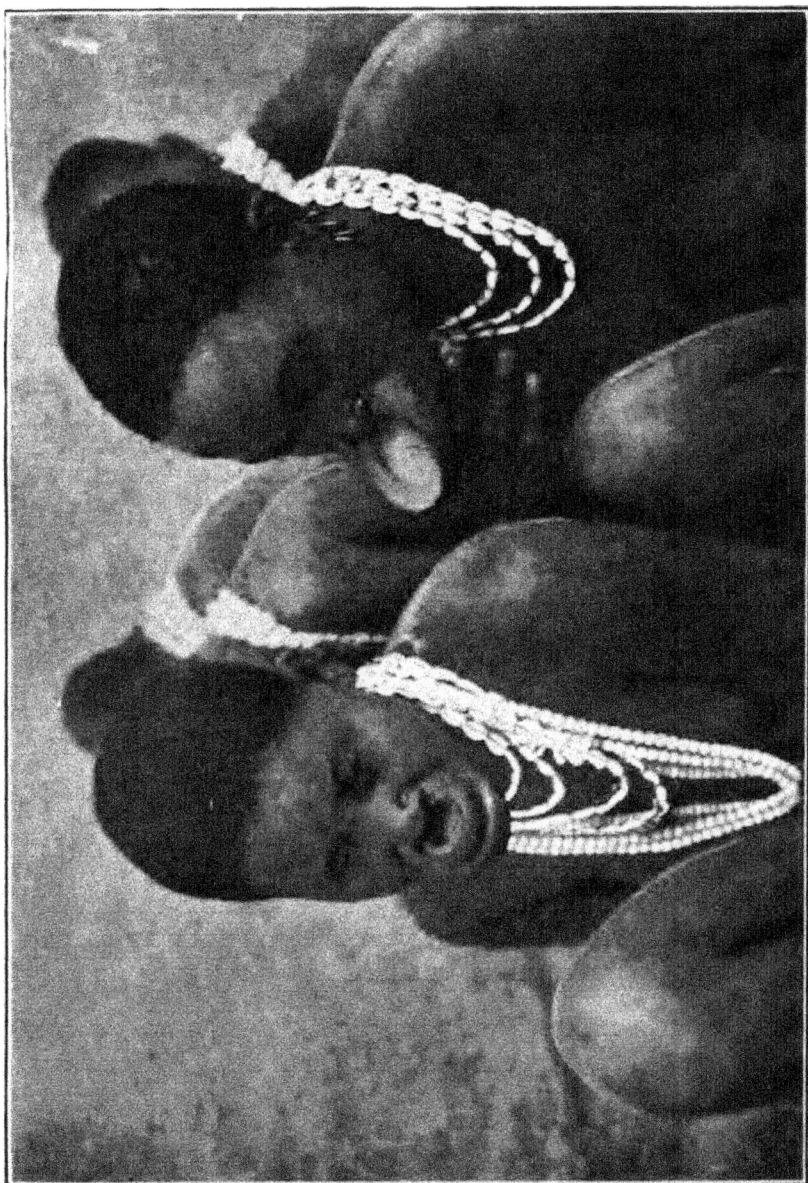

Women with elongated lips (Shari river).

they are a more finely built people than most of the tribes on the Ubanghi. They have extraordinarily developed lips, the upper lip in its normal state sometimes reaching further out than the tip of their noses, while the lower lip frequently stretches further out for ward. The upper lip possesses a formidable curl over the lower one, which gives them an appearance of sulkiness and disappointment, even when they are pleased.

Most of them have horrible skin diseases—herpes, itch, and other complaints being extremely common among them. As with most tribes we have met, their blood is in a terrible condition.

The eyes of these people were somewhat more luminous and intelligent than those of other negroes, the nose much more prominent and aquiline, well-rounded at the base and not so broad, showing evident signs of an infusion of Arab blood in the race. This could also be noticed in the whole formation of their body, although naturally this was tempered by local conditions. Unlike most other tribes, the lobes of the ears were not attached.

To a casual observer they frequently possessed what appeared to be a large tumour in the lower jaw, or possibly a much-expanded gland, and one was rather astonished to find that this large abscess or gland or tumour suddenly disappeared from one individual and equally suddenly appeared on the jaw of his neighbour. This was due to the local habit of chewing a ball of tobacco. The masticated tobacco ball, one inch in diameter and larger sometimes, was passed from the mouth of one friend to that of another for several days until its flavour became exhausted.

The chief peculiarity of the Sara men, who went

about naked, was their method of hiding their genital organs before strangers, by drawing them backwards and keeping them firmly in that position by a most characteristic walk.

A triangular cloth like a tail, or else a piece of leather, was hung behind, but never in front.

These people, like the Yacoma, spend much time in their boats. While rowing they kneel down, which causes their knees to be much swollen and wrinkled, and their feet also become somewhat distorted and swollen.

We left Fort Archambault on July 30th. Lieutenant Causeret, in charge of 150,000 thalers, proceeded down the river at the same time. In our steel boat we carried some forty cases of silver, together with ten Nielim *pagayeurs*, three soldiers and a Senegalese boat captain. So laden were we that only one inch of our boat was above water.

On leaving the high bank of the river on which the post is situated, sixty feet above the river (the river itself being at an elevation of 1,236 feet), we began to lose sight of the clay stratum, which was replaced by great patches of sand stretching for a great distance inland along the stream. Further back was heavy forest. Game abounded in this region, and in the evening when we camped on one of these great sandbanks we saw hundreds of antelopes.

We left at sunrise the next morning, both banks of the river being low and sandy, and as usual the sand spreading far inland. In some places on our left extensive regions were inundated; others seemed likely to be under water soon, as the rainy season was progressing.

Lieutenant Causeret, who was an ardent sportsman,

Women with elongated lips (profile)

Women of Gribanghi.

bent on killing anything he saw, shot three or four flat-headed crocodiles that morning. We saw hundreds of them lying asleep with open mouths upon the sandy banks. As we proceeded, the sand extended further away on both banks, no trees being visible on the left bank during that entire day. Only a few could be distinguished upon the right bank a great distance from us.

At noon we saw a herd of elephants, over one hundred of them, and we hastily got out of our boats and struggled through sand and large pools of water. In my haste not to get wetter than necessary I jumped on the back of one of my *pagayeurs*, asking him to ferry me across. To my surprise, when we were well in the middle of a swamp, I discovered that the man was covered from head to foot with large patches of itch. The herd had sentinels at each corner, while the other elephants were grazing peacefully. As we approached, the sentinel nearer us stood on a high dune, a gigantic mass against the sky-line, and lifted now one ear and then the other to catch the sounds of approaching danger. As we had to go over a flat stretch of sand before getting to them, he raised the alarm, and unfortunately on that occasion they all got away. On returning to the boat we saw some large hippopotami out of the water and we had good sport.

There were innumerable sandy islands in this part of the stream. In one spot, which we reached at 4 p.m., having rowed some fifteen or sixteen hours from Fort Archambault, was a cluster of rounded volcanic rocks, some standing up on the right bank, others half submerged in the water. Further down I noticed a slight attempt of the clay stratum to reappear, with a deep layer of sand upon it ; immediately below followed almost uninterrupted sand, with short grass upon it here and there.

The Nielim *pagayeurs* were great, big, powerfully-built fellows, but with no strength at all in their arms.

Late in the afternoon we perceived before us to the north-west two short but high ranges of mountains rising somewhat abruptly over the absolutely flat country all around. The first range, the larger of the two, was divided by three distinct depressions which, however, did not reach as far down as the flat horizon-line. Then there was a long flat gap of horizon between this range and its lesser neighbour.

The river here was from five hundred to six hundred feet wide. We made camp at about sunset on a sand-spit. Before dinner we killed an antelope and a wild hog. In the evening we had an uninvited concert of lions, elephants and crocodiles.

We started at sunrise again, the current in the river being slow, and the country inundated to some extent. We had to wade some hundred feet or so to get back to the boat.

It was towards 8.30 when we passed close to the Nielim mounts (or Togbao), on the left bank, a picturesque, semicircular mass of volcanic rock, with gigantic boulders in the central portion. The highest point was some three hundred feet higher than the level of the river. It was at this place that the French had a battle against " Rabah the Terrible," and the plucky Lieutenant Bretonnet, after a desperate defence, was killed.

The river was getting now from eight hundred to one thousand yards wide. Two hours later I visited the battle-field of Kouno, three-quarters of a mile from

en on the Shari river showin exte ion of li

the river, where Rabah sustained a severe defeat from the French. His stockaded and entrenched *zeriba* was still to be seen. Out of this he made a *sortie* against the French, but had to retreat and continue the battle within the stockade. Human bones were scattered upon the millet fields all round, and several trees showed bullet holes.

In the *zeriba* stood now a Kaba village, each house or group of houses being enclosed in a high mat wall forming a spiral and with a narrow passage closed by a mat door.

Further on we came to another larger village, where under a shed sat Chief Batchen or Bassen. (It was most difficult to write these names with our alphabet, as no two people pronounced them in the same way, and also because in their languages, although primitive in a way, we find many half tones, quarter tones and inflections, which cannot be transliterated with the letters at our command.) Chief Batchen was a powerful, jovial-looking creature.

These people resembled the Sara, and, like them, had adopted the fashion of hiding their genital organs.

Many of the round roofs in these villages were decorated with ostrich eggs.

Arab influence was getting stronger and stronger in the types of these people as we went further north, although the characteristic flatness of the face had been preserved to a remarkable extent in this particular tribe. They possessed well-developed chests and largish heads, but the legs and arms were seldom in good proportion with the body. The arms and legs were smaller and shorter than they should be, the knees bulging out considerably. This tribe only removed one front lower tooth, while the Sara removed two or more lower incisor teeth. All these people along the Shari were extraor dinarily tall, especially the men. They cultivated the ground to a great extent, and possessed large plantations of millet.

At six o'clock in the afternoon I arrived at Dumrao, a well-kept post, where I had the pleasure of meeting Lieutenant Mailles and a sergeant, who had just arrived from the German Cameroon territory across the river. They had been occupied in defining the oriental frontier between the German Cameroon and the French Congo, under the leadership of Commandant Moll, and with the assistance of Enseigne de Vaisseau Dardignac. The Germans employed Hauptman Freiten von Seefried, Ob.-Lieut. Winckler and Lieut. Freisher von Reigenstein.

Lieutenant Mailles had his instruments ready to take an occultation of stars in order to establish the exact longitude of Dumrao where the work of the Franco- German frontier delimitation had ended. He told us how genial were the relations of the French and German officers. The Commission, I understood, had spent a year in establishing a careful geometrical provisory boundary defined by straight lines of meridian or parallels, the extent of frontier to be determined being great; this boundary was in no way final.

Dinner was excellent, the sky beautifully clear, and everything promised well for the occultation, but, un- fortunately, shortly before the hour when it should have taken place little cloudlets began to travel overhead, and, as is usual on such occasions, one, about the apparent size of a loaf of bread, obscured the particular stars to be observed. So Lieutenant Mailles struck his hand

Store-houses in a Sara village (Shari river).

upon his forehead and exclaimed in resignation, mixed
with despair : " Me voici encore pour un mois dans ce
sacré Dumrao ! " The weight of these words can only
be gauged when one knows the place. Three or four
mat sheds, with thatched roofs, formed the military
post ; five Europeans formerly resided there. Four out
of that number were dead and buried in a melancholy
little grave-yard upon the river bank. The country all
round was flat and uninteresting.

CHAPTER XV.

I WAS sorry Lieutenant Mailles could not take his occultation, but in a way I was also glad, because the time
which would have been spent in taking the observation
and working out the long calculation was employed
instead in a most interesting conversation about the
various tribes which Lieutenant Mailles had visited
with the frontier delimitation expedition.

I was chiefly interested in the description he gave
me of the Kaka, the Baya and the Kirdi. He told me
that as far south as a place called Bania one began to
find a few Haussa, a powerful race of traders with whom
we shall get better acquainted further north. He found
many of these people even at Cariot, north of Bania
on the Sanga river. On German territory was the
great town of Ngondere, also inhabited by Haussa.
The river Sanga flowed practically from north to south,
east of the former geographical boundary between the
German Cameroon and the French Congo on the 15th
degree long. east of Greenwich. Bania was slightly
north of the limit of the great equatorial forest, approximately between the 2nd and 3rd degrees of lat. N.

The Kaka dwell east of Bania, and the Sanga within
the German Cameroon boundary, whereas the Baya
are found to the east of this boundary and somewhat

further north than the region of the Kaka. The Kirdi
(or Lakha, as they are called by the Fulbeh) inhabit a
region north of the Logone river and east of the town of
Ngondere.

These three tribes go in for fetishism. The Kaka
are confirmed cannibals. The Baya were so formerly,
and some indulge to this day in meals of human flesh ;
whereas the Kirdi have given up anthropophagy.

In the Baya country were to be found curious colonies
with small groups of negro tribes, different altogether
from the local predominant race. These colonists call
themselves Yanghere. They were members of a conquering race which once came from the north and,
owing to their courage, vanquished the Baya. Having
come in too small a number, they were unable to keep up
their victory, and they now lived secluded and peacefully
in the small colonies which they had formed slightly
west of the Sanga river.

Their type, not unlike that of other tribes we have
met, exhibited Asiatic, almost Mongolian, characteristics
in the formation of the skull, such as the slanting eye,
the bizygomatic breadth of the face, and the scanty
moustache and beard, worn in a point as with the
Asiatic people they resemble. I had been able to trace
right across Africa types undoubtedly of remote Asiatic
origin, and the remarkable fact was that the tribes
showing these characteristics were always of a greater
intelligence than the pure negroid types. Upon the
Ubanghi I saw a great number of such persons. Their
skin was not black, but of a yellowish-chocolate colour,
to my mind a mixture of the blood of yellow and black
races. Of course, there were also a great number of
people who dyed their skin of a light brown colour, but

I am not referring to those. I mean the naturally light-coloured specimens well known to traders and officers in those regions.

The Baya, among whom these colonies of Yanghere were to be found, had curious confraternities called the *labi*. In villages where these confraternities existed a large hut was set aside for them, built in the shape of a horseshoe and divided inside into sections, each member living in a small cell. Children were brought up in these confraternities and were taught a different language which was only understood by themselves, but not by the inhabitants generally.

Lieutenant Mailles, who studied these people carefully, told me that these confraternities had an occult aim, which he could not well define, as the natives and the members of these sects maintained strict secrecy regarding their beliefs and doings. Children entered these societies' schools at the age of ten or twelve and remained there until the age of seventeen or eighteen. They were easily recognizable when they had joined these sects by the cicatrices on the face and body, especially round the waist, on the abdomen and on the forehead, where, owing to some herb they placed inside the wound when fresh, the cicatrice remained in high relief.

In war and in the troubles of the Baya with other tribes, the people thus brought up took a lead. They daily exercised themselves in archery and spent hours in practising contortions and dancing in a circle round a teacher who beat the *tam-tam*. One of their favourite exercises was one calculated to develop the suppleness of the waist, and consisted in wearing a belt of a number of large dried hard-skinned fruits, inside which the seeds rattled when the lower portion of the body was thrown violently backwards and forwards without moving the position of the chest.

The Kaka were mentally on a lower level than the Baya, brutal to a degree, and, like all brutal people, degraded cowards; whereas the Kirdi were fine-looking, brave people, although their bravery was of little use to them as they possessed no organization. They had, therefore, been imposed upon by the people from Reiboubé and Ngondere, who constantly made raids upon them in search of slaves. They were inveterate drunkards, and in order to satisfy their craving for drink cultivated large quantities of millet, the greater part of which they used for distilling alcohol.

Like many other tribes we had met south of the Kirdi country and south-east, they had various kinds of spears and throwing knives which they used skilfully.

Women among them were bought, or rather exchanged, but not here for oxen and cows nor cloth or beads, but for horses, the horse being worth in that country, on an average, about ten thalers, or about twenty-five or thirty francs (twenty to twenty-four shillings).

The Dumrao post was built on a cliff somewhat higher than the swamps and sand-beaches on the water-level, perhaps some thirty feet or so above them. There were three main buildings and a number of conical-roofed huts for the soldiers and militiamen.

The population on that side of the river was mostly of Baguirmi, particularly towards the north.

I left on August 2nd, the country being flat on both the French and the German sides. Nearing the German post of Miltou, the German banks became much higher, and the German military post actually stood on a cliff thirty to forty feet high. There were no hills on the French bank, such as are marked on many maps, but one could just see in the distance to the east six conical hills with broken tops, which appeared of a beautiful cobalt blue.

The appearance of my boat as I landed on the German side created excitement in the military post; but I received a hearty reception from Sergeant Giller, who rushed down with open arms to greet me. The post was beautifully kept. The buildings were put up inside a protecting mud wall, the central position being occupied by an imposing flat-roofed residence.

At the two sides of the quadrangle inside were rows of neat, cylindrical huts for the soldiers, twenty men all counted. The post was an absolutely military one, and no cultivation of any kind was attempted. As far as military purposes went, the post was certainly exceedingly well built and could make a strong defence against native attackers.

Low sand-banks faced us on leaving Miltou. I camped two hours further down on the German Cameroon side.

More sandy patches were seen the next day. Occasional forest stood in the distance, and here and there high vertical banks, twenty feet or so above the stream; but generally we traversed flat, low country, liable to inundation at high water. Innumerable were the sandy islands, which were gradually getting submerged. The river was very wide in many places.

On August 4th we came in for such torrential rain that we could not see the banks of the river. The Nielim paddled their hardest, shivering with cold in the heavy rain. After twelve hours' steady rowing we arrived at Busso, also called Fort Bretonnet, the post being in charge of a French sergeant.

There were two Baguirmi villages, one on each side of the post. They had low, hemispherical roofs neatly made, but the post itself had no great attractions, except that there were fine palm-groves all along the banks on the French side.

From this point the river had nothing of interest, as we had desert sand almost all along. We amused ourselves killing hippopotami, the meat of which made delicious eating, especially the younger ones, as tender as, and superior to, the best beef.

We were now at an elevation of 1,206 feet on the water-level, the river when we reached Mundo being extremely wide, almost like a lake, with islands and shallow water in places and tufts of grass sticking out here and there. Above the grass emerged a gently-sloping embankment some thirty to forty feet high, of a beautiful emerald green, on the summit of which were beautiful deep-green masses of foliage such as one might see in the finest English parks. Upon heights like these one saw a lot of domed roofs, which, at a distance, appeared not unlike umbrellas spread out to dry. Behind and at the sides of them were masses of trees in clusters with plenty of grass between.

The river was here no less than a mile wide. There was a long sandy island between the German and the French side, both being here thickly wooded. As we went along, the banks got higher, with the usual strata of clay and sand. The top of these higher banks was dotted quite picturesquely against the sky-line with small villages, of which Guleh and Balegnereh were the principal, with minor ones all along until we arrived at Honko, a most picturesque-looking place upon a precipitous cliff of reddish sandstone. There were *zeribas* and domed roofs. Hundreds of people assembled upon the edge of the cliff to see the steel boats approach.

The current was strong here, especially in the channel nearest the bank. There were many sand-banks in mid-stream. The river was wide. By a slippery path we ascended to the village. The neighbouring country was swarming with guinea-fowls, hundreds and hundreds of them running about, mingling gaily with goats and cattle, which were here plentiful.

By a regular maze of narrow passages walled with strong high mats, seven feet high, we were led into the village by the sub-chief, the head man being absent in the German Cameroon. By winding passages we entered several *zeribas*, each family possessing a separate enclosure. In each enclosure was a mud-walled cylindrical house six to ten feet in diameter (walls seven feet high), with a flattened spherical roof, the summit of which was ornamented with ostrich eggs. Ostriches were scarce in this region, but these eggs came mostly from Wadai. The natives valued them.

The houses had oval doors five feet high. In front of each house was a quadrangular mat shed, open on one or more sides, under which the men sat in the daytime, while the women pounded millet in wooden mortars.

In the interior of the houses directly upon entering the door was either a wall or a mat screening one-third of the interior, and in the portion behind this screen, which was used as the sleeping-room by the

Woman of the Lower Shari. Two wooden discs were inserted in the lips.

family, was also found a tall earthen urn, the *dabanga*,
five to six feet high, where millet for the daily consumption was stored.   The fireplace was in the centre
of the hut, as usual.   Over the fire were one or two elevated shelves where articles in daily use were kept and
fish and meat were placed to dry.   Except for a pile of
cooking-pots and drinking-bowls, a broom, and a knife
or two hung upon the wall, there was nothing of interest
in these dwellings.

Honko, as well as other villages I visited, was extremely dirty.   Inside the huts lived not only the people,
but calves, goats and chickens, sharing the home of their
masters.

The leading characteristic of all these establishments was the small *mezjid*—or praying-site—attached
to the outside of the hut.   It consisted of a quadrangle
three to four feet square, bordered with stones and filled
in with sand.   There in the morning, noon and evening
people said their daily prayers in good Mussulman
fashion.   No mosque existed in the village.

The Baguirmi were strongly under Mussulman influence.   Most of them were clothed.   They had made
large clearings in the forest with extensive plantations
of millet, and they possessed well-cared-for horses and
cattle.

Refinement of race and joviality of temper showed
in their faces, and they had quick, intelligent eyes with
the sparkle of life in them.   The bridge of the nose
was depressed in the lower classes and the nostrils were
broad ; whereas the better people, who were lighter
in colour, had aquiline noses, not so prominent, however, as those of the pure Arabs.   They possessed beards
on the chin and small moustaches, large lips and a well

overlapping upper eyelid. Arab influence was also strongly marked in their manners and general customs; but although they followed the religion of Islam, they did not keep their women in strict seclusion.

We had camped on the edge of the cliff, some thirty feet above the level of the river and had a glorious feed upon hippopotami, *double gras* and steak. My men stuffed themselves with a variety of meats, such as antelope, crocodile and wild hog. The odour of roasting meat over the various fires in camp was well-nigh suffocating. During the night a fierce tornado did us damage: it blew down my tents and many things flew into the river.

For a while after leaving Honko we passed villages upon the higher points of the elevated land, among these being Makle, Muola and Anja. After seven hours' journey we came to a village of great length, Mandjafa, along the top of a high vertical cliff, reflected in long broken deep-green lines in the yellowish water of the running stream. With high, big, green trees towering here and there above the domed roofs and the peculiarly grooved cliff, Mandjafa was quite picturesque. A few hundred yards down was the French military post, now abandoned and in ruins.

On the German side the country was mostly flat, with extensive sandy patches and forest in the distance. On the French side, too, there were great stretches of lowlands with sand upon them. On the river a few fish-snares stood out, and a fisherman or two passed by in gondola-like canoes with curled-up front and stern.

On August 9th we left at six o'clock in the morning, and by noon were caught up by one of the two small steam launches, the *d'Uzès*, which the French military

have on this river, and which was conveying Colonel
Largeau down to the headquarters of Fort Lamy. He
had been making a remarkably quick journey from Paris
to Lake Tchad.

Colonel Largeau kindly insisted on taking me on
board, so I was able to reach Fort Lamy late that afternoon instead of the following day. The country was
sandy on both sides of the river, with many villages,
the principal of which were Bonguman, Balamassa,
Kuldji, Asse, Darda, Odje, Mileh, Murgu, Djalali and
Klessem.

Innumerable were the crocodiles on the sand-banks
on either side of us, and a constant fusillade was kept
up from the launch. When shot in the neck they died
open-mouthed as if sleeping.

The French have two little steamers on the Shari
which have done wonderful service both on the Congo
and now on the Shari river. Though the *d'Uzès*, while
being conveyed from the Kemo and the Gribanghi
rivers, had been left in pieces in the bush for some
months, she had eventually been put together again on
the Gribanghi and had worked successfully since the time
of Monsieur Gentil's expedition against Rabah, for which
purpose these steamers were conveyed to the Shari basin.

We arrived at Fort Lamy shortly before sunset and
met with a charming reception from the officers there—
about twenty of them—this being the headquarters of
the military command of the entire French Sudan and
the Congo, as well as of the three sultanates on the
Mbomu. Although from a military point of view this
was, next to Dakar, the most important post in the
West and Central African French colonies, and was the
capital of the French Tchad territory, Fort Lamy was

unattractive as a residence. There was not sufficient accommodation for the officers, and huts were being put up in a hurry. Hence the irregularity of the houses and the streets. The terrible weather which prevailed in this swampy district was chiefly to blame for the bad condition of the place. Buildings collapsed as soon as they were built.

Much to my sorrow, Colonel Gouraud, who was then in command of the place, insisted on placing a whole house at my disposal, while I knew some of the officers must be put to inconvenience, three or four in one house, in order to allow sufficient space for me. The kindness I received from all officers in this place was unbounded.

Colonel Gouraud's work is too well known to military men of all countries for me to refer to it at great length. In the Tchad region and among the Tuareg his military *rôle* has largely helped the extension of civilization in the heart of Africa. His magnificent work in subduing the warlike Tuareg requires no words of praise from me, nor does his later tactful and firm policy on the frontier of Wadai, where a belt of military posts, upon the strategic value of which there is no question, has now been established by the French.

I have serious doubts whether the Wadaians and the fanatical Sinoussi who live north of that country in the desert will not some day need severe punishment before they submit entirely to the French. No one has so far been able to penetrate their country and return alive. The peaceful conquest of Wadai—a dream of many people unfamiliar with these regions—will always, in my opinion, remain a dream. The Wadaians are so fanatical, so assured of their own importance, and entertain so much contempt for white men of any

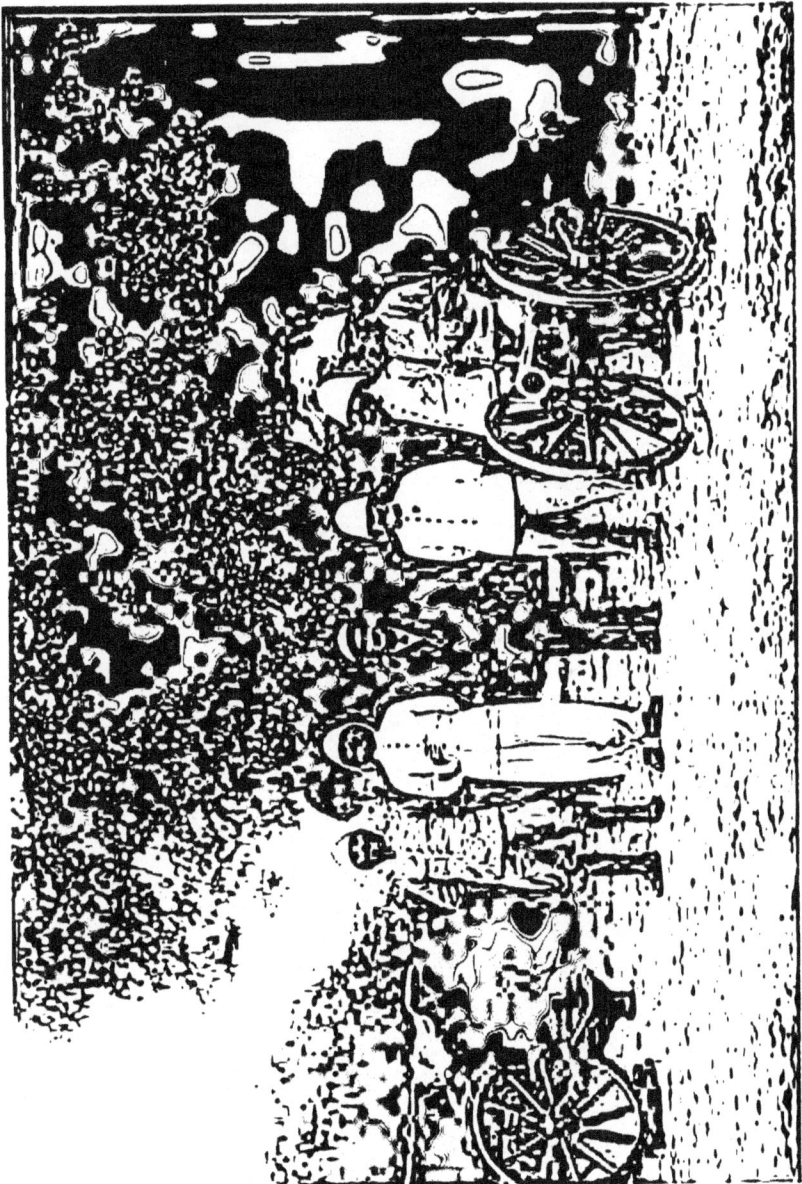

nationality, that only one thing will bring them to reason, and that is a thorough defeat. The Wadaians are better armed than people suspect, and may give a great deal of trouble. The most practical way of destroying the power of these raiders and brigands would be by a combined movement of the Anglo-Egyptian forces on the east and the French on the west. It must come sooner or later, the sooner the better.

The French are well prepared for contingencies. The belt of posts already established on the western boundary is quite sufficient for defensive purposes, as we shall see later, and with the magnificently trained, practical, plucky officers stationed in these regions the French have little to fear except a general Islamic movement of those troublesome tribes from the east and north-east.

The White Arab tribes are held well in hand by the French, who have mastered the geography of the desert and defined the exact position of wells and oases, and who hold the key of the various routes by which the desert tribes of Tuareg and Arabs provision themselves; but the Marabu (the priests) are constantly blowing up the fire of discord and sedition. A fanatical general war might have serious consequences in so distant a country.

In the group reproduced in the illustration facing page 206, another distinguished officer is represented, Colonel Largeau, a man of extraordinary coolness and with a well-balanced head. He accompanied Marchand on his famous expedition across Africa, and has done excellent work in the Tchad region.

Another interesting figure in the group, on the extreme right of the observer, is Commandant Gaden,

notable for his work in the region of Zinder, where, with
Colonel Peroz, he succeeded in conquering the Tuareg,
controlled the pillaging proclivities of the local sultan,
and established the administration on a firm basis in
the country.

There was at Fort Lamy a market-place where good
milk, butter, delicious onions of immense size, and
vegetables of all kinds could be purchased, besides fresh
meat, chickens, eggs, millet, rice and fruit. Women
as a rule did all the selling. The market-square looked
picturesque. In the centre of it stood a monument
to the officers and men who fell in the battle against
Rabah. Fort Lamy had grown around a huge tree,
under which Monsieur Gentil, after the battle had been
won on the opposite side of the stream in the German
Cameroon (before the German occupation), retired with
his officers to rest. He had for ever broken the
backbone of the fanatical hordes which accompanied
Rabah.

Arab influence could be felt more and more strongly
as we proceeded north. The women here, for instance,
in the market-place, had fine features, only somewhat
marred by long vertical cuts upon their cheeks. They
squatted round the market-place in lively groups, selling
milk and butter in large gourds strengthened by tightened
leather straps.

These women had long plaits of hair on both sides
of the head and two on the top ending in a curl on the
nape of the neck.

Arab and Bornu merchants found their way to this
place from the north and west. Low sheds had been
erected for them, where they sold quantities of matches,
dyes for the eyelids and beard, looking-glasses, leather

Women in the market at Fort Lamy.

top-boots, well adapted for that country, wooden bowls, ropes of tobacco, dried fish and meat.

Further along were merchants selling lambs, sheep and cattle, a big bullock fetching at Fort Lamy the equivalent of thirty-three francs. Forty-six chickens could be purchased for three francs (two shillings and fivepence) during the good season, but only twenty-three for the same amount during the wet season, owing to the difficulty of conveying articles to market.

CHAPTER XVI.

FROM Fort Lamy I went into the German Cameroon,
proceeding on the river Logone as far as Fort Kusseri,
the strongest in the Tchad region on the German side.
As one approached it from the river, a huge white house
with large wooden shutters and two lower houses were to
be seen, with a long castellated wall beyond on the river
front. The *ensemble* resembled an imposing Italian
villa. The main entrance, with double doors and guard-
room, was on the opposite side, away from the river.
A tin plate with the black German spreadeagle in all its
grandeur informed one that this was a German fortress.
Under it, exactly as one would see in any military post
of Emperor William's country, was a letter-box, which
told us that the mail went and came regularly and
quickly. What was more, this was an absolute fact.

Although the Germans possess only a very small
portion of the coast line on Lake Tchad, as compared
to the French and the British, they are geographically
most conveniently situated—as far as means of transport
in their own territory are concerned—for reaching
the lake comfortably and quickly. The French captain,
Lenfant, some years ago discovered a route from the
Niger to Lake Tchad, entirely by water except for a
distance of some thirty kilometres.

During three months of the year it is possible—in
fact, quite easy—to reach Lake Tchad by water from

The fort of Kusseri (German Cameroon)

the Atlantic Ocean *via* the Niger, the Benoué, the Tomburi and the Mayo-Kebbi. With the exception of some thirty kilometres of porterage—between the high waters of the Tomburi and the upper waters of the Mayo-Kebbi—further north changing its name into Logone river—the entire journey can be performed by steamer. The short land journey is in French territory—south of the tenth degree of lat. N. defining the Franco-German frontier—while the first part is in British territory, the last part on the Logone is in the German possessions.

The French have of late made some highly successful experiments in provisioning their garrisons on Lake Tchad by this route, which has saved much expense and time. Barring some international complications which may arise—not because the navigation of the rivers is not free, but because it is necessary to land on other people's territory for fuel, food, etc.—the Benoué-Logone route is by far the most convenient for reaching the lake. The Germans use it extensively for their mails, which arrive in Europe months before French mails, which, unluckily, have to travel either by a roundabout way *via* the Congo or else across the desert on camels *via* Zinder to the Niger, where they are either despatched through the Senegal or the Dahomey.

A second high wall, half ruined, encircled once the old town of Kusseri, which no longer exists. This town was within a large semicircular enclosure and possessed its own fort. Between it and the German fort was a big swamp, which the Germans had so far been unable to drain, as it was lower than the level of the Logone river at high water.

The inspection of the fort and barracks proved highly interesting, and it was a pleasure to see how beautifully the buildings were kept. The flat round houses for the soldiers, the kitchens and the stables, were all excellently built, and kept spick and span. Everything in the way of sanitary arrangements was up to date. The dispensary was provided with an inviting dissecting table— for anybody on dissection bent—with all kinds of knives and forceps and remedies of all sorts, really too many. A fine live lion was tied at the gate of the officer's house, which grunted as one approached.

I was hospitably received by Lieutenant Schipper, who took great pride in showing me everything. His house was excellently built for colonial purposes in two stories, with large windows and spacious verandahs, which made the rooms extraordinarily cool. The flat roofs were supported upon beams of palm-wood, which were not attacked by ants. Ingenious furniture had been constructed of horns and palm-tree wood.

The prison was in one of the turrets of the house, and there were neckrings in the wall for prisoners—who, however, were only taken there when violent.

Even an improvised shower-bath had been constructed—quite a luxury in the heart of Africa. This I had to use when I least expected. Having gone out to photograph Lieutenant Schipper in front of his fort, and being unable to obtain a satisfactory general view, I got a ladder and climbed on the thatched roof of a cowshed, on which I sat. In a moment big black ants swarmed inside my clothes and bit me furiously all over—as only African ants know how. I had to tear off my garments and rush under the shower-bath, when I began to live again. Several soldiers were summoned

at once to search my clothes and kill the hundreds of ants which had found their way into my sleeves, pockets, and everywhere, and which ran about, excited and vicious, as if the clothes had belonged to them.

There were five sultans in that portion of the German Cameroon—three Kotoko sultans, the Logone, Kusseri and Gulfei ; one Bornu, the sultan Kamori, who formerly came from the Kanem ; and one Mandara. All these sultans were fervent Mussulmans.

I met several of these sultans during my stay in the German Cameroon. Sultan Mussa of Kusseri sat like a statue, with five Kotoko behind him, when I photographed him. In this photograph, which is reproduced in this volume (facing page 212), will also be seen two other figures sitting down, one of the tribe Kanuri from Dekoa ; the other a Haussa from Kano.

The Bornu were at one time the rulers of all this country, with Kuka for a capital.

The extensive wool and leather industry in that country would, I think, bear developing and be profitable. The officer in charge of the district did all in his power to further progress in that direction.

Germans are not agriculturists by nature, but they are good traders. Taking things all round, perhaps more immediate profits are to be got out of a new, semi-barren country by well-conducted trading than by developing agricultural resources. The latter, after all, are merely of moderate assistance to the local natives without encouraging a demand for foreign imports, nor is the locally-grown produce of sufficient value to bear the expense of freight for export.

On August 15th, in torrential rain, I continued my journey towards Lake Tchad in the steamboat *Jacques d'Uzès*, kindly placed at my disposal by the French authorities. The river had now fairly low banks, very grassy at the water's edge. The channel was narrow, and naturally deep. North of Fort Lamy the Shari formed a delta with two principal arms. The eastern channel was the larger and deeper of the two. It was navigable by the small steamers even during the dry season when the western passage had but little water.

On the left bank of the Shari dwelt the Kotoko ; on the right were the Dagana and some Kotoko tribes.

I left the French government boat and went by canoe to visit the large walled town of Gulfei in the German Cameroon. On the French side at this point there was only a small village. There seemed to be a good deal of excitement when I crossed over, as, although the relations between the French and Germans are cordial, no social intercourse takes place and the officers refrain from landing on each other's territory.

Gulfei was an impressive place when seen from the river. It possessed a mud wall twenty feet high, extending for over one thousand yards along the river front. This wall was in a dilapidated condition. Hundreds of goats could be seen climbing on its slopes or perched on the summit against the sky-line in company with vultures. Along the river front the town could be entered by four gates.

Upon landing I was at once conveyed before the sultan, as there were no German officers here. Within the city gate one was rather surprised, after the shabbiness of the town wall outside, to find oneself among neatly-built mud houses tightly packed together on both sides of narrow winding lanes. I was struck by the architectural lines of these well-constructed edifices, which suggested a strong influence from the north and east. The doors, characteristic of this town, were V shaped ; they gave entrance into a vestibule from which a small court was reached, the residence itself, either square or cylindrical in shape, being found at the further end of this court.

Followed by hundreds of excited natives we arrived in the market-square, where stood the sultan's palace. Sultan Jaggara came forward with extended hand to receive me. An armed rabble surrounded him, and a number of prisoners lay chained on the ground. The sultan beckoned me to enter his palace, and by a maze of narrow winding passages at sharp angles we reached his private room—a small chamber with a large door, the walls hung with rifles, revolvers, cartridge-belts, rugs and swords.

The sultan seemed puzzled at my visit, especially when I told him I was a British subject. He seemed even more puzzled—almost disappointed—when I began my conversation by making it quite clear to him that I had no secrets to communicate to him, nor intrigues ; that I considered his religion (the Mussulman) quite as good as mine ; that when men were honest, just and generous to their neighbours, when they were not addicted to drunkenness or objectionable vices, it little mattered what their religion was or what coloured skin they possessed. German, French, English, were all equally good. I had only come to visit him and his town for my own gratification, and that was all.

Sultan Jaggar spoke highly of the treatment he received from the Germans. His own people were savages who sometimes behaved badly because they knew no better, but they were gradually understanding

that what was being done was for their own good, and
of late years, since the arrival of the French, the
Germans, and the British on Lake Tchad, all had been
peace where before death and terror reigned, especially
in Rabah's days.

Trade was improving gradually and steadily, tribal
raids had been put a stop to, and the people's property,
owing to the protection of the white people, was now
quite safe.

He detained me some time in order to give me
presents of chickens, eggs and pots of honey for my
journey. He was, indeed, most civil, and escorted me
out into the square, sending many of his suite and
soldiers to see me safely back into my canoe.

The sultan's palace was evidently built on strategic
principles. He explained to me that were an attack
to take place it would be impossible for the assaulters
to fight with their swords in the extremely narrow
passages. One could hardly squeeze through. In
addition to the various heavy gates in the angles, bar-
ricades would delay any armed mob endeavouring to
enter.

By the river was a regular fleet of fishing boats, each
boat having long angular arrangements like gigantic
horns, to which a net was attached, and which, being
balanced upon a pivot, allowed the net to be raised or
lowered into the water with the minimum of exertion.

On August 17th, embarking once more in the despatch boat, I left the Arab village of Jimtiloh, situated
on a smaller arm of the delta (the right arm, flowing
in a direction of 20° bearings magnetic, roughly north-
north-east). At the estuary of this arm we collected
quantities of firewood for the boilers and then pro-

ceeded down the main river, one hundred yards wide at this point, and flowing in a direction of 30° bearings magnetic.

The principal of the two greater arms of the delta, three hundred yards wide, flowed to 60° bearings magnetic ; the other to 25° was slightly narrower. The main arm had low grassy banks on either side.

I entered Lake Tchad an hour after leaving Jimtiloh. There were thousands of ducks and cranes, and innumerable hippopotami and crocodiles upon the banks and in or upon the water. We saw quantities of papyrus and swamp vegetation and a thick growth of reeds. A few low shrubs grew on land. The water upon entering the lake was of a yellowish colour for some distance from the mouth of the Shari, and we had before us four low islands on the horizon-line north-west and north. East of the fourth and smallest island a pole marked the route to be followed when approaching from the second important mouth of the Shari, which we had not followed. We steered due north between the two middle islands.

At the mouth of the Shari where we emerged was a low island. To 110° bearings magnetic could be perceived Mount Algeru Lamis, isolated and dome-shaped, the only mountain visible in the neighbourhood.

From a pictorial point of view Lake Tchad is disappointing. With its very low banks and flat desert country all around, the dirty colour of the water and the low islands which hardly rise above the surface, it was of all the lakes I had seen in my travels the most insipid-looking.

In the north-north-east part of the lake was another long, low, flat island with a number of smaller ones by its side. Soon after leaving the Shari one had the impression of being at sea, as there was a great expanse of clear water before us, and north, north-west and north-east we could see no land beyond the above enumerated islands. But the depth of the lake was not great—about one fathom.

We crossed a large stretch of open water and proceeded due north, with slight deviations of a few degrees (not more than five to ten degrees) either east or west in order to keep where the water was deepest. In the middle of the day we passed between two islands—the first of a series—mere sand-spits or accumulations of sand and decayed vegetation rising a few inches above the water, and smothered in thick reeds and grass. Islets were met which were now quite submerged, merely the vegetation upon them showing above the surface.

It was not till 2 p.m. (having left the mouth of the Shari at 10 a.m.) that we entered the extensive archipelago of islands, most of them hardly above water, with a thick growth of *ambatch*, the shrub we have already met with in the Bahr-el-Ghazal (of the Anglo-Egyptian Sudan). With it the natives make themselves what they call water-horses. They ride astride upon a large trunk of one of these trees, and they either paddle themselves with their hands or else punt themselves along with a long pole. Dozens of natives could be seen crossing the Shari river in this manner, and the Buduma use this method frequently in order to cross from one island to the other of their archipelago.

We proceeded all the time among low islands with an occasional high growth of *ambatch* in the water, and at 4.30 p.m. we reached the Buduma village of Momo.

Upon these islands is to be found a plant locally called *chok-choku*, said to be beneficial in spinal, liver complaints, inflammation of the kidneys, and a safe cure for gonorrhœa and allied troubles. The fruit of this plant is a small oblong bean. The *kusai*, a large-leaved plant, with fat grey leaves and light wood, has a pretty flower partly violet-coloured. The white latex which flows in abundance when a leaf or branch is cut is used by some of the tribes for poisoning their arrow-points and spears. So far away as in Somaliland, where this plant is also common, the skin of the stem is used in rope-making.

The Buduma village was untidy in the extreme, and had been surrounded by a wall of papyrus reeds. The huts were domed, with a pointed cone rising above them, also thatched with papyrus. They were badly constructed, regardless of symmetry or straightness of lines. In the interior was a semicircular partition three feet high, a kind of screen, and also another quadrangular partition, higher than the semicircular one. In this was a doorway leading to a bed of *ambatch* for the owner of the house. Another similar bed was outside, and over it hung neatly-made baskets containing butter. By the door was always found an earthen jar of water as well as a bundle of rolled mats. There were here, as among the Baguirmi, open shelters where people spent their time during the day, and during the hot season the nights also, upon the beds of *ambatch*.

Great excitement prevailed when the *Jacques d'Uzès* arrived, men waving their hands and screaming, the women hopping up with considerable lightness, tapping their lips rapidly with the open hand, giving a tremolo to their shrill ululations of welcome, which were identical to those employed in the British Sudan. Arabic influence was, in fact, strongly shown by the Buduma both in their manner and in their clothes — the latter absolutely Arab in design—and in their bracelets, as well as in the amulets they wore round the neck.

The population on the islands and some of the coast of Lake Tchad is principally *Yedena* or *Buduma*, who are subdivided into *Guria, Madjogogia, Dalla, Buja, Margana, Uarsoagana, Uarsoa, Direma, Kadjijena* and *Jela* —all tribes of the same family, and who, with some slight variations, speak the *Kuri* language.

There is a second race, the *Kura*, or *Kurawa*, subdivided into *Daghela, Dagoria, Kalia, Tossiman* and *Media*, the people of this district using the subtribal name with the generic name of *Kura*—the mother race of which they all form part—prefixed.

Close to the mouth of the Shari river in the southern portion of Lake Tchad we find the *Kalia*, with no subdivision of tribe, who speak the *Kuri* language like the *Buduma*. Then the *Kelea*, or *Keleoa*, who also speak the *Kuri* language, and of whom a single tribe is found. They are in many ways akin to the *Kalia* and the *Buduma*.

Somewhat different are the *Kanembu*, subdivided into *Kadjirabu*, large groups of *Gheloa, Kadia, Madaah* and *Ngalamabigu talfu*. Very important is the great family of *Kanembu*, the *Ngalaga* ; the *Ngalaga* of *Tala*, the *Ngalaga* of *Djabu*, and the *Ngalaga* of *Lerebu*.

The third kind of *Kanembu* are the *Surumu*, subdivided into *Surumu* of *Limina, Surumu* of *Lamindam, Surumu* of *Malummussa* and *Surumu* of *Seghendah*.

We have a fourth division of *Kanembu*, the *Katiti*,

with the following subdivisions : the *Katiti Galana*, the *Katiti Kuga*, the *Katiti Joa* and the *Katiti Kelemia*.

Less extended are the fifth, sixth and seventh tribes of *Kanembu :* the *Manigabuh*, the *Kailogoma*, and the *Kenghena*, near Kulua. In the north-east part of Lake Tchad one finds the *Kuburi* of Kiska, and near the *Kellu* the *Kuburi* of Kologa, both making a part of the *Kuburi* family. Also another not clearly defined tribe living at Tagal near Bol.

In the northern part of Lake Tchad we find the *Toumagheri* and the *Nguigmi*.

Among the most important people after the *Buduma*, we find in the Kanem, east of Lake Tchad, some *Tubu*, in the proximity of Dossolem, and the *Bornu*, who have a fixed abode at Ngorodugubé. Scattered about we have the *Duggu*, called *Haddad* by the Arabs, a race formerly of blacksmiths, but now degenerated into mere pariahs.

Lieutenant Hardellet, who travelled for the Government in those regions from the years 1902 to 1904, was able clearly to define all these tribes and subdivisions of races. Then Lieutenant Freydenberg was sent over to survey Lake Tchad, and he also made important studies, not only of the hydrography of the lake, but of the many tribes living upon the coast and in the neighbourhood.

The *Kanembu* of Lake Tchad (apart from those *Kanembu* who are dependent upon the *Guria* [*Buduma*]) are the people under Chief Abba, the people of *Mateguh*, and those of *Kamba*. Those of *Mateguh*, who go by the name of *Khinghina*, came formerly from the Solo country east of Rig Rig, in the western portion of the Chitati. According to local history they were driven away by

Chief Bulalla, and some fled to Bornu, the others migrating to Lake Tchad. The latter are known as the *Kenghena* of *Danda*, of *Abba* and of *Kabulu*, the tribes as usual taking the names of their respective chiefs. When the *Kenghena Maghenu* left Solo and went to Rig Rig they continued their migration still further towards the Bornu, and remained for a long time at a place called Bolongo ; evidently dissatisfied with this new country they eventually returned to Rig Rig after Bulalla's occupation, and there established themselves. Mateguh, one of the villages in which they took refuge, was also abandoned when danger threatened again, and it was not until 1901, after the French had taken Bir-el-Ali, that they finally settled down. The *Abba*, whom we have mentioned above, migrated well south-east to Bol, where they conquered the local inhabitants named the *Korio*. To this day one finds a few *Korio* among the *Kabulu*. One of the chiefs, Kadalla Far, the father of Abba, left the Kabulu country in 1893 in order to proceed to Kanassorem, as a racial hatred existed between the *Danda* and the *Abba* people, which was much intensified by some murders that had taken place. The *Kenghena* (or *Kinguina*) had a severe fight about the year 1899 against the Wadaians who had come on a raid as far as Danda. They were brought to Kubulu by the *Kotoko*, a powerful race who had fled to the southern part of Lake Tchad during the approach of the barbarous hordes of Rabah to that region. The *Guria* also came to their assistance, and eventually the Wadaians retired to their own country.

The *Kanembu* of Kambu came originally from the Bahr-el-Ghazal, an effluent of the Tchad, but they were driven away by Bulalla. They established themselves

Kanembu women making "spaghetti."

in the land of Folé at Kamba, on the east of the road
between Bol and Kulua, in order to escape the raids of
the *Tubu*, their neighbours, a warlike and troublesome
people. They have, up to the present time, succeeded
in keeping the land of Folé as far as the Oasis of Tagum,
near Dossolem, which I visited in my journey, on the
east of Lake Tchad. Formerly, these people were
numerous, and the *Buduma*, their foes, had never been
able to conquer them. They derived most of their
wealth from the great deposits of sodium carbonate
found in the region inhabited by them. These deposits
were of considerable thickness ; the crystallized carbon
was cut by the natives in large slabs, weighing about
fifty pounds each, two of these slabs making a full load
for an ox and four of them for a camel.

The *Kamba* people derive a good income from the
sale of the sodium carbonate, chiefly to the *Bornu*, who,
in their turn, sell it further west. On Lake Tchad
twelve slabs are sold for one Maria Theresa thaler, which
has a varying local value of from two francs fifty to
three francs. By the time one of these slabs has reached
the market of Zinder, west of Lake Tchad, half way
between Lake Tchad and the Niger, its price is increased from twenty to twenty-four times its original
value, one slab being sold at the Zinder market for
one thaler—a thaler being worth in Zinder from five
to six francs, as the natives, the Tuareg particularly,
prefer these less valuable Maria Theresa coins, if not
damaged, to French five-franc coins.

The *Kamba* are too lazy to go in for trading on their
own account or to send out caravans with salt, so the
Wanda are the people who convey it, mostly by means of
carrier oxen. There are from two to three hundred

oxen going backwards and forwards on the road under *Wanda* caravan men.   These *Wanda* people when coming to the mines are made by the *Kanembu* to pay a tax of five thalers for every hundred oxen brought to be laden with sodium carbonate—*sesqui*, as they call it.

In the desert and in parts of the Tuareg country, as among the Haussa, sodium carbonate is eaten mixed with tobacco.   The natives relish this mixture, which, no doubt, brings about many of the intestinal, liver and bladder complaints which are so frequent among them.

In the Kanem oxen form the greatest part of the people's fortune, and they are—as among the *Shiluk*, the *Nuer* and other tribes we have already met further east—used as currency in matrimonial bargains, as well as in purchasing slaves or paying tribal fines.

When getting married a man buys his wife direct from her father, the value of the young lady varying, not according to her family's fortune, but according to the wealth of the purchaser.   A good healthy wife will vary from the cost of two shillings (one silver thaler), to such an exaggerated sum as ten oxen.   Most people, however, in the Kanem, only pay the two shillings— and the wives are dear at that price—as but few men can afford a larger fortune for matrimonial alliances.

Wounding or killing a fellow-tribesman comes more expensive than buying a wife.   For wounding, a carrier ox must be handed over as a fine to the wounded person, as well as a young cow.   A good carrier ox is valued locally at from three to twelve thalers, and a cow at about ten thalers.   For killing a man, no less than a hundred oxen must be paid over to the family by a man who possesses them ; but no such penalty is incurred when one kills a *Haddad*—one of the pariahs I have already mentioned (*Duggu* as they are locally called by the Kanembu)—who are greatly looked down upon by the natives, and can be killed with impunity without the murderer having to disburse a farthing or give away cattle.

Of course, where there are marriages there are bound to be divorces. The simplest form of divorce among the Kanembu, when the husband does not wish to live with his wife any longer, is to drive her away from his home and give her nothing ; but when the woman seeks the divorce and wishes to remarry, she cannot do so unless she pays a number of oxen to her first husband, the number of oxen depending, as usual, on how many the second husband can afford.

As with the Buduma, the reasons for which a divorce on the husband's side can be obtained are the following First, if the woman talks too much ; second, if the woman refuses to cook ; and, third, if she has lovers. The first and second offences are generally forgiven, and the third also is overlooked if a suitable payment of oxen is made by the co-respondent.

In cases of adultery, according to the law of the Kanembu and the Buduma, the husband is allowed to act on his own judgment. He has a right to kill his rival if he wishes, but if he is not bent on murder he generally satisfies himself by claiming all the other man's possessions as a compensation for the wrong he has received. Should he, however, have neither sufficient courage to kill the offender nor sufficient influence to confiscate all his possessions—as in the case of a chief, who, whether in the wrong or not, would have the support of the entire population—the offended husband has to be satisfied with making the culprit pay a fine, generally of one ox.

A woman can obtain a divorce if she can prove the following points : If the husband beats her too often and too violently ; if he talks too much ; if he does not give her sufficient clothing and food ; and if he is impotent or unfaithful. In the first instance of the latter case, the husband is usually advised by the chief to make an arrangement with his wife by which she may enjoy life and procure the birth of children who may be recognized as his, unknown, however, to all the other members of the tribe. But if the husband is not satisfied to agree to these conditions the father of the girl is allowed to take her back to his home and marry her to a more suitable husband.

In any case, when domestic quarrels occur, both the Buduma and the Kanembu invariably try to avoid a scandal. The chief and the older men of the tribe endeavour to reconcile the unhappy couple. The Koran is produced and an attempt is made to make them swear that they will never quarrel again ; if they refuse, then they are allowed to separate.

In the case of a woman's adultery, it is generally a relative of the husband—possibly the brother or the father—who goes to confabulate with the wife, trying to bring her back with persuasive ways and more frequently with a few touches of the *courbash*. Should she, nevertheless, be found at fault a second or third time no pardon will be granted.

The men of that region can be quite accommodating for a consideration, and if a rich man wishes to possess the pretty wife of a poorer tribesman, all he has to do is to come to a suitable arrangement with her and her husband, and he can marry her on paying back to the first husband the sum which he had paid for her, *plus* a present according to his generosity. If the husband is unwilling to do this openly, the bargain is made in a more indirect fashion by paying back to the father of the girl the oxen which had been paid to her, and the father—also for a small consideration—eventually hands back his property to the first husband.

All these people belong to the religion of Islam, and children are circumcised at the age of eight years— an operation which is performed by a *Haddad*, who receives in payment for his work two calabashes of millet and one calabash of butter or grease. In the case of orphans the village pays for the operation at the rate of one calabash of millet.

No sooner does a person die among the Kanembu than, if the death occurs in the daytime, the body is placed in a shallow grave, lying extended, with the head to the south and the feet to the north, the face turned towards the east in the direction of Mecca. People dying at night are buried at sunrise.

The laws of heredity are somewhat complicated. If a man dies leaving no sons, it is the brother of the deceased who inherits everything. If there is only one son, he becomes the owner of the property ; if there are two sons the property is divided equally, except for one extra ox, which is the right of the eldest. Should there be a cow above the division of property—which generally consists of oxen—the eldest son becomes the owner of the animal, but he must give each of the brothers in succession a calf when born until all have their share. If there is a horse, all in the family have the right to use it.

The daughters have no right whatever to the succession, but in the case of a single brother coming into the property, he generally gives each sister an ox as a present.

Slaves are divided in the same manner as oxen.

The widow has no right to anything, but the sons are obliged to feed her during her lifetime unless she remarries.

In the case of landed proprietors, the eldest son takes the portion of land which has been cultivated by the father, and the rest is divided equally among the younger brothers.

CHAPTER XVII.

THE customs of the Buduma vary somewhat from those of the Kanembu. Although most are Mahommedans, we find many are fetishists, especially the Dallakuta, the Madjogoja and the Maibolloa, north of Lake Tchad, near Kulua. The Dallakuta, for instance, a race of pirates, under Chief Tiari Dongola, who inhabit the northern part of Lake Tchad, have as fetishes the spear and the sword, emblems of the gods of war ; whereas the Madjogoja worship water and a cane, the *folé*.

There is a quaint ceremony among these water-worshippers : in the morning they place a leather belt round the waist and attach to it a small calabash full of millet. They go to the nearest pool of water or to the lake and throw some of the millet into the water, invoking favour and the protection of " their mother," for they say that they are the sons of the water. If fish come at once and eat the millet the people return happy to their homes, as they believe their prayers or wishes will be fulfilled. That these people worship water is not strange, for, indeed, they spend most of their time on or in it.

As we have seen, there exists on Lake Tchad a peculiar wood (the *ambatch*), which grows to a considerable size, and is infinitely lighter than cork. A piece of this

wood, twelve or fifteen feet long and six or eight inches
in diameter, can be lifted up with one finger like a feather.
Although this wood has no great resistance for building
purposes and quickly rots away, it is nevertheless useful
to the natives for getting about from one island to
another. Every man carries his water-horse of *ambatch*
wood upon his shoulders.

The other fetish, the *folé*, is used as an amulet. A
section of it is hung by a string round the neck. The
folé is a reed used by the Buduma in making canoes. It
is tied into fascines. With these, boats similar to those
of the Shiluk on the Sobat and in the Bahr-el-Ghazal
(Egyptian Sudan), are constructed. The lightness of
the material gives these boats a good floating capacity.

The people who need amulets go into the lake, fill
their mouths with water and sprinkle it twice on the cane
which they have selected. It is only after this graceful
performance that it is gently pulled out of the water
and carried home to be divided among the people of
the family to whom it is to bring luck.

The Maibolloa worship mostly a gum-tree, which
they call *caraku*, and in whose protection they thoroughly believe. This tree is never cut down by them
and never burnt as fuel. In order to keep in its good
graces and to be everlastingly protected, they pour
calabashes full of grease and flour over the roots, so as
to nourish the tree, and on passing near they throw small
pieces of wood at it.

As among the Kanembu, dead people are buried
immediately after death, the body lying from north to
south, but the Buduma place the head instead of the
feet to the north. The face, however, is always turned
towards the east. Men are dressed up in their best

clothes when buried, but no jewels, weapons or articles of any kind are placed on the grave.

The grave is cut in a particular fashion among the Buduma. First, a large rectangular hole is made, at the bottom of which a second and smaller chamber—the actual grave—is dug. In it the body is placed wrapped in a sheet. The aperture of the second chamber is then covered with pieces of wood, with a layer of straw above. A thick layer of sand is then deposited ; next comes a stratum of mud, and on the top dry earth is placed.

An ox is sacrificed and eaten upon the grave and another ox in the village. According to the wealth of the children and the love they bore to their parent or relation, more or fewer oxen are despatched. As many as fifteen or twenty oxen are sacrificed in this way.

Among the Buduma, the land and pastures did not belong to private individuals, but were the property of the tribe. Until the French occupation, and, indeed, quite lately, these people, who were of a piratical nature, were given to extensive raiding both on the lake and on dry land. Only a few weeks before my arrival one of these raids had occurred, and the natives were duly punished for it.

Their raids consisted mostly in seizing oxen, extremely numerous in that country, belonging to some weaker tribe. They had fixed regulations for the division of the booty. Two-thirds of the stolen oxen were divided, in equal shares, among the people who had taken part in the raid ; the other third was taken by the chief of the expedition. If clothing and money were also obtained, they were divided into two equal shares : one for the leader and the other for his followers. The Buduma obtained a further profit by selling back to their own tribe the people they had made prisoners, the ransom received being divided in the following way : one-third to the chief of the expedition, one-third to the individuals who made the capture, the other third divided among the other raiders. A curious point in Buduma laws of brigandage was that when dividing booty, a horseman received three oxen to every two of an infantryman's. If the horse on which the rider rode had been lent him by a friend not taking part in the raid, the horseman must give two-fifths of his share to the proprietor of the steed.

The Buduma were polygamous, but every woman had to have a separate household. The husband had to stay two days at a time with each of his wives, the first married having the precedence. If this rule were not observed, divorce could be obtained by the neglected wife. No Buduma ever married in his own clan. After reaching the age of reason he had no relations whatever with the women in his village. No reproach was made for keeping concubines galore in other villages, but he was not allowed to bring them to his home.

There were strange rules among the Buduma regarding the morality of women who should by mishap have an infant. The illegitimate infants of young unmarried girls were at once killed, but a divorced woman or a woman with no relatives was free to give herself to a fast life. She took the name of *dagaram kogoï*, or " woman-hen," and was looked down upon by other women in the village.

Marriages among the Buduma were somewhat more lively and elaborate than among the Kanembu, although they were carried out on the same principle of purchase.

Brides who were virgins fetched a higher price than those who were not. Nearly all women got married when about twelve years old, at which age they were fully developed. They cohabited at once with their husbands.

A Buduma man bent on marrying was compelled, first of all, to pay for a feast with much beating of drums and dancing. Then he must pay the father the purchase price, which varied from a loin-cloth, made of bands of *gabaga* sewn together (costing about one thaler), to as much as six oxen.

Girls in the Buduma country were permitted to have a will of their own, but only to a certain extent. If her family wished a girl to marry a man whom she did not love, and if she would not acquiesce, severe punishment was administered. Were that not sufficient, first her brother and then her *fiancé*, the latter by way of ingratiating himself, gave her a thrashing. If that did not produce the desired effect she was left alone.

The reasons which could be produced to obtain a divorce were the same as with the Kanembu with some extras. A woman demanding a divorce invariably began by receiving a volley of the *courbash* upon hemispherical parts of her anatomy from her father, who would have to take his daughter back and return the purchase-money which had been paid for her. If the husband demanded a divorce, the father or the brother of the woman gave back the purchase amount, or more frequently the sum was kept by the woman until she had found a second husband. He was the person who eventually had to pay up the marriage money to the first husband.

When a Buduma married a slave, the offspring were slaves, and had no right to inherit their father's fortune.

They became the property of the eldest son by a non-slave wife. A certain consideration, however, was shown to these children, and ultimately in reality, if not nominally, they became free.

When Buduma women were raided from their villages and, later, were recovered, children conceived during the interval became slaves ; but when a Buduma woman had been seized in a raid and had been married by her captor, the children were free. This, of course, in the case of a woman who was originally free and not a slave.

Family rows among the Buduma were frequent and generally about oxen. The father did not always occupy a position of respect or fear in the family. The sons often endeavoured to seize the father's property, and family fights took place in which the greater number of the relatives joined, the brothers of the father taking the part of the older man against the sons and their friends. The villagers endeavoured to prevent a battle and took the matter into their own hands. The property was divided. Half was given to the children. The other half was not handed back to the father, who was held in contempt for not being able to hold his family in check, but handed over to his brother, who was expected to support the disgraced man until his death.

The division of property among the Buduma was as follows : If there were children by several wives, all the children of the same mother were treated as one unit in the division. The eldest of all had the right of *folé* and of the *kam kolarum*, symbolical words which mean " the man who is in front," or, in other words, " the man who has the precedence in the hereditary rights." The daughters had no claims whatever. The widow usually married the brother of the deceased, whose property she became at the death of her husband. If he did not want her he had a right to marry her to any man he chose ; but in this case all he could demand in return of the value which had been paid for her was a young cow and a carrier ox.

Among the Buduma, at the death of a man with no sons, the eldest brother of the deceased inherited everything if the deceased were a younger brother. In case of the eldest, his younger brothers divided the property into equal shares. When there were sons the eldest of these became nominally the chief of the family, although in reality he had but little influence over the others. At his father's death, the eldest son took all personal effects, including the family canoe and one slave. After that came the division of the cattle in a complicated fashion. One animal was taken by him as his right of *folé*, and he was allowed to select for this right whichever animal he chose. Then he appropriated another animal as " the man who walks in front," the *kam kolarum*, chief of the family. After this came the actual division, and he was permitted to choose the best animals of the remaining lot. After the selection of the first ox by his younger brother, the eldest received an extra head of cattle. So that, for instance, if there were five animals to be divided, the eldest received three extra animals and then one for his share, which would make four out of five. In a larger number of animals the same rule was applied, and the eldest son would only benefit to the extent of the three first extra animals.

If at the time of the husband's death there were suckling children, they remained with their mother during lactation, after which time the eldest brother was obliged to give a sufficient number of cows or oxen to

supply the wants of mother and children, the latter
having no share in the succession. The moment the
child was weaned, it was taken over by the eldest
brother, and the mother, if she wished, was allowed to
remarry.

No special diet or special precautions were taken
by Buduma women during pregnancy, nor were difficult
labours common in the Buduma country. Far from it.
A Haddad, or pariah woman, was generally entrusted
with all arrangements during confinement, and in her
absence a Buduma woman operated. For her trouble,
a present was given to this midwife. For the birth of a
boy she received one pot of butter, a calabash full of
millet, one roll of tobacco and a spear ; for a daughter, a
similar amount minus the weapon.

Festivals and rejoicings took place at the time when
circumcision was practised on boys at the age of six, a
tenderer age than among the Kanembu. Girls were not
excised among the Buduma. First of all, free children
underwent the operation also at the hands of a Haddad,
then slave children. The operator received a fixed
present for each boy of one calabash of millet, one of
butter and a spear.

We remained the entire night upon one of the islands,
and when we left early in the morning we passed between
the islands of Iba and Kormiron. Picturesque horsemen,
mounted on beautiful animals, galloped along the shore
waving their hands at us, while crowds of people followed them, leaping in the air and yelling, partly
delighted and partly frightened at the uncommon sight
of the little steamer.

To the east, in which direction we were travelling,
was Gurguliah island, flat and with scanty vegetation

when compared with other islands.   On Isa island could be seen a small wooded mound about thirty feet high. We went round the eastern end of Gurguliah, following a course of east-north-east.   North of us we now had Kugudu island, and east of it Iru.   We passed between these.   Behind, west of Kugudu, was Wiua island.

I took several boiling-point observations.   Water boiled at this point at 213° Fahrenheit, with the temperature of the atmosphere at 79°.   My aneroids registered the elevation of the lake's surface at 956 feet.

After that, Melia island and Jiburu were to our left, on the west, and Irbu to our right, our course being 323° bearings magnetic (roughly north-west).   To the north-north-west we had Murikutta island, and beyond to the north-north-east Murikura.   On the eastern part of Melia stood a large settlement.   Altering our course to the east, we now had Murikutta to our right (on the south) and Murikura, whereas to our left a grassy island became disclosed, whose name I could not ascertain.

We altered our course again at this point to east-north-east, going round Murikutta island, on the north end of which stood a small village.   East-north-east we had Kalinduah, and steering a course of 70°, we left it on our left, with the small island of Madiruh on our right.   We met here many Buduma, with beards in tiny curls upon the chin and shaved heads.   They had two small incisions, one inch long, near the temples, and two on each cheek quite close to the nose.   Most men wore a black armlet above the elbow.   We stopped at this village and were well received by Chief Adigakabu, from whom we bought provisions.   There was a narrow channel not more than fifty yards wide between Kalinduah and Madiruh.

Madiruh-Gana and Tumburah were close together to the south-east of us and Kutkuh was to the north-east. From this point Komi rose to the east-north-east, with a village on the summit of a grassy mound, this island being higher than most of the others, with fine pasture meadows almost devoid of trees.

We were now following a course due east. Several villages were noticeable on Komi, and the mound on this island rose some sixty feet above the level of the lake. We went again 20° (north-east), Tendal island standing now to the east of us and Komi (or Somi) to the left. The channel between Komi and Tendal was hardly twenty yards wide. Cotton was grown in small quantities by natives, these people being mainly shepherds. They derived their wealth entirely from their cattle.

In the afternoon of August 18th I arrived at Bol on the northern bank of the eastern bay of Lake Tchad. It is in this basin that the greater number of inhabited islands in the archipelago are to be found. It was my intention not to continue my journey directly from this point towards the west, but to describe a loop in a north-easterly direction in the desert, in order to visit many interesting tribes in the Kanem. I also wanted to study the peculiar geological formation of that country, with its curious *cuvettes*—deep hollows of immense proportions, which some people believe have been formed by infiltration from Lake Tchad, a theory which I think is not altogether correct, except perhaps in regard to a few of the depressions nearer the lake.

In many parts of Lake Tchad I drank some of its water. Far from finding it heavily salted, as it is supposed to be, I found it extremely sweet. The quantity of reeds and vegetation of all kinds gave the water quite a sugary taste. Even without this the water, at least in the two southern basins, showed no traces of salt, and I rather doubt whether in the northern portion it would have a brackish taste, except perhaps directly over or near the deposits of sodium carbonate, which are frequent in the northern portion.

CHAPTER XVIII.

IT is perhaps true that many travellers are responsible for mis-statements regarding countries they visit by not taking sufficient care to check their observations, because of insufficient education or lack of observation, ignorance of the local language, and so forth ; but I think that great confusion in geographical problems is principally caused by the theoretical stay-at-home geographers, who base their theories upon imaginary notions and false calculations, and who end by misleading themselves and the public at large.

Lake Tchad is perhaps the one of the lakes of Central Africa about which more nonsense has been spoken and written than about any other. Of late years, however, a few French and German travellers have done magnificent work in that region. Among these may be mentioned Barth, Overweg, Nachtigal, Colonel Monteil, Messieurs Foureau-Lamy, Gentil, d'Huart, Captain D'Adhemar, Captain Hardellet, Lieutenant Audoin and Captain Tilho. The latter gentlemen lately made a hydrographic survey of the lake, and by including additional surveys made by other travellers produced perhaps the most accurate map so far published of that region.

Colonel Largeau, who succeeded to the command of Colonel Fourneau at Fort Lamy, continued the serious study of the lake in order to establish its navigability

and the exact extent of the eastern archipelago with its numerous islands. Lieutenant Audoin's expedition, sent out by Colonel Largeau, carried on this work.

The lake is an irregular polygon, with a surface of some twenty thousand square kilometres. It has no well-defined boundary, except on the western coast, where the shore remains fairly parallel to the dune which marks the limit on that side. The lake may be divided into two basins, one that of the Komadugu, the other much larger, with an eastern and a western basin filled by the waters of the Shari. To the east and north-east we have absolute desert. To the west we find a narrow band of vegetation seldom more than four hundred yards wide extending all along the shores of the lake. This is perhaps because of the great evaporation from the lake during the *harnattan* winds coming from the north-east, which evaporation settles down again upon that particular part of the coast on coming in contact with the radiation of the sandy soil.

There are people who believe that Lake Tchad is drying up fast, and is likely to disappear altogether, this because the lake has shown certain tendencies to diminish its surface. In fact, for some years the level of the lake had become lower, especially in the northern part, which had actually dried up to such a degree that a French officer, Lieutenant Freydenberg, was able to walk on foot from the northern dune (the former limit of the lake) right into the centre, and to explore, still on foot, the north-eastern part of Lake Tchad as far as Kulua, practically without getting his feet wet.

Naturally, like all lakes which depend for their supply of water upon streams with no outlet into the sea, and which are situated in climates where the evaporation is extraordinarily rapid, where the absorption of the soil is considerable, and where rainy seasons are not alike two years running, Lake Tchad is liable to variations. It is obvious that when the rivers flowing into and forming the lake do not carry the same volume of water, the level of the lake cannot always be the same. The two principal rivers bringing water into Lake Tchad are the Shari river, coming from the south-east, and the Komadugu, coming from the west; the latter flows into the northern part of the lake. The Shari brings the largest volume of water. In fact, Shari is a word coming from the Bornu language, which means " great river," whereas Komadugu in the same language means " small river " The Buduma call the big river *Ndjeri*, which is nothing but a corruption of the Bornu word *Tchari*. The Baguirmi call the Shari *Bahn'goloh*, which also means " great river," and the Arabs call it Bahr-el-Kebir, which means the same.

Naturally, following the custom of the country, the river takes different names in different sections—for instance, the Bahr-Busso, etc.—the names being those of different chiefs inhabiting along its banks. Lake Tchad is called *Tchuku* by the Buduma, from which word I think the corruption Tchad has been derived.

What happens is roughly this. In seasons when the rains are not abundant in the hilly regions of the Gribanghi and in the Wadai, from which several important tributaries run into the Shari, and when there are no heavy rains in the Haussa and Bornu countries west of Lake Tchad, neither the Shari river nor the Komadugu brings large volumes of water, and the lake naturally does not rise to its maximum level. It is well known that the water of the lake does not reach the same height in any two consecutive years. In fact, the natives say that for seven years the level of the lake keeps decreasing and they relate various legends regarding the fluctuations of the lake. Whether the figures they state are absolutely correct or not is difficult to say, but there is certainly a foundation of truth in their accounts.

Fluctuations certainly occur in the lake, and people believe that it has tides like the sea, but it has been proved that although these movements on the surface do occur, they are caused by the north-easterly wind forcing the water towards the south-west, during which periods the coast is left dry to a corresponding extent on the east side of the lake. This phenomenon can with considerable certainty be attributed to the influence of the *harnattan* (north-east wind), since it only occurs when that wind prevails.

Lake Tchad is on the limit of two zones, one extremely humid, the other, and larger, of dry, hot, desert sands. Climatic conditions of this kind are bound to cause daily variations in the level of the lake, especially during the dry season, owing to extreme evaporation during the hot hours of the day when the north-easterly winds are blowing. This action does not take place at night, when the fluctuation caused by the evaporation does not take place to the same extent, and is at any rate counterbalanced by the amount of water conveyed into the lake by the rivers. This produces variations of flux and reflux, which have no relation whatever to tidal movements. During the rainy season, in fact, when the sky is always cloudy and the temperature comparatively cool, this phenomenon of a constant change of level is not noticeable at all.

It is perhaps due to these fluctuations that whatever

salt exists in the lake—if, indeed, it is salt in the common meaning of the word—is pushed back towards its banks by the incoming water of the two streams. Lake Tchad being situated in a zone of transition between tropical Africa and the desert, we are bound to find an abundant growth of reeds, grass, papyrus, and all sorts of water-plants in the swampy parts of the lake and upon the low islands. This thick vegetation decays when in the water and settles at the bottom of the lake. The winds from the desert bring over a quantity of sand, which settles down at the bottom of the lake with the decayed vegetable matter. Therefore, the bed of the lake is constantly and, comparatively speaking, rapidly rising. In the central portion of the lake we find a broad barrage of grass and mud forming a number of small islets hardly above water. This barrage extends from east to west of the lake, but south of it we find two large basins of clear water which are always filled by the normal supply of water brought by the Shari River. Again, in the north-westerly part of the lake north of the barrage, we have another basin of clear water from three to six feet deep, the water of this being supplied by the Komadugu. In the northern part of this basin we find banks of grass, some islets in course of formation, and others already formed and definitely emerged. This region of islets is situated almost entirely north of another barrage of grass and mud of a similar formation and almost parallel with the larger one we have found stretching across the lake. In the south-west corner of Lake Tchad is a great swamp of reeds and mud, so thick that the Germans, who own a portion of the lake's coast, are quite unable to get to the water.. There are a great many islands in the most easterly part of the lake, and these islands, as we have seen, are inhabited mostly by the Buduma and the Kanembu.

The natives declare that Lake Tchad fills up to a maximum height every twenty-five years, the water reaching to the dune all round the lake, after which the water gradually retires and portions of the lake actually dry up. Whether this period of twenty-five years is correct or not, I could not ascertain. What was more, I had no idea whatever of remaining in those parts long enough to solve the problem; but all the natives were unanimous in stating that every seven rainy seasons (years) or so there was a partial flood, which half filled the lake, and every twenty-one to twenty-five rainy seasons a great flood which filled it entirely.

This is just what occurred last year—1906. The Shari brought so much water owing to an abnormally long and abundant rainy season that, soon after I left, the entire lake, I am informed on good authority, filled up again.

It is, nevertheless, beyond doubt that the lake must centuries ago have been of much greater size than it is at present. Lieutenant Freydenberg has been able to demonstrate this important point. He dug a well at Kulua, now some distance north-east of Lake Tchad, and in digging he came across a deep layer of sand, under which he found a comparatively small layer of decayed vegetation. Under that he again found another layer of sand, these layers of sand being deposited, as we have seen, by the wind, chiefly during the period of the sub-sidence of the water. Then he found another layer of decayed vegetation, and again another layer of sand above another layer of decayed vegetation, which shows how the bed of the lake is gradually being raised.

In its broadest southern portion Lake Tchad is
about 170 kilometres wide, and its length from south to
north is about 180 kilometres.

From the mouth of the Shari to the eastern extremity
of the lake runs a current, which is evidently caused by
the force of the Shari water rushing into the lake, and
which continues along the coast among the many islands
of the archipelago. This current, still following the
coast-line, proceeds around the basin, and then in a north-
westerly direction, until it loses itself in the northern
basin of the lake, where it comes into contact with a
counter-current from the Komadugu. This current at
very high water occasionally invades the valley called
Bahr-el-Ghazal (not in any way to be confounded with
the Bahr-el-Ghazal we have crossed in the Anglo-Egyptian Sudan). The Bahr-el-Ghazal, in the Tchad region,
is a channel which proceeds towards the north-east for
several hundred kilometres. For some years it has been
absolutely dry. The geographical problem of whether
the Bahr-el-Ghazal is an effluent or a tributary of Lake
Tchad has puzzled geographers. When the level of the
lake was stationary the water in it, if there was any, did
not move either one way or the other. When the level
of the lake rose, water flowed up the Bahr-el-Ghazal,
and flowed slowly down into Lake Tchad when the level
of the lake became lower, so that, personally, I have
little doubt left in my mind that this was merely an
effluent which had bored its way along one of the great
depressions that are common enough in that region.
It has been said that the water in this channel had been
known to travel simultaneously in double currents,
both upwards and downwards at different periods of the
year, which fact might be responsible for the shape of

the banks at the mouth of the Bahr-el-Ghazal, the shores being pointed instead of rounded, as might be expected of an effluent. The fact that the water flowed down the channel towards Lake Tchad on the surface, and up the channel away from Lake Tchad underneath, was probably due to the strong current from the Shari, which I have mentioned above, and which forced its way up underneath while the surface water flowed back as the level of the lake gradually got lower. This phenomenon of the double current was only noticed, I think, in the vicinity of the mouth of this enigmatic channel. According to French observers, who have studied the Bahr-el-Ghazal valley when dry, water supposed to be caused by infiltration from Lake Tchad is to be found at a lower depth the further away one goes from the lake. Further still it actually appears on the surface, forming extensive *mares*.

During the season of floods fresh water is to be found all over the lake. The maximum level is generally reached in December, when, during ordinary floods, the level of the lake does not rise more than three feet eight inches. This gives rise to another question regarding Lake Tchad. Some people maintain that its waters are salt. In no place where I visited the surface of the lake was the water salt or brackish. Others maintain that except in the basins of the Shari and Komadugu the water is extremely salt. The observer who most forcibly maintained this point was at the time of his visit laid up with fever. I do not know whether he discovered the water to be salt by chemical examination or by simply tasting it. I think that the latter case is the more probable of the two, and as he was not in good health, and probably taking medicines liable to affect the palate, I think his statement should be tested before accepting it.

Other travellers—Barth is one of them—who were in excellent health, as I was when I tasted the Tchad water, found the water extremely fresh and in no way salt. Perhaps, as we shall see later, there are certain pools in the northern part of the lake directly over deposits of sodium carbonate, where the latter becomes dissolved in the water and gives it a brackish taste, but the water of the lake as a whole is undeniably fresh. The lake, as we have seen, is absolutely fed by the above-mentioned rivers which bring down fresh water. I tasted the water many times in the eastern archipelago, where it was practically stagnant in the inner channels among the islands, and there, as I have already stated, I am positive that it was not only fresh but actually sweet.

The navigation of Lake Tchad is not always easy when the north-easterly winds blow, causing heavy waves sometimes as much as two feet high, particularly at the mouth of the Shari. The wind is generally much stronger in the daytime and subsides at night.

The temperature of the atmosphere in the Lake Tchad region during December and January is seldom more than an average of 29° Centigrade (84¼° Fahrenheit) during the day, descending to an average of 9° Centigrade (48¼° Fahrenheit) during the night. This is the cool season, but in April and May the heat is intense both day and night with an average of 40° Centigrade (104° Fahrenheit).

There is yet another problem, more difficult to solve, regarding the formation of the curious *cuvettes* of the Kanem and Bornu. At the bottom of some of these, as we shall see, we shall find pools of water. The *cuvettes* nearer Lake Tchad are certainly fed by infiltration of the water from the lake, but whether the supposed subterranean channels feeding the *mares* of these *cuvettes* with the waters of the present lake actually exist or not, is difficult to prove, and I will only state what I observed.

The *cuvettes* which I visited and which showed pools of water were, according to the natives, filled with rain water during the rainy season. Most of them dried soon after the rainy season was over. The elevation of many was higher than that of the lake.

The *cuvettes* themselves had the appearance to me of having been formed chiefly by the erosion of wind in the softer upper layers of sand until the moist and harder under-stratum of the *cuvette* had been reached, which remained flat and quite clean, freed from movable surface sand.

In several of the *mares* in my journey across the Kanem and the Chitati we shall find crystallized deposits of sodium carbonate, some of which are worked successfully by the natives.

In the neighbourhood of Bol there were lagoons which were then full, and which, according to the natives, had never been filled with water before, which would show that far from drying up, the lake in some parts is actually extending. Of this, I think Captain Hardellet, who made serious studies of that region, could give clear proof.

The flora round the lake was not luxuriant ; acacias, the *hadjelidi*, palm-trees and gum-trees, mostly in the northern region, formed the greater part of the vegetation. The islands in the eastern portion presented more the forest character of the Kanem, while the others, more recently emerged, were formed solely from alluvial mud and marsh deposits of decayed papyrus, reeds, shells and sand.

Professor Ehrenberg, who examined specimens of sand from Lake Tchad sent home by Barth and Vogel, found in them one hundred and thirty-three well-determined forms of infusoria, the same sand infusoria which are found on the Atlantic coast during sand-storms. Ehrenberg explains that these deposits of sand are carried by the vigorous atmospheric currents due to the rarefaction of the heated air over the Sahara desert.

The islands could eventually be profitably used for the culture of cotton, which seemed to grow well in that soil. The natives produced small quantities of cotton, which they used as currency in the form of narrow strips locally woven. Only eighty islands of the entire archipelago were inhabited by some fifty thousand people all counted. These people possessed between seventy and eighty thousand oxen, according to French estimates.

The French give the elevation of Lake Tchad at 275 metres.

The appended table of elevations taken by Captain Mangin, in a north-easterly direction from Lake Tchad in the Kanem, Djourab and Borku will be of interest, as showing the considerable differences of heights in that desert portion of the country.

It will be seen that the greatest elevations are between Mao and Mount Mandara, where a table-land is to be found.

ELEVATIONS TAKEN BY FRENCH OFFICERS IN THE REGION OF LAKE
TCHAD AND BAHR-EL-GHAZAL.

Lake Tchad	275 metres
Mao	315
Mount Mandara	345
Limit of the Kanvas plateau (Kanvas Boufournine)	305
Hacha (Zgrei)	265
Redinga	285
Manzao (Toro)	245
Chicha (Toro)	240
Korotoro (Bahr-el-Ghazal)	270
Kizimini (Djourab)	235
Mole'dinga (Djourab)..	230
Chicka (Djourab)	207
Touhorde (Djourab)	200
Voan	230

CHAPTER XIX.

THANKS to the energy of Lieutenant Gauckler, who obtained for me a number of oxen at a moment's notice to carry my loads, I was able to leave Bol on August 19th. There was nothing interesting in that place. Two hours after my departure, a first depression and then a second, separated by a dune, were reached. We crossed the second with water up to our waists. This channel occasionally makes Bol an island when the water of Lake Tchad rises sufficiently, but when the water is low in the lake one can get across quite dry. Several gulfs of Lake Tchad extended along the Bol peninsula.

On the opposite side of the water, separating Bol from the mainland, we rose some thirty feet upon a sand dune, and then upon a flat plateau, with only a few tufts of grass. We halted at Dossolem, a Tubu village of millet planters. These Tubu went in extensively for cultivation, and supplied the country round with millet. They had convenient folding houses covered with mats sewn together, each mat about eighteen inches wide. They frequently shifted their quarters from one place to another; hence the necessity of having easily removable residences. Their more permanent huts were hemispherical. In the interior of the folding huts were palm-tree forks supporting long bags of matting filled with millet. A few pots and pans constituted the entire possessions of these people. In the more permanent homes partitions were found, each with a bed, in each of which one wife of the owner slept.

These Tubu came originally from Bir-el-Ali, when the Tuareg invaded the Kanem in 1901. The Tubu hated the Tuareg, and for protection fled to the neighbourhood of French posts.

The women wore their hair plaited in small tresses, like the Kanembu and the Buduma.

During the journey many dunes were encountered, some with a flat, uninterrupted sky-line, others undulating on the ridge. Great stretches of flat sands with tamarinds and mimosas and tufts of grass formed the landscape. In depressions we found during the day no less than six lakelets, some with water tasting strongly of sodium carbonate, others, on the contrary, with excellent water.

We left at sunrise on August 21st, and went over immense stretches of pampas grass, flat, or sometimes with slight undulations. In one spot for some hundreds of yards we found upon the ground lumps of ferruginous gneiss. It was of so brilliant a red that the natives had a legend of a great battle which took place at this spot between the Tubu and the Bulalla, when, according to the Tubu, the Bulalla were exterminated and the red blood of the Bulalla coagulated into rock. This is the local explanation of the rock being found in the sand. The Bulalla version of the battle is, of course, the same, except that it was the Tubu blood which produced such an extraordinary geological phenomenon.

There were great flat plateaus of sand, with here and there a tiny mound or an occasional undulation. Then we began to find high dunes, characteristic of the Kanem. In the depressions between one dune and the next there was generally a certain amount of moisture filtering through, which gave birth to deep-green grass and occasional reeds. We then went many hours without finding water. We reached the village of Miyu upon a high dune, where we halted for the night.

On August 22nd great sand dunes were encountered, over which we went, these dunes being now more regular in shape and quite horizontal in their upper profile line. Sand had filled in a good deal between these dunes, and we began to find the elongated oval depressions regular *cuvettes*, or basins, usually with beautiful green grass at the bottom, or else with layers of sand. Locally the set of two dunes with the depression in the centre is called *djirghi*. *Kangar* and *tchongo* trees generally dotted these depressions prettily, and palms were also frequently to be seen.

That day three of these *cuvettes* were observed, two of a most regular, long, oval shape ; the other shaped in a double inverted coil like the letter " s," with beautiful grass at the bottom of the depression, where antelopes grazed peacefully.

Beyond these we passed the Kanembu village of Medighih, with domed huts and the usual bedding, bags of millet on shelves, a few pots and an outer fire-screen of reeds. Most of these Kanembu had taken to themselves Arab wives.

The village stood on a high dune, overlooking a fourth basin, the Nangibediro, also called Kudu, deeper and broader than the three we had already met earlier in the day. A fifth *cuvette* was passed and then a sixth of great length, called the Kiri, only an hour or so distant from Mao, the military capital of the Kanem. In this place a well was to be found at the bottom of the dune

Cuvette at Mao Kanem

at an elevation of 950 feet. The dunes had a general direction from north-west to south-east. The depressions between were not only interesting because of the problem of their formation, but also were most refreshing to the eye, as grass of a deep-green colour covered the bottom of the *cuvette*. As we were going further east on the edge there were palm-trees in abundance right round the huge basins, a great contrast to the hot yellow sand on the upper surface of the plateau. In this region there were a great many *siwak* trees, from which the natives extracted potash which they used as a substitute for salt by washing the ashes. The fruit of the *siwak* had a taste like watercress.

We arrived at Mao, where Captain Bordeaux, with several non-commissioned officers, was in charge of the post. When I arrived I was surprised to see in camp many redcoats, which reminded one forcibly of British uniforms; but on getting nearer I discovered them to be one hundred and twenty spahis, Senegalese mostly drawn from the Saracolle, Bambara, Ouoloff, Djerma, a few Bahr-Sara men and a few from the Bahr-Salamat.

Although the Senegalese were better as infantrymen than upon horses, I could but admire the way in which these men had been trained by their excellent Commandant Devedaix and Lieutenant Godart. Three platoons of spahis were stationed at a post called N'gouri, south of Mao, and one platoon was at Bukkoro, in the Fitu, on the Wadaian frontier.

The French, well knowing the treachery of their eastern neighbours, the Wadaians, had wisely established a strategically excellent belt of military posts along their Wadaian frontier, extending from Fort Archambault on the Shari river to Dumrao, Melfi, Tchekna, Fort Lamy, and Massa Kori, with outposts at Bukkoro, Abourai, N'gouri, Mao and Bir-el-Ali. The northern posts of this belt commanded all the principal wells in the desert, and the southern ones made it impossible for the Wadaians to come on raiding expeditions without finding immediate and severe punishment.

The Wadaians were extremely troublesome. When I was at Mao the spahis had been summoned. A raid from the Wadaian side seemed imminent, and the post was deemed in danger. In fact, Captain Bordeaux, who was in charge of the post, detained me several days, as he feared some misfortune might happen if he let me go towards the north without a large escort. I intended visiting some of the tribes of white Arabs, interesting as far as my work went, but treacherous to a degree.

The country all round was in a commotion. All the tribes were restless owing to renewed rumours of a coming raid. Many of the tribes had folded up their tents and vanished. Others were on the point of removing their quarters.

The detention of several days at Mao was profitably spent in studying the Bornu, Kanembu and Arab tribes which form the population around Mao. Khalifa (or Halifa, as it is locally pronounced) Mahommed, a Bornu whom I met, was the former chief of Mao, supplanted now by Khalifa Mahla, a pleasant fellow, who had for a second brother Khalifa Kerrer. Portraits of these men are to be seen in the illustration facing page 256.

Mao was charmingly situated between two *cuvettes*, one to the south-west of us and another north-east of the post. The latter was a *cuvette* of great beauty. Both *cuvettes* had small lakelets in the depression. The lake

A charge of Senegalese Spahis at Mao (Kanem).

Senegalese Tirailleurs scouting.

to the south-west was not a permanent one and filled only during the heavy rains. The dune between the two *cuvettes* followed a direction from north-west to south-east.

In the northern part of Mao was situated the fort, a castellated structure, twenty feet high, affording good protection against the attacks of local populations. It was ingeniously loopholed, and near access to it impeded by barbed wire obstructions. Mao as a military station consisted merely of four or five houses in the post.

South of the military settlement was the small village of Bornu. South-south-east of the southern declivity of the greater *cuvette*, but east of the Mao post, was the large and quite important Kanembu village of Mao.

To the west of the post the view was extensive, miles and miles of greenish dunes being visible as far as the eye could reach. To the north and east the view was more confined, being obstructed by a high dune. The trail northwards to Bir-el-Ali ascended the northern dune in a straight line. To the south the view extended uninterrupted. In the scorching sun an immense stretch of grass, endeavouring to look green and growing upon hot sand, was dotted scantily with round spots of a darker colour which one suspected to be trees. In a south-easterly direction, in the depression between two dunes, trees, mimosas and palms were somewhat more prominent, and formed a dark-green line. More poetic writers than I have called these few trees " magnificent forests."

In the native village straw was plaited, somewhat after the Italian way, and the people made elaborate oval mats, interlaced in a most artistic manner. They also plaited straw in lengths, of which picturesque hats were made, with conical crowns surmounted by a red leather knot. Two broad straps under the chin were interlaced in a dainty pattern on the side. These broad hats were evidently suggested by the Arabs, and were not dissimilar to the hats found in certain parts of Algeria and Tripolitania.

Perhaps the most surprising of all industries in that country—certainly the one that astonished me most—was to find a hard-working factory of vermicelli inside a house, where women crowded together, some sitting crosslegged upon the ground, others upon a spacious native bed. Others sat in a row outside the domed hut. All possessed curly heads, with silver ornaments tied in the back of the top hair. Children helped in the work. They rolled a lump of cornflour paste between both palms over a basket or plate resting upon their knees. Friction reduced the lump into a thin uniform thread, which, when cooked, tasted like vermicelli. Grease and occasional spitting upon the palms facilitated rotation of the paste threads.

The elevation of Mao by hypsometrical apparatus was 1,148 feet.

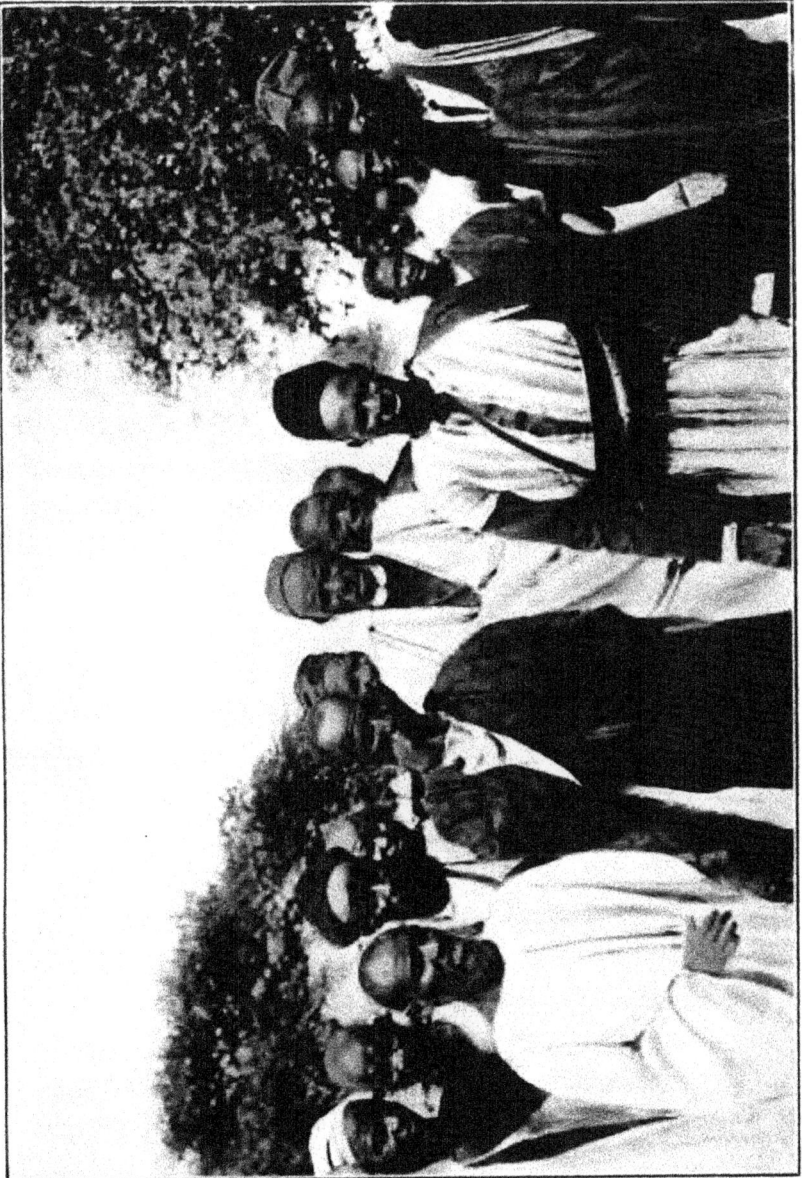

CHAPTER XX.

As the raid was not forthcoming and the Arabs with their camels had all vanished from Mao, I decided to go northwards into the Uled Suliman country in order to see whether I could obtain camels from the White Arabs, as I intended to cross the Tuareg country as far as the Niger.

Captain Bordeaux kindly sent Lieutenant Gauckler with an escort, so that no evil should happen, and on August 25th I left Mao with a big caravan of oxen, and travelled in a north-north-westerly direction, crossing a valley—quite a beautiful oasis of palms of a deep green and some large trees. One never appreciates trees so much as in places where you do not often get them. Personally, after crossing the tropical forest with its stifling intricate vegetation, I was so tired of green foliage that it was a great relief to me when I got into the desert and only saw sand. But when I had seen sand for several days, and had been roasted by the sun and the refracted heat and glare from the yellow soil, it was refreshing to see a few neat trees.

We rose over a dune of a slightly undulating character, where good pasture land for camels was to be found, reaching the village of Gunzu two hours later, and shortly afterwards the Kanembu village of Sumtara, with its half-tumbling-down huts. There were sandy *mezjid* enclosures in the centre of the village, where the people assembled to say their prayers, a wall of reeds enclosing these improvised mosques.

Beyond this village was high undulating country with good pastures for camels. We left Farei village to the west of us in the depression of a great dune (with a direction from west to east). At the eastern end of this deep depression, in the pretty oasis of Tefe (or Tufo) were a lot of palms and sweet-scented acacias near a well of excellent drinking-water.

Having gone over a handsome plateau with fine, silky grass, dotted here and there with black, dense foliage of trees, we examined (west of our route) the *bulla*, or basin, called Adgilum, extending from south-east to north-west, and having at its bottom a magnificent green lawn enclosed in a natural square of deep-green trees. We got here at sunset, and having filled our canvas bottles and skin bags with water from the well, went on and made our camp at the top of the eastern dune enclosing the Adgilum.

We generally selected high places for our camps, as we were then comparatively free from mosquitoes.

On August 26th we passed many depressions, the Burcabulum being the most notable, with a well of drinkable water and a lakelet, and with a number of *kiuh* (*capparis soda*) and *tchumbo*, a tree forming blackish spots in the Kanem scenery, where it is common. This basin extended from south-east to north-west, and some three hours later we reached another similar basin, the Shala, where we found another well. Half way between Burcabulum and Shala was the boundary between the Kanem and the Chitati. The *cuvettes* were now beginning to be scarce and the land flatter, only slightly undulat-

ing in portions and with hardly any vegetation except
a few tamarinds, which here took the place of the *kiuh*
and the *tchumbo*.

At eight in the evening, having marched since six
in the morning, we arrived at a Tubu village of folding
huts, but we had some difficulty in discovering its
real name. Some called it Irre, others Naga, others
Irulum.` The village stood on the crest between the
bullas of Irre, which we crossed to the east, and the
bulla of Urah on the west.

Having left again at sunrise, we travelled once more
on undulating, slightly grassy country and soon came
to Suero, a small *cuvette*, and later on to a very large
one extending from south-east to north-west called
Moito. On the prominence north-west of this great *bulla*
we found the new encampment of Mayuf, the White
Arabs.

We had had a good deal of trouble in tracing these
people, as, hearing of the raid which was about to be
made on the Kanem, they had suddenly shifted their
quarters. They had abandoned their old encampment only the night before we arrived. As these people
possessed thousands of camels, oxen and goats, we could
easily track them, and, in fact, we were able to catch
them up just as they were making their new camp.

Some of the camels were surmounted by strange, high,
circular cages, curtained over. In these they conveyed
their women. The men were dressed up in the usual Arab
fashion in ample white trousers, a kamarband, and white
bernous.

East of this new encampment was a great *bulla*
stretching from north-west to south-east, called Lasfar
by the Arabs. Another large *cuvette*, the Kulla, was to

the south-south-west of us, this particular *bulla* showing huge cracks in the red earth forming its sides. The Arabs called the Kulla also by the name of Wadi, which meant " the valley with holes."

It was interesting to watch these people putting up their tents and building their huts. In a moment dozens and dozens of skin tents and thatched huts were erected. This spot was the former encampment of the Nuku Arabs, and stood at an elevation of 1,120 feet.

I had a good deal of trouble with these Arabs before I could get the old chief, Mayuf, to come to a suitable arrangement to form a caravan of camels for me, to take me half way across the desert as far as Zinder, where I expected to get another relay to proceed to the Niger.

The tribe of these Arabs was called Miaissa. They formerly lived in Egypt, which they called " Massar," and they professed to have migrated to this part of the desert about a century ago. The Miaissa and the Uled Suliman were the same people. The Uled Suliman came directly from Tripolitania and the Miaissa, who were also formerly in Tripoli, went there first from Egypt and then migrated to the place where I found them.

There was also another chief called Salem-bel-Hadji, a cousin of Mayuf. These Arabs were strict Mussulmans. They repeated the morning prayer, the Salet-el-Fadger, four times; the Salet-el-Dohor four times, at 1 p.m.; the Salet-el-Acer four times, at 4 p.m.; the Salet-el-Moghreb three times, at sunset; and the Salet-el-Arché no less than seven times in the evening before going to sleep. They always constructed a *zeriba* in their encampment, which they used as a *mezjid*, or mosque.

These people married when about fifteen or sixteen

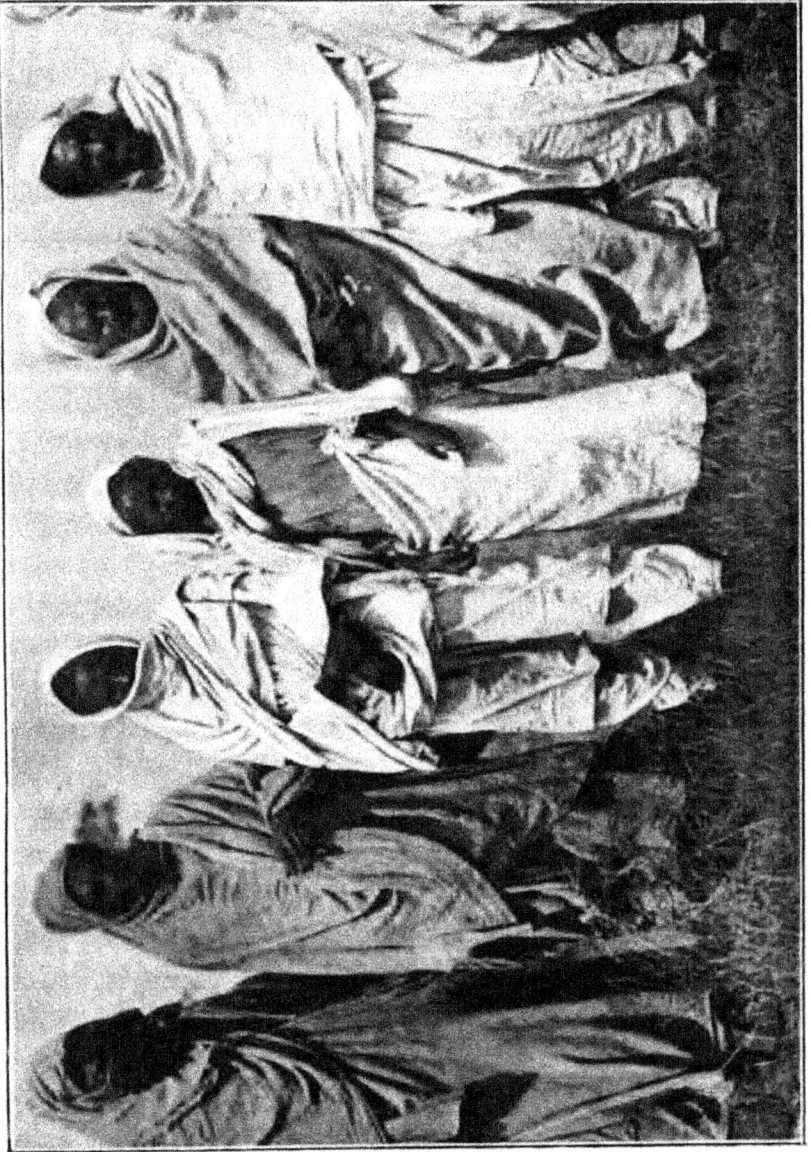

Магуг.

б.

years of age and always married women of their own tribe. According to the Mussulman religion they never indulged in more than four wives.

They arranged their life to suit the convenience of their numerous animals. When the pasture got exhausted in one place, they changed their encampment for another.

Before marriage the men wore a short pigtail under their *tarbouches*, but after marriage the head was shaved clean. The dowry consisted of eight camels and a woman slave, the latter, when about thirteen years of age, valued at the rate of six camels. Miaissa Arabs were charitable when marriages took place. An ox was usually sacrificed for the benefit of the tribe. When a woman gave birth to a boy, the husband presented two extra camels to the father of the girl. In case of divorce, the woman did not return the purchase-money paid by the husband to her father. In cases of adultery, the woman was deserted or driven away from the hut (or even from the tribe), but was never killed.

These people were extremely superstitious. Chief Mayuf told me that water was full of evil spirits, the wells simply swarming with them. These evil spirits often made people ill, even caused death. In their superstitions these people came nearer the truth than many a man of science.

Illness they also attributed to evil spirits entering the body. The insides of camels, they said, often enclosed one or more evil spirits, especially camels who held the head high. Crippled men were people whose body had been entered by an evil spirit.

They were strong believers in the evil eye and they could not endure being looked at or having people point at them. It rendered them extremely nervous. At the time of my visit there were four Miaissa accused of casting the evil eye. Mayuf told me in all seriousness that one of his female camels had died instantly upon being looked at by an " evil eye " person.

In the desert, according to them, evil spirits prowl about, who, unseen, mount and ride their camels, making them very tired. Other spirits come to put out fires during the night, and others, more mischievous still, throw stones at passing Miaissa. Sometimes, they say, these evil spirits take the shape of men, goats or dogs. Certain mystic marks, however, drawn upon the ground make these spirits vanish.

These Arabs seemed highly strung and subject to melancholia. Suicide was common among them. When all the goods of Miaissa were confiscated for some offence, and they had not sufficient power to make up their losses ; when insulted, with no means of obtaining a revenge, or when sons were harshly spoken to by their fathers, they frequently killed themselves rather than bear the shame. During the last year alone, Mayuf told me, four suicides had taken place in his tribe.

Lunacy was frequent, and was believed by the Miaissa to be another kind of devil which entered the brain-case of the sufferer. There were five cases of insanity among the Miaissa at the time I visited the tribe. The treatment they received was not likely to improve their mental condition. Mystic circles with a cross inside were burnt with a red-hot iron on the back of the neck, while the patient was tied fast by the legs and arms.

Many of the men were, to say the least, eccentric in their manner. I know it to my cost, because Mayuf passed on some of these lunatics to me as camel-men. One of them became raving mad during the journey across the desert.

When a man died among the Miaissa, he was wrapped in a new, white cloth, spotlessly clean. Then a grave was dug, in which a layer of wood was deposited at the bottom, then a layer of grass above it on which the body rested, the head to the south and the feet towards the north with the face looking east towards Mecca. Small wooden rafters were placed above and across the body of the deceased so as to leave a small air chamber. The grave was covered up with sand, and a camel was sacrificed over it, the meat being dispensed for charitable purposes among the poorer people of the tribe. For women, only three pieces of wood were placed at the bottom of the grave. Two upright wooden posts were stuck on a man's grave, three on a woman's.

The Miaissa were at one time well known for their *harka*, or raiding expeditions, against the neighbouring tribes.

Chief Mayuf was an intolerable beggar. He spent his entire day bothering me to give him now one thing, now another, that I possessed, notwithstanding that his boy, about twelve years of age, was in a dying condition in the chief's tent. Tetanus had supervened. The combined strength of Lieutenant Gauckler and myself was not sufficient to make him open his teeth. The tongue had, unfortunately, been caught between and was being severed. The poor child was in terrible agony, and although we tried to do what we could for him, Lieutenant Gauckler having a lot of remedies at his disposal, the child died after a few hours. Mayuf, I suppose, was sorry for the death of his son, but not a

266 ACROSS WIDEST AFRICA

sign could be detected upon his stolid face. He continued to amuse himself, and just as the child expired he merely glanced at him as if he had been a dog. A few seconds later he was again importuning me to present him with a lantern I possessed.

A curious incident happened during the night. During a terrific storm, lightning struck Mayuf's camp two or three times. One Arab was struck so badly as to become absolutely paralysed, partly by the electric shock received, but mostly, I think, by fright. We were called at once to restore the man to his former health and vigour. Lieutenant Gauckler and I were puzzled as to what was the best cure for the effects of lightning. The man, quite rigid, complained of terrific pain in his digestive organs. I thought if we could relieve him of that it would be a good beginning, so a dose of castoroil—my universal remedy—was applied, and we left the man alone. To our amazement the next morning, he was walking about the camp, somewhat limp and martyr-looking, but quite on the way to recovery after his narrow escape.

There were, in the desert, two powerful religious confraternities, or two great families, of Marabu, who held nearly the entire population of the Sahara under their religious ascendancy. The Tedjajina, the oldest of these confraternities, was based on the True Light of Islam, and was principally created to unite all the people of the Sahara, with the further intention of spreading its influence among the black races of Central Africa. The second division, the Sinoussi, was organized after the conquest of Algeria by the French in order to fight against the ever-increasing European influence over Mussulman countries and to preserve the people of the

Sahara and Central Africa from European contamination. Fanaticism of the most exalted kind was preached by the latter.

Duveyrier, who went fully into the history of these people, tells of how Es-Sinoussi (a man whose origin is somewhat disputed and who came either from Djalo in Tripolitania or from the Beni-Sinous tribe southwest of Tlemcen) was a learned man who had long lived in such sacred places as Mecca and Medina in company with most advanced champions of the religion of Islam, and who was particularly wounded to see Constantinople and Cairo adopt European costumes, customs and institutions. With European ways spreading in all the African countries nearer to Europe, there remained nothing for him but to make his way into the desert with a following of fanatics and to found there a suitable abode of isolation from the contamination of white people's ways. He founded several *zauiya* (monasteries or religious centres).

The word *marabu* (priest) which we shall often hear from this point of the journey, comes from *merabot*, plural *merabotin*. According to Duveyrier, Djebel-el-Akhdar was the first central seat of the institution, which met with a hearty reception all over the Sahara. Helped by Mohammed-Ben-'Abd-Allah and the *Taleb* Hadji-Ahmed-el-Touati (better known as El-'Aalem), Es-Sinoussi invested the latter with the title of *Mogaddem*, or Vicar-General, for the region west of Djebel-el-Akhdar, or country of the Tuareg, and the Touat.

These two fanatics together, having joined their forces, developed their entire influence, the one recruiting *khuan* (agents), the other enrolling followers under his banner for the Holy War. So fast did their

influence spread that new *zauiya* were built at Sokna,
at Zuila, at Murzuk, at Ghadames and at Rhat. Shortly
before his death Es-Sinoussi ordered a new *zauiya* at
Jerhajïb, slightly north of the route leading from Sïaua
to Odjlela, which afterwards became the centre of the
order. Others were subsequently built, and in less than
fifteen years eight well-provided centres of fanaticism
were founded in the desert.

In 1859 Es-Sinoussi died, his son succeeding him.
El-Hadji-Ahmed-el-Touati, or the *Mogaddem* of the West,
became the leader of the Sinoussi people and went from
town to town preaching the Holy War and pressing
Mohammed-Ben-'Abd-Allah to fight, so organizing the
well-known movement which in 1861 troubled the
entire Algerian Sahara, and which eventually ended in
the capture of Mohammed-Ben-'Abd-Allah.

The Tedjajina sect was founded in 1775 by Sidi-
Ahmed-el-Tidjani, of the Marabu family of Aïn-Mahdi.
Unlike the Sinoussi, the members were tolerant, and their
only aim in life was based on such sound principles as
that " right follows right," and " all that comes from
God must be respected."

Sidi-Ahmed had two sons, Mohammed-el-Kebir, the
elder, and Mohammed-es-Seghir, the younger. The elder
brother, being betrayed by the Hâchem, died in the
plains of Eghreis. The second brother on coming of
age succeeded to the chieftainship of his sect, and
afterwards to that of the *zauiya* of Temassin. Sidi-
Mohammed-el-Aid, the Marabu, had been regent during
the time the two brothers were under age.

At the *zauiya* of Temassin, Duveyrier found a
sumptuous palace, with Venetian glass and imported
European furniture—quite a surprise in the middle of

the desert. It was principally this centre which extended its influence as far as Timbuctu on one side and the Borku and Tibesti on the Egyptian side. These people had recruited many black agents to make active efforts in bringing all neighbouring races into the religion of Islam.

Two secondary *zauiya* had also been established, the " Timassanin " between the Azdjer country and the Ahaggar Tuareg, intended as a conciliatory intermediary between those two antagonistic tribes ; and another at Gurara, in the Touat.

There were also *khuan* of the Tedjajina sect in the Bornu, Timbuctu and Futa, but the most important were El-ouad, Temassin and Chinguit in the Adar, between Timbuctu and the Atlantic.

In the region of Timbuctu we have a third influence, the Bakkay, their *zauiya* receiving numerous disciples from Morocco, from Touat (where they also possess much property and *zauiya* have been built), from the Senegal, and other black tribes. The Bakkay was a family descending from Ogba-ebu-Nafa-el-Fahri, a religious potentate who maintained himself independent of the Fellahta as well as of the black states surrounding his country. These Bakkay are immensely wealthy, and possess great herds of jebus, camels, sheep and horses, as well as slaves and serfs, belonging to the Arab tribe of Mahr-Rhufa. A good deal of their wealth has been accumulated from the nominally voluntary tribute paid by caravans and native travellers passing through their country.

There remains another important *zauiya* on the Algerian side of the Moorish Algerian border. It was founded at El-Abiodh by Ulad-Sidi-Sheik, a lover of peace, who gave happiness and shelter to all who shared his honest ideas. Duveyrier, who visited these people, speaks very highly of them, and their sect has rendered valuable services to the French in capturing the Sinoussi Mohammed-Ben-'Abd-Allah, who for some time gave unbounded trouble in the Sahara.

North and East of Mao is interesting country, but perhaps the most interesting region of all is that which includes the Borku, Ennedi and Tibesti. In the Borku, sedentary tribes, such as the Teda, are found. Their country is one of fine oases. To the east, in the Morcha, beyond the channel cut by the Bahr-el-Ghazal, is a region of winter marshes along the caravan routes followed by Mahamid tribes.

The Borku is practically the granary, with plenty of wheat, millet and dates, of all that region. The dates are excellent. Cattle and sheep are bred. Tobacco is grown. The Borku feeds a population of about 40,000 persons, belonging to the Tibesti and Ennedi, two sterile countries. Under the administration of the Sinoussi agriculture flourishes. There is some degree of trade with the Ennedi, from whom the Borku people purchase salt and red gum, and with the Wadai, to whom the Borku sell millet, oxen and sheep. There is a direct route *via* Bokalia to Arada and Abesher (capital of Wadai). Situated as they are between the desert of Libyia on one side and the Wadai, it is easy enough for the Sinoussi to exercise their influence strongly upon the Wadaians and the people of Darfur, the effects spreading to the neighbouring French Kanem and to Baguirmi.

In other words, the Borku is the " relay " spot of all caravans proceeding to and from all the Sinoussi

stations either towards the Kanem or towards the Wadai
and Darfur. By various routes from Tripoli, Egypt
and Kuffia a serious importation of improved firearms
is taking place both into the Darfur, and especially into
the Wadai, to be used in defence against, and, perhaps,
some day, in attack upon, the British on one side and
the French on the other.

The Sinoussi have sent several embassies to Darfur
in order to attempt a *rapprochement* between those
people and the Wadaians to encourage them in combined action against white neighbours. The Germans
and Turks are suspected of wire-pulling in those regions.

Sidi-el-Mahdi, the Sheikh of the Sinoussi, has of
late years proceeded towards the south, and since the
Borku occupation by the Sinoussi has now established
himself at Guro, in the Borku, evidently with a firm
intention to cement a Sinoussi alliance of the Kanem-
Baguirmi-Wadai peoples. Combined Franco-British
action will some day be necessary in those regions, if
the importation of arms is not suppressed.

The Borku is perfectly unknown in its north-eastern
part, and the Ennedi is but vaguely known. It is a
rocky region, with a population akin to the Tubu ; fierce
people at best.

Nachtigal and Captain Mangin, who have studied
these regions, state that the Egueï and the Bodele
formed depressions north-east of Lake Tchad, and an
ancient lake basin at a lower level than Lake Tchad.
That these were at one time supplied with water by
the Bahr-el-Ghazal as well as by the drainage of the
Tibesti and Ennedi. The Borku is higher than the
Bodele, according to Captain Mangin, who also suggests
the possibility that in remote times the waters from

these marshes flowed into the desert of Libyia, into the
" chelonide marshes " of Herodotus' map and into those
of Ptolemy (north-east of the Borku).

In the Tibesti hot springs are to be found and salt
deposits. The country in some parts suggests a volcanic
upheaval. Perhaps, when Europeans are able to make
their way across that country, mineral wealth may be
discovered.

The routes most followed by caravans in the Tchad
region—before the Sinoussi's interference—were : the
one from Kano (in British Nigeria), viâ Zinder-Agadès
and Rhat to Tripoli ; and second from Kuka (west of
Lake Tchad), viâ Nguigmi, Bilma, and Murzuk, also to
Tripoli.

Colonel Gouraud was able to reopen the former
route, and the present occupation of Bilma by the
French, with its probable gradual extension to the Borku,
will facilitate the re-establishment of the other. Eventually the routes from Abesher, viâ the Borku and Tibesti
towards the north-west, will again be frequented by
caravans, all these routes being of great importance in
developing the commerce of the Sahara. Much of
the trade of Sokoto and Bornu would find its way towards Tunis if the trails were safe, and not only would
southern Tunisia greatly benefit by it, but a brisk trade
might be carried on by the populations of Uled Suliman
Arabs, by the Tubu and Kreida, the Mahamid (of the
Bahr-el-Ghazal), the Teda of Tibesti and the Tarawia of
the Ennedi, who possess immense herds of camels and
some cattle.

CHAPTER XXI.

On leaving Mayuf and going south-west, I had to the west a *cuvette*, with an almost dry lakelet. This *bulla* (with a direction of north-west to south-east) was extremely pretty and possessed wonderful regularity of lines. Then we went over undulating country until we came to the Larghegi, another *cuvette*, with wells of good water. In torrential rain during the afternoon we passed another *cuvette*, the Marara, on our right, and one to the left, the Mumunu ; half an hour later, yet another one to our right, the Artugri.

We stopped for one night at Khaber, a Tubu village of folding huts similar to the Arab tents of the Miaissa tribe. These Tubu huts were covered by a mat over a wooden frame. The entrance was either at one side of the hut or at the end, according to the people's needs. The Tubu were tall, thin people, dressed in long blue robes, instead of in white, like the Arabs. They had shaven heads and slightly-bearded faces. Their countenances strongly resembled those of the Arabs, their neighbours, except that their skins were of a dark chocolate colour instead of the white-yellowish tinge of the Arabs. They possessed high cheek-bones, slightly oblique eyes and long faces with a long nose in good proportion to the face. The upper teeth were prominent.

On leaving this camp at sunrise we at once crossed the

Chindi, two *cuvettes* joined together, and two hours later we passed on the left side of our trail the Chillagu basin, absolutely circular. We crossed the well-beaten trail of Jili-Kurei. From this point we began to find a number of *gabudo*, a taller tree than others we had met belonging to a similar family, not unlike a weeping-willow, and also a great many *kindil* trees.

We then marched towards the south-west across country, as no trail existed, and near the *cuvette* of Diseroh we came upon plantations of millet. We descended into the Tegal *cuvette*, with a picturesque group of *kindil*, a mimosa with long white thorns. Another kind of mimosa, the *col-col*, with most minute leaves and white flowers was also to be found in this *cuvette*.

Then in examining the vegetation we found some *kusullu*, a plant with a small flattish oval leaf, and some *chongu* trees, usually smothered under masses of creepers.

We passed another village that day, a village of tents, Yalmini, with a *zeriba* of thorns for cattle, sheep and goats. Then, later, we came to a small encampment at Adegada, and further on to the small village of Yuro with a good many sandhills to our south-west.

We were marching due west. A Tubu guide I had employed to convey me to Kulua in the north-eastern part of Lake Tchad, instead of guiding, was trying to mislead us all the time as to the direction in which we intended to travel. Lieutenant Gauckler and I took matters into our own hands, and over undulating country, fairly wooded with short trees, we went right down into the Yuro basin, west of the last village we had passed. There we found a well of good water. Having filled the skin bags we carried, we continued our march. At sunset we had to make camp, our carrier oxen being worn out. That evening we found no water.

On August 30th we travelled over flat ground, with lots of trees similar to those we had found the day before. We crossed the high trail from Gum to Khaber, the route going from north-east to south-west. We had altered our course and were marching now south-south-west, then south-west. We came to curious irregular sand-dunes and mounds with deep and frequent depressions between, in which we encountered troublesome fine sand, most annoying for our animals. In this place we struck the high and well-beaten trail from Gum to Rig Rig (1,000 feet), which passed south of the village from south-east to north-west.

A most beautiful oasis with cultivation was near the village of Rig Rig, and wells, with a similar arrangement for drawing water to that frequently to be seen on the Nile. A long rod was balanced upon two high posts, and to it a heavy stone was attached at one end, and a rope with a bucket at the other. There were plenty of trees here, and any amount of millet, green beans, maize and wheat.

On leaving Rig Rig on our left high columns of smoke rose from the big village, Mategu—two hundred huts or so—which lay on the direct route between Rig Rig and Mao, and from which village a trail bifurcated to Bol.

Late in the afternoon we came upon another and rather shallow *cuvette*, the Borku. We were now going over undulating sandhills, with unpleasant *kram-kram* thorns attaching themselves to our limbs each time we got off our mounts, and with tamarind bushes brushing and lashing us as we rode by. We were going across a trail-less country, with long-thorned mimosas tearing our clothes mercilessly, and sometimes our faces and hands.

The vegetation here, although of no great height, was quite thick. We found large basins which had the appearance of having been filled up to a certain height by sand, accumulating in small successive rounded mounds, not only on the shallow bottom of the basin, but upon the surrounding wall of the *cuvette*. These deposits of sand made the inner curves of the *cuvette* irregular in shape, and unlike the smooth well-rounded ones we had so far met. Spurs projected in the bottom part, while the sky-line was undulating instead of absolutely flat as in the more regular *cuvettes*.

Towards sunset we descended into another *cuvette*, somewhat deeper than the average, and with a luxuriant growth of thorny mimosas in the northern part of the depression. Here was a well of good water. We halted on the dune of the Lahr, in which *cuvette* more wells of good water were to be found. We had been travelling between two dunes, the greater to the north of us. The heat during the day was intense.

On August 31st, at sunrise, we were moving over irregular sandy undulations of rounded shape. While we were travelling south-west we had on our left a long dune extending from east-south-east to west-north-west. We found the Lugundom that day, a lake-bottom three hundred yards in radius, absolutely flat, and of a dirty raw sienna colour, owing to the sand which had been deposited and mixed with wet sodium carbonate. Around the circumference of this lake-bottom was a white edge where the moisture had not reached. Big fissures had been opened by the heat of the sun. An outer

Author's caravan of oxen in the Kanem and Chitati.

fringe of high reeds within a dune surrounded the lake. Some water was visible in the southern portion of this *cuvette*.

We were now travelling amid tall grass, seven feet high, locally called the *sugul*, the seed of which when squeezed had a strong scent of turpentine. The shorter grass, the *murku*, was of a light silky green and produced feathery flowers, which were whitish in colour, and which gave the appearance of frost over the landscape, although the heat was somewhere near 40° Centigrade (104° Fahrenheit). We next came to another *bulla*, the Gababu, also with a flat, whitish-yellow lake-bottom of sand and sodium carbonate. I think that the infiltration from Lake Tchad, at high water, fills both the Lugundom and neighbouring depressions.

The Wayieh was a group of three *cuvettes*, one square-bottomed, the other two well-rounded, also with a bottom of sodium carbonate and sand. Then came the pretty little *cuvette* of Duwai to the south of our route. Further on we descended into an extensive basin, and shortly after into another one much elongated from south to north, but not more than twenty to thirty feet deep, the lower portion of which was covered with reeds and high grass, indicating abundant moisture. In fact, in all these *cuvettes* water could be found by digging only a few feet, sometimes only a few inches, below the surface.

We steered our way for a dune between the *cuvettes* of Bilam (on our left) and Mallam (on our right), trees getting scarce again, the few we saw being small and young. There was here an abundance of *kalam* grass, with its many ears of small green seeds.

We crossed, in a westerly direction, the northern

end of the huge, horseshoe-shaped Yarta *cuvette*. It was divided by a narrow dune not more than twenty feet high from another great basin, of the same name, but circular in shape. The latter had a luxuriant growth of reeds in the *mare*, as the French so appropriately call these swampy places.

In the Tirguggiri *cuvette* we again found deposits of sodium carbonate. Then we came to the great circle of Sagur, where, in the western side, a well three feet deep had been dug. Near it was a pool of undrinkable rain-water on the extensive sodium carbonate deposits. There is a theory that when these subsidiary lagoons of Lake Tchad become saturated with sodium carbonate the water does not evaporate so quickly as when in its normal condition. As far as I could judge, it seemed to me just the other way round.

The Sagur was separated from a smaller depression north-north-west of it—this also having sodium carbonate deposits—and another small pool of water, by a dune two hundred yards wide, going from north-east to south-west. Our way, after crossing the Sagur, proceeded over this dune, and we travelled westwards until we came to the Toro, which had an undulating sand bottom, and which formerly was actually a portion of Lake Tchad. The highest water-mark on the banks of this depression, evidently of no remote date, were fully twelve feet above the bottom. Lakelets were still to be seen in the deeper depressions, and also the bed of a channel, the Sao, as it was locally called, now quite dry, lined on either side by a thick growth of high reeds. This channel was three hundred yards wide, and its bed consisted of black mud and sodium carbonate.

We followed the northern bank of the Sao, which

here went due west into the lake. The dune, called by the people the Kri, went practically all round Lake Tchad, and was some twenty feet wide here.

From this point we left the Chitati country, which we had crossed, and were in the Kuburi country. We crossed the Sao, in the centre of which we found the Kudulul encampment upon a mound of sand that rose out of the former bed of the lake. The hemispherical huts were constructed of mud over a wooden frame.

From this point we proceeded first along the dune which bordered Lake Tchad on that side, then we descended into the actual bed of Lake Tchad, now absolutely dry with the exception of a few pools like the Toro, and further on the Tori. The formation of the lake-bed was curious. There were rounded mounds of sand, deposits of sodium carbonate, and ancient decayed vegetation, which formed an undulating surface on the lake-bottom. Not so, however, on our left along the broad channel, the Sao. Where we crossed this channel we found two wells of fairly good water only slightly impregnated with sodium carbonate.

On the opposite side of the Sao we perceived large herds of cattle and flocks of goats. On the top of the dune was an encampment of some forty huts, hemispherical, with the upper part of the dome plastered over with mud, while the lower was left open for ventilation's sake. Other huts were thatched with grass, and all were constructed on a frame of reeds or of *ambatch* wood. We received a warm greeting from the natives, but we did not stop. We found one or two more pools, the undulations in the lake-bottom giving place to an absolutely flat surface of mud and vegetable matter reduced to black powder when dry and forming dark patches. Here and there could be seen yellowish and white patches of mud and sand mixed, evidently reduced to this very fine form by the shifting action of water.

We had marched now west, then south-west and west, owing to deviations forced upon us by the country. On nearing Kulua, after marching fourteen kilometres, upon the absolutely dry lake-bed, we came to extremely flat country in terraces. In the well-rounded curves of these terraces could plainly be perceived the action of the retreating waters of the lake at various periods. The small settlement of Kulua (970 feet) stood upon one of these terraces. Not a tree could be seen on either side, and the horizon-line was perfectly straight, like that of the ocean in its calmest moments.

Kulua, which at one time was at the edge of the lake, is now many kilometres from the water. Lake Tchad, according to the older natives of Kulua, has risen and fallen twice during the last thirty years or so, but the greatest fall they had known was during the last six or seven years, when the northern portion had practically become dry, and it was quite possible to walk into the centre of the lake on foot without getting wet, except for one or two channels in which the water was one or two feet deep.

The brother of the Chief of Bossu states that when a boy he saw the lake quite full as far as Kulua. Then it gradually became empty in the northern part, then full once more ; then empty again.

There are immense deposits of sodium carbonate, especially near Kamba, some forty-five kilometres from Kulua, but *mares* of sodium carbonate are to be found as far as Wanda. Others are also to be found nearer Bol, but they are not of sufficient value to be worked. The people of Wanda carry on a brisk trade in sodium carbonate in its crystallized form, as do also the people of Kindiria, a village eighty-five kilometres south of Kulua, in the neighbourhood of Wanda. These villagers, who own innumerable carrier oxen, make constant journeys to Kamba, where the Kamba people charge them a tax of five thalers (about fifteen francs or twelve shillings local value) for every hundred fully-laden oxen. Every ox carries eight rectangular slabs, weighing altogether about 160 kilos (approximately 352 lbs.).

The post of Kulua was established in 1904 by Lieutenant Hardellet, and was being reconstructed at the time of my visit by Lieutenant Gauckler, whom I left there. It had been merely a temporary post, but was to be converted into a permanent station, principally for purposes of tariff, but also to keep a watch on the Tubu, who inhabited the country for a hundred kilometres eastward under Chief Issa Maimi, and who were restless people. They were much given to raiding when opportunity offered.

The heat in the desert at the northern part of Lake Tchad had been great, and as I had marched long distances every day my men had suffered considerably. My faithful Somali, owing to several accidents and the strain, was giving signs of insanity. It had taken the form of a religious mania, the many wonderful sights he had seen on our journey across Africa having preyed heavily upon his mind. He wanted to be killed, so that he could proceed direct to Heaven, for which place he thought himself quite ready. I begged to differ from him. Patience was required, although his conduct was trying in such tropical heat ; but, poor fellow, he was not responsible for his actions. Time after time he refused to come on and entreated to be shot, but I am not in the habit of murdering anybody, particularly faithful servants, so I put off the operation indefinitely. At Kulua one day he disappeared, saying he wanted to die of starvation, and gave me no end of anxiety until a search party was sent and he was brought back to camp. Maybe, the hot sun had also affected his head, especially since I had presented him with a black London bowler hat, which he insisted on wearing in the desert. Here was another indication that protecting the head was sometimes worse than not protecting it at all.

I was sorry to say good-bye to Lieutenant Gauckler, who had been a most thoughtful and kind companion during the journey north of Lake Tchad. On September 2nd I left Kulua with my caravan of camels and Miaissa attendants, riding across the dry bed of the lake, a flat, treeless expanse, with large shallow depressions and regular terraces, the depressions being filled with tall reeds owing to the moisture which still existed.

An hour west of Kulua we passed the very large village of Kiska or Kiskaua, inhabited by Kuburi, Kanembu and Buduma people. Later, we came to the small village of Djakar, a Kanembu village, from which place I marched in a north-westerly direction over soil of a blackish colour (sand, sodium carbonate and decomposed vegetable matter). We came to a sand-dune east of, and parallel to, a channel running from south to north, and connecting several basins ; then travelled over flat terraces of sand, with well-rounded banks dipping into these basins. When Lake Tchad reached

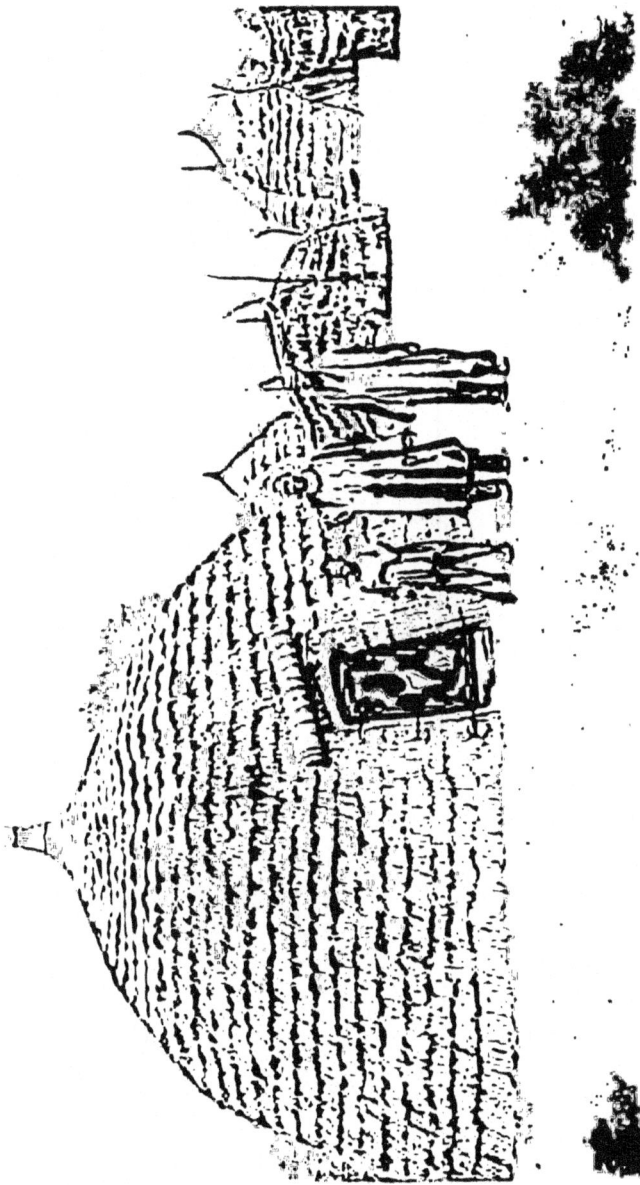

Habitations in the Chitat

its maximum height, all these terraces were evidently islands.

Upon these we found large-leaved latex-ejecting ferns like those which we had seen on the islands near Bol, and which are called *ushar* in Arabic, *kayo* in Bornu, *kobai* in Buduma, and *bouada* in Somali.

By noon we had ascended and were travelling over an immense barren stretch, with no vegetation at all except *ushar* plants here and there. In a small depression was a well two feet deep, the water saturated with sodium carbonate. Later on we continued over the same barren, black soil on a flat stretch, with a dune north of us. This barrier, not more than fifteen feet high, was the northern limit of Lake Tchad at high water.

I travelled north-west until 4.30 in the afternoon, having left Kulua at seven in the morning, and then I came to a well four feet deep in a great expanse of grey sand and alluvial deposits. I found another well an hour and a half later, and yet another at eight in the evening, when I halted, still in the lake-bed upon black soil, with a few young tamarinds growing on spots which formerly had been islands. Before making camp, I crossed a depression with a dune on each side, both the depression and the dunes having a direction from south-west to north-east.

On September 3rd I left at sunrise, six o'clock, with the northern dune sometimes nearer, sometimes further away, according to the line of the water which it had followed, and varying in height from fifteen to forty feet, the greater heights being found principally in the latter part of our march in the afternoon of that day. Its summit was irregular, and generally undulating. Small trees could be seen on the top of it all along, and on those formerly existing and now distant islands which I have mentioned above, but there were no trees whatever in the part where we were marching, the actual bed of the lake. In fact, from six in the morning till one in the afternoon we did not pass a single tree. There was only short grass and either accumulations of sand or grey alluvial deposits.

A shrub, called the *radem* by the Miaissa Arabs, was plentiful in some parts of the lake-bed, and was much relished by my camels.

We came to a well at half-past two in the afternoon, approaching it over a low, flat stretch, and at 4.15 I arrived at Nguigmi, a large and wretched-looking place of miserable sheds, some conical, some domed, all more or less tumbling down. In the market-place, which had a shelter in the centre and was slightly more picturesque, were a few Haddad at work, and merchants selling cloth, rope, and slabs of sodium carbonate displayed upon the ground.

The village was screened all round by a large plantation of millet. Each little *zeriba* had its own further plantation within the little enclosure. Some of these *zeribas* were not more than thirty feet in diameter, and contained one or two houses besides the plantation.

The inhabitants were Kanembu. Chief Malem despatched men in all directions to bring firewood and water, and help us to make fires.

The huts were fenced off with tall reeds. As my caravan passed through the village, the women, with their long hair in oily locks and huge silver earrings, looked in astonishment at us, while the children, with their big paunches, fled at the sight of the camels.

The elevation of this place was 1,050 feet.

Upon the dune a few hundred yards from the village was a French military post, now abandoned, the remains of the few cylindrical mud structures being still visible.

Nguigmi, the most north-westerly post of Lake Tchad under the French Congo administration, would be the last post to which we should come, and we were now entering what the maps call the French Sudan, and what is now styled by the French, the *Territoire Militaire de la Nigerie Française*. This was at one time the country of the warlike Tuareg, and of the Bornu, the Manga and the Haussa, all people excessively treacherous.

Anxiety was felt by the French regarding my safety, as I travelled with a comparatively small caravan and with an escort of only one soldier. I positively refused to take more with me. I think that my safety in uncivilized countries has mostly depended upon the speed at which I generally travel, and on the absolute secrecy of my movements, none of my men ever knowing when or by which route I shall proceed. No information is, therefore, conveyed to natives which could enable them to prepare an ambush for us. My arrival was always a surprise to everybody, and before their surprise was over I was off again.

I left Nguigmi on September 4th, and about one mile beyond I crossed the dune, after having gone over inclined deposits of sand and sodium carbonate extremely hard on the surface. The dune was low where I crossed it—not more than ten to twelve feet high. Upon reaching the summit of the dune we found ourselves upon a flat stretch, with mimosas in abundance. We went through large plantations of millet, then through a regular forest of mimosas, the *balha* of the Miaissa Arabs.

I travelled west-south-west for some two hours, when I reached the large Tubu village of Leskerih, where lived Chief Mahommed Kossuh, the son of Keshirda. At this place were to be seen interesting appliances, furnaces and conical baskets used in extracting potash from the ashes of certain plants, a process which we have already examined.

Once over the dune, we had before us yellowish sand and *cuvettes* almost entirely filled up to the summit with irregular mounds of sand.

On leaving Leskerih I went first west, then south-west, and two hours later I found two deep depressions, one some fifty feet deep, with dunes in a direction from south-west to north-east. Then came a third immense *cuvette,* showing subsidiary minor depressions. None of these depressions were as deep as the first we had met that day, at the bottom of which was an abandoned settlement with conical mud roofs. The name of this place, they told me, was Kuritoah.

We marched on in a most erratic fashion, the guide I had employed having lost his way during the evening. Towards eight o'clock we came to another abandoned village, Kinzerram. Over undulating ground we arrived towards nine in the evening at Wudi, where we fortunately found a well of fair water.

At this well we expected to fill all the water skins we possessed, as we should be for at least two days without finding water if we marched briskly for the 105 kilometres which separated us from the next well. On September 5th, at 1 a.m., I left Wudi, meaning to march the 105 kilometres without stopping.

The country at this point was flatter and clearer of tall mimosas, which tore one's clothes to pieces when the camels passed near them, the camels pushing along unmercifully when they felt that the thorns had caught hold of the riders. All my men were mounted, so we progressed quickly.

We marched all night in glorious moonlight, mostly over flat or undulating sand-hills, and crossed several dunes all stretching from south-west to north-east. We came to a deep *cuvette* with a grassy bottom and with dunes round it fifty feet high.

By four o'clock in the morning we had come to another *cuvette* upon our trail, and an hour later to another one to the left of our route. We were travelling slightly south of west. A lot of *mbarkat* trees were passed.

Steadily moving along till nine o'clock that evening, that is to say, for twenty-one hours, we let the camels rest for four hours, and started again in the night of September 6th, this time crossing undulating country. Six deep consecutive *cuvettes* were passed. All were sandy. The vegetation was sparse, except in the *cuvettes* themselves, where plentiful grass was to be found. At five in the morning we came to a seventh small *cuvette*, and at 6.15 to a perfectly circular basin, the strata of which were shallow, distinct, superposed and horizontal, giving the appearance of steps like those in an ancient Roman amphitheatre. This particular *cuvette* made part of a series of depressions on the east side of a high and important dune, also with a direction from south-west to north-east. Two more *cuvettes* were found beyond this dune, also not unlike amphi-theatres, and at 8.30 in the morning we came across yet another huge *cuvette* of light yellow sand, with mimosa trees along its banks, and a flat, hard bottom of mud and sodium carbonate.

At 9.40 we had on our left another huge *bulla*, this one having level terraces of grass of different shades of green. Between one *cuvette* and another as we went westwards the ground was only slightly undulating, but on some of the flat stretches we crossed there were occasional mounds and subsidiary dunes. We then came to plenty of grass and plenty of mimosas, and by ten o'clock to another *cuvette*, this time almost circular.

A characteristic of the *cuvettes* west of Lake Tchad, as compared with those east of the lake, was that, while the latter were generally oval in shape, the former were almost always circular.

The heat during the day was intense, and it affected my poor Somali, who was by now a raving lunatic. He now insisted on remaining in the desert to die. To make things worse, the insane camel-man given me by my friend Mayuf, the Miaissa chief, also had a relapse, and I had indeed a terrible time with these two monomaniacs in that portion of the journey. During the long uninterrupted march I had fallen fast asleep on my camel. When I woke I found the mad camel-man had disappeared; the Somali, in a state of beatitude, had been stargazing, and we had strayed and did not know exactly where we were. Fortunately, the soil was soft and sandy, and it was not difficult to discover the footmarks of the Miaissa. After marching back and wasting considerable time, I found the rascal spread flat upon the sand, saying he would die and would not come any further with the camels. Allah was good and he would go to Allah.

Author's caravan cross ng a " cuvette " in the dese

"Allah is good, true enough, but I am not so good," I explained, giving the man a violent shaking as I conducted him by the nape of the neck to the caravan, to which I bade him attend at once.

Watch had to be kept upon him, as he invoked Allah for hours in a loud voice, tearing off one by one his turban and clothes and brandishing his sword in a dangerous manner.

All these excitements sound well on paper, but in the terrific heat of the sun it was no laughing matter to me to keep the camels going and keep an eye on my perambulating lunatic asylum.

Both the Somali and the camel-man were next on suicide bent. I promised them, if they came quietly as far as Zinder, I would allow them to kill each other if they chose to their mutual satisfaction. As the Somali hated the Miaissa, and the Miaissa loathed the Somali, they would not hear of so unsatisfactory a death; the survivor would feel so happy at the death of the other. I think the incessant quarrels between these two distracted their minds and eventually drove the suicidal mania from them.

At three o'clock in the afternoon we came to and crossed a most beautiful *cuvette*, perfectly circular in shape, with a bottom of white clay and sand.

PLANTS BETWEEN LAKE TCHAD AND ZINDER.

LOCAL NAME.	DESCRIPTION.
The *kaigo* tree	Plentiful in this region; from the ashes of it the natives extract potash. It has a fatty leaf one and a half inches long.
Kindil (in Bornu), or *bul bulla*.	A mimosa, with tiny leaves at the top of the tree, and innumerable thorns upon most elastic branches.

PLANTS BETWEEN LAKE TCHAD AND ZINDER—*continued.*

LOCAL NAME.	DESCRIPTION.
Kabi	A tree common in the desert, ejecting a white sticky latex when cut. The oval leaves polished and spoon-like, especially when young.
Kalimbo	A kind of tamarind much loved by the camels; also quite common.
Col-col	Long, hook-thorned mimosa. The grain of its wood is extraordinarily close.
Subucal	Tall grass, common in some parts of the desert. The ends of the ears form a regular *panache.*
Subuh	Another tall grass, the ears of which are enclosed in long, pointed leaves.
N'ghibo	A short grass, with a feathery white *panache.* Also found further east.
Kussulu	A strange plant, with three-ribbed leaves, and a tiny yellow flower, the red seed of which is good to eat.
Kurgunoh	A short plant, to be found in patches under the shade of trees. It has a small violet flower and star-shaped leaves.
Kamangar	A small plant, producing yellow flowers and comparatively large pods containing tiny beans. All the joints of this plant are of a deep yellow colour upon a general tint of faint green. It is used medicinally by the natives as a purgative.
Mghiri	A ball-like tree of thorns and tiny leaves, fairly common.
Nghiziri	A clean-stemmed plant, with small, fat, oval leaves, four or five growing together quite crowded, directly along the main stem.
Tambar	A ground creeper, with a pretty, much-fretted leaf. It produces a fruit not unlike a miniature water-melon.
Kanoski	A small plant, with long arms shooting skywards almost directly from the ground, and with a six-section leaf, each section forming a leaf in itself, the group of them upon a long common stem. Near the top, tiny leaves

LOCAL NAME.	DESCRIPTION.

grow all along the main stem and at the summit is an elaborate flower. Yellow buds are held in the centre in a group, in green receptacles. These, when burst open, show a white flower upon a violet stem, inside which are long violet stamens coiled in graceful curves.

Morauah — A small plant, with velvety stem and elongated leaves growing in sets of twos along the stem and its offshoots. It produces a small light-green pod and a tiny violet flower.

Pagam .... — Grass common in the desert, with a starry flower of four points, each point being composed of hundreds of tiny triangles, making a wonderful design something like filigree, only finer.

Nganzano .... — A delicate herb, which easily fades and dies on being touched. It has long, flimsy leaves, with a fretted edge.

Cayei .... — A small untidy and *antipathique* plant, with small white thorns on an unwholesome pink stem. The leaves are in sets like those of mimosas. It produces a most unwholesome-looking fruit of a bilious green, shaped not unlike a miniature tomato in five sections and covered all over with a whitish down, plus half a dozen long and strong thorns, one on each section. It is most difficult to open one of these fruits.

Purah .... — Grass plentiful in the desert, short, and of fine texture. The long-bladed leaves, when rubbed downwards, cling to the fingers like the teeth of a small file. It has a greenish panicle within a circle of dark, violet-coloured filaments, each seed of the antennæ being enclosed in a heavy envelope.

Chungo .... — A tree, with branches at right angles, of a beautiful emerald green, with formidable spikes at intervals of half an inch, the spikes in relation to one another being at an angle of

PLANTS BETWEEN LAKE TCHAD AND ZINDER—*continued.*

LOCAL NAME.	DESCRIPTION.
	fifty-five degrees. These spikes, one and a half inches in length, are green in colour, with a yellow point, and as hard as bone. Their resistance is amazing and the sharpness of the points notable. At the base of each point is a set of two rounded waxy leaves.
Jibby (in Bornu), *ascagni* (in the Miaissa tongue).	The well-known *kram-kram* of French Colonials. These tiresome little balls of thorns which make life unbearable in the desert are perhaps the most common plants in the French Sudan desert.
Nduko vine	A climber, with three-pointed leaves and the usual spirals. Gives a perfectly oval fruit of a deep yellowish red, soft-skinned, about one and a half inches long, not poisonous, but quite insipid.
Kaggigi	A grass, each blade of which separates at the top with five or six stalks, each ending in a star. The star develops into an ear containing brown-and-white striped seeds. The ears form a sphere.
Gantesku	A fine and flimsy grass, with long, pointed leaves keeping close to the stalk. It has tiny ears containing grains, hanging from numerous offshoots at the summit of a stalk.
Kakkara	A tall oat, not unlike the *avena* of Central Italy.
Korgunoh	A short grass, with violet flowers.
Krisumkuri	Has long, narrow leaves quite fat and furred with tiny white thorns. The flower bud is enclosed in a large calyx, three-tiered, and in four fluted sections, each leaf of the three growing above the fourth having hard curved spikes round its edge. The four flowers, one in each section, are white.
Kalabul	Grass, yellow and thorny, with seeds in ears enveloped in white, fine down.
Karago	A tree, having contracted branches, and a mass of thorns, but no leaves.

LOCAL NAME.	DESCRIPTION.
Glei	A palm, the leaves of which are used for making ropes (*dum* in Arabic). The *burr* is the date from this palm.
Cridjum............	Also a palm.
Daghdaguh	A creeper, with minute leaves, four-leaved yellow flowers, and a fruit like an inverted double pear of a rich cadmium yellow, with a vermilion tint at the broader part. Its envelope is quite frail. The seeds, also brilliant crimson, are good to eat.
Tumpapia (in Haussa), *barambatch* (in Arabic.	A large-leaved ficus, common near Lake Tchad. Its leaves and branches eject quantities of white latex.

The zone of Africa I crossed was not attractive in the way of flowers. The desert, where one had tropical vegetation, was, of course, worse. In French posts I occasionally saw some of the more robust European flowers growing in abundance, but in the desert, with the exception of a few flowers upon trees generally extremely small, I only saw a few upon the ground These were mostly of a dirty white, or else of a violent and unpleasant violet tone, which set one's teeth on edge.

CHAPTER XXII.

AFTER passing chiefly over flat country, we arrived at
Mir at 6 p.m. on September 6th.   There we found merely
the small mud fort in charge of a Senegalese sergeant
and five Senegalese soldiers.   There were a few mud
huts inside the fort wall, the fort itself being situated
on a hillock of sand over a substratum of rock (1,150
feet), overlooking an extensive but somewhat flattish
cuvette to the west, with patches of white crystallizations
all around it.   Otherwise there was absolutely nothing
to interrupt the level horizon-line all around us, and at
night one had the impression of being in the middle of
the sea, so uninterrupted and flat was everything.   There
were no villages in the neighbourhood, the only population being found south of the British Nigerian boundary,
where the Bornu lived.

The Bornu to this day use bows and arrows, both in
war and in hunting, the bow being made of hard wood
with a leather cord.   A piece of hard leather is placed
where the hand grasps the bow.   The arrows, which are
poisoned with the *debi*, a concoction of several deadly
herbs, are extremely light and made of a reed with a
long iron head double-barbed.

I continued my journey from Mir, going due west
across a *cuvette*, then slightly north-north-west.   After
that it was flat, with only a few undulations and hardly

any vegetation at all with the exception of a shrub or two or a tree here and there. Grass was plentiful, but not fit for grazing purposes.

Going over a dune we met two Bornu sportsmen, wild-looking fellows, with bows and arrows and an axe. They ran away.

At sunset we came across another small *cuvette*, although *cuvettes* were now getting scarce. After that all was flat and barren until we arrived at 8 p.m. at an encampment, where there seemed to have been a raid, or perhaps the people had been scared of a coming raid. We found numbers of pots and pans and bundles of rope abandoned in the encampment of a dozen huts. Dangaliah was the name of this deserted village, where a deep well was to be found. The inhabitants belonged to the Manga Dagra tribe.

There were in this neighbourhood numerous robber tribes. They were taking advantage of the ill-defined boundary between Great Britain and France in that region, which left a neutral zone, upon which neither the British nor the French exerted their influence, as they were not quite certain to whom it belonged. Bornu robbers therefore raided, now on one side, then on the other, of this neutral zone, to which they then retired, thus escaping punishment. The new boundary has now been clearly defined, and in due time all this will be mended. With the complete accord which characterizes the relations between English and French officers in those regions, that country will eventually become safe.

Later we came to another encampment, also deserted. We found no water in the wells.

We halted at 1 a.m. on September 8th and left

again at six o'clock, finding a little more vegetation upon our trail on this march. We crossed two small *cuvettes* almost entirely filled up with sand. By 10.30 we crossed two more twin *cuvettes* beside each other, and we then reached Karkaro (1,230 feet), where a tumble-down camping ground was to be seen with a few mat sheds which afforded us a shelter from the intense heat of the sun. We were marching at a great speed, my camels being lightly laden. I had by now finished most of my provisions, and all my heavy and cumbersome baggage had been sent home, some by the Nile, the remainder down the Congo river. The camels which I possessed were excellent, and, although my head camel-man was liable to fits of lunacy, I had one or two other men fortunately possessed of sound sense.

During the night we were startled by the sibilant hissing of a *serpent souffleur*, a large serpent which makes a curious noise like a howling wind being forced through a slightly open door. All the camels stampeded, throwing off their loads. The serpent was as scared as we were, and hastily beat a retreat. We eventually got the animals back and loaded them again.

Snakes were plentiful in this part, the larger ones not nearly so dangerous as the little vipers, which were deadly.

In the afternoon at five o'clock we came across a large *cuvette*, quite devoid of trees in the southern half, but the northern section crowded with shrubs. Shortly after, at 5.15, a smaller circular *cuvette* with plenty of green reeds and grass at the moist bottom, was passed on the left of our trail. During that march we came across other depressions of no great importance. The country was mostly flat with short *kurgunoh* grass. Yet another *cuvette*, quite circular, was found at six o'clock, and another, quite shallow, at 6.10.

The typical peculiarity of these *cuvettes* towards the far west of Lake Tchad was that they were now nearly devoid of trees, quite unlike those of the Kanem and the Chitati.

At 6.30 we were compelled to stop by a severe storm which overtook us. It first raised clouds of sand and dust in the violent gust of wind which always precedes the rain that presently falls in bucketfuls.

One of the principal things which characterized my march across the desert from Lake Tchad to the Niger, and which astonished people whom we met on the trail or in any of the posts, was the rapidity with which we moved and the little rest which I allowed my men, animals, and myself on this march of 1,415 kilometres. I used two separate and consecutive caravans of camels.

There is a belief in Europe that to see or learn something about a country you must remain there all your life. Of course, this may be imperative in people who have no experience of foreign lands. Personally, I cannot see what is the use of wasting one's life in places where there is absolutely nothing to see, and where even the profoundest studies on the earth's surface could, if one wished, be carried out in a few hours' observation.

There were no people in that country and no vegetation to speak of. The *cuvettes* and sand-dunes and other accumulations of sand were the only things of interest.

We left again at three o'clock on the morning of September 8th, the country being more broken up. No sooner had we left than we saw another *cuvette* at 3.15 and another one at four o'clock. At 5.30 a circular *cuvette* with palm-trees was encountered and at six a *cuvette* with an old well at the bottom. At 6.45 we arrived at a shelter which rejoiced in the name of Pompom Cabran Bokhar, and was now in ruins. To the west of it was a small *cuvette* with many palm-trees, and at 8.15 and at nine o'clock two small *cuvettes* were again met only five kilometres from Shirmalek. At 9.45 another *cuvette*, with lots of palm-trees in its depression, was visible on the right of our trail.

The post of Shirmalek was situated high up on an elevated dune, and looked quite imposing as one approached it. I arrived at the post at ten o'clock in the morning. A square block-house had been erected with a *zeriba* of thorns all round. A small village stood at an elevation of 1,270 feet. One white sergeant was in charge of the post with ten Senegalese soldiers. The post was situated between a *cuvette* to the east-north-east, and a smaller one south-west. I only stopped at this place for four hours to let my camels graze.

An hour after leaving, I came to a high dune with a direction from south-east to north-west, and with an elongated *cuvette* on its eastern side.

Innumerable plants were to be seen here of the ficus *tumpapia* (in the Haussa language ; *barambatch*, in Arabic), the fibre of which is used, as in Somaliland, for rope-making.

At five o'clock we crossed a small *cuvette*, and at 5.45 another long oval basin. At six we were in a great and more irregular *cuvette*, with mounds of sand in the centre and a group of palms at the northern end. From this point great undulations occurred in the ground and trees ceased almost altogether until we reached the Farlala shelters towards nine o'clock at night. Mosquitoes at this place were innumerable and troublesome.

On leaving this camp by a steep descent we found ourselves in a deep *cuvette*. One hour later, just as the sun was warming the landscape with its golden rays, we were in an elongated and most picturesque basin, with a small lake in the centre encircled by groves of palms. Later, at 7.10 and at 7.30 respectively, we met two similar basins, and at 7.45 we came to a great dune, the direction of which was from south-east to north-west. At 8.10 another dune of great proportions, running parallel to the preceding one, was reached. On the other side of this dune, at 8.30, we went across an immense *cuvette* full of palms and large deposits of white sodium carbonate, causing these palms to appear as though growing in snow. The west side of the *cuvette* was formed by another dune parallel to the one on the east side.

At 9.45 we reached the village of Marikuramalek (elevation, 1,400 feet), a " Berberi " village, situated upon a height. Berberi is the name applied to all those inhabitants who are neither Haussa nor Bornu. Each two or three houses in this village were enclosed in separate *zeribas* of wooden posts and matting. The low conical-roofed huts were miserable-looking. The people inside shared their homes with numerous goats and some chickens.

Two *cuvettes* in succession were found west of the village, the first one with water and good grazing. Both these were shallow basins.

At 4.30 another large but equally shallow *cuvette* with a big millet plantation in it was reached. At

5 o'clock, 5.10, and 5.30 more *cuvettes* were found, the last one with water. Then came a long dune (from south-east to north-west), our course being here due west. The depression along these dunes was deeper on the east side than upon the west.

We arrived at Tamashuka at 7.30, and there we found a Mangawa village of over a hundred huts. A large *cuvette* with a well lay to the west of the village, to which we had come across undulating country.

By September 10th we were in a region of great dunes, mostly running in a direction from south-east to north-west, but many of them showed a tendency to a crescent form, describing immense arcs, within which we generally found villages. Some of these dunes were under cultivation and had enormous plantations of millet.

We passed the Sannanaua camping ground at 8.20, and from this point we did not find any more well-defined *cuvettes*. We constantly encountered crescent-shaped dunes, with depressions between, where numerous palm-trees and mimosas grew among minor hillocks of sand.

At 9.30 a.m. we perceived in the distance to the south-west-west the mountains on which Gouri stood. At 11.30 we came to a beautiful basin with small palm groves ; then more great crescent-shaped dunes, with valleys of palm-trees. After that, to a flat expanse with huge millet plantations, and at 12.45 we came to the village of Wajengoni, inhabited by Manga or Mangawa people.

Although this portion was called a desert by many people, it was not really a desert in the proper sense of the word. Indeed, the soil was extraordinarily fertile.

Were it not for the scarcity of water almost anything could be grown there, the climate, though hot, being at no time unbearable. In the winter months, in fact, there were nights when it was quite cold and the thermometer descended to 50° Fahrenheit (10° Centigrade), sometimes even lower.

On leaving this village we descended at 3.30 into a most beautiful and immense grove of palms by the side of a dune (south-east to north-west) which ran parallel to it. There was a well of capital water in the depression. An hour later, at 4.30, another great dune (also south-east to north-west) was found. Then we came to a series of wide but shallow hollows, with mimosas, *tindil*, *col-col*, and *chungo* trees.

At 5.25 there was a great valley to the north of our trail, and at 5.45 we struck an irregularly-shaped depression. We arrived that afternoon at Gouri, in what is termed the district or province of Mounyo.

The British Nigerian frontier lies on the 13° 20′ lat. N. and the latitude of Gouri is exactly on the 14th parallel of lat. N. The province extended from Moa, which ought to belong to Mounyo, as the inhabitants are all Mangawa as far as Nguigmi, which we had visited on Lake Tchad.

North of Gouri we found the Kontouss, a plateau, or rather a mountainous mass inhabited by the Dagguera, people akin to the Mangawa. They chiefly inhabited the highlands, but two villages of these people were also to be found further south-east, at Tamsoukoua and Mallam Goullamary. The most important mountains of that group were the Mia Mountain, and west, towards Zinder, Mount Guedio, north of the trail, about twenty kilometres west of Gouri.

South-east of Gouri, at Gourselick, were salt-marshes. The salt was extracted mostly by a primitive process of ebullition. The natives took the dry earth mixed with salt crystals, and boiled all in earthen pots, pouring in water constantly, until the earth was washed away and the salt, in a more or less dirty form, was eventually collected.

There were also salt-marshes at Karangaoa, at Kailaram, at Karagou, etc., east of Gourselick. The Boue mines, west of Gourselick, were now exhausted.

At Abque quantities of carbonate of soda were to be found.

The region south of Gouri was infested by brigands, as although the convention for the new frontier was made in 1904, it had not yet been ratified, and the actual boundary pillars had not been erected. The officers, both on the French and English sides, had orders not to interfere with the people near the approximate boundary. In the new delimitation the zone near Gouri will form a long rectangle. The only important places in the district which have been ceded to the French are Khabi and Budum, Khabi being formerly a great slave market.

Much discussion has taken place regarding a quick route to Lake Tchad which would be reached by water down the Komundugu; but as Lake Tchad itself is not navigable in the northern part, except under exceptional circumstances, this route would really be of little assistance to the French, especially when there is an infinitely better route by the Niger, the Benoue and the Logone, by which Lake Tchad can be comfortably reached the entire way, except a few kilometres, by steamer.

The Mangawa who inhabit the region of Gouri were docile people, timid to a degree and suspicious. They avoided Europeans as much as possible. They seemed uncertain as to what the British and French were going to do with them. Neither morally nor physically were these people strong enough for well or ill doing.

Near the marshes they cultivated wheat and a kind of sorrel, called by them the *yawa*, a small quantity of cotton which they used in their bartering transactions, a little tobacco for their own consumption, onions, potatoes, great quantities of millet and a lot of beans.

Although these people belonged to the religion of Islam, they were in no way fanatical, not even fervent in their prayers, which they frequently forgot to say in the morning and at night.

No commercial movement worth mentioning was to be noticed in that country. The land had been subjected to much devastation and the people possessed no wealth. What little commerce there was consisted in the export of salt and sodium carbonate, which found its way mostly to the great city of Kano, in British Nigeria. From there, notwithstanding the high tariff in British territory, it was conveyed south and southwest, as markets were nearer in that direction than they would be to the north in French territory, where the salt would have to travel across the central Sahara to Tripoli or Algeria to find a suitable market.

A camel charge of salt was valued locally at about three francs (2s. 5d.). The imports which found their way from British Nigeria into the Mangawa country were mostly Manchester cottons, fancy cotton materials, shockingly bad matches, and Kola nut, the latter much valued by the natives, who made constant use of it. The hunger-appeasing qualities of this nut were, I think, much exaggerated. It did in no way feed one, or keep one's strength up, but it certainly had the power of stopping digestion, which allowed people to go long periods of time without eating. I once or twice tried it, but with most disastrous results. It made me very sick, and when I recovered after a few minutes I became ravenously hungry and had to eat double the quantity of food that I should have used under normal conditions.

The Mangawa people used leather trousers, because of the innumerable *kram-krams* which attached themselves to their legs when they walked about anywhere. They carried numerous leather amulets slung to the neck, arms, chest and belt. The women placed a red coral bead generally in the left nostril.

The Gouri fort, beautifully constructed, stood on a rocky hill at an elevation of 1,570 feet. North-west of it was another rocky hill with huge boulders. Due west was a long high plateau, while south-west of the post was a native village in a depression with an extensive plain before it. To the south-west, in the background, beyond the village, there was a hilly region in the distance, and to the north-west, also in the distance, rose the plateau of Kontouss, only broken up in one or two places.

When I walked into the fort in a blue serge suit and my straw hat, Lieutenant Faulque de Jonquières, who was standing there, as well as Captain Chambert who was in command, were both staggered. They were not aware that I was on my way there and could not at first make out where I had dropped from. They were extremely hospitable and kind and insisted on my remaining there four days.

I left again in the afternoon of September 14th, and for several kilometres went up and down among rocky hills both to the south and north of my course, naked granite rock showing through the sand, with crystallizations in the greyish mass dotted all over with black spots. The Kontouss Mounts, with a grey strata of clay, showed a curious erosion in some places. This erosion seemed to me to have been due mostly to the action of water, but no doubt it had been continued not only by the action of wind, but by the action of the sun, the moon, and the electric currents which predominate in the desert.

Nights in the desert during the good season have a great fascination. The average non-travelled northern European cannot imagine the immense number of stars and planets that can be seen dotting the sky over the desert, nor their amazing beauty and brilliancy. Shooting-stars, leaving streaks of fire across the immense vault overhead, can be perceived in hundreds on some nights. The moon, too, owing to the great clearness of the atmosphere, is very beautiful. It generally rises in a huge red disc upon the horizon, the redness being due to the sand in the atmosphere up to a certain elevation, then becomes of a beautiful golden colour as it gets higher, and of a luminous metallic white when it is directly overhead.

Lunar haloes are frequent, and I have often beheld circular luminous rings of immense diameter and beauty round the moon.

Everybody is aware that sunlight is extremely powerful in the desert. Many a native is blinded by the effect of the sun, together with sand entering the eyes, or if the eyesight is not absolutely lost the vision is affected even in comparatively young people. Opacity of the cornea and paralysis of the ciliar arch are common complaints due to the powerful rays of the sun. Sunstroke is common among the natives, and more common still among white people who do not understand suitable ways of living in tropical climates. But not many people are aware that moonstrokes are also frequent, especially in the desert, and are sometimes as dangerous as sunstrokes. I myself, who, without protecting my head in any particular way, was never affected in the slightest degree by the rays of the sun, was always somewhat inconvenienced, especially when the moon was full, if I sat outside my tent without my hat. On one or two occasions, when I neglected this precaution, I felt a peculiar sensation in the nape of my neck and very nearly dropped backwards ; for two or three days after, I experienced in my skull an uncomfortable sensation similar to that felt when parts of one's body have been exposed too long to the X-rays.

Anyone who has lived in the tropics can vouch for the remarkable effects of moonlight upon human beings, and any student of the various phenomena in the desert is aware that lunar light has a strong effect, not only upon people, but even upon the disintegration of certain rocks. Moonlight seems to act in the desert with greater force than elsewhere. This, I believe, is caused by the abundant electricity which is generated all over the surface of the dry, hot sands, and which, when intensified by lunar influence, affects the components of certain rocks. The action of the sun is, of course, one of the principal agents in geological changes. To it

Making a trail in the desert French Sudan

may be added the great fluctuations in the temperature; wind storms, the chief generators of enormous electric currents, and, last but not least, the torrential rains which have undoubtedly a greater action upon the disintegration of rocks than either lunar light or electricity.

According to some geologists the formation of the numerous dunes in the desert is due to disintegration and destruction of matter constituting primary rock. It is due, they say, to friability of rocks in which gypsum is present, under the action of atmospheric agents, and principally to alluvial causes, which reduce rocks of carbonate of calcium and gypsum to powder. This disintegration of the rock brings about a fusion which develops an internal pressure under which the hard layers of the plateaus are completely broken up.

In the country which I traversed between Lake Tchad and Timbuctu I saw but little calcareous rock, encountering mostly sandstone in various stages of formation and of various colours according to locality. I am told that in the North Tasili sandstone and clay of a beautiful rose tint are to be found. In some quarters gypsum is noticeable, and clay is abundant in the lower stratum of dunes. Calcium, I am told, is also abundant and of excellent quality in the country round Ghadames but too far off to be of any use in the southern part of the French Sudan until the ways of communication and means of transport are simpler than at present.

Saltpetre is fairly plentiful, and also alum, especially in the mountainous portion of the Tuareg country, while sodium carbonate is only too frequently met with near Lake Tchad and in neighbouring parts of the desert.

In certain parts of the western Sahara one finds many fossils, which show plainly that at one time the sea must have reached thus far. Natives speak of the remains of huge animals in a petrified condition to be found here and there, and a gigantic pre-historic mammal is said to exist at Tadohayt-tan-Tamzerdia.

Near Rhat, sulphate of lead and sulphate of antimony, which certain tribes use for blackening the eyelids and eyebrows (the *kohl* of the Arabs) is found in some quantity.

Although in various parts of the desert one occasionally finds beautiful crystals of all colours, I never personally found stones, precious from a commercial point of view, but it is not improbable that in the mountainous region, such as in the Touat, emeralds might be discovered, and possibly even diamonds.

As in nearly all the central zone of Africa, iron is plentiful, but of no commercial value, as the difficulties and expense of transport are too great.

CHAPTER XXIII.

THERE were two *mares* near Gouri, one most picturesque at sunset, recalling bits of Egypt, with its tall palms reflected in more or less limpid waters. Camels, cows and horses took cooling baths in this pool, and the water was fetid, especially near the shore. The kitchen-garden of the post was in this depression, but although the soil of clay and sand mixed was sterile, they managed to grow all kinds of vegetables introduced from France.

Three or four kilometres from the post we left the heavy undulations and came out altogether of the hilly region. From this point we obtained a fine view to the south-west of higher hills of a well-rounded shape. The surface rock appeared of a rich brown colour owing to being hard-baked by the sun. Underneath was erup- tive rock. We had been marching slightly south of west over a plateau, first extremely undulating, then almost flat, with big, isolated, volcanic boulders showing through the sand in one or two places.

At 6 p.m., three hours after leaving Gouri, we sud- denly descended into a huge plain, fairly wooded with low shrubs. We were moving along the diameter line of a great circle of hills around us.

The French captain at Gouri had provided me with a picturesque guide carrying a formidable sword slung to a most elaborate bandolier. Innumerable tassels, and amulets by the dozen, were tied to his right arm, to his wrist, above his elbow, and round his neck, while countless mascots were sewn in front and at the back of his coat, and dozens hung from his belt. It so happened that upon the road this man had to undress. He took off one after the other a multitude of shirts—seven or eight, all of different colours, the under ones in rags, the outer new and smart. Whenever he became possessed of a new shirt, he never discarded the old, but covered it with the fresh one. This fellow looked a perfect giant when I first saw him, but there was but little left of him except his height by the time he had removed everything. His strength, however, was enormous. His amulets—leather cases containing verses from the Koran on a folded piece of paper—were of considerable weight, and his sword, his numerous garments, heavy leather trousers reaching to the waist, and huge straw hat with leather attachments, brought the total weight of what he carried upon him to at least forty to fifty pounds.

A notable feature in the south-western hills were the broken cones forming the spurs of the hill-range. Some way off there were isolated conical sections of this hilly mass which had evidently been detached from the main range by the erosion of water, of wind, or of both.

I found upon our trail huge upright pillars resembling gigantic monoliths, especially when we got out of the circle within the hills. There were masses of great boulders in that part. No sooner had we come out of the circle than all of a sudden we came to a steep and stony descent of some length. After that the trail became good and level until we neared the big village

of Tchangari.   Here again we found a number of basins
and *cuvettes* and two conspicuous undulations in the
ground.

We arrived at Tchangari on the morning of September
15th at 7.30, and at eight we were on the march again.
Between Tchangari and Ouargelé we found mostly a
series of great dunes and deep depressions, the dunes
as usual having a direction from south-east to north-
west.   They appeared from this elevated point like
a series of great waves.   Ouargelé village looked like a
beehive, the cylindrical walls of the huts being close
together, and suggesting a gigantic honeycomb.   The
architecture was mixed in this place, some of the huts
having conical roofs, others elongated domes, but all were
shabbily built and in a tumble-down condition.   The
usual *zeribas* of matting were found.

The natives, tall and bearded, were garbed in the
typical long blue Arab shirts.

In the afternoon we had again a series of long sand
waves (south-east to north-west), but at somewhat
longer intervals than in the morning.   We then came to
a regular barrier of isolated rounded mounds connected
merely by an irregular ridge.   From this point we had
before us a steepish descent leading into a vast plain
below us to the west, and only interrupted at the
horizon-line in the south-western part by a long distant
range of hills extending southwards.

In this plain we found the miserable village of Wurua
and also a small well.   Wretched plantations of millet
were to be seen, but in this part the soil was much covered
with sand and quite sterile.   The millet looked yellow
and sickly and the plants were ugly and far apart.

That same evening we descended from the third

terrace since leaving Gouri into another fairly flat
expanse, and arrived at Kakkara at eight o'clock in
the evening, after having gone over a number of
undulations.

From Kakkara we went over dunes (south-east to
north-west) with gentle slopes on either side, the depressions showing a stratum of grey clay mixed with
sand reaching half way (some fifteen feet) up the side
of the dune. We then came to a rocky hill and *débris*
about one hundred feet high, the first of a series which
extended mostly north of the trail. We were travelling
at this point in a south-westerly direction. There were
accumulations of sand on the north-east up to half the
height of the hills. South-west of us stood massive
hill-ranges.

Two hours and a half after leaving these hills we
passed close to gigantic domes of volcanic rock on the
north side of the trail, some quite smooth, others sponge-
like, having apparently been subjected to great heat.
Some distance to the south-west were peaks of a conical
shape.

Having left at six o'clock in the morning, we found
ourselves by 11.30 between two hill-ranges. Near
Zermou was another dome of rock on the left of the
trail.

We travelled over flat country as far as Gafati,
where we arrived at ten o'clock at night. Near Nono
we had to cross a small lake of rain-water, two or three
feet deep. The camels, quite helpless in water, fell down
one after another as they were pulled along upon the
slippery clay bottom. We arrived wet all over at

From Zermou the trail went to the south-west with

hill-ranges on both sides. Another dome was passed on the left of the trail.

Later in the morning we were moving west-south-west on the trail along great plantations of millet, with low hills to the south and north.

The mad camel-man was again taken with one of his fits. A few yards from where we had pitched our tents a number of deep holes were to be found in the ground where natives had endeavoured to find water. Some of these holes were of great depth. There was no protection at the mouth of these wells, and, when abandoned, grass grew near them and it was difficult to see them.

In the Kanem once one of my oxen, while playing with another, walked backwards into one of these holes and gradually slid down, much to the excitement of the Buduma who owned him. All hands in camp seized him by the horns, which, fortunately, spread out to a greater diameter than the aperture of the well. There the ox remained until we could get ropes round his front legs, which also protruded, and round his head. Then all pulled and pulled until the animal's head nearly became severed from its body, when it was discovered that the ox was so jammed that all our strength could never get him out. So the digging process was adopted, and after hours of labour my men had dug down to half the animal's body. Then more ropes were put around him and a greater pull was obtained, and the ox was eventually pulled out, the air resounding with shrieks of delight from the Buduma. So alarmed was the animal that he could hardly stand upon his trembling legs. I had seldom seen an animal in such terror.

To return to the Miaissa. He had that evening a

similar experience. He dashed away from camp in the middle of the night, again invoking Allah, and disappeared in a millet plantation. A few moments later we heard faint cries as if out of the bowels of the earth. We listened, and sure enough it was the voice of the Miaissa calling for help. I knew that he was out of his mind, and did not pay any attention until the cries became so distressing that I thought something serious must have happened. In fact, guided by the voice, I found that the Miaissa had dropped into a deep well. I sent for help at once, for ropes and lights, but all our ropes fastened together in sufficient strength to haul him up did not reach to within two feet of where he was, so we had to send to the village for more. After some hours of hard work the Miaissa was pulled out again, much shaken and scared, but none the worse for his twenty feet drop.

From Gafati to Zinder (Damanga, as it is called by the natives) there was a succession of millet fields all along, the millet of poor quality. Clouds of locusts had paid a visit to that country, and most of the millet had been destroyed. Normally, this region produced immense quantities of millet and almost wholly provided the market of Kano in British Nigeria, as well as many of the oases of the desert on the north in the Tuareg country.

I arrived at Zinder (elevation 1,650 feet) in the morning of September 17th.

The post of Zinder was established in 1903, but the actual occupation dates from 1898, from the time of the Foureau and Joalland expeditions. Joalland arrived from the west and Foureau from the north (Algeria), Lieutenant Joalland continuing towards the Kanem,

Zinder, within the city wall.

whereas Foureau came two or three months later. The two expeditions, having accomplished a junction with the Gentil expedition from the Ubanghi, fought and destroyed Rabah's power on Lake Tchad.

Captain Bloch and Captain Lefebvre were responsible for the construction of the handsome post, with its elaborate buildings of mud bricks.

Captain Gaden, who at one time commanded this important place, is well known in France for his successful undertakings, from Zinder as a centre, against the Tuareg; the work of Lieutenant-Colonel Peroz is too well known for me to refer to it.

There is a native town within a castellated mud wall, called the Birni, where a market is to be found. A breach has been made in the wall on the west side, where a heap of gigantic boulders are to be found within the city wall. At the other end of the town are a few huts and a market-place. This walled town has practically been abandoned, and the greater part of the population is to be found in the commercial village of Djanko, only a short distance away, with a population of Haussa, Arabs, Tuareg and Bella.

A high marabu, called Malam Settima, who is the chief marabu of the three adjoining towns, lives there. In Djanko all the trade was in the hands of Arabs and Tuaregs, with one or two Haussa merchants. The Haussa only carried on trade on a small scale with cotton goods of inferior quality, red-tanned skins and ostrich feathers. The red dye for the skins is obtained from the stem of millet soaked in water.

Numbers of ostriches were kept in this village, and it was amusing to see these long-necked birds peeping over the high fences inside which they were enclosed.

Their valuable feathers found their way northwards by Arab caravans. The ostriches were despoiled of their plumage twice a year and brought their owners an income of from fifty to sixty francs each (£2 to £2 8s.).

Not far from the commercial village was Garimalamassa, the religious centre, where all the Marabu have collected and have erected two mosques. The only important mosque in that part, however, was to be found in the Birni, the others being merely miserable enclosures.

The marabu, a corrupt lot, derive a considerable income from the manufacture of *gri-gris*, the leather amulets worn round the arms, legs and neck, or sewn in such quantities to the clothes of the people that they form a regular cuirass.

Perhaps the most attractive people in and near Zinder were the Tuareg, and I much enjoyed meeting Moenson Mahamma, their official representative in Zinder, a man of distinguished, dignified manner and business-like instincts.

The lower part of his face was covered, in the distinctive Tuareg fashion, by a thick black veil, so that only the eyes could be seen. Squatting upon valuable carpets imported from the north, he received me on more than one occasion in his fine house.

This man was useful to the French, as all transactions with the Tuareg were carried on through the agency of this fellow, who was sensible, intelligent and quick.

There were several merchants in the place, quite enterprising people considering that Zinder was a city in the middle of the desert. There were three native chiefs at the time of my visit, Tchikama, the chief of the province, Bellama and Galadima Yaro.

The sultan of Zinder was in prison for high treason, as, shortly before I went through, he had been implicated in a plot to murder all the French officers in the post. Malamiero, the richest merchant in the place, a Bella by birth, was also in chains with him.

It was by a mere miracle that the officers escaped assassination, the plot having been discovered only a few hours before it was to have been carried into effect. The beginning of this rebellion, which was to have extended all over the country, came from Sokoto, in British Nigeria, where, as everybody knows, a number of British officers were murdered. On the French side of the boundary one officer, as well as the natives who accompanied him, were murdered upon the Niger by fanatics, and the bodies mutilated. Another French officer was killed in a fight with the rebels.

The well-conceived plan in Zinder was to attract the attention of the French towards the west in order to drive the soldiers in that direction, and to profit at the same time by the yearly movement of troops towards the north. This would allow the post to be taken by surprise, and they expected to seize all arms and ammunition. Taking advantage of the unexpected success of the rebels at Sokoto and at Bubu, near Niamey (upon the Niger), the rebellious movement at Zinder was to have been hastened.

At that time the sultan of Hadeija, between Kana and Kuka, had already disobeyed English authority, and twenty days after the sultan of Zinder had been imprisoned an English column took possession by assault of the walled town of Hadeija, the sultan's seat.

The movement undoubtedly originated among the

marabu. It was regrettable that the French authorities were unable to deal with the culprits in the summary way which we adopted in Sokoto. Everybody implicated in the movement, and even the assassins of Lieutenant Fabre, were merely waiting comfortably in prison while the case was being fought out in one court after another, much to the damage of the white people's prestige in that country. In cases of that kind immediate hanging of the leaders is the cheapest and only salutary method of impressing the mob.

Perhaps, with the Islamic movement brewing and getting stronger and stronger every day in the northern part of Africa, and spreading fast southwards, England and France, who have great possessions in the central region, will some day have a difficult problem to face. The marabu, at best a most unscrupulous lot, are blowing the fire with all their might, and the time will come when they will feel strong enough and will make a firm stand against Christianity and the civilized ways of Christians. In consequence of foreigners instructing the people, the marabu rightly feel they are gradually losing power, which they formerly easily maintained over the ignorant masses. Superstition is rampant and is carefully nursed by them among the people. The sultan of Zinder himself tells a story in all seriousness of a marabu being transformed into a lion under his own (the sultan's) eyes. In order to be able to accomplish a similar feat of transmigration, the sultan had been smearing himself with powder for three consecutive months.

A strong dislike to civilized ways was in that region also felt by the Arabs, who formerly benefited by raids and slave-trading, and whose income had been greatly

Interior of the fort of Zinder French Sudan

decreased by the adoption of civilized restrictions. They were, however, too clever to join openly in a rebellion until they knew themselves powerful enough to emerge victorious.

The Tuareg, after the severe punishment inflicted upon them, were easily held in check by the able tactics of the French military; the position of all the wells and of the markets where they provisioned themselves had been accurately established. They could now, at any moment, be brought back to reason if they did not want to be starved to death or die of thirst.

Commandant (now Colonel) Gouraud and Captain (now Commandant) Gaden came to Zinder on the departure of Colonel Peroz. Colonel Gouraud fought bravely against the Tuareg Kelgress at Guelma, where they displayed extraordinary bravery.

When I was at Zinder Commandant Gadel—no relation to Commandant Gaden—had been sent to occupy the oasis of Bilma, as there were curious rumours of an attempt of the Turks to occupy that place.

The five French officers at Zinder, Captains Lefebvre and Lécrivain, Lieutenants Aubrion, Petitperrin, and the *officier interprète*, Landeroin, formerly an officer in the Marchand expedition, showed me considerate and charming hospitality.

Thanks to the kindness of Captain Lefebvre and the Tuareg Moenson Mahamma, I was able in three days to make up a fresh caravan of excellent camels, with Tuareg in charge of them, and in the evening of September 20th I took my departure westward.

There were marshes round Zinder, in which the curious *ghewa* (mud fish) was to be found, which lives during the dry season walled up in the mud in a lethargic state, but regains its life in a few moments when placed in water. It possesses four long tentacles instead of fins, and can live for several months in the dried mud.

There were a lot of *calgoh* and *sahbara*, the large-leaved mimosa *markeh*, *zekekkia*, *dashih*, *carammioh*, and the big *annu* trees ; *gheza* were plentiful, as well as *tammioh*, olive-coloured trees, acacias and mimosas of various kinds; then the *faru* trees, the *danyia*, a kind of acacia; the long-leaved *dureh*, the long-thorned *adduah* (also an acacia), and the *syriah*, with tiny leaves. There were quantities of tall *gamba* grass and tiny-leaved mimosas called the *dafora*. The *dugniya* possessed large circular leaves. Although this was a desert there was, indeed, a great botanical variety. Shrubs of all kinds abounded.

From Zinder I descended a dune, at the bottom of which was the garden of the post under fine palm-trees. The garden, although on extremely sterile soil, was beautifully kept, and should be an object-lesson to many a military officer who has to spend his life in the colonies of what can be done in that direction.

All the officers accompanied me for ten kilometres, when they bade me farewell. I continued the journey during part of the night, and on September 21st I left Termini at 5 a.m., crossing flat ground with a dune to the north. Another northerly dune was flat-topped. Water and the erosion of the wind had cut a series of separate hills in it, all identical in shape. There was a dune also to the south composed of many accumulations of huge boulders.

At 9.30 I passed, on the south of the trail, a curious flat mountain in terraces of a brilliant burnt-sienna colour, and later others of a similar character but not quite so much eroded.

Takieta was reached at 11.20, a most charming camp with magnificent *gantchi* trees. Between Takieta and the next camp, Kurnawa, the country was uninteresting and flat for ten kilometres. We proceeded to Garagounsa, where beautiful *samia* trees stood near the camp, tall and with dense foliage.

On September 22nd we came to great undulations in the ground and immense dunes, this time in a direction from south-west to north-east, with deep depressions between until we arrived at Kongomeh. A lot of red sandstone with perforations was noticeable, and travelling over this we came to a most picturesque cañon, a great rock in horizontal strata surmounted by vivid burnt-sienna sandstone. It formed a fissure in the earth's surface in a direction from south-west to north-east, and was some fifty feet deep. This cañon was to the left of our trail, and wound its way through the valley. This was the only bit of natural scenery I had seen which was of any intrinsic picturesqueness since leaving the Nielim mountains in the Shari basin.

We found near here quantities of *gonda*, a small yellow fruit of the desert, extremely sweet and juicy.

Shabareh village was passed, and after ups and downs we descended into a vast plain, where the Magirgui village and a really delightful rest-house were found.

In the afternoon of September 22nd, at seven o'clock, by a well-marked trail with nothing of interest on the way, we arrived at the post of Tessaoua.

Both the Mangawa and the Haussa who inhabited these villages saluted by shaking their right fist as if threatening, or else by placing one or both hands spread wide behind the ear, the thumb directly under the lobe. Another salutation was by squeezing the lobe of one's own ear and wringing it violently.

These troublesome people were kept in good order by the French. One never met a man upon the trail or in villages who did not rise to salute as one passed by.

I was riding a Tuareg camel-saddle, one of the most torturing and unpractical arrangements I have ever come upon in all my travels, although, I agree, it was most picturesque, even elegant, to look at. Moreover, should the tiny strap which keeps the whole affair in position upon the front slope of the camel's hump break, one would be precipitated head first from a height of about ten inches above the highest point of the camel's back, and not less than ten feet above the ground.

Tessaoua was at an elevation of 1,370 feet.

In the afternoon of September 23rd I went through the walled town of Sultan Serki Bahnnuh, the wall being a heavy wooden stockade plastered with mud. The principal houses were also of mud and showed a predilection for roofs with pointed corners and flat terraces. The humbler homes, however, were merely mat-walled, with thatched conical roofs. The interior was divided into two sections, one a sleeping-room, the other a room where the people spent the day and did the cooking. The roofs were generally covered with a large-leafed creeper producing gourds, used by the natives for making drinking bowls, vessels, etc.

Within the small *zeriba* of matting round each house was generally a tiny garden, with two or three stalks of millet and a vegetable or two.

The country was flat all along. About sunset I had reached the village of Rabah with extensive plantations of millet. Later on, on the left of the trail, was the village of Kainko Sao, our trail being now mostly over slightly undulating sand. We arrived at the large village and rest-house of Kanambakachy towards nine o'clock in the evening, having marched twenty-one kilometres in the afternoon.

Haussa pack-saddles interested me. They consisted of two skins filled with millet, these two bags being placed one at each end of the camel's hump. Two supplementary rolls of matting were then placed across these alongside the hump on either side. If the camel had to carry extra heavy weights, then a stick was laid over each mat roll. The loads when going over fairly level country kept their position safely enough upon these improvised saddles.

At sunrise we made a start, going first over flat, then over undulating, country, travelling due west over a dune, and leaving the village of Anagodaye on our left, three hundred yards off the trail. Haussa villages were frequent now, and near them wells were found.

At Degaba was a picturesque crowd of half-naked women drawing water from the deep wells. A rope of great length was used, to which was attached a parachute arrangement of skin, a folding bucket which turned the other way round when filled with water. Rows of red spherical earthenware jars, gourd cups and vessels of all sizes lined the sides of the wells.

Mayahi village, with some four hundred inhabitants, was reached next. We were now marching north and only a few yards from the boundary of British Maradi, north-east of Sokoto. At Goumsa we were even nearer the boundary, as the trail converged towards the frontier, which there formed an angle.

At Zaburi village, where, for some reason or other furious drum-beating was going on, at Gamussa and at Megabbai only a few sheds were found.

I reached Goumsa at nine o'clock in the evening. On September 25th the following villages were passed : Al Mocktar, Ghidentino, with many store-houses ; Idankana, a well patronized market ; and further along, in a trailless plain, Guidam Haussa. We were travelling mostly over flat ground. Two villages on the right of the trail and one on the left were passed before we arrived at Guidam Salifou (elevation 1,300 feet).

After Guidam Baua and some minor villages, I arrived at Kornaka at nine o'clock in the evening. I had the great pleasure of meeting Colonel Lamolle, commanding the region, and his A.D.C., Captain Bouchez, two officers well known for their excellent work in the French Sudan.

The Haussa tribes were at that moment fairly quiet, and there seemed to be a possibility of the country west of Zinder getting repeopled to some extent. It would certainly become relatively prosperous if the natives could be made to return to their former homes. They were beginning to see that the French were in no way inclined to do them harm. The definite ratification of the new frontier between French and British territory will do much towards settling difficulties regarding villages and tribes in that region. They have been until now divided merely by an imaginary astronomical frontier which did not suit local necessities. Many of the tribes were divided in two by this imaginary line. Half the people of one tribe were under British rule, the other half under French. Necessarily this involved different taxation and different methods of administering justice. The result was that both sections of the tribe were dissatisfied. Brigandage, as we have seen, had been going on extensively all along the frontier while the question of the new boundary was being discussed, and this zone treated as neutral.

The difficulties of developing such a barren, inhospitable country were great, but Colonel Lamolle told me that, notwithstanding everything, the region was already paying its own expenses. The natives paid their small taxes quite regularly. The Tuareg, particularly, were most punctual in paying what was due to the Government.

CHAPTER XXIV.

THE Tuareg found in this region had mostly inter-married with black tribes and were dark-skinned, but those further north, many of whom I saw, had white skins like the Arabs. They were undoubtedly the most attractive and noblest people of the desert in the French Sudan.

We have a curious way in Europe of always calling non-European races by the wrong name. This is the case with the word "Tuareg," which is rejected by the Tuareg themselves, and is only applied to them by the Arabs. In the singular it is *Targhi* (feminine : *Targuia*), plural, *Tuareg*, meaning " the abandoned by God," or " the God - forsaken people." This because for a long time they refused to adopt the Mahomme-dan religion brought over by the Arabs. After they had accepted it they discarded it on more than one occasion. Their language is *Targuia*.

Locally, the Tuareg go more by the name of each large division of the tribe, such as *Imohagh, Imocharh, Imajirhen, Temahaq, Temacheq ;* several of these words are evidently derived from the word *iohagh*, meaning " free, frank, independent, with a slight inclination to raiding."

The word *Kel* is often used as a prefix to the name of the tribe, and means " the people of." There are

Tuareg caravan of oxen.

four great divisions of Tuareg : the *Kel-Azdjer*, occupy-
ing the north-east of the desert and a plateau of the
North Tasili ; the *Ahaggar*, north-west, in the Ahaggar
Mountains (called Hoggar by the Arabs) ; the *Aïr*,
Kel-Aïr, or *Kel-Oui*, south-west in the mountain mass
of *Aïr* (or Azben) ; then the *Oelimmiden*, south-west in
the mountainous mass of Adghagh and the plains of
Ahanag.

The *Azdjer* and the *Ahaggar* are, consequently, the
Tuareg of the north and the *Aïr* and *Oelimmiden* are
the Tuareg of the south.

Each great division of Tuareg has adopted as a
refuge a distinct mountainous region ; two at the cul-
minating points of the central plateau of the Sahara
and in the regions of the watershed between the
Mediterranean Sea and the Atlantic Ocean ; the other
two belong to the basin of the Niger.

The limit of the Tuareg country on the north is a
line from El-Hesi in Tripolitania to Ghadames and a
line from Ghadames to the northern limit of Touat.
The western boundary is formed by the eastern and
southern side of the plateau of Tademayt and by the
caravan route from Agabli to Timbuctu; that on the
south by a line from Timbuctu to Ungua Tsammit
(north of Zinder). On the east their boundary runs
parallel to, but fifteen to twenty miles west of, the
route from Kuka to Murzuk ; and from that point along
the direct route from Murzuk to Tripoli as far as
El-Hesi.

In other words, the Tuareg inhabit a quadrilateral
country known by European geographers as the central
plateau of the Sahara. The general Tuareg name for
their country is *Adjema*, a synonym of the Arabic word

Sahara, which means hard soil. In fact, their country consists mostly of vast plains and deserts, sometimes sandy, sometimes rocky, sometimes of clay, showing in places alluvial deposits similar to those of the salt basins of Sebkha, but more frequently showing stony, hard soil.

The proper and purest Tuareg are really those of the north. According to a learned Tuareg Sheik, Ibrahim-Ould-Sidi, the Tuareg are derived mostly from the Edrisiens of Fez; some from the Ech-Chinguit (between Timbuctu and the ocean); others from Adghagh (between the Niger and the mountains north of it).

The *Ifogha* and the *Imanan* are of as great and noble a family as the *Maghreb.*

In the *Azdjer* there are four tribes. The *Imanan* are half Edrisien of the reigning family of Fez, half *Alouyien,* descendants of Sidna-'Ali, grandson of the Prophet. The *Es-Solatin* (the sultans) are pure *Chorfa.* The *Oraghen* are half noble, half of low origin. The *Imanghasaten,* who come from the Arabs of the east, are of doubtful nobility. The *Ifogha* at one time constituted the bulk of the population at Es-Souk, a big town on the old border between the white races of the desert and the black races of the south.

According to legend, this place had been destroyed three times—first, by envy; second, by the well-known *kram-kram,* the wretched thorny little ball we have met in the desert. It became so plentiful that no room was left (the Tuareg say) to kneel for prayer. This punishment was brought about by heresy. The third time the city was destroyed by an inhuman enemy. It was razed to the ground by the black army of King Gogo. The surviving inhabitants dispersed, the

Juadalen and the *Idaura* towards the Adrar ; the *Ignuaddaren* settled near Timbuctu ; the others went north.

When the Tuareg captured Es-Souk they are said to have embellished it greatly, but, curiously enough, no one seems to know exactly where the ruins of this formerly important city are situated.

After the *Gogha* we find the *Kel-Izhatan*, the *Imettrilalen*, the *Ihadhanaren* (of quite low extraction), the *Ihehauen*, and the *Ilemtin* (west of Timbuctu).

The Tuareg of the north can be divided into two great sections : the *Azdjer* in the eastern portion of the northern country and the *Ahaggar* (or *Hoggar*) in the western portion. Each section has subdivisions : one is the *Ihaggaren*, or nobles ; the other, the serfs, or *Imrhad*. Then come the *Marabu*.

In the *Azdjer* the noble tribes are the *Imanan*, the *Oraghen*, the *Imanghasaten*, the *Kel-Izhaban*, the *Imettrilalen*, the *Ihadhanaren*. The mixed tribes are the *Ilemtin*, the *Kel-tin-Alkoum*. The *Marabu* tribes are the *Ifogha* and the *Ihehauen*.

The *Ahaggar* are subdivided into some thirteen tribes, or practically fourteen, because the *Inemba* tribe has two subdivisions : the *Tedjché-Mellen*, the *Tedjehi-'n-u-Sidi*, the *Ennitra*, the *Taïtok*, the *Tedjehe-'n-Eggali*, the *Inemba* (subdivided into *Kel-Emoghri* and *Kel-Tahat*), the *Kel-Rhela*, the *Irechchumen*, the *Tedjehi-'n-Esakkal*, the *Kel-Ahamellen*, the *Ikadeen*, the *Iboguelan* and the *Ikerremoin*.

In a remarkable work the young French writer, Duveyrier, who is probably the greatest authority about the Tuareg of the northern part of the desert, shows the probability of an affinity between the modern Tuareg and the Autochton people of Greek and Roman times. The Berbers of Morocco call themselves *Amazigh* (or free people), and their language *Tamazigh*. The Berber genealogists of the Middle Ages called them *Mazigh*, or *Tamzigh*, and Greek authors describe them as *Maziques*, evidently a slight mispronunciation of *Mazigh* and *Amazigh*. It is certain that the Tuareg should really be called *Imazighen* or *Imohagh*, and their language *Temahaq* or *Temacheq*.

The Tuareg say that before their arrival a race of giants lived in their country, and we find among them legends similar to those of the Bornu, the Kotoko, Baguirmi and other tribes of the Shari and Lake Tchad basins.

There is little difference between the manners and customs of northern and southern Tuareg. Each tribe is divided into nobles, serfs and slaves. The nobles are usually entrusted with the political powers and rights of each division, and are expected to protect the country. They take command in time of war. Common interests are discussed in public meetings called *mia'ad*. The life of a nobleman in the Tuareg country has charm, but is more tiring than that of inferior tribesmen. The nobleman does not look after the little agriculture there may be in his district, but is expected to roam thousands of miles about the desert to report on the state of the various markets, to attend the feasts of different chieftains and to reconnoitre and spy upon the movements of caravans and of unfriendly tribes, in view of possible raiding if opportunity offers. The chief of all his occupations is to keep all trade routes free for the commerce of his own tribesmen.

Although the Tuareg are Mahommedan, they are

not so strict as many of the Arab tribes north of their country. Even the *inislimin*, their priests, do not attend to religious duties so much as to the public instruction of the young and the administration of justice.

The largest class of individuals among Tuareg is the *Amrhid* (plural *Imrhad*), including the slaves and serfs. Among these *Imrhad* some are busied in agriculture on a small scale, others work in the camps of the nobles looking after camels and other possessions of the richer folk. The nobles live upon the labour of these *Imrhad* and upon the *dhifa*, the gifts or offerings of travellers and passing traders—gifts occasionally willingly offered, but more often extorted by threats or force. Certain it is that if no *dhifa* is forthcoming to the various chiefs upon the road, trading caravans run a fair risk of coming to an untimely end.

No confusion must be made between serfs and slaves in the Tuareg country. The serfs are transmitted by heredity or donation, but are on no account sold or bartered, whereas the actual slaves are constantly being exchanged for money or goods. In many cases the serfs are a white-skinned people who have demanded the protection of the nobles, or black slaves who have been liberated at the death of their masters. The actual slaves, on the other hand, are generally persons who have been seized during raids.

The population in the Tuareg country is, I think, rather on the decrease, but it is a difficult matter to obtain accurate statistics about the ratio of births and deaths in communities, and, therefore, the above remark is merely a surmise based on what the older Tuareg relate of their former power and number.

It is also impossible, when merely passing through a country, to deal accurately with such difficult problems as the fecundity of pure types, of pure types crossed with mongrels, or of pure types crossed with pure foreign slaves or serfs.   As far as I could notice, the mixed types seemed, in the case of male children, physically stronger and mentally more intelligent than the pure Tuareg of noble blood, or than their slave or serf parents.   Such crosses of superior male types of one race with inferior female types of another race, or else superior female types with inferior males, were certainly more fruitful than when pure types of either of those races intermarried.   I had no opportunity of checking by statistics the precise relative degree of the fruitfulness of these unions and of those of pure-blooded individuals.

A characteristic point in Tuareg social conditions in some tribes, called Beni-Ummia, is that children take the social standing of the mother and not of the father. For instance, the sons of a slave or serf father and of a noble mother are nobles, whereas the sons of a noble father and of a serf or slave mother remain serfs or slaves. There is a philosophical saying in the Tuareg country that it is the direct and unconfuted origin which stamps the child ; according to them—and they cannot be contradicted—there never can be a misunderstanding upon who the mother of the child is.   We have already seen how this custom has spread among some tribes far south of the Tuareg country.

There are, however, exceptional tribes where, following the rules of Islam, paternal succession is adopted. These are called the Ebna-Sid.

With the Tuareg, as in most cases, beauty and refinement are more frequently found in the better classes than in the lower. With the Tuareg this is particularly the case. As far as endurance is concerned, the nobles, owing to their stronger will, can accomplish feats which their slaves are incapable of imitating, but perhaps in momentary outbursts of physical strength the lower classes may be superior.

By constant intermarriage a family may become half-noble, and eventually even noble altogether. Slaves in the Tuareg country are treated with the greatest consideration and actually make part of the family. Marriages of noble Tuareg with slaves (mostly black and coming from the French Sudan) are not unusual, and although the slaves act as servants, when needed, the women are often employed in the double capacity of servants and concubines, and are eventually married.

Woman among Tuareg occupies a high social position. There are few countries where she is treated with so much benevolence. She is considered equal to man and even superior. When young, she is educated better than her brothers, and is free to give her hand to whom she pleases, the father being allowed to interfere only to prevent a disastrous marriage. It is not considered a disgrace for a free woman to fall in love with a slave, although this is not usual, as women in the Tuareg country are proud and ambitious, and generally prefer to marry in their own rank. Woman has gained so much authority that she has been able to impose monogamy upon the polygamous Tuareg—quite a remarkable feat among Mussulmans. Monogamy is now unreservedly respected by Tuareg men.

The Tuareg marry comparatively young, as soon as they feel inclined, and, as far as one could judge from superficial observation, the number of males in the population seemed slightly larger than the number of females.

Infanticide is common among the Tuareg, and owing to the life led by these nomad people the natural mortality of children, especially during the cold winter months, is considerable. Mothers are fond of their children, whom they invariably suckle themselves. They seemed to bear children from an average age of fifteen to an average age of thirty-eight or forty years. The formal marriage ceremony generally took place when the women were about eighteen or twenty and the men twenty-five to thirty years of age.

When married the wife of a Tuareg controls her personal fortune and contributes in no way to family expenses, so that almost the entire wealth in the Tuareg country is in the hands of women. Of course, this wealth consists mainly of accumulated products rather than of solid cash.

The women of the Tuareg are quite free up to a certain limit. They go where they please and do what they like without having to answer for their behaviour to their husbands; that is to say, provided their motherly duties are in no way neglected, and these they perform most willingly.

In councils of the tribe the Tuareg woman takes a leading part, and her influence in these councils is enormous. It is the Tuareg woman who makes war or peace between tribes; she is responsible for many feuds; and often, when her ambition is not satisfied with what she possesses, she is at the bottom of the raids upon passing caravans or upon weaker tribes.

Some writers maintain that the monogamy of the Tuareg dates from ancient times, and was one of the

principal reasons of their long rejecting the religion of
Islam.   One thing is certain, that it is the firm influence
women have in that country which has been able to
preserve that state of affairs.

Contrary to most migrations, the Tuareg migration
has evidently been effected from north to south.   The
tribes of the north are more civilized and stronger than
those of the south, partly because they have been in
longer contact with European civilization, partly because, having been settled in those regions for a longer
period of time, they have been able to devote themselves
to educating their young.

The pure Tuareg is a born nomad.   Raiding and his
pastoral instincts make him necessarily nomad in the
first instance, while the agricultural pursuits of his serfs
and slaves—quite unimportant—as well as the difficulty of finding wells in the desert, place a check upon
his nomadic habits, and he has to settle periodically upon
favourite pasturages and near known wells.

The average Tuareg lives under a tent, covered with
skins stretched upon a framework of wooden sticks.
These tents are easily packed or taken down, and are
carried from place to place on camels or sometimes on
oxen.   The distance travelled by Tuareg with their
paraphernalia in one day is not great—only a few miles,
probably eight or ten.   But when the Tuareg travel
light on their raiding expeditions, or in war, they will
go on continuously for two or three days, giving their
camels little rest until they have accomplished what
they wish.   Only then do they halt to rest for long
periods until their animals have recovered from the
strain.

I have not visited the Tuareg of the north, but I was

impressed with the magnificent appearance of the southern Tuareg I came across. Generally tall—some regular giants—thin, nervous and wiry in the extreme, they possessed skins as white as those of the Latin races of Southern Europe. Young people, particularly in *Targuie* families (*Targuie* being the correct way of speaking of them), were extraordinarily white.

The type was quite Caucasian : a long, oval face, spacious forehead, deep brown eyes, fairly prominent cheek-bones, a well-chiselled nose with well-defined, small nostrils, the mouth well cut, with medium-sized lips, firm enough and not unduly prominent ; the glabella (or central boss) in the supra-orbital region more prominent than the brow ridges, and the forehead as well as the entire cranium well formed, although in many cases not finely developed. The profile was convex, as with European people. The ears were small enough, with attached lobes, but somewhat lacking in delicate chiselling. Owing to their headgear pressing down upon them they were generally flat. Taking things all round, the face was of a meso-prosopic form, not unlike the Celtic type.

Like all people who take constant exercise and who live out in the open air, the Tuareg possessed beautifully white teeth of great strength, tribes in regions of the eastern part of their country excepted, where the wells frequently contained a superabundance of sodium carbonate, which had disastrous effects upon the digestion and on the liver, and was destructive to the enamel of their teeth.

It was not unusual to find persons with blue eyes among the Tuareg, although I was told that blue eyes were more frequent among the northern Tuareg than among those in the southern part of the desert. As with nearly all people who live in tropical climates, a distinct discoloration of the upper part of the iris is noticeable in the Tuareg eye. This discoloration is frequent in a slight degree with Europeans, but with people living in brilliantly-lighted countries it affects nearly one-third of the circle forming the iris. The Tuareg live in a country trying to the eyes, not only because of the powerful rays of the sun and the refraction of the light upon the yellow sand, but also because of the grains of sand which accumulate upon the eyeball during the high winds and the irritation of the caruncle thus caused. Therefore, we find that, although when young many Tuareg possess extraordinarily beautiful eyes, magnetic and velvety, they are soon injured by the above-named causes, and the eyes become dull in individuals of thirty-five to forty years of age. Cataract is frequent, and the Tuareg have no way of curing it. Myopia and ophthalmia are common in young and old ; uneven focussing of the pupil is very common, even in comparatively young people ; also uneven and independent motion of the eyeball is frequently met with, and a squint is not unusual. Blindness is prevalent.

The Tuareg possess black, smooth hair upon the scalp, and a thin black moustache and beard upon the upper lip and chin.

The body of the Tuareg is well developed, with long, well-formed limbs, muscular and not overburdened with extra flesh or fat ; the hands and feet in the purer types are delicately formed, except the big toe, which is somewhat deformed owing to the prominence caused by their footgear.

The endurance of the men is considerable, especially

in camel-riding. They can cover enormous distances on relatively small quantities of food. Their arms are not strong, but as the people are extremely supple and quick, they know how to use to advantage whatever strength they possess. The arms of Tuareg are well-rounded and absolutely lacking the abnormal muscular development which is much admired in Europe. In fact, the arms of Tuareg warriors are sometimes as delicately formed, if not more delicately, than the arms of women in many a European country. It is somewhat of a surprise to see these delicate arms brandish a sword with a vigour disastrous to their enemies, or inflict amazing wounds with their heavy spears.

The practice of spear-hurling and their sword exercises are to a certain extent responsible for the strikingly dignified bearing of Tuareg men. They are at once recognizable among less noble and distinguished tribesmen. Their slow, grave movements; their long, firm steps upon the broad-soled sandals they wear when walking upon the sand; their characteristic, gentle swing of the arms, and the head carried high in sign of defiance; their quiet, slow way of talking, are indeed most impressive when you first come across the better types of Tuareg. It is seldom that one finds weaklings among them, as these people lead a hard life and only the strong and healthy survive.

There are many qualities of the Tuareg which commend themselves to Englishmen. We will not speak of their bravery, which is proverbial. A guest of the Tuareg must be defended at all costs and against anybody—a quality which has so far rendered possible whatever commerce has gone through the Sahara desert. The word of the Tuareg is his bond, and it would be difficult to find on the surface of the globe people more faithful to their promises than these veiled men of the desert. It is true that in return they exact, by force if necessary, the rigorous accomplishment of promises made to them by others. In order to be certain that he will fulfil any promise he makes, the Tuareg is always careful to undertake much less than he is really able to do, always relying on a good reserve, as he does in battle when fighting an enemy.

The real Tuareg fights his enemy in the noblest of ways. He never poisons his spears nor his arrows, and disdains to carry firearms. He looks upon them as being weapons of treachery. With them, he says, you can kill your enemy without being seen and run no danger to yourself.

As any friend can trust a Tuareg, the Tuareg in his turn trusts his friends without reserve. For instance, when a man goes on a long and dangerous journey, he has no compunction in leaving his wife and family under the protection of a neighbour, who is expected to defend them—and does defend them—from affront. It is in distress that the moral qualities of individuals can be better gauged than under normal conditions, and I was always much struck by the patience, fortitude and resignation of Tuareg under such circumstances.

Of course, we Europeans, the English and French particularly, as well as our cousins in the United States, have curious notions regarding slavery. Perhaps slaves of white people have been cruelly ill-treated, but slavery in Africa is different. In the case of Tuareg nobles, their kindness towards faithful slaves and serfs has no bounds. Indeed, if one felt induced to make a comparison between the way slaves are treated in the Tuareg country and the way some servants are treated to-day in England, we should find that the Tuareg would be fully justified in sending missions over to teach lessons in kindness and goodness of heart to some people of Great Britain. Slaves in the Tuareg country partake of the food of their master as well as sharing anything he possesses, and they divide with him and his family the joys and griefs and the many vicissitudes of life.

The Tuareg carries on commerce and raids in combination, but he has no corresponding industrial capacity, although to a certain extent he is ingenious enough with the materials which he possesses. These materials are usually imported, as no primary substances worth mentioning are to be found on the spot. Leather articles, such as saddles, harness, pouches, etc., are made by them with some artistic skill.

The Tuareg have been frequently described as "the brigands or thieves of the desert," but these thieves are, as a matter of fact, more honest than a great many honest people nearer home. If goods or money are confided to a Tuareg they are as safe as, or safer than, if they were deposited in a bank vault. He will on no account dispose of them, and will guard them more jealously than if they belonged to him. You can lend money to a Tuareg on his word only and no security, without witnesses present, and he will never fail to return it. He has been known to travel for two or three months to reach the person who had lent it to him, and if he himself cannot do so his children or some of his relatives will do it for him. He is not unlike the Chinese in that respect.

When I say this I am not speaking of the disguised gifts which the Tuareg frequently ask from strangers, whether traders or travellers, as loans in order to protect them while passing through their country, and which are understood to be actual presents.

If you treat a Tuareg fairly he will never betray you. I myself have employed Tuareg in my caravan, and I have never in all my travels in any part of the world met with more faithful, hard-working and thoughtful followers. They carried out their contract with me to the letter, and, having well explained to them in the beginning what I required of them, I never once had occasion to find fault with them. Cool and collected at all times and in any circumstances, dignified in all their doings, they were ever ready and apparently delighted to obey, although when I had these men in my employ we were making forced marches across the desert, which was very trying for them and the animals. These Tuareg had no rodomontade about them ; they never showed fear, although the country we crossed when they were with me was in a disturbed state, and their thoughtful manner was indeed quite refreshing after the brutal treatment one received from nearly all black tribesmen closer to the equator.

Even when the Tuareg goes on raids to capture an enemy's cattle, he would never dream of appropriating the baggage or merchandise left on the road by a caravan in distress. As for actual theft among themselves, or abuse of confidence, I do not believe that even the words exist in the Tuareg language. If the words do exist they can certainly never be used in relation to Tuareg themselves. The Tuareg are frank and truthful, and I am told that if by chance an escaping criminal were caught by his own tribesmen, he would at once confess his crime, although he well knew his life to be at stake.

Let us examine Tuareg camps. As I have said, the Tuareg are nomads with pastoral habits. In a way, we find some analogy between these people and nomad Arab tribes of neighbouring regions in the desert. The Tuareg have two kinds of camps—the stationary or semi-stationary camps and the marching camps. The *amezzagh* is the name they give to a great camp ; the *erheuen* is a small camp. The stationary camps are generally selected near good pasture lands and where sufficient water can be obtained from wells.

The Tuareg make themselves some fine tents of straw or reed matting, or more frequently of skins dyed red, or of woollen material, not unlike in shape to the Arab *kheima*, only somewhat smaller. The nobler people inhabit these tents, but the serfs usually improvise for themselves huts or sheds thatched over with grass. The tents are usually constructed in a circle in groups of five to ten or twelve, according to the number of families they are to contain. Within these circles the animals they possess are kept at night.

Inside the tent one does not find elaborate furniture, and all one can see are a tanned skin spread in the centre as a dinner-cloth, on which are placed various bowls, iron vessels, gourds, etc., used by the Tuareg during their meals ; a dromedary cage or two, the *takkauit*, cages covered with a cloth, used by Tuareg ladies when *en voyage*, and camel-saddles.

These riding saddles, perched up on the top in the fore part of a camel's hump, over which they are raised upon a small wooden pillar, are not unlike a wooden soup-plate with a high cross in front and a tall piece of wood behind. They are called the *ataram*. The legs of the rider are supposed to be gracefully crossed on the camel's neck,

A portion of Author's caravan arriving at Tamaske French Sudan) (Showing Tuareg riding-saddle.

when they can reach that far, as the saddle is stirrupless. The saddles are held in position by a girdle, a chest string and a back fastening which catches the camel just under the front part of the hind leg. Ornamental leather is stretched upon them, but it is difficult to imagine a less practical and more torturing saddle than these. I rode on one of these saddles for nearly a thousand kilometres, and suffered constantly up to the last minute of my journey as much as I did when I first got on it. The Tuareg themselves say that these saddles are made on purpose to hurt the rider, as the Tuareg generally march during the night, and were it not for the excruciating pain which they have to endure when upon their animals they might fall asleep and be caught in ambush by inimical tribes. Whether this is the case or not I cannot say, but certainly, if that is not the reason why the Tuareg have made such absurd riding saddles, I am at a loss to find a better explanation. The saddles injure the back of the camel to no small extent on long journeys. They are most difficult to keep in their right position upon the camel's hump, and if one of the three strings which make it fast gives way, you have a spill from the height at which you are perched that you are not likely to forget in a hurry.

Another kind of saddle is the *arhazer*, copied, I think, from the Arabs.

CHAPTER XXV.

ONE of the things which astonished me most among the Tuareg, and even more among the lower tribes in Central Africa, was the wonderful knowledge of local botany these people possessed, and the richness in their languages of words for each plant. The Tuareg, being more civilized and more observant, have an extraordinarily rich vocabulary in that direction, and it was amazing to me to see how the Tuareg in my employ at once identified the most minute plants found in the desert, and could tell me without the slightest hesitation the evil or good properties of each plant ; the kind of soil on which you generally found it ; which produced fruit and what kind of fruit, poisonous or edible. In order to prevent possible fraud in their statements, I frequently asked them over and over again the name and properties of each plant when I detected it a second or third time in different regions. The Tuareg always told me right, and they invariably repeated the same statements for each plant.

The Tuareg have also a good deal of unconscious geological knowledge—a knowledge which has been gained, I believe, greatly by long experience in digging wells in the desert in order to obtain drinking water. They are wonderful people for locating spots where water is to be found without the difficulty of digging a well, and they show remarkable observation in examining the various strata, especially the stratum preceding the one where water is reached.

We civilized people pride ourselves on our telegraphs, telephones and wireless telegraphy, but anyone who has travelled in Africa or Asia away from civilized centres will tell you of the marvellous way in which news is transmitted great distances with accuracy and at an incredible rapidity without any apparatus being used for such transmission. The Tuareg are particularly good in this respect. In many cases, of course, tidings travel quickly by word of mouth from tribe to tribe. But these tribes also possess a method of thought transference, perhaps because they have learned the power of intense concentration. Many of these people were unconsciously adepts at telepathy. The desert seemed particularly well adapted for telepathic communication.

Duveyrier tells of interesting hallucinations which he observed among the Tuareg of the north, especially in women under mental strain. When their beloved sons or husbands were on a journey to distant lands, the women went to pray heartily on their ancestors' tombs. Immediately afterwards they retired to sleep, when the invoked *Idebni* appeared to them and either gave them the news required—which the Tuareg said always turned out to be quite accurate—or, if displeased, would give no answer but would strangle the praying women. This is quite curious, as it would seem as if a sort of mental telepathy were established, leaving out the additional superstition—at any rate, among people either closely related or fond of one another. The strangling part of the communication, according to the Tuareg, would generally take place in case of disaster or similar causes, which irritated *Idebni*.

The Tuareg, with their constant marching at night, have become students of the stars, and in their own way were well versed in astronomy. Naturally they applied their own doings to the movements of planets ; for instance, an eclipse was for them only a raid of one planet upon another.

It was interesting to notice that the Tuareg was well able to determine the exact local noontime by planting a vertical rod in the sand and calculating the length of the shadow. Similarly, when a Tuareg wanted to know the exact time of day, he not only looked at the sun to judge of its height above the horizon, but would first look at the sun and then at his own shadow to establish a further accuracy in his observation.

In the way of religion, as I have said, the Tuareg have nominally adopted the Mussulman religion, but they are not observant of the strict laws of the Koran. They have no mosques in their country, no *Imam*, or High Priest, and no *Mufti*. They still cling to a great many of their superstitions, some of which are interesting. One finds a cross on nearly all articles made by the Tuareg. There is a cross as a pummel on their saddles; cross ornamentations are visible upon their clothes ; the hilts of their swords are cross-shaped ; crosses can be seen on their shields, in their alphabet, on the tattoo on the back of the hand, as well as on the tattoo upon their foreheads. There is a good deal of controversy regarding the origin of the Tuareg cross, and I think it might be unwise for me to go into it in the present work, although I may entertain my own ideas upon the subject.

It is curious to note that the Tuareg firmly believe in the spirits of the mountains, as well as in the spirits of the oases. It is not uncommon in the desert to strike rocky places where the wind and water have worn the rocks into fantastic shapes. These places, the Tuareg say, are the haunts of evil spirits. They will on no account approach these spots, which they avoid by making great détours on their journeys.

They call their only god *Amanaï*, and *Iblis* is their reigning devil. According to the great authority, Duveyrier, the northern Tuareg speak of a heaven, *Adjenna*, and of a hell or last fire, the *Timsi-tan-Elakhart*.

Duveyrier says that the Tuareg of the north also speak of other genii, human in form, but with additional horns, a long coat of hair on the body and a tail. These are *Alhin* or *Alhinen*.

I always found the Tuareg reluctant in giving information on these spirits, but they were all unanimous in asserting their existence. Indeed, they often gave trouble in life. In fact, it was but seldom that a Tuareg could be persuaded to sleep under a solid roof, as they attributed all illnesses to these evil spirits. They entertained an idea that they might be imprisoned under the roof by these devils and never escape alive. This was to a certain extent due to the feeling of suffocation experienced by all people who live in the open air when entering a building.

They believe in sorcerers who, by certain exorcisms, can cure most evils, and who by their friendship with good and evil spirits can at will change men into beasts and beasts into men. The *Aissaua*, who claim the ability to charm vipers, might be classed among these magicians.

It is because of these superstitions that the Tuareg are simply laden with charms and amulets upon the arms, head, neck, chest and round the waist, in order to be preserved from accident or misfortune, but not to escape death. Most of these charms are in the shape of leather satchels more or less ornamented, or else small metal cases strung together which contain verses from the Koran or cabalistic signs.

The marabu do a great trade in these amulets, which they spend all their time in manufacturing. There are, of course, various kinds of amulets : some designed to fulfil the wishes of the possessor; others to bring everlasting happiness, others to protect from illness ; yet another kind to be used as a lightning protector, a fifth kind to keep away all sorts of evil spirits, a sixth to bring victory in battle, etc., etc. In fact, the marabu make these charms to order, and get what they like for them from the credulous Tuareg.

There are, of course, no native scientific doctors in the country, but one finds medicine-men. Besides, nearly all natives think they know of treatments for the ill-nesses common in the region—such as ophthalmia, intermittent fever, smallpox, rheumatism, skin diseases, the very troublesome guinea-worm, which bores long channels under the skin, and the *bouri*, a kind of violent madness common among the lower classes, such as slaves and serfs.

Among the affections of the skin, some are traceable to the worst of hereditary venereal complaints; others are caused by local climatic conditions; others by parasites which find their way into the skin. Among the most common is the itch, which the Tuareg profess is contracted from camels. They nearly all suffer from it, many in quite a repulsive degree. Only a few are free. It begins at the joints, generally at the elbow and under the knee, as well as between the fingers. Whether the camels got it from the Tuareg or the Tuareg from the camels I do not know, but it is certain that you cannot get on a camel in the Tuareg country, even with all precautions, without running a great risk of contracting this unpleasant complaint. The camels of my own caravan had it too, and I had a great deal of trouble to keep free from it. It is true that the form of itch found in the desert is not of such a virulent kind as that found in Europe. Strong carbolic soap and strong solutions of permanganate of potash proved beneficial for the treatment of my men. The Tuareg say that camels can never be cured of the itch, but in the case of men they believe that the sting of scorpions—when it does not kill the patient—invariably cures him of the tiresome complaint.

A kind of herpes is occasionally found among the Tuareg, an inflammation of the skin in red patches. Ulcers and watery blisters appear at the joints of the fingers. From the latter I also suffered while crossing the desert.

Leprosy of the anæsthetic and sometimes of the tubercular type is to be found among the lower classes, especially with those tribes living closer to the Niger. Leprosy is not looked upon as infectious; lepers live like other people, and even marry non-lepers if they have a chance.

Lupus is not so frequent except in a mild form, but ulcers inside the nose are common enough, and occasionally take a virulent form. The natives attribute the latter to the sand, but in addition I think the bad condition of their blood is responsible for them, as well as the breathing of vitiated air from camels' lungs, emitted during the process of rumination.

Long journeys on camels are also responsible for three more nasty complaints of the Tuareg: hernia, both inguinal and umbilical, frequently congenital, but more often acquired; rheumatism, with its usual resulting deformities of the hands, feet and knees; and renal and vesicular calculus, which frequently forms in those who spend much of their time on camels.

Insanity is common, frequently taking the form of melancholia and monomania, with proclivities towards suicide. The Tuareg know of no remedy for insanity, the lunatics moving about with other people, except in cases when they become violent, when they are fastened with ropes and beaten.

As is the case with many Asiatic and African tribes, fire is used as a remedy, and often with considerable success, especially in snake bites or scorpion stings. The Tuareg tie the injured limb tightly with a ligature and apply the fire cure to the injured spot. Occasionally, in cases of the richer people, an extraordinary remedy is used : a sheep or a goat is seized, and the poisoned spot placed in immediate contact with an open wound inflicted on the animal, as the Tuareg believe that the blood of a healthy animal will absorb the poison.

Tubercular diseases are rare among the Tuareg living far in the desert, but not so with those living nearer the water. Abdominal diseases, complaints of the liver and of the kidneys, are frequent; also nervous and mental diseases, such as convulsions, paralysis and idiocy.

Many are affected by the worst of complaints of the blood, in most cases hereditary, but this terrible com-

plaint is in no way so general as with the black tribes
further south. I think that their life in the desert with
the powerful sun as a disinfectant has to a certain extent
stamped the disease out of the country, and it never
shows itself in such a violent form as in more tropical
zones.

The Guinea-worm, as you know, is a small tape-like
parasite which bores its way under the skin, generally
on the legs, and gradually becomes of great length. It
is easily recognizable by the swelling of the skin all along
its subcutaneous passage. Occasionally one of these
parasites will get to other parts of the body, or even into
the head. The latex of the *Calotropis procera*, a tall
plant, also used as a purgative by the natives, is said to
kill the parasite. A more frequent cure consists in
making an incision in the skin, seizing the end of the
worm and slowly twisting it round a small stick, the
twist being slowly repeated day after day until the entire
worm has been drawn out. Great care must be taken
not to tear it, or else, they say, the worm proceeds to
escape in the opposite direction under the skin, causing
intense pain to the afflicted person.

For people living in the desert, the diet of the Tuareg
is quite varied. Dates, figs, millet, onions, a few wild
vegetables, milk, butter, cheese, gum from the *Acacia
Arabica*, grain and flour are much relished by them.
Among the delicacies are worms and locusts, the latter
salted and preserved in oil, a great dainty for the people
of the desert. Meat is generally roasted or made into a
stew, the heart and liver of animals being eaten by men
only, possibly with the idea of giving them additional
strength and courage in war. Unlike most Mussulmans,
the Tuareg eat with their wives, and what is best of

their food they give to their women. Milk may be said to be the most essential food of the Tuareg at all periods, but although they will eat almost anything else, they will not touch fish, nor flesh nor eggs of sacred birds. The few marabu in the country will partake of any food not forbidden by the Koran.

On the march the Tuareg often uses the *kola* nut, which is quite expensive, and is imported from the south. He shows great firmness in abstaining from food or drink when taking exercise. On his long marches the Tuareg only eats once in twenty-four hours, always at night ; but when settled anywhere he generally has two meals a day. The belt-tightening process is well known by the Tuareg when hungry and unable to satisfy his appetite.

The Tuareg are fond of tea and coffee, which are drunk by the richer men. All more or less make use of imported tobacco.

The Tuareg, while alive, never washes his person nor his clothes, which are full of parasites, in water, but he never looks dirty. Even his religious ablutions are made with sand, or else by rubbing face and hands with sand-stone. Only when dead is the Tuareg's body washed by his relations with hot water and garbed in clean clothes.

The funeral is more or less in the Mussulman fashion, and the body is buried. The relations of the deceased do not cry or make any fuss about the loss of the departed, but as soon as the burial ceremony is over a feast is offered to his friends, and from that moment they all endeavour to efface from their memory the remembrance of their lost friend. The encampment is abandoned and another site selected. For this reason one never hears of a Tuareg being called " So-and-so's son," as living on the memory of ancestors is quite out of the line of a Tuareg.

In ordinary life the Tuareg who can afford it dye their arms and hands with indigo to prevent the action of the sun upon the skin, but also, I think, to allay the irritation caused by itch or inflammation of the skin. The women occasionally smear the face with ochre.

We find among the Tuareg the habit so common in many parts of Northern Africa of delicately applying by means of a small rod (the *tafendit*) a thin layer of sulphate of antimony to the eyelids to add expression and luminosity to the eyes. This habit, common also to many people of Asia, has been frequently described as necessary in order to preserve the eye from the strong glare of the sun. Personally, I never saw that it was used for that purpose, and always heard from the natives themselves that it was only a fashion adopted in order to add beauty and sentiment to the expression of the face.

The Tuareg men generally shaved the head, except for a bristly comb which they kept over the top of the skull. They called this the *ahoggot*. According to them it served the double purpose of leaving a ventilating space between their head-covering and the skull, and of providing after death a suitable hold for angels to haul them up to heaven.

Following the Mussulman custom, male children were circumcised. Marriages were celebrated in the usual Mussulman fashion, the ceremony being presided over by marabu, the people abandoning themselves to songs, dancing, and sports on their camels, before and after the ceremony.

In their assemblies, called the *mia'ad*, the Tuareg, usually of two tribes, sit in two semicircles facing each other, and, after swearing at the devil that he may not give evil advice, tribal matters are discussed with diplomatic skill, strengthened here and there by fierce threats. Men under forty years of age are not admitted to discuss or control public affairs, but women have a great deal to say in these matters, and they often incite their men to deeds of bravery, improvised music and poetry of more or less refined quality being used in the process.

The visual acuity of the Tuareg is fair but not extraordinary, and, as I have said, the vision even when good is rapidly injured by the abnormal conditions of their life in the desert. The strain of night marching should be added to the other causes I have enumerated. The hearing of the Tuareg is, taking things all round, more acute than their sight, and they are able to distinguish sounds at great distances, a sense which serves them well in their raiding expeditions.

The strategy of Tuareg in surprising the enemy is good, scouts being selected from among their most intelligent men, who play an important part in tracking the enemy. In battle the men fight from the height of their camels, their throwing-spears being used first, and fighting *corps-à-corps* with their swords coming later. The fights of a most violent character are long, but few are killed or wounded, owing to their extraordinary skill in defending themselves. To show the typical shrewdness of the Tuareg, it is sufficient to say that, when surprised in camp, flight is generally preferred to fight. The Tuareg takes no odds, and he prefers to abandon his baggage and goods, arranging for a suitable revenge when convenient. Friendly tribes willingly join in these expeditions, and owing to the facility of tracking one's enemies in the desert and the necessity of stopping at wells and grazing grounds to feed up one's animals, it is an easy matter to catch up the enemy and recover the baggage.

The language of the Tuareg has many dialects with many notable variations, the Tuareg of the south having adopted a number of useful words from the negroid races of Central Africa. One of the most notable differences is that the Tuareg of the north use in their language the aspirate "h," and those of the south replace it by "ch" or by a "z."

Although the spoken language is practically different with each large division of Tuareg, the written characters of the *Temacheq* language in general use are the same in all tribes.

Only women can read and write in the Tuareg country. They teach the young, whereas the men are almost invariably illiterate.

Duveyrier, in speaking of the Tuareg of the north, says that both *Tefinagh* in the north and *Temacheq* in the south can be written either vertically or horizontally, or from right to left, or *vice versâ*, either like Arabic or Hebrew. Characters can be written in any position. I think this statement is based mostly on some inscriptions which he found in the desert upon rocks as well as upon weapons, shields or ornaments. The Tuareg are also given to occasionally ornamenting rocks with allegorical scenes. But I think perhaps that, although Duveyrier was absolutely correct in his observation and actually found the characters turned in any direction, it was due to the ignorance of the Tuareg writer rather than to an actual rule in Tuareg graphology. But I am not sufficiently versed in the Tuareg written language to decide this point definitely.

The Tuareg alphabet seemed to me somewhat inadequate, even for local literary wants, and, in fact, their more serious books were invariably written in Arabic. Their calendar and divisions of the year were practically the same as with the Arabs, their *azhoum* corresponding to the Arabic *ramadam*.

One of the most typical habits of the Tuareg is the wearing of a veil over the face, which has gained them the name of *Ahel-el-litham*, or "people of the veil," or the Arabic name of *Molathemin*, " the veiled." This veil is worn at all times by the Tuareg, and they never remove it either to eat or to sleep, when at home or on a journey. Only the eyes are visible, the other parts of the face being hidden by the turban and by the *litham*. Nobody seems to know exactly the origin of this habit, or the reason why it has not only been kept up by the Tuareg, but has been copied by many other tribes in the Niger valley and all over the desert. Some people say that it is because the brigand-like Tuareg do not wish to be recognized by their enemies; others maintain that the Tuareg hide the nose and mouth to prevent the fine sand from entering their lungs ; others, more scientific, say that it is in order to keep moisture at the entrance of the respiratory organs in a climate where the atmosphere is so extremely dry. Personally, I think all these theories are inaccurate, and I believe it is nothing more nor less than a fashion, as the women of the Tuareg, for instance, never wear a veil at all, and they seem in excellent health. Tuareg never remove the veil from their faces even to meet friends or relations, and were it done among themselves it would be considered an insult.

There are "white-veiled" and "black-veiled" Tuareg. The white-faced Tuareg of Caucasian type,

Tuaregs with their typical face screens.

particularly the noble classes, have entirely adopted the black veil ; whereas, for the sake of contrast, I suppose, the lower and blacker people generally put on a white veil. It is because of the colour of the veil, and not because of the colour of the skin, that the Arabs call the serfs "White Tuareg" and the nobles "Black Tuareg," although, as we have seen, the face of the White Tuareg is black and the face of the Black Tuareg is white.

The veil covers the lower part of the face, the back of the head, the temples and the forehead, the portion covering the forehead taking the name of *itelli*.

There is little difference in the costume of the Tuareg all over the desert. The men wear a long white cotton shirt, the *tikamist*, or else an ample blouse, the *refirha*, over large trousers (the *karteba*). Over the *tikamist* is the *tikamist kore*, an over-garment of indigo-blue, decorated with simple but artistic embroideries. A kamarband of blue cotton, the *tamentika*, is worn at the waist. The women wear two or three long blouses tied at the waist by a red woollen sash; the hair is made into tresses and covered over with a piece of cloth, the *ikar-hay*. Their chief ornaments are metal rings, glass bracelets and beads. The children in the Tuareg country wear one great ring of metal, horn or wood.

The most characteristic ornament of Tuareg men (except the marabu) is the green serpentine marble armlet, which they wear from the tenderest years and which is never removed. It is on the right arm, and is kept there in order to brace up the strength while striking a blow with the sword, and also to be used in hand-to-hand fights as a means of striking mortal blows on the enemy's temples. The Oelimmiden and the Azdjer are the manufacturers of these bracelets.

The Tuareg in general do not work, although there are a few *inat* (smiths), who make and repair spears and swords, and the *sefel*, who can skilfully tan and dye skins.

The *telak*, which is a typical Tuareg weapon, consists of a long, flat dagger fixed to a large wristlet, and carried along the lower face of the left arm, reaching from the tips of the fingers to the elbow. The sheaths of these daggers are generally of green stamped leather with silver fastenings and ornamentations.

This dagger is used as an auxiliary to a heavy, long sword slung over the shoulder, the *takoba*, which cuts on both sides, and has a straight, long blade. A nobleman of the Tuareg country is not supposed to carry firearms, although occasionally he may carry a beautiful rifle which has been presented to him by a friend. The *imrhad* are the carriers of most of the weapons, such as the spears, about three yards long, made entirely of iron with side barbs at the point ; and the throwing-spears, with a wooden shaft and also a barbed point. In battle the *imrhad* occupy the front rank. Disc-shaped shields, of antelope hide, are used in battle, and among the southern tribes of Tuareg a bow and iron-pointed arrows are sometimes used.

The footgear of the Tuareg is extremely sensible, and takes the shape of a solid sandal with extra broad soles held firm to the foot by well-placed straps between the big toe and the next and at the instep. These sandals are very practical for walking on the sand. At Kano, in British Nigeria, a great leather market, the shoes, called *irhattimen*, are manufactured in quantities, and are much used by the Tuareg.

Transmissible property is divided by the Tuareg

into legitimate and illegitimate. Legitimate property acquired by individual work or inherited is quite sacred, and includes such things as money, weapons, purchased slaves, flocks of sheep, camels, provisions, crops, property acquired by raids, by force, or by taxes exacted from passing travellers and caravans. In the second are included the "tribute for protection," the *imrhad*, or rights over serfs; territorial rights and right of command. At the death of the head of the family all legitimate property is dívided into equal parts among the children. The illegitimate rights, which only apply to the noble classes, descend entirely to the eldest son of the eldest sister, in order to ensure the transmission of blood.

The law among the Tuareg is simple enough, and the punishments simpler still. Flogging and fines are inflicted for smaller crimes, and for graver misdeeds the parents of the injured person can apply their own punishment, on the favourite principle of "an eye for an eye, a tooth for a tooth," and so on.

CHAPTER XXVI.

THE French are doing all they can to develop the country. I am informed that a telegraph line with iron posts is to be made shortly from the Niger to Zinder, and later it may be pushed on as far as Lake Tchad.

Having stayed a whole day with Colonel Lamolle, who was on a journey of inspection in this country, at the small sheds of Kornaka, I left on September 28th, passing over undulating country, and in the morning marched twenty-three kilometres to Amonkaye Ourroua, where hardly any water was to be found. The trail became bad, with large pools of rain-water in two places filling depressions. There were undulations, and in places deep grooves had been cut into the trail by passing caravans where the sand had subsequently been hardened by the action of rain and sun-heat. Tuareg caravans have as many as three or four hundred animals sometimes.

My camels had the greatest difficulty in proceeding along these grooves and crossing the pools. When we arrived at Korema Alba, twenty-seven kilometres further west, we found the village abandoned and the camping-place fallen down.

In some of the valleys there were thorny plants and palm-trees. Further on we proceeded over hilly country, positively hills and not dunes.

Kankara, where we arrived at one o'clock in the morning, after having marched through the night, was a fine oasis of palms. From this point we were troubled by thorny plants in profusion, which tore one's clothes as the camels made their way between them. For desert plants, they reached a considerable height.

Between Kankara and Amaschi we had first come over a few undulations, then over level country. At sunrise on September 30th we left Amaschi. A few kilometres west of camp, from the crest of an undulation, I obtained a view of a hill-range of some height. It was a dune of gigantic proportions eroded here and there into well-rounded banks and hills, but connected in the north-western portion, and extending as a mass in a general direction from south-west to north-east Looking back towards the east we had an immense stretch of flat horizon-line with only a high hill-mass rising prominently on the south-west, and some lower distant conical hills to the south.

On September 30th we arrived at the post of Guidam Bado, in charge of a French sergeant. The fort of Guidam Bado presented an imposing appearance, standing as it did on a rocky height, and with rocky hills forming a picturesque background. For some miles before reaching this post, loose stones and great boulders of volcanic rock were to be found, and after going over a hilly region this rock became plentiful.

I left that same afternoon by way of a high rocky pass on the hills to the north-west. The camels climbed the steep incline with difficulty, and experienced more difficulty still in descending on the other side, where stones rolled under their feet and they slipped and stumbled. I was severely hurt when my camel stumbled down the steep incline and fell, the back plate of the Tuareg saddle hitting my spine with terrific force and causing intense pain. It so happened that the piece of wood struck my spinal column exactly at a spot where I had sustained severe injuries in Tibet some years previously. From this moment marching became extremely painful, and it was all I could do to keep on the saddle.

After climbing the first hill-range I found myself at the summit upon a flat plateau, on descending from which we crossed a plain; then we climbed over a second steep hill-range, similar to the first, with another plateau on the summit. Beyond, at a lower elevation, we reached the camp of Deoulé.

On October 1st another rocky pass had to be negotiated, the camels giving us endless bother up and down these inclines. After that, fortunately, the trail became fairly flat and good. Camp Laba, forty-three kilometres from Guidam Bado, was reached, with its village of one hundred and fifty huts in a sinuosity of the hills. The entire valley of Laba was encircled by hills.

We were caught in a tornado in the afternoon. On resuming our march the ground was extremely slippery and made marching painful, the camels stumbling all the time and slipping on the bad trail.

We went along intricate sandy beds of torrents, where during the night we lost our way and wasted considerable time until we struck a village called Mansalla, and, later, one called Tarrawadda, reaching Onagher at midnight. From Onagher the trail was quite good again. We were now in a region of elongated, flat-topped tablelands. Marching in a north-north-westerly direction, we followed one of these, which was not unlike a huge dune south of the trail. The exact direction of this dune was south-east to north-west. Then we crossed over a rocky pass, and proceeded along another huge dune north of us, this one north-east to south-west.

We arrived at camp Tamaské at noon, the village being situated in a charming nook upon the hillside with two other villages, Jiankarata and Samangheda (west of Tamaské). The elevation of Tamaské north-east, close to the rest-house, was 1,450 feet. Tamaské stood on a prominence, and was protected by a bastion and watch-tower. A most beautiful view over the entire valley was obtained from this high point. In the village close by were visible the elongated domed roofs of huts, beautifully constructed, and rising above circular walls made of alternate layers of mud and stone. The roof was built separately upon the ground, and then raised bodily upon the structure, the entire population taking part in lifting it up.

The chief, with a picturesque sword attached to a bracelet upon his wrist in Tuareg style, came to pay his salaams, a habit common to all these villagers as soon as one arrived.

Sometimes we were able to purchase milk, chickens and eggs. Chickens fetched from twopence to threepence each, the eggs about threepence a dozen. Unfortunately, the natives had a way of keeping eggs for weeks, and they were generally bad.

Late in the afternoon we were again on the march. From the rocky hill-range north-west of us we obtained a panoramic view of the plain we had crossed on the south. In its eastern part the plain showed three distinct dunes, two of which were almost parallel to each other, with headlands towards the south-west. The direction of the dunes was north-east to south-west.

We found another extensive flat plateau on the top of this hill-range. We crossed it and descended beyond by a steep trail into a comparatively flat valley, only to climb another steep hill later on, to yet another plateau with many large villages upon it, collectively called Kalfu (elevation, 1,550 feet).

It was 10 p.m. when we arrived, and as I was greatly in need of provisions, the whole town was awakened by the sound of drums, the chief taking special delight in rousing everybody in order to obtain chickens and eggs for my men.

On leaving Kalfu we went along the plateau, which was quite flat; then by an extremely rocky descent we went down into another plain. Three hours later we were climbing up to another rocky table-land, again quite flat on the summit for some kilometres, where we found the village of Polema (1,500 feet).

At sunset of October 3rd I arrived at the French post of Taua, in charge of Lieutenant Edouard Bigolet. The post was built in Gothic style of mud and palm-tree rafters, with tidy quarters, consisting of a lot of little square houses, regular and clean, on its eastern side, for the Senegalese *tirailleurs*. (Elevation, 1,270 feet.)

South-west of the post was a large village of six thousand inhabitants. The post itself was built on a small hill and had outer rest-houses for travellers. In the market enclosure traders were often to be seen from British Sokoto, from which place there was a direct route to Taua, *viâ* Mogher, Illela, Danfora, Kurfey, Konni, Torkei, and Godebaoa, 186 kilometres altogether. The trail ran almost due south from the new frontier at N'kara Talle.

Traders generally came for the Sunday markets.

An enterprising French trader was transacting business here. This post was generally in charge of a captain, but as that officer had been sent to Bilma it was now in charge of a lieutenant.

I left Taua in the evening of October 5th, on a good new road from five to ten yards wide, travelling over undulating ground, and arrived at Magher at 11.10 at night.

On October 6th, when we left, I had before me to the south-west—the trail followed a southerly direction here —a long table-land in four flat-topped terraces (south-east to north-west), with quite a high hill at its north-western end. There were also a number of conical hills and a distant plateau in the far background to the west. The high hill was formerly a continuation of the range, and formed in reality a fifth terrace. It had evidently been separated from the range by erosion of wind and water. On the circle formerly drawn at a radius of a hundred miles from Sokoto we passed a roughly-made cairn indicating the Franco-British frontier. Part of this circle has now been ceded by Great Britain to France. I entered the circle, marching almost due south, then slightly west, until I arrived at Illela, a large village forty-seven kilometres from Taua, (elevation 1,070 feet).

The Haussa who lived here constructed high-domed store-houses of mud for millet, these huge receptacles having an aperture at the top, with a removable cover of mats or of thatch. Another aperture was also made on the side in order to allow an entrance to the store and also for ventilation. Others of these store-houses were cylindrical or hemispherical, others not unlike gigantic ink-bottles. All of these were raised about one foot above the ground and rested on stone supports.

By six o'clock in the afternoon we had reached the hill-range to the west. We were now encircled by flat-topped, isolated hills. Before us to the south-west we could count as many as six or seven of these curiously-shaped mounts. West of us there was the long unin-terrupted line of a plateau. To the north (we were now going west), almost in the centre of the basin we were crossing, stood a conical hill, behind which could be seen another long plateau. To the north-west in the distance were hills with less-marked characteristics, their summits being more broken up into irregular shapes. We passed close to a high dome-like hill to the south. In this basin the steamy heat was suffo-cating. Only low shrubs seemed to grow there.

We reached Agurmi by the side of two hills at 10 p.m. On our next march, due south, we had before us a hilly barrier much eroded and divided into three principal sections and some minor ones.

We passed through the good-sized village of Dongoua, with its enormous store-houses, and afterwards perceived to the north-west nine horizontal sections of cones rising sheer from the flat. Several others had tops slightly more rounded. All around us in the distance could be seen more of these peculiarly-shaped fragments of cones.

On the north slope of a rocky hill we came to a fair-sized village, and after rising upon a dune formed by accumulations of sand north of the village, we descended into a deep hollow where wells were to be found, close to the rest-house of Durereh. One or two Tuareg caravans, with hundreds of oxen and camels laden with cotton goods, were passed on the way.

Gongufema was reached late at night, a poor village

of three hundred inhabitants, with no trade of any kind. There was a small post here in charge of a non-commissioned officer with four *tirailleurs*.

Having rested but two hours during the night at this place, I proceeded once more on the tedious march, over uninteresting country with thick shrub and high grass all along.

A herd of a hundred half-wild oxen afforded amusement when they charged my camels and kept circling round us at a gallop—now boarding us on one side, then on the other. The camels looked first perplexed, then, for lack of a better remedy, they all sat down.

Dimkin (1,050 feet) was reached by noon. No more hills were near except a small range to the north and a small rocky, isolated hill on the left of the trail.

On October 9th we had a long plateau to the south-west in the distance, and smaller sections of this plateau extending south. Three hillocks in a group were to be seen near Kauara, where we arrived at noon. The wells in this part of the desert were either dry altogether or else the water was brackish and quite fetid.

I met here a company of Senegalese soldiers bound for the Kanem, under Captain Jérusalémy. These men had made a wonderful march across the *boucle* of the Niger during the rainy season when the country was swampy. Although one of the French officers and a sergeant had died from the terrific hardships, most of the soldiers and the surviving officer seemed in excellent condition.

We crossed the hill-range we had perceived in the morning to the south-west, and we found on the top of it a flat plateau. By nine in the evening we had arrived at Tongana. The two marches between Gongufema and

Tongana were troublesome. On one march of forty-five kilometres we did not find a drop of water. All the time we were compelled to carry water on our camels, as we never knew whether we might find the wells dry.

On October 10th I enjoyed my march a little more, although I was still in intense pain owing to the injury to my spine. We were again on undulating country until we descended by a very steep and rocky path from the flat highland to which we had climbed the previous night. A gorgeous panoramic view of the great flat expanse to the south-west and a high, flat-topped barrier to the south opened before us, with great black boulders in the immediate foreground. To the west-south-west was a group of cones, with whitish summits above a stratum of rich red. By the side stood a three-peaked hill of a similar formation.

This group demonstrated clearly enough the process of erosion which goes on in that part of the district. The cones at the southern terminus of the dune were of a light yellow in the lower stratum. The top layer of red earth had been eroded at the sides, chiefly by the action of water in this particular part. The line of sun-baked rock and the part of the stratum which had been submerged were clearly defined. This was even more evident in the southern part of the range, where a thin stratum of greyish clay, perfectly rounded and smooth, with perforations undoubtedly caused by water, could be noticed. Above it was yellow sand, and above this blackish rock or rock burnt dark red.

The village of Matamkari had some three thousand inhabitants. There were narrow streets, filthy in the extreme, and running crooked between zeribas of matting. In sharp contrast with this dirt was the cleanliness pre-

The fort o Matamkari.

vailing within the enclosures and in the interior of their huts. The huts were cylindrical, with conical roofs, the doors fairly high. A separate hut was used as a kitchen, while numerous *canari*, or large mud vessels for millet, stood at the entrance of each hut. Slings hung from the ceiling, to which were suspended gourds cut into bowls or preserved in their natural shape and used as bottles.

The houses were divided inside into two sections by a cane screen, each section containing a bed, a mere mud frame with two hollows in the middle. A flat reed mat was spread over the top of these double hollows, which were designed for coolness. The hollows when not in use were turned into wardrobes.

The chief's house possessed a high, castellated mud wall, with a grandiose entrance, quite out of keeping with the general squalor of the village. Two great mud columns reminded one strongly of the architecture of Egypt. From this point onward we shall notice Egyptian influence not only in the architecture, but we shall also find it in people, quite different in type to the local inhabitants, and with manners and a language of their own. These people formerly migrated from Egypt as far west as the Senegal.

Dozens of broad-soled sandals formed a row in front of the chief's door. When Chief Kotchi came out to greet me, a number of sub-chiefs and important people reclaimed their footgear, which was of a most practical kind for walking on the sand, the soles being as broad as six or eight inches.

After a profusion of handshakes with all present and a mortal fear on my part of contracting the itch from which all these people suffered, Chief Kotchi took

me round his village and spoke eloquently of the doings
of his tribesmen.

He showed me how the richer people buried their
relations within their own *zeribas* directly in front of
the habitations. They were agriculturally inclined, and
cultivated millet and cotton, the latter in small quantities, only just sufficient for their own needs. The
women spun it in the usual fashion, only they chalked
their fingers and thumb, between which the thread was
revolved, in order to preserve its pure whiteness.

The Haussa of Matamkari belonged to the Maori
(no relation whatever to the Maori of New Zealand)
class. They were fairly bright and intelligent, jovial,
with long, well-shaped faces, often bearded. They were
tall and slender, and had adopted the garb of the Arabs.

They extracted sodium carbonate from the *mares*
in their neighbourhood when these were dry in the hot
season.

The post of Matamkari (950 feet) was interesting,
as it stood exactly on the curve of the former Anglo-
French boundary. It rose on a small mound higher
than the surrounding wall of the fort.

The natives of this region had many ostriches in
captivity.

Sergeant Gauthier was in charge of the place.

I continued my journey, rounding the headland of
the range, which was so eroded that it had the appearance of a fortress in ruins. A portion of its side was quite
vertical. In the distance upon another hillock could be
perceived the ruins of the abandoned British post.

Passing over undulating ground, and suffering intense pain, I arrived at Banigombo, a distance of thirty-
four kilometres, at 1.30 in the morning, having marched

six hours in the morning and eight hours in the afternoon. Unluckily, we found no water at this place, and I had to proceed as far as Mayakikuara, where I only arrived at noon the next day, animals and men being worn out. We had gone seventy-seven or seventy-eight kilometres, with a halt of only two hours.

At this place we found Djerma instead of Haussa. On the trail we saw many natives returning from the Matamkari market carrying long cones of salt either upon their shoulders or else laden upon oxen, donkeys, or camels. Each man had a spear, and many had a bow and a holder filled with poisoned arrows.

The Djerma have few industries, the chief being leather-tanning. Iron is worked by them neatly enough.

Another night march from Mayakikuara brought me to Gambadie at 1.15 a.m. on October 12th, in drenching rain, which lasted the whole night. At sunrise we were off once more, leaving the small village of Gambadie and then Loga behind, the latter at the foot of a dune with a breach in it some hundreds of yards wide through which we passed. We first came across the *baobab* trees here (locally called *coggioni*), which had immense trunks, six or seven feet in diameter. When compared with other trees of the desert, these appeared giants. The *cof*, sometimes larger than the *coggioni*, was another tree—quite scarce—of this region, which had great breadth of trunk and massiveness of branches.

Sargadié was passed next, nineteen kilometres further. An afternoon march of sixteen more kilometres over flat, uninteresting country took us to Gubegeno. Going towards the west we saw a long dune before us. At the village of Lahmudi there were quantities of palm-trees.

We reached the small post of Sandireh at an elevation of 750 feet. To the south-west, west, north-west and north, was a long, flat-topped dune describing a curve as far as the north-east.

We had descended, on coming to Sandireh, into a depression which had the appearance of having formed an ancient river-bed, either an arm of the Niger itself or of an affluent, or perhaps it was at one time an arm of an inland sea. The western dune had battlements. One could plainly detect the erosion by water half way up the dune. This erosion was not such as could be entirely caused by the running water of a stream, but looked more like the erosion by waves such as one sees on a sea or lake shore. Due west of Sandireh was a wide opening eroded by water in the dune.

Djerma village was south of the post, which consisted of a few thatched houses close to a marsh. Everything was sadness when I arrived, two white men out of three being in a dying condition. In fact, during the night one, a lieutenant, died, and shortly after I heard that the other, a sergeant, had also succumbed. Dr. Vallet, who was looking after the patients, was also very ill. The post was in charge of Lieutenant Fourcade.

Having spent the whole day of October 13th and all of October 14th until 5 p.m. at this post, I continued towards the Niger, the trail from this point going south-west through the large opening in the dune. On getting nearer one noticed a grey lower stratum with cavities, generally at an angle of forty-five degrees to the ground, the openings of them being round and the surfaces polished. Above this was a stratum, some twenty feet deep, of sandstone, also with numberless perforations and cavities, most of them facing downwards, and produced by water dashing against the dune. Many of these cavities were shown in the concave shape of the lower portion of the coast-line, especially on headlands, whereas in the many small bays formed between the headlands the erosion by the slackened movement of the waves had left a far less perceptible trace and in some places could not be detected at all.

To the east of us and extending from north-north-east to south, we had another long dune, which gave the impression that the flat space between might have been the bed of a stream, a tributary of the Niger. In fact, this channel extended somewhat circuitously in a northerly direction for a great distance. The surface sand was of a light-grey colour, in great contrast to the rich burnt-sienna of the sun-baked sandstone, and was identical with that found in the lower stratum of the cliff.

When we rose on the passage between the two sections of the western cliff we again found richly-coloured sand in the upper portion. Undulations in the sand, regular waves, occurred all through the march that day. At midnight we arrived at the camp of Tonde-kiboro, thirty-two kilometres from Sandireh. From this point there were continuous transverse undulations across the trail, the course we followed being now slightly south of west. There were deep depressions between dunes, especially north of the trail.

One or two small villages were met with before reaching Foulanke, twenty-two kilometres further (850 feet), and between that place and Barkoggal we travelled for fourteen kilometres across flat desert.

On October 16th, having left at sunrise, we descended considerably by a succession of terraces, descending practically all the time with the exception of one or two undulations, until we arrived at 10 a.m. at the post of Niamey upon the Niger (750 feet above sea-level— 80 feet above river-level). Before us all through the march we had a long dune on the west bank of the Niger, with three broken flat-topped cones in two successive terraces at its northern end. Another long dune could be seen north of this one, and must formerly have been a continuation of it. On the south a third dune was noticeable. The large dune directly in front of Niamey, on the opposite side of the Niger, showed, like those at Sandireh, erosions half way up its height.

I had been suffering from the blow received on my spine, and I was glad when the Niger was reached and I could say good-bye to camel-riding and Tuareg saddles. I was compelled to lie on my back for several days, the pain being so intense that it caused strong fever.

DISTANCES BETWEEN LAKE TCHAD AND THE NIGER.

Nguigmi to Wudi..	25 kilometres	
Wudi to Mir	105	,, (no water)
Mir to Shirmalek	100	
Shirmalek to Gouri	75	
Gouri to Zinder....	.. 150	
Zinder to Tessaua..	160	
Tessaua to Guidam Bado	200	
Guidam Bado to Taua	140	
Taua to Matamkari	240	
Matamkari to Sandireh	120	
Sandireh to Niamey	.. 100	
	————	
Lake Tchad to Niger..	1,415	,,

CHAPTER XXVII.

SINCE leaving Lake Tchad on September 5th I had travelled 1,415 kilometres to the Niger in twenty-five and a half days' actual marching, or forty days, including halts of fourteen and a half days in various posts, in order to rest my camels and obtain fresh provisions. When French officers were sent out to their posts in the desert the distance from Zinder alone (half way) to Niamey occupied fifty-eight days' actual marching. To Lake Tchad, if I remember right, four months were allowed for the journey. In my case, I actually covered an average of fifty-six kilometres daily. Considering the distance I had already travelled in the deadliest parts of the continent, the intense heat in the desert, the slowness of progress with camels marching, which had to be made up for by marching more hours a day, and the scarcity and foulness of water all along, this was quite a record march in the matter of endurance.

At Niamey I made arrangements for a steel Government canoe to take me up the Niger, and after enjoying the hospitality of Commandant Dardignac and the other officers in that post, I proceeded towards the north-west by river on October 21st.

I think that Niamey will eventually be abandoned by the French. Gao, further north upon the Niger, is more conveniently situated to be the terminus of the

Lake Tchad military route, and will take its place, as we shall presently see.

I heard at Niamey that yellow fever had broken out badly in the Senegal and that communication had been interrupted. Officers returning to France were not allowed to proceed that way, but were obliged to take the Dahomey route to the south. I continued, however, northwards.

Along the stream, when I left Niamey, were men, women and children in great numbers bathing in the river, and smearing one another with native soap. Further on were fishermen drawing big fish out of the stream ; then, upon dry land, strings of women with well-developed chests carrying large yellow calabashes upon their heads, or picturesque men in long blue robes and white turbans and black or white face-screens.

Pictorially, this was a more interesting region than any I had met in my journey across the continent, these veiled men in their loose robes being artistic enough, and the women of a far higher and more refined type than those of the black tribes of Central Africa. Remains of an ancient civilization of some sort could be traced here, and in many spots one could detect a Moorish influence from the north, as well as a strong Egyptian influence which had come over with the Fulbeh, a pastoral race, the members of which declared that their forefathers had migrated from Egypt.

The first halt on the Niger was made at Bubu, the spot where Lieutenant Fabre had a short time previously been assassinated by the natives.

I had an excellent crew. The current was strong, and we were compelled to punt all the time. The French officers have a fleet of steel canoes on this river, the shape of which has been copied from the native wooden canoes. They are well adapted for the navigation of the stream. They draw little water even when heavily laden, and can thus go easily over the many rapids. They are of great length and narrow, the only drawback being that they roll extremely when being propelled first on one side and then on the other, so that people who suffer from sea-sickness can hardly travel by them. Personally I liked them.

On the left bank was a long dune, with occasional villages picturesquely situated half way up the slopes or else along the green line of the water, grass and reeds growing along the banks. On the right bank were several large Djerma villages, with domed roofs and mat walls, and immense well-made egg-shaped store-houses for their foodstuff.

We saw here our first rice-fields, which excited my Somali intensely, poor fellow, as we had been out of rice for some time and he was longing to get some.

Two great rocks, one on each side of the stream, interrupted the monotony of the scenery, and small rapids were occasionally gone over. I was travelling at high water, and these rapids were easily surmounted with a few occasional bumps.

Between Bubu and Karma were two brown sister-hillocks, with a row of smaller ones further back on the right bank.

I could not help admiring the six men who were punting my boat among plentiful reeds in the water. In a stifling heat of 120° in the sun, not a drop of perspiration could be perceived on their backs or foreheads. The captain of the crew, a great swell, was garbed in a heavy old military overcoat and an admiral's cap.

Near the villages were groups of bathers, mostly women and children—the women being quite good-looking. They were delicately shaped, with long faces, the eyes slightly more expressive than those of pure blacks, and the nose, though still depressed at the bridge, not so ill-shaped as that of the races on the Ubanghi or the Shari. The skin was not of a jet-black but of a medium chocolate colour.

We halted at Sorbo Haussa at 6 p.m. We generally made a start between 2 and 2.30 in the morning. On October 23rd we had flat shores on either side with immense anthills upon them. Sansan Haussa, a large village, was passed on the right bank. The chief's house showed mud towers and a wall round it, but the other structures were built of thatch, with cylindrical walls and flattened domed roofs.

There were long dunes in the distance all along the right bank. We stopped at Kogomani village on October 23rd, the air being absolutely foul and reeking with miasma.

River navigation was unpleasant to me. I was still laid flat on my back, trying to recover from the injury to my spine. When we halted anywhere in the inundated country the boat had to be left a long way from the shore, and it was impossible to get out of it without wading in water and mud sometimes for fifty or sixty yards, and I frequently preferred to remain in the canoe. Myriads of mosquitoes made life miserable.

High dunes were again seen on October 24th, one with a cylindrical natural pillar at the summit, and with typical battlements projecting all along quite close to the river bank. There were many villages, especially on the left bank, and lots of cattle and horses grazing

in the half-inundated country, where there was only an
inch or two of water and nice green tender grass.
Many of the houses closer to the shore actually stood
in the water, and were appropriately constructed for
that purpose. There was nothing in Djerma houses
which actually stood upon the floor, the great pot of
millet near the door resting on high stone supports.
All implements, such as spinning-wheels, work tools,
calabashes, spears, etc., hung from the ceiling. Two
beds, one very long, occupied almost the entire length
of the left section of the hut, and were constructed to
accommodate several persons. They were raised three
feet above the ground on forked posts. The larger bed
was curtained off. On the right side of the hut was
another broad bed, also raised, but only constructed
to accommodate two. At the end of the hut were high
shelves with foodstuff, clothes, etc.

The noises upon the water at night were innumerable.
The humble and solitary cricket began earliest of all,
at sunset. Then came the acute hissing of a kind of
nocturnal cicada. Suddenly one heard a clear, sharp
" quack-quack " repeated at once in a perfect chorus by
innumerable frogs all along the swampy banks. There
was also another kind of smaller frog, the voice of which
exactly resembled the prolonged distant whistle of a
railway engine. A kind of insect which is found in
swamps in this country produced a jingling sound like
that of mule-bells. All these noises together, with the
more suave tones of mosquito melodies and of other
insects with solo songs of their own, produced together
a really weird and quite beautiful soft music, not unlike
a chorus of a multitude of distant voices with an
accompaniment of the æolian harp. It was a pity that

all this poetry only meant death to white people, for it was in the country where malaria was most deadly that this music was to be heard.

The air was stifling among the vegetation stewing in the tepid water of the Niger. Decayed reeds floated and were entangled in the florid growth of all kinds of water-plants. Where there were patches of water clear of vegetation, big oily circles or rings, and floating balls of sickly yellow froth floated on the impure water. All the water of the Niger was of a sickly greenish-yellow colour. A good deal of time was spent in endeavouring to force our way through thick reeds, the river being broad in many places, with large expanses of rock both above and slightly under the surface of the water, and on the shore. Great dunes stood along on the right bank, their direction being from north-west to south-east, eroded as usual in several places along their length where they occasionally formed separate cones.

At Dirawami, on the left side of the stream, the canoe had to be towed over some rapids. Punting and paddling were impossible, and I had to land all my men, about a dozen, with a long tow-rope, in order to pull the canoe up the steps from the lowest to the highest point of the rapid. There was a high step to get over with a violent rush of water flowing over it. The men from the land were pulling their hardest, while I, alone in the boat, did the steering with a long paddle. We had got the canoe nearly one-third over, and then we stuck at an angle of about thirty degrees, but with every prospect of the prow of the boat describing still a wider circle in mid-air. The canoe was full of heavy baggage, which, unfortunately, slid in confusion from aft to stern, causing a bad list. The canoe swung violently and was caught

Giant mud jars for storing grain on the Upper Niger.

sideways by the chute of water. It was washed away
with great force, dragging into the stream most of the
men who were pulling the tow-rope, some of them
narrowly escaping getting drowned. The canoe floated
down sideways at a good speed for some thirty yards,
when it collided with two rocks and became full of
water. As she was about to sink, we just managed to
pull her on the shore and save the baggage. The elevation of the rapids was 750 feet above sea-level.

The Djerma construct canoes in two equal sections,
one aft and one forward, sewn up in the centre by means
of strings, the holes where the stitches are passed through
being further stopped with mud.

After passing Mallighikoira village we went over more
strong rapids with a violent current, which gave us no
end of trouble. Then we passed Tilla and then Jute,
and other large villages on both banks of the stream.
On the right, particularly, the villages were more
numerous, Zinder being a regular town with hundreds
and hundreds of *bua*, the huge earthen receptacles for
storing millet and rice, which had stone steps stuck in
the sides of them and an earthen slab used as a cover
for the upper aperture. There were a number of these
receptacles near each hut. We found there many
hemispherical huts made of pretty mats with black
designs on them.

An hour or so beyond Zinder granitic rocks stood
out, rising from the river and of the same formation as
those we had found at Gouri in the desert.

Tiesa village was left behind on the left shore. Then
we arrived at Gari, also on the left bank. At Usuli
village (right bank), we were fortunate enough to get
a little wind, and we put up a sail, but the boatmen had

had no experience in using canvas, and, as the wind was squally and powerful, we were nearly capsized on two or three occasions. The canoe got so full of water that at one time we had to land and take all the baggage out before we could continue our journey.

On October 26th we passed Namarigungu during the night, and then Farca on the left bank with a background of low hills. Then Sarakoire, Satoni, and Desa. We went up several rapids on October 27th. Now on one side, then on the other side of the stream, we had rocky banks with high slopes of well-rounded boulders, which looked as though they had been brought down and stopped in their course by a barrier of ferruginous rock.

At this place were the famous Tentaji rapids, which we had difficulty in surmounting. The men were again overpowered by the current, and, as on a previous occasion, the canoe swung round and drifted swiftly away until there was a terrific bump, and she got full of water. After an hour's work we succeeded in pulling the canoe over.

In the village of Desa, when I was going round with the chief, he took me to his mud enclosure, which had secondary enclosures within. In the last of these, in the open air, was seated upon a black and white mat a woman of immense proportions, quite picturesque in her repulsiveness—her fat limbs being so well proportioned and the skin, oiled all over, wonderfully smooth and free from blemishes, marks or scars. Her hair was elaborately done in the shape of a Greek helmet, with huge sidelocks fastened under the chin. The massive but simple and beautiful decorations of brass and silver which embellished her *coiffure* produced a really artistic effect. A large necklace of metal adorned her neck and chest. Armlets and bracelets of shining silver embellished her arms. There was no clothing to speak of between her neck and her feet. Just above the latter brass circlets, weighing no less than ten pounds each, adorned her lower limbs. She was the first fat woman I had ever seen who was graceful and dignified. She sat motionless in Turkish fashion, as the last rays of the sun shone brightly upon the jewels of her head.

Sitting by her were three slaves, similarly but not so lavishly decorated with ornaments of metal. One was polishing with the palm of her hand the numerous rings, including a thumb ring, worn by her mistress. A fourth maid, a young girl of graceful lines, stood on the left fanning the fat woman's ample cheeks.

On October 28th we came to a series of bad rapids. It was only after three or four attempts that we were able to get the canoe over. As far as the villages of Aiaru, one on each side of the river, the navigation was indeed difficult. After passing these villages we had to negotiate first a low but swift waterfall, where, for the third time, we nearly got wrecked. We had got over fairly safely, when the men became unable to hold the canoe in the strong rush of water, and down we went again and drifted for a couple of hundred yards. Finally we had to find another passage on the left side of the stream, which turned out to be comparatively easy.

We eventually arrived at the large military post of Dunzo (elevation, 760 feet), with a village and market, with Captain Buck in charge, the only other white man in the place being a French merchant.

It had taken us seven days and a half to reach this place from Niamey, owing to the many rapids we had encountered.

From **Dunzo** the scenery on both sides was absolutely flat. At the village of Firigul, on the left of us, I saw a wonderful collection of magnificent black and grey ostriches. From this point the natives in nearly all the villages had many of these birds in captivity.

We went on, forcing our way all the time through grass and reeds, as we kept mostly on the inundated country, where the water was shallow, which allowed the men to punt. After passing a solitary hill-range with much-rounded slopes and top, close to the right bank, we saw a dune further back on the same side. The river and inundations here extended to a great width. We were crossing an almost treeless region, and the river was so broad at Katongo that the current was hardly felt.

The Labesango rapids (760 feet) had to be got over on October 30th. The water had a heavy chute one and a half feet high. With the help of volunteer villagers we negotiated this exciting passage safely, although these were supposed to be the worst rapids in the northern portion of the Niger. The *lapto*, my boatmen, who had deposited their mascots in various parts of the canoe during their ordinary work, were so afraid of this particular spot that they put them all on again round their arms and neck in order to protect their lives.

North of Dunzo the navigation was slightly pleasanter. The air was getting dryer and less stifling. There were fewer villages and the river was broader, with sandy shores on either side and not so much putrid vegetation.

Tiny humming-birds, some golden-yellow, some of a deep Prussian blue with most beautiful iridescent tints, some with heads and breasts of the softest Indian red,

Author's stee canoe being hau ed up over rapids upon the Niger.

were to be seen. Then there were myriads of birds of mixed brown and white and of all other colours. The variety of beautifully-coloured insects was also immense, brilliant vermilion, green and yellow being the prevalent colours. Softer and better blended browns were noticeable in moths, butterflies and dragon-flies. Giant green specimens of the orthoptera order (*saltatoria*), similar to, but larger than, the *monachelle* of Italy (four or five inches long), sometimes dashed into one's face. Worms of extraordinary shapes and tints, earwigs in quantities, and beautifully coloured beetles and hard-shelled insects of most fantastic shapes constantly dropped into the canoe when we forced our way through grass.

Fish were also plentiful, and impudent enough to jump into the canoe, especially at night when I burnt a light. This was a great nuisance, because sometimes unseen they would stick between packages and become decomposed.

Towards evening, exactly at the same hour, about sunset, a pretty sight was always noticeable as we were punting along. An escort, or rather an advance guard, of thousands of red, blue and black dragon-flies sped along in front and at the sides of the canoe. The moment the sun disappeared they immediately vanished. Then innumerable mosquitoes came.

There were hundreds of ostriches, with beautiful grey or black feathers, in captivity at Garon, a large village on the left of us. Some of the birds had been partly divested of their plumage. Their skin was sore, of a brilliant vermilion, quite a ghastly sight, their thorax and neck quite naked and inflamed. Only a small ring of feathers was left half way up the neck.

The natives along the stream worked iron with a forge. Double bellows cleverly handled produced a powerful draught. Blacksmiths and their assistants were generally lepers covered with ugly sores. They seemed to be a hard-working and suffering lot. One of them, a mere living skeleton, was sharpening spearheads and knives by hammering them upon a small iron anvil. Although his fingers were in a distressing condition, parts of his phalanges having dropped off, he was dexterous at putting a sharp edge on these weapons. This particular man had a poor, wretched, half-blind little boy as an assistant, with a huge paunch and atrophied legs, but he seemed to possess wonderful strength in lifting up and pressing down the bellows. The bellows were similar to those used in the Congo Free State.

Fortune attended us that day. A fair breeze allowed us to cover a long distance, reaching Koatagana, on the left bank of the river in lat. 15° 7′ N.

On October 30th curious black and red rock in thin waved strata prevailed for a long distance on our left. At noon we had arrived at the renowned rapids of Fafa. Although we expected trouble, we were able to get over them safely, owing to the skill of my pilot.

The Niger here formed a big delta with two large islands in the centre, and one on the left, on which the village of Fafa was situated, with minor islets near it. On each of the larger islands were masses of ferruginous volcanic rock surmounted by boulders in heaps.

We had come in the morning through paddy-fields where men were up to their chests in water taking in their crop of rice. Then we had plodded through submerged millet fields and through dense grass.

In order to prevent fish destroying their rice, the natives made great *barrages*, regular walls of entangled vegetation and reeds, below the surface. These stopped us a good deal, as sometimes we had to cut them or tear them apart before we could proceed.

There were white lotuses, the flat circular leaf fully six inches in diameter, fluted slightly at the centre, and very deeply at the circumference.

After Fafa more rapids had to be gone over. We soon arrived at the village of Beltia, upon the right bank, the journey being uninteresting that day, for we went all the time through grass and submerged millet fields, with only here and there a lot of granitic boulders, similar to those we had seen at Gouri. We halted at Firchindi, which stood upon a height. Then, on October 31st, we passed the village of Karo, and later a rocky, curiously-rounded mountain of volcanic formation, quite high for this region. Deep black holes and perforations like small craters were visible in the top and sides. A long flow of solidified lava dipped into the river. This was called by the natives the Ghidi-ghidi.

Shortly afterwards we arrived at Bura, situated among a lot of black volcanic rock. A hill-range, with two high towers of natural rock upon it, stood on the opposite side of the stream, forming a peculiar sky-line.

The people of this region showed a strong Moorish influence in their type. They had long faces, heavy in the lower part ; long, prominent noses, with broad nostrils, eyes well covered by a well-developed brow, and an expression shifty in the extreme. The mouth generally reached almost from ear to ear. They possessed slightly curly beards upon their chins. The younger folks had arched eyebrows and a strong Jewish look about them.

At Gandakoro were extensive plantations of millet. Where the right bank of the Niger described a loop, there was a village of Haussa ; and on the left bank stood a high dune all along between Bura and Lelehoï. The rapids came to an end when we reached Ansongo on the left bank, a long string of houses and stores along the river front.   Here and there beyond Ansongo we could see upon the banks a few movable huts, dome-like, and covered with mats.   Occasionally larger groups of huts were to be seen, as at Barbi, but after Ansongo we found no more Djerma.

Again we proceeded among thick grass, which, as we brushed past, filled the canoe with dirt and insects of all kinds.   The heat was stifling, sheltered as we were by a high dune on the left bank, which took away from us what little wind there was.   Occasionally we saw portable native huts and piles of rice collected in bags of matting containing some two hundred pounds each. The portable huts of these people were not of interest. The bed, which occupied all one side of the interior, was raised above the ground.   Beyond a few calabashes, a wooden pestle and mortar, and a few baskets, there was no furniture in any of these habitations.

When quite young the women were good-looking, with regular features, reminding one strongly of the ancient Egyptians as we see them on sculptures.   The men bore a striking resemblance in type and manner to the Abyssinians.   Perhaps they came from the same stock, although now living so far apart.

By November 2nd we were still proceeding through rice fields, high grass and submerged millet fields.   There

Women constructing a hut on the Niger.

were high dunes on both banks. At no time were we on the Niger itself, but always proceeded over flooded country. Here and there on the high points slightly above the water were encampments of natives harvesting their crops. On these small islands they stacked away their millet and rice in huge baskets of matting.

Since entering the rice-eating country I had found leprosy not only prevalent but extremely common. Numerous lepers came under my observation every day, even among the well-to-do people of that region ; whereas I found that leprosy was scarce in countries where people ate millet. Many lepers whom I saw on the Niger had lost their fingers and toes. Two lepers were one day put on board my boat by a local chief to whom I had applied for a guide to lead us through the inundation as far as the next village.

Somehow I seemed to have a great attraction for lepers, drunken people and madmen, all of whom I loathe. They were always inflicted upon me, and I hated to offend their feelings by driving them away.

On November 3rd I arrived at Gao, having travelled the entire night. Here I found a fine post built on the pattern of an old castle. The Tuareg often came to the river at this place, as their country practically began from this point northwards. Since the French occupation, however, they did not show themselves along the river banks as much as they used to do.

CHAPTER XXVIII.

IMPLEMENTS of stone and flint are to be found near Gao, in the sand, where battles have taken place, and in camps where people who used these implements lived during the stone age. It is a puzzling thing that these arrow-heads and axes have not been buried in sand, unless, indeed, they have been buried and have come to the surface again owing to erosion of the wind. Along the loop of the Niger, especially northwards, we shall find some of these implements and camps.

I possess many flint and stone weapons from this region, and in the Paris Museum the French have a complete and representative collection of stone axes, hammers, arrow-heads, pestles, knives, etc., sent over from there by officers who have made archæological studies.

In a zone two hundred kilometres east of Gao and further east than that, one finds a great many sea-shells, where another portion of the great depression can be identified which I had met at Sandireh. This would tend to confirm the theory that at one time that region formed part of a sea, or, at least, of a salt-water lake.

The natives have various theories and legends regarding the bed of the Niger, which they say was not in olden days where it is now. They also maintain that the country east of them was at one time covered by water.

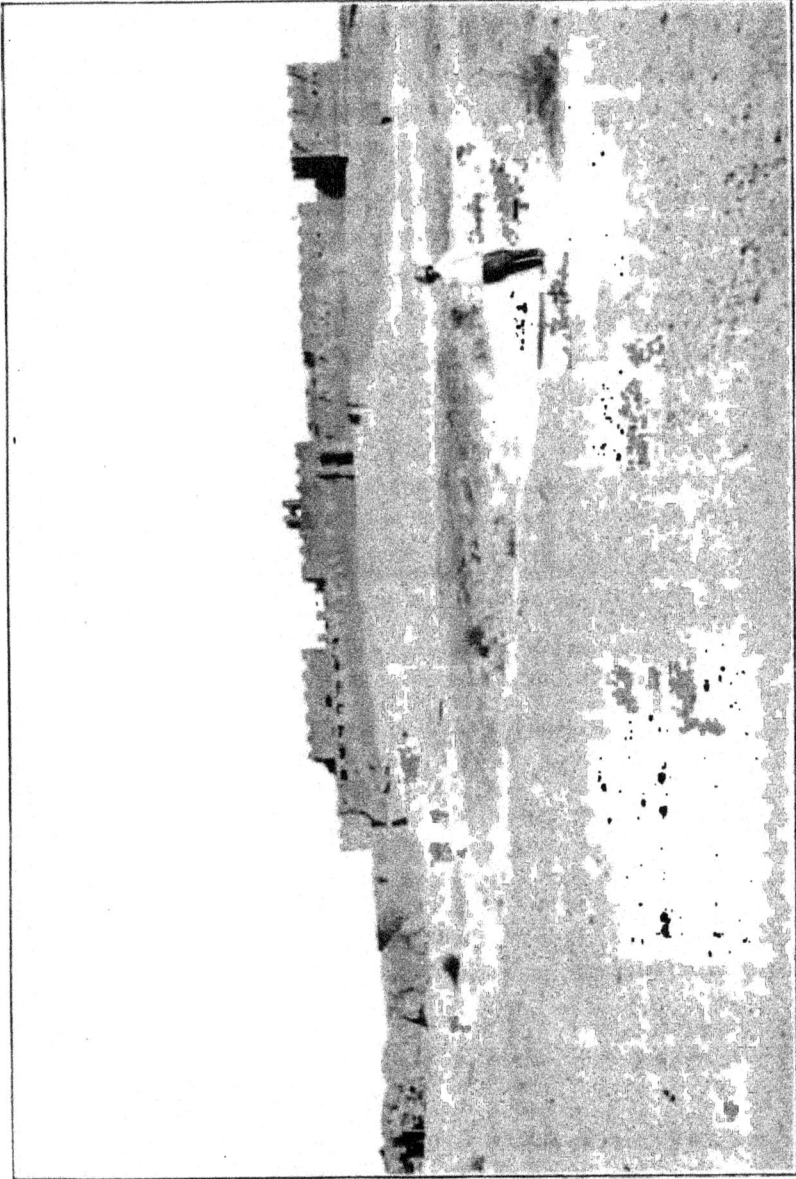

Fort o Burem, Upper Niger.

According to Pliny, the Niger was not a river but a large basin; but he knew of the existence of two great rivers in Libya, the *Nigris* and the *Ger* (or *Gir*) in the west.   Ptolemy, who seemed to possess exact topographical information for those days, says that the River *Nigris* ended on one side at Mount Mandress, at the other at Mount Thala, forming Lake *Nigris*.   As far as one can surmise, Lake *Nigris* was nothing else than the present dried-up depression of Touat.   Ptolemy, too, writes of the *Gher*, in the east, and the *Nigher*, west. Both Pliny and Ptolemy believed the *Nigris* lost itself in the sand only to reappear further on.

In the various dialects of Libya, in Berber or *Temahaq*, we find that *gher, ghar, ghir* and *ghor* mean " running water," and in many North African languages *Nil* or *Ni* means " great river," so *Nil-gher* or *Ni-gher* stands for " great river of running water."

The tribes found in the neighbourhood were the Inkari, the Telatai, the Inuellen, the Ebback, the Emaka, the Tidorome, the Taghibat and the Asighi. South of this line (16° 12′ lat. N.) none of these tribes of Tuareg were to be found.

Gao, formerly the capital of Mohammed Askya, emperor at the time when Soñgoy power was at its height, will again some day be a place of importance because of its geographical situation, and because it can be reached by water, in nearly all seasons, even by steamers of shallow draught.   If the route from the Niger to Lake Tchad had Gao instead of Niamey for a terminus, it would be longer overland perhaps than the route further south, but easier, wells being found all along which are now used by the Tuareg.

One kilometre from Gao was an ancient mosque of

pyramidal shape, with a minaret upon its blackish summit. A red mud wall encircled it. It was quite picturesque at sunset. Many of the older inhabitants went within the enclosure to make their salaam towards Mecca.

There were many Tuareg in the neighbourhood of this place. There was a small market. Captain Pasquier was then in charge of the post with seventy Senegalese infantrymen and seventy *méharistes,* or " camel corps men."

On the left bank on leaving Gao was a dune with an undulating top. There were a great number of camps near the water. Most of the inhabitants spent the entire time in the water taking in their rice.

Facing this page a photograph is reproduced showing women building a movable hut. In a moment they will bend the sticks, fasten them, and spread the mats over them. In less time than it takes to describe the process they will make quite a comfortable and watertight structure, firm even during comparatively heavy gales of wind.

On November 5th we were all day beside a low sand dune on the left bank, the canoe being forced as usual through high grass. No villages were seen and only a small encampment on an island was passed late in the evening.

I received that day the only wound I had sustained in the entire journey—quite a prosaic one, but one which might have been serious all the same. In opening a box of sardines my hand slipped, and I sawed my thumb in two. The vein which is directly under the skin at the joint was severed, and I had difficulty in stopping the bleeding, which lasted some hours.

I should not mention this incident except that people

talk so much of antiseptics and disinfectants, bandages, filtered and sterilized water, etc., without which people cannot be cured, and none of which things I possessed at the time. All I did was to rinse the bleeding thumb in the dirty water of the stream. We were at that moment going through a lot of putrid vegetation. After this immersion the thumb was wrapped in a piece of cloth which my Somali used for cleaning rifles, the only cloth I could get hold of at the moment, as the blood was squirting out with some force. Next day the healing was beginning. Five days later, although a notch remained, the wound had healed perfectly, leaving the thumb stiff for some weeks. Now, however, I suffer no inconvenience from it.

Mind you, this is not treatment that I would suggest to everybody for a similar wound; but I think that when the blood is in a healthy condition an exaggerated importance is attributed to antiseptics and disinfectants, which, instead of decreasing the natural healing power which all healthy people possess, stop it and increase the suffering.

On November 6th I reached Burem, in the country of the Oelimmiden Tuareg, a beautiful fort, built of sun-baked bricks by Lieutenant Barbeyrac de St. Maurice, at a cost of a few thousand francs. It was amazing to see what French officers could do with practically nothing. Although the work cost little, it was magnificently carried out considering that the only materials at disposal were sand and mud.

The fort of Burem, on the summit of a high dune, was a strong position with excellently loopholed, stout walls. All the buildings in the interior were connected by elevated bridges from roof to roof.

The Arabs who were found near Burem were the remainder of the first invasion of the Arabs towards the seventh century under Sidi Oga, who came from Tunis, and was eventually killed at Biskra. A second invasion by the Ben Hillal, who came from Egypt under Khalifa Fatemi, took place in the eleventh century. There were three divisions of these invaders, two of which sacked the Maghreb (Morocco, Oran and Algeria); the third crossed the Sahara and reached the Niger. The Moors say they are the descendants of Beni Hussein, that is to say, of the third division.

The Arabs of this region called themselves Kuntah. Then we found Tuareg, Soñgoy and Arma. The Tuareg in this region belonged to the Oelimmiden tribe, a great and noble group. The Kel-Essouk, noble, marabu, and warriors, were also located here.

Along the Niger from this point we came across the Fulbeh, a name merely the plural of *Peuhl* (or *Pulloh*). These people had better-chiselled features than any of the tribes in the Niger valley and an undoubtedly higher intelligence. They generally did not live in the villages of other tribes, but habitually built their huts some way off. They, nevertheless, intermarried freely with members of local tribes. They were nomads at heart. Their mental qualities were well recognized by other tribes, who made constant use of them. They were said to have come from Egypt, where they were the Fellahtas. They had mixed a good deal during their migration west. The mixed race of Fulbeh and Nigerian tribes was generally called Tukuler, which by some was supposed to be a name derived from the English " two colours " ; by others said to be from the French " *toutes couleurs* " ; but which was really only a native name which happened

Head-dress of Fulbeh women on the Niger.

to have a resemblance to English and French words, but had nothing to do with their meaning. These Tukuler, the mixed race, owing to their superior intelligence, became powerful in the eighteenth century. Abdu-el-Kader actually founded a Tukuler State in the Senegal. During the second conquest, also in the eighteenth century, the Tukuler founded Fouta Jelma in the loop of the Niger, and a third conquest occurred under Almami-Ibrahim, a Bunda Mussulman. At the beginning of the nineteenth century Otman Fodia formed the Empire of Sokoto and Gando. Also, at the beginning of the nineteenth century Ahmadu Labbo founded a Fulbeh State between Timbuctu and Segu. Between 1857 and 1861 El Hadji Omar, pushed hard by the French in the Senegal, conquered Karta and Segu.

Some eighty kilometres or so east of Burem were to be found quantities of flint arrow-heads and stone axes. Along the top of the dunes in that region were also camps where arrows were shaped by special workmen. These places can be traced to this day.

The district of Burem was interesting geologically. Here again I found the same formation as at Matamkari and Sandireh, except that in this place additional ferruginous rock was to be found. There were dunes here with a lower stratum of hardened white or grey clay, and an upper stratum of sandstone, over which in many places was a layer of ferruginous rock. Where this ferruginous rock existed, or had at one time existed, it had given a warm, rusty tint to the layer of sand below it, and had even given a beautiful violet colour to the clay of the bottom stratum. This clay was excellent for building purposes. The river had made many breakages into these clay dunes, the clay being gradually

washed out by the current, the sand above collapsing
and being also washed away.

Further up-stream I found these same three strata
in a vertical position instead of the normal horizontal one.
This might have been caused by a subsidence of the soil
or by a volcanic commotion.   Personally, I am under the
impression that it was a subsidence, caused possibly by
volcanic action, for close by I found a large expanse of
ferruginous volcanic rock which seemed to have been
subjected to intense heat and at a comparatively recent
epoch.

I left Burem before sunrise on November 7th, and
two hours later I passed the Tussa pillars in mid-stream
—the only picturesque sight I had so far seen on the
Niger. A high sand dune was on our left, but on the
right the land was almost flat. We were still proceeding over inundated country.

Having landed in several places to examine the geological formation, I came across curious camps with
marble anvils, which had evidently been used for shaping
flint heads for spears and arrows. Pieces of silex were
to be found, some in a chipped condition, and also fragments of pottery with angular ornamentations and
parallel lines. A huge block of yellow sienna marble
was peeping out of the sand. Crystals and stones of
beautiful colours were scattered upon the sand everywhere. Gold, I believe, existed inland not far from
this place.

The natives in this part of the Niger constructed
canoes in small sections of wood—as there were no big
trees about—sewn together. The holes through which
the stitches were passed were of great size. When
navigating the river these holes were stopped up with

mud and grass. A deep layer of grass was then laid at the bottom of the canoe, partly because the leaking was considerable, and also because it was necessary—Irish as it may sound—to have several inches of water inside the craft to make it quite watertight, as in absorbing the moisture the wood expanded and became close at the fissures.

In constructing these canoes the natives make a mould in the sand, laying the various pieces one next to the other in the order they should go, this method considerably facilitating the sewing of the pieces together.

The country was flat and desert on either side. Fortunately, we got a breeze which pushed us along across clear water instead of our having to punt through the interminable inundations among thick grass, which was tiresome. On November 8th we travelled northwest all day, until we passed Amgudie on the left of us, where, at a point called Aguadesh, the Niger described a big curve due west. This was one of the most northerly points of the Niger. There were three or four collections of domed mud huts, and a lot of cattle grazing along the water's edge. To the south was a long barren sand dune with an undulating summit. The river with the inundations had an immense width at this place.

I arrived at the post of Bamba on November 10th. Captain Cauvin and Lieutenant Langlumé interested me so much with the work they were doing that I remained until November 16th, also partly in order to wait for the arrival of Commandant Mezillier, of Timbuctu, from whom it was necessary for me to obtain a permission to travel across the country between the Niger and the Senegal, which was infected with yellow fever.

Captain Cauvin was employed in forming a camel

corps, as it was found that horses were practically of no use in that part of the country. They became greatly fatigued by plodding through the sand of the desert, and suffered greatly from the want of water and the badness of it when it was possible to find any. The corps of Captain Mangin in the Borku had done such excellent work that the French were now establishing these *méharistes* in the various posts where they would be useful in policing the desert.

I left Bamba on November 16th, making a halt the first night at Kennashoui, the second night at Rergho, the third upon barren land in the region of Tumeneshâht, Commandant Mezillier, who had joined me at Bamba, travelling along in his own boat on his return to Timbuctu.

Three Tuareg tribes were found between Bamba and Timbuctu—the Iguaddaren, the Keltamulaït, and the Irreghenaten.

All along the stream as far as Gunda we found the Soñgoy Gabibi, who, under their ancient Moorish conquerors, were locally called the Arma. Next to the Soñgoy were some groups of Puehl or Fulbeh. In the lake region were Tele, Oro Fati and Garu, on the right bank, mixed with the Soñgoy, and still more with the Fulbeh, especially in the larger villages. In the region of Lake Fakibin the Kelantassar were met, some Soñgoy and some Arabs, of whom the principal were the Tormoz, the Usra, the Mborade and the Sherfigh, all descendants of the Sherifs. These were generally shepherds.

I arrived at Kabara in the afternoon of November 19th, the journey by canoe from Niamey having occupied thirty days.

Along the Niger a great variety of animals is to be

Senegalese infantrymen   Bamba, Upper Niger

found. Perhaps the most familiar to travellers is the repulsive hyena, which, with its weird cries, prowls around camps at night in search of food. Wicked little jackals are fairly common, while many varieties of antelopes and gazelles are known. Near Gundam giraffes are plentiful, and in certain parts wild boar have been killed. Here and there one hears of panthers, or of the more easily-tamed cheetahs. In fact, I have seen one or two of these in captivity in French military posts.

Maneless lions (the *guhn*) were common enough, but their skins, with short hair, were valueless. Alive, these animals were not so impressive as their hairy fellows of the Algerian desert. Elephants were getting scarce, but inland herds were still to be found. The ivory was not of such good quality as that of the Ubanghi and Mbomu regions. I was told that rhinoceros exists, especially on the right bank of the river, but I never saw it in that region. Hippopotami (the *bañga*) were to be seen in certain localities where they possessed favourite pools ; they were shy and it was difficult to get near them.

The most characteristic and most remarkable mammal on the Niger was the amphibious *ayuh*, a mammal which the natives say is half-woman, half-fish, and is described as a mermaid by early travellers on the Niger. Near Gao there was a family of these *ayuh*, and I believe they were common enough further south and in some of the tributaries of the Niger. They resembled a large seal. The head and upper portion of the body had some sort of a resemblance to a human being. The females, they say—I never saw one myself—had well-developed breasts, like women. I possess pieces of the hide of one of the *ayuh*, or *lamantin*, as the French call them. The thickness and elasticity is amazing ; of a light amber colour, it becomes quite transparent when trimmed and polished, and can be made into beautiful walking-sticks.

There were many legends among the natives about these mammals.

In the stream crocodiles and caimans were plentiful; while on land sand-lizards were extremely common, the *jecko* and the beautifully-tinted chameleons. Horned vipers and other specimens of the ophidian family were frequently met. Numerous hares swarmed over the country, and various kinds of rats and mice, such as the *koro-sinkara*, the *tendjela* or *jerboa*, and the *ntjom*; also hedgehogs and bats of various sizes.

There was an immense variety of birds upon the Niger, some of infinitesimal size and with plumage of indescribable beauty, with magnificent metallic tints iridescent in the sunlight. Egrets with valuable feathers were common enough, but were fast being killed off. White and black storks, pelicans, crowned geese, numerous ostriches — especially in the southern and western portions—martinets, green and grey parrots, wild pigeons and doves, owls, snipe, guinea-fowl (very plentiful), teal, duck, black and also white-collared crows, vultures, eagles, pretty tiny red and black birds, swallows, sparrows and partridges.

Most interesting to me were the tiny *oiseaux mouche*, in myriads along the banks of the stream. They were so small and so light that they could land on a blade of grass without causing the slightest oscillation, and they could fly away with equal facility without creating a disturbance. Some were of a brilliant crimson, others of a glorious blue, changing in the light into yellow and greenish tints. Then there were others of a deep rich velvety black—quite a gorgeous colour.

A native of the Upper Niger.

I saw red birds, yellow birds, and I believe that all colours and tints of the rainbow—only ten times more beautiful and vivid—could be found in the plumage of the minute birds of the Niger valley.

In the way of gorgeous metallic tints, these birds had rivals among the coleoptera (some being of enormous size), and the remarkable varieties of scarabs.

We will not speak of the flies and mosquitoes, of all kinds and sizes, millions of which were to be found upon the river ; nor of the slightly less numerous lepidoptera, of which I saw no very striking specimen. In the evening, slightly before sunset, it was a great amusement to me to watch the swarms of grey libellula, the *hanga-hanga*, or " pursuing libellula," and the green *iblisi-bari*, the " devil's horse," the two most common kinds upon the Niger, which followed my canoe for long distances until night set in.

In rice-fields upon the inundated country and upon the great swamps of *borgu* thousands of these beauti-fully-coloured dragon-flies were to be met. Not so beautiful were the clouds of locusts which travelled almost yearly over the country, doing great damage to the crops and leaving a rancid odour behind them. There were two principal kinds, one smaller than the other, but both destructive.

Yellowish-brown scorpions, four to six inches long, were common inside huts, but they were not deadly, although their sting gave excruciating pain and caused intense fever for a few hours. Spiders, big, small or flat-bodied ones, were not generally to be feared in that country. Some, large ones with hair upon their backs, were most repulsive to look at.

Of parasites, found in villages or in or upon natives,

we had a good variety. The Guinea-worm was not uncommon. Lice, intestinal worms, ticks, which get under one's feet and anywhere on the skin of men and animals, were plentiful, but fleas, curiously enough, were less frequently found.

The Yobou-Ber, or great market square, Timboctu.

CHAPTER XXIX.

I ARRIVED at Kabara at 3 p.m., and, thanks to Commandant Mezillier, at once obtained from the soldiers good horses and donkeys to convey men and baggage.

On leaving the fort at Kabara, an interesting view was to be obtained of the inundated country to the south. A tortuous canal which allows navigation at low water from the Niger to Kabara was quite perceptible from our high point of vantage, as well as a trail leading to Koroyume on the Niger. Upon the seven kilometres between Kabara and Timbuctu depressions were visible, showing plainly how far the inundations spread when the Niger is extraordinarily high and Timbuctu can be reached entirely by water. On the right of the traveller on going towards Timbuctu, and somewhat higher than a depression liable to inundation, were many small trees.

I cannot say whether I was disappointed or not in Timbuctu. I certainly was impressed when I first approached it, riding across the desert from Kabara. One does not get a glimpse of Timbuctu until within half a mile or so, when, getting over a high dune, the entire city spreads out before one's eyes. It was sunset when I got on the top of this dune. A heavy, bluish curtain hung over the horizon; the upper portion of the sky was tinted with a greyish red reflected from the last rays of a dying sun. Undulating masses of yellow sand, with mimosas and thorny shrubs, were in the immediate foreground. Caravans of men and boys on donkeys galloped wildly on their return from the Ramadan feast. Timbuctu, the mysterious, a greyish-yellow mass of mud buildings, stretched thread-like upon the horizon-line to the north, and was more impressive from this point than when I actually entered it. Fort Bonnier, built by the French, the minaret of a mosque at one end of the city and the arcades of the hospital were the only places which stood out prominently.

There were no walls round the city. A few minutes after obtaining this first sight I found myself in the largest square of the town.

At an elevation of 800 feet above sea-level the town was built on the two sides of a dune running from east to west, and on the westerly side of a second dune to the north parallel to the first. Timbuctu formed a triangle, with its base towards the south.

There was absolutely no mystery left about the place, and as soon as one entered the town the observer was forcibly struck by how much overrated this sacred place had been. From an artistic point of view there was not a single building in Timbuctu worth a second look. Even the three mosques were of little interest as far as the architecture went, but were, of course, interesting from the historian's point of view. In the southern part of the city stood the *Djingery-ber*, or Big Mosque, built in the eleventh century by an Alfa marabu called Alkali-Alakeb. This mosque had inside it a series of remarkable arcades and pillars supporting a heavy mud ceiling with a flat terrace above, the whole made of white

The Djingery Ber, or Big Mosque, Timboctu.

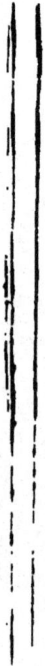

stone and clay mixed with flour of the *baobab* fruit. Not far from this mosque was the *yobu-ber*, or great market, by which I had entered the town—a vast rectangular square, the two sides of which showed arcades with square pillars. In these buildings merchants and pedlars had their stalls, whereas in the square itself dozens of women squatted on their haunches selling coal, wood, articles of food, cheap ornaments, etc. Formerly the market consisted entirely of straw huts. The bigger merchants transacted business in their own private homes. The local civil and military club was also in this square, and Fort Bonnier, with its handsome buildings and barracks, stood prominently on the southern side of the town.

The Catholic Mission of the White Fathers, established in Timbuctu in 1895, also had its establishment in the great square. A church and tower had been built, but shortly before my visit the tower, imitating the example of the Venice Campanile, collapsed, and was a mass of mud *débris* when I visited it.

. Stone was scarce near Timbuctu. Except the Big Mosque, all the houses and buildings were constructed with sun-dried bricks and balls of clay. There was no architectural beauty to be detected anywhere, the greatest effort towards decorating a house-front being made by flanking the façade with large pillars and by raising flat vertical bands upon the upper storey in relief; between these bands were small windows with wood *musharabeah* work in imitation of the Moorish style. These square columns have occasioned people to say that this architecture has found its way from Egypt. Personally, I think that the real origin of the application of these columns to the façade is rather the necessity of strengthening the outer walls, as mud walls in Timbuctu have a way of washing off and disappearing during the rainy season unless properly protected.

In the southern part of the town we still find the *Alfasin-kunda*, or Moorish quarter, inhabited by the people from Fez, in Morocco; the *Sirfa-kunda*, or quarter of the *Sirfa;* and the *sarey-keyna*, or small graveyard. On the highest part of the dune is the *Chirfa-kunda*, or quarter of the infidels ; the *Wangara-kunda*, or quarter of the Wangara people ; the *yabu-keyna*, the small market, by far the most picturesque spot in Timbuctu ; and near it the *Sidi-Yahya* in the centre of the town, a small mosque built in the fifteenth century by Omar, Governor of Timbuctu, by special order of Gogo King of Gao. There is a curious superstition regarding the *Sidi-Yahya* mosque, the greater part of which is now buried in sand, but the minaret is still in good preservation. Slightly above the level of the road is a small window overlooking the grave of a saintly marabu inside the tower. When a man is accused of crime and his guilt or innocence is to be decided, he is brought to this window and his head is thrust inside until he can see the grave. They say that if a man is guilty and does not confess, he will die at once ; if he is not guilty, he will show no fear.

Further to the north and built about the same time as the *Djingery-ber* was the *Sankore* mosque, now almost entirely buried in sand except the minaret shaped like a pyramid. It was built by a wealthy lady. Near the *Sankore* was the North Fort, where spahis had been stationed. They had lately been withdrawn It was found that soldiers mounted on horses, in the desert took longer to march than infantry soldiers ; the horses were difficult to feed, and long halts were necessary for

The Sidi-Yahya Mosque, Timbuctu (showing window, nearest the ground, where those accused of crime are brought to prove their innocence.)

the horses to recuperate their strength even after comparatively short marches in the sand. From the North Fort, now half abandoned, one obtained a good panoramic view of Timbuctu. East of the town, and separated from it by a wide avenue, was a settlement of hemispherical thatched huts harbouring a portion of the transitory population. Towards the west another similar suburb was gradually forming.

The environments of Timbuctu could not boast of luxurious vegetation. There were dunes of sand on all sides, a few mimosas, and nothing more. To the west, the fingers of both hands were quite sufficient to enumerate all the palm-trees in sight, mostly near wells. Two historical palm-trees were perceptible in the pretty garden of the *Cercle*, towering over a pit laid out in small rectangles with all kinds of vegetables, which were compelled to grow by constant water poured upon them from the well at the bottom of the pit. Each rectangle had a border of bottles upside down. I do not know exactly where those bottles came from, but in their last state and position they were certainly useful in preventing sand from sliding down the slope and carrying away with it the horticultural efforts of the garrison.

On the north slope of the dune was the *banga-djindeh*, generally abbreviated into *badjindeh* (or marsh of the hippopotami), the *Saney-Goungou* (the island of North Arabs), the *Timbuctu-Koy-Batuma* (or the court of the Timbuctu chief) and the *Biti-Batuma*.

On the slope of the second dune was the *Birinka-kunda*, or quarter of roasters of sheeps' feet. There was a caravanserai, the *Albarradjuh*, the *Taka-bunder*, the *Sargu-kunda* (the quarter of Tuareg and their slaves), as well as the *Sankore* mosque.

Three hours at the most should, I think, provide ample time for the casual observer to see everything in Timbuctu, but if one wishes to go into architectural details and study the customs of the natives, one should stay a little longer. I remained some ten or twelve days, and every minute of my time was fully occupied. Being the guest of Commandant Mezillier, and through the great civility of the officers and civilians in Timbuctu, the entire premises of the club were placed at my disposal—much, I fear, to the inconvenience of the members. I appreciated having such comfortable quarters, for I was able to develop several hundred negatives taken on the journey, and got my notes and baggage straightened up.

I looked upon Timbuctu as the end of my journey, as from this place I should be able to travel by what people call civilized ways—perhaps sometimes far more uncomfortable than primitive methods of locomotion.

I was interested in visiting the natural pools and artificial wells bored round Timbuctu in order to furnish water to the inhabitants. The pools, or *banguh*, as the natives called them, were not to be relied upon for a constant supply, as they depended chiefly on the high water of the Niger for their refilling. When the flood did not reach so far, nor the infiltration extend to the locality where these pools were to be found, they gradually dried up. The water became undrinkable, quite fetid.

Near the hospital, south of the town, the French were, at the time of my visit, boring a big well which ought to be useful to the post. Digging a well in the desert involves a deal of work. This particular well was forty feet deep and double that measurement in diameter at its mouth. The sand constantly slipped and refilled the aperture of the well. Hundreds of men were at work, and the supply of water obtained was constant and plentiful.

The climate of Timbuctu was healthy and dry, except from June to October, when the wet season set in. In the shade the temperature varied from 4° Centigrade (39½° Fahrenheit) during the coldest months of December and January, to some 46° Centigrade (114½° Fahrenheit) during the hottest months of May and June. From October to April north-easterly winds were prevalent, then for the next six months the winds blew from the west. Violent storms came chiefly from the north-east, but sometimes also from the east and the south-east.

Timbuctu was nothing more than a city of transit and exchange, with a fixed population of about five thousand and a floating population of some four thousand people. The floating population consisted of Arabs, Moors and merchants from Tripoli, many from Ghadamenon, Tenduf, Tadjakant and Touat, who came every year. From the south, many people found their way to this big centre, and as one walked about the narrow lanes of Timbuctu one frequently saw Bambara, Fulbeh and Mossi types. This shifting population might be called more exactly " semi - stationary," as all these people remained for several months in Timbuctu, often intermarrying with people of a different race, and then returned to their homes. There was, indeed, a great mixture of types in the Sacred City, quite interesting.

The two principal elements were distinctly the Soñgoy, perhaps the most ancient race, and the Arma, their conquerors, who came from Morocco.

From an intellectual point of view, Timbuctu was

the most important centre of Mussulman science in the
French possessions in Western Africa. Numerous schools
were frequented, not only by young people of the town,
but also by strangers from neighbouring countries, who
came to this big centre in search of education, to be
afterwards imparted to their respective tribesmen.

One of the most influential classes in Timbuctu was
that of the *alfa*, or learned men, who had arrived from
all parts of Africa to study or to teach. These men,
generally of strong Islamic principles, had at one time
great power over the population. The Mussulman religion prevailed, although I cannot say that these people
impressed me as being particularly observant of the
Koran's laws. Except some of the older men, I seldom
observed individuals making their salaam at sunrise or
at sunset. The usual ablutions were omitted—occasionally, as with the Tuareg, a sand friction was substituted—and I believe there were but few who knew
their daily prayers accurately. Mosques were not well
patronized, except on grand occasions when the priests
collected considerable crowds.

The *Imam* of Timbuctu, Hammaduh-Umar-Jidji, a
man somewhat morose and ill-tempered, had lost most
of his power over the masses, and his deputy, Khadi-
Hammed-Baba, though less inclined openly to show his
contempt for white people, was none the less afraid of
being contaminated by them. It was always a great
amusement to me while in Timbuctu, whenever I met
these ecclesiastics in the street, to grasp them by the
hand, which I shook in a hearty manner. Their faces
became horrified, and no sooner had I released them than
they rubbed their hands upon their clothes in order to
remove any taint the difference in our religions might

Digging a well in the Deser

have caused. After the first two or three meetings, whenever the high priests perceived me in the distance, they vanished inside a doorway or round a convenient corner. With some ill-will they one day took me, by order of the commandant, into the *Djingery-ber* (Big Mosque), and showed me what little there was in the various court-yards and between the long colonnades. With the *Imam* were several high priests, equally suspicious, as well as a man who acted as interpreter and whose hands were affected by leprosy. I noticed that whereas the *Imam* and the high or religious authorities showed repugnance in shaking hands with me, the leper took every opportunity of showing his friendliness by grasping my hand with his crippled and decaying fingers. It was fortunate that I did not share the general idea that leprosy is contagious—in fact, I am certain it is not, except in cases when a sore spot upon a healthy person is placed in immediate contact with the sore of a leper.

The chief of the town was an *alfa*, called Saïdu, a somewhat insignificant person, but quite respectable as far as I could judge. He had little to do, as the entire management of the city was in the hands of French officers. Hence the excellent way in which the town was kept and everything regulated in as sensible and sanitary a fashion as was possible in the circumstances.

We have a notion in England that the French occupy their colonies by mere brute force, by keeping a large staff of officers and a strong force of soldiers in all their military posts; but indeed no nation in the world does things in a simpler and more practical way than the French in their African colonies.

If one takes the trouble of examining the work done

by French officers, without regard to racial jealousy or preconceived notions, one can only express the most profound admiration. The enthusiasm, energy and practical methods with which they carry on their work are amazing. They administer justice, build houses, make roads, build boats, make irrigation works, develop the commercial possibilities of the country, and make excellent maps of the regions they open up.

I must confess that I was not astonished to find the French officer such an admirable person, but I was surprised to notice how intelligent non-commissioned officers were in the French colonial army, men of no higher grade than sergeants possessing sound technical knowledge of surveying, road and bridge making, and engineering in general, that many a superior officer of some other countries I know would have difficulty in emulating.

In the way of colonial wars, it is surprising what the French have done in Africa, and how they can keep their colonies going with so few officers and men. In the Senegalese soldier, the French have perhaps the finest black soldier of the entire zone of tropical and semi-tropical Africa. With a handful of these men it is safe to go anywhere.

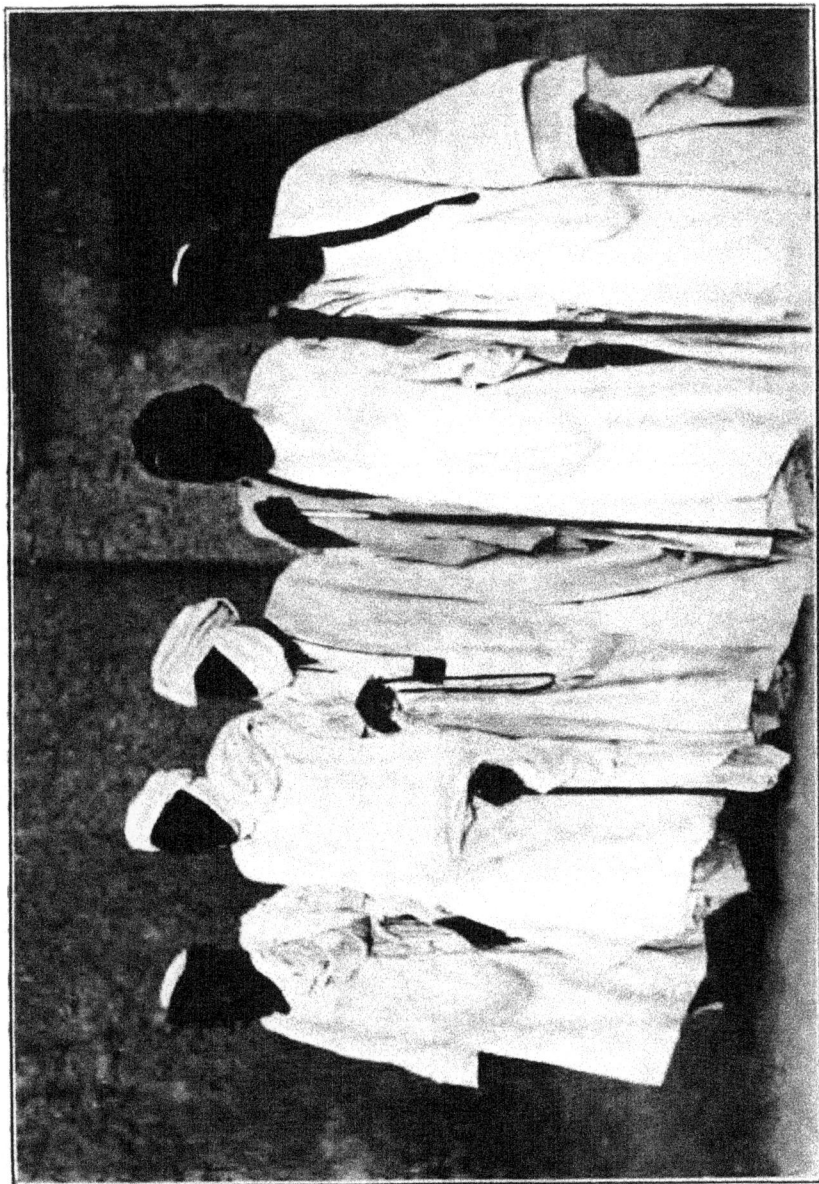

The Imam, Khadi-Hammed-Baba, and Head Marabu, of Timboctu.

CHAPTER XXX.

TIMBUCTU is a good exchange market, but little is actually produced there. For seven or eight months out of twelve the region south of Timbuctu is inundated. When dry it is suitable for pasture land. Rice is cultivated on a large scale and the process of its cultivation is ingenious. The seed is sown shortly before the flood, then, by means of ably-constructed dunes, water is let in gradually. The crop is brought in in November and December according to the season. During that time hundreds of men and women can be seen in the water cutting the rice. I think the moisture absorbed in spending many hours of the day for some weeks in the water, as well as a fish and rice diet, are responsible for the amount of leprosy noticeable on people whose blood is much impoverished and not in good condition. I had noticed an appalling number of lepers in villages upon the Niger.

White and black millet of the giant and of the small variety is cultivated on dry land, or in the country liable to inundation shortly after the waters have withdrawn.

In Timbuctu we find ovens in the streets. They are constructed of mud, and are of a conical shape somewhat rounded at the top and lined inside with baked bottoms of broken earthen vases. In these ovens the natives

bake their small round loaves—quite good, were it not
for the quantity of sand which gets mixed with the flour
of the inferior kind of wheat locally grown. The wheat
is ground between two stones, the lower one larger than
the upper. These stones are imported at great expense
from the mountains of Sahel in Morocco. After the flour
has been coarsely ground it is passed through a thin
material, and then rolled between the hands until it
becomes fairly fine. Both in the big and the small
market-places one sees dozens of women selling bread.

The Timbuctu people do not possess many cooking
implements, if the inevitable mortar and pestle for rice
and millet are excepted. An earthen fire-pot, the *fema*, a
large earthenware vessel or two in which water is kept,
known to the French as *canari*, and a similar perforated
vessel used as a strainer form their *batterie de cuisine*.

Principally since the French occupation the natives
have taken to growing vegetables, and some of them
own small gardens where beans, onions (quantities of
these), tomatoes and red and yellow water-melons are
produced and consumed in the town. The millet and
rice grown are not sufficient to provide for local wants,
and much is imported from Djenne, the sister city of
Timbuctu, and from Djimballa. It is generally during
the months of November and December, when the water
is high and navigation easy, that large provisions of
foodstuff are collected.

Boats such as those we have seen on the Niger, constructed of small planks of palm-wood sewn together
with pieces of string, were so heavily laden with grain
to be conveyed to Timbuctu that it was a wonder to me
they did not sink.

A lot of meat is eaten in Timbuctu. Good mutton

Caravan entering Timboctu from the north.

and goat are sold cheap enough. Beef is a little dearer. Large herds of cattle are owned by Tuareg tribes and by the Foulame.

Antelopes, gazelles and hares were formerly abundant in the immediate neighbourhood, but are not so now. Of domestic animals one finds camels, horses, the *yedji* and the *hau*, two kinds of humped ox, the first used mostly as a beast of burden and the other for riding. Then there are quantities of the useful and powerful little *farka*, faithful donkeys, which do all the daily work in and about Timbuctu. They are taken with the large *canari* on their backs to the pools and wells to fetch the water ; with a large basket slung on each side they trot along to fetch mud in order to build houses ; they are brought to market with loads of wood for fire-making ; and when the day's work is finished they are mounted by the younger members of the family to go racing along the big boulevard round the city or upon the Kabara road.

Sheep, with or without wool, goats, dogs, cats, numbers of pigeons, chickens and ducks are kept.

Whenever you want to please a native of Timbuctu with a present you should give him some kola nut. He loves chewing kola the whole day long. When he wishes to confirm a sale or any commercial transaction he gives a present of kola, and even when he is about to get married the wedding agreement is not complete until some kola nut is handed over as a present. I have already referred to the nourishing qualities of the kola nut. It affects the gastric juices and takes away the appetite. People therefore can go for longer periods without feeling hungry, but not, I repeat, without considerable damage to their health and constitution.

The people of Timbuctu generally take three meals a day—at about seven or eight in the morning, at about two in the afternoon, and at nine o'clock in the evening. Bread soaked in honey, or a sort of stew of millet or flour, cheese and spices, is taken for breakfast. For lunch and dinner they have the usual *kuss-kuss*, which they locally call *tasso ;* sometimes also meat, mutton, beef, birds, or fish with a spicy sauce over it ; the leaf of the *baobab* as well as the flour of its beans are eaten. The leaf of the *djisuma* besmeared with butter from cows' milk or else with the *boulanga* butter from the *karité* nut, as well as all sorts of spices, are much relished in the diet of Timbuctu people. Coffee is scarce and too expensive for most people, but great quantities of tea of inferior quality are consumed.

Although Mussulman, the people do not abstain from intoxicants as much as they should. The rich people indulge in foreign imported spirits, such as absinthe and gin, while the poorer folks make themselves a strong drink with fermented millet and honey, or with the stems of the *borgu* (the *kundi-hari*).

A good deal of public cooking is done in Timbuctu, especially for the benefit of the transitory population. Nearly all the butchers prepare cooked meat for sale. Very appetizing *bundia* (or *brochettes*), small pieces of meat passed through a rod, roasted sheeps' feet, mutton cutlets, sheeps' heads, legs of mutton and a small sausage called *djinana* can all be purchased.

In the way of sweets, the most suitable for a European palate are the loaves of rice cooked in *karité* butter; the *fourmé*, a similar kind of paste made of wheat instead of rice ; the *filati*, a puff-paste steamed ; the *djimita*, sweetened with a thick layer of honey, and the millet

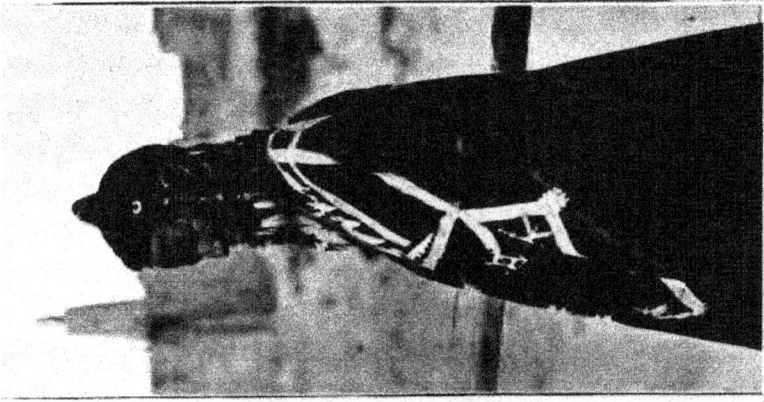

Fu beh-Soñgoy lady.

Fu beh woman.

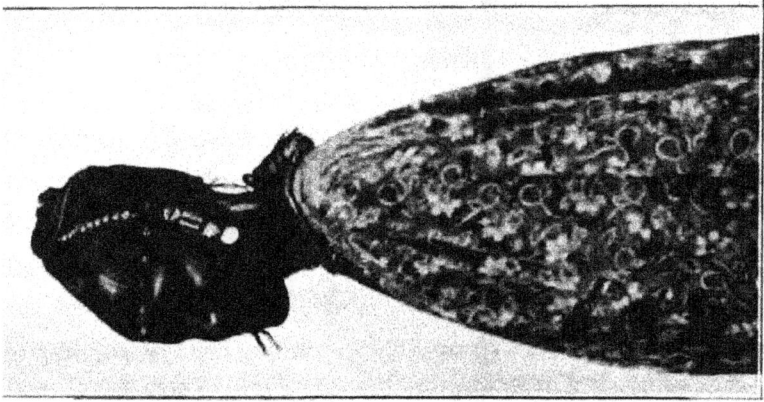

A lady o Gao.

balls called *nempti*. *Kolo,* or beans cooked in water, are also devoured in quantities.

I was fortunate in meeting in Timbuctu an extraordinary man, who now goes under the name of Yacoma, and who piloted me all over Timbuctu and gave me no end of useful information about the town and its people. This gifted man has now been employed as official interpreter to the military. His faithfulness to the French government, combined with his marvellous knowledge of the country around, and of the various tribes, whose languages he speaks fluently, are, I am sure, of great assistance in the dealings of the French with the natives. He commanded great respect in the town and seemed to be the adviser of everybody in the sacred city.

I always found the information he gave me regarding anything connected with the country accurate. On one of our walks I asked Yacoma what were the principal trades of Timbuctu. He told me that everybody in Timbuctu had a trade, which descended from father to son.

" The *alfa* people are all tailors. The *Arma* go in for shoemaking, while the Soñgoy," said he, as he pointed first at one group, then at another, then at a third, " are butchers, blacksmiths, locksmiths, goldsmiths and manufacturers of weapons. Then," he added, as he made me peep into a house, " there you see some Soñgoy weavers, and over there "—he made me describe a semicircle on my heels—" there is a Soñgoy carpenter."

" Look, look ! " he exclaimed in excitement, " do you see that man scraping the skull of a student ? " (Barbers always carry on business at the corner of two streets) . . . . " That is a Soñgoy barber."

As he was saying these words a lot of donkeys went by raising clouds of dust. Two or three men followed them with long sticks, which they used freely on the animals' backs. Those were Soñgoy donkeymen.

"Yes," said Yacoma, "the Soñgoy do pretty well everything."

We had hardly gone a few yards when Yacoma, catching hold of my sleeve and pointing with his finger to the top of a mud wall being constructed, drew my attention to some masons who, by the use of a small flat pick and a minute wooden implement, were doing their work with considerable precision "Those," he said, "are also Soñgoy. Do you see," he remarked to me, "how straight that wall is ? They are building it without using a plumb-line. Do you not think that is wonderful ? "

Well, it was wonderful, because the wall had already reached a considerable height and was absolutely vertical.

There are certain guilds for each trade in Timbuctu and each one of these corporations has a chief, or Emir The Emir of the butchers, for instance, controls the quality and the price of meat, and has the right of confiscation if the meat supplied to the public is not good.

Naturally, in Timbuctu, none of the trades are highly developed, as the local wants are small. One thing that astonished me greatly was the simplicity of the tools used by all people in their work. The carpenters, for instance, who spent most of their time making massive doors and the green, red or yellow musharabeah screen for the windows, only seemed to possess one tool, a combined axe and pick. The weavers did their work on primitive looms worked by two strings fixed to the big

The small market-place, Timboctu.

toes which served to move up and down the two sets of threads that were woven into narrow bands of cotton with simple but regular ornamentations upon them.

Jewellers occasionally worked in silver and gold from French money or Maria Theresa thalers, but most of their time was occupied in converting empty sardine-tins into cheap ornaments, sometimes quite interesting in shape.

Blacksmiths did the greatest variety of work ; they manufactured picks, axes, knives, spears, swords, nails, locks and padlocks out of iron imported from Morocco and Mussi.

The manufacturer of jewellery was not always the salesman, but there were *teyfa,* or middle-men, who sold jewellery on commission in the market-square.

There were many dyers in Timbuctu, men who came mostly from Sansanding. The favourite colours were red and blue.

One of the most flourishing businesses in the sacred city was that of the donkey-men. There was a constant demand for their services between Kabara and Timbuctu during the wet season, and in the dry season they went as far as Day and Koroyume. Most of them were un-scrupulous scoundrels, and besides their pay they generally managed to rob their employers of part of the goods entrusted to them.

" They are bad, bad men," said Yacoma to me. " If you give them pots of honey to carry they will drive holes in the pots and lick the honey as it comes out. If you give them bags of millet and rice, half the grain has disappeared by the time it reaches the other end of the journey, and with slabs of salt they will chip them and make an extra profit from the stolen property."

The transport of salt from the mines of Taodeni to Timbuctu is done entirely by the Arab nomad tribe, the *Berabish*, for whom Arauan is a centre. They go twice a year to Taodeni and bring the slabs of salt to Timbuctu. These slabs, weighing about sixty pounds each, are sold in Timbuctu at from fifteen to thirty-five francs each, according to quality. The slabs of salt which are sent from Timbuctu to various parts of the country towards the south, south-east and south-west form the greatest part of the Timbuctu carrying trade. In exchange for this salt come from the south a good deal of millet, rice, *karité* butter, honey, kola nut, dried fish and iron. From the north, besides the salt, come cotton and woollen stuffs, leather, tanned and in its natural state, weapons, gunpowder, glass-ware, knives, tea, sugar, coffee, dates, etc., by caravan from Morocco, Algeria, Tunis, Tripoli, the Sudan and from the oases in the desert.

The salt mines of Taodeni are north of Timbuctu. Their position is not properly marked on maps, being generally put down as south of lat. 22° N., whereas it is twenty or twenty-five kilometres north of the 23rd parallel.

Captain Cauvin took an interesting journey to that little-known region, accompanied by twenty *méharistes*. He found that there were two routes from Boudjebiha leading to Taodeni, one by the wells of Arauan, the other by Inichaig. Vegetation ceased altogether in that desert country between one hundred and one hundred and fifty kilometres north of Arauan. Then the trail went through an opening in the dune called Foum-el-Alba. The shift-ing sands north of the dune were troublesome, the camels having great difficulty in pushing through. North of this dune it seemed as if a cataclysm had taken place, rocks, mostly sandstone and quartz, being dispersed over the landscape in the greatest confusion.

A great caravan, called the *Azalay*, goes once a year to Taodeni from Arauan, and then on its return breaks up, the salt finding its way to Timbuctu, Djenne and into the interior of the " loop " of the Niger.

Between Unan and Taodeni the country is at first hilly, some of the hills being high, then numerous *oued*, or river-beds, directed towards the west or to the south-west, are found. Near Taodeni a great depression is found about 780 feet lower than the wells of Unan.

A legend of the nomad tribes in that region says that in ancient times the Niger flowed towards the north and eventually into the depression of Taodeni, where it formed an immense lake. North of the dune Fum-el-Alba, they say, it is easy to recognize the passage of the Niger through that region. There are evident signs even near Timbuctu that at one time the Niger, or a portion, at least, of the water of the Niger, flowed northwards instead of towards the east. Certain dunes near Kabara show indisputably that a channel northwards existed.

The village of Taodeni itself was small, one hundred and ten yards long by eighty yards wide, and built of sun-baked bricks.

The salt mines of Taodeni were celebrated all over Western Africa, especially upon the Niger. There were only one hundred and fifty inhabitants in the place under Chief Kaïd, a descendant of the Kaïds installed there by the Sultan of Morocco during the time of the Timbuctu conquest by the Moors. Some of the houses were actually constructed of slabs of salt.

Southwards was an *arête*, which was merely a ramification of a rocky mass, and which was the boundary of the region of El-Djouf. Only a small region of dunes existed.

Great suffering was experienced by the Cauvin expedition from want of water. Many of their camels were lost. They were able to map accurately 1,200 kilometres upon their road, and it was wonderful that a newly-formed company of *méharistes* could accomplish such a hard journey without losing a single man.

Captain Cauvin gave me these interesting barometrical readings :—

		mm.
The barometric pressure of the well at El-Hadjiou	..	739·1
Arauan	..	734·5
Bir (well) Unan	..	736·0
,, Taodeni		748·5

The exportation of salt from the Taodeni mines takes place from four kilometres south-west of the village, where the mines are to be found at the foot of a mount. Well-marked stratifications are noticeable in the landscape all round, and south of Taodeni is a stream-bed going westwards. Anyone can exploit these mines by paying to the Kaïd one bar of salt for every ten exported. Every worker makes a rectangular ditch eight metres by ten. One has to dig from three to four metres in the clay and gypsum in order to find the strata of salt. There we find first a stratum of hard crystal impurities which are not suitable for being cut into slabs. This stratum is considered useless and is abandoned. Under this useless layer are three distinct strata of salt easily detachable by using a lever. The first and the third layer are fifteen to eighteen centimetres thick. The middle one is somewhat thinner, hardly more than half the size of the first and third. In fact, the first and third layers are actually double layers, stuck fast in the middle. They can be detached by hammering hard. The second one consists of only one slab, undetachable, of course. Under these three layers there is another layer not workable, under which extremely brackish water is found.

In digging, the natives say, they have found in these deposits a mummified camel, as well as footmarks of men, sheep, well-preserved pieces of wood, remnants of places where fires had been burnt, and the footmarks of elephants and hippopotami. The inhabitants declare that if one were to dig deeper one would go through the earth's crust and die in the water below, which is extraordinarily deep.

Strangely enough, any amount of botanical fossils like tamarind beans, stones of dates, and fruit from tropical palms have been found in extracting the salt. In the sandstone schists large stones of some fruit, resembling the stones of mangoes, have also been discovered.

The Arab merchants send workers to the mines under a contract to extract one hundred slabs, after which, if the man works hard and can get more, he may barter them as his own private property.

Formerly all trade in Timbuctu was carried on in the streets or in private houses, whereas now much business is transacted in the two market-squares, where merchants spread samples of their goods on mats, in baskets and calabashes. The men mostly sold woven materials, salt wholesale, meat and shoes ; other articles were sold by women.

Tobacco was grown in fairly large quantities and was mostly consumed in the town. Ostrich feathers and

white and brown rubber were sold direct to French
exporters and seldom found their way to the market-
square. Ivory, which was plentiful at one time, is
never to be seen in Timbuctu now.

Here again could be plainly noticed how mistaken
people's ideas are in Europe regarding slavery. In
either of the markets in Timbuctu were plenty of women,
nearly all slaves, selling goods which were entrusted
to them by their masters. They did pretty well what
they pleased and were practically free in their actions,
occasionally being even allowed to trade on their own
account. Not infrequently these slave women, if they
showed good business capacity, married their owners,
when they received their liberty on the birth of children
from the union with a free man. The sons of slaves,
born in the house, were seldom sold, and remained
slaves of the family, of which they practically formed
part, living with, and as well as, their masters.

The price of slaves until quite recently was about
fifty shillings for boys not older than eight or ten years.
A man in good health might fetch as much as £12
sterling, or its equivalent in merchandise; whereas
girls of from eight to ten years of age were sold for £4
sterling, and young women for from £14 to £18.

The Mussulman rule was applied to marriages in
Timbuctu. A man could take to himself not more than
four wives, if his means allowed him such luxury; each
wife, of course, to live in a separate home with her
private cooking materials.

There were no harems. Yacoma told me that
divorces were common, owing to the great opportunities
which women had of being unfaithful. Personally, I
was not struck by the standard of morality of so

sacred a place, but on my travels I have always been impressed by the fact that the greater the sanctity of a place the lower the morality.

"Come along to see some of the schools," said Yacoma to me, and along we went, winding our way along the narrow streets until we came to some of the houses where we could hear children chanting their lessons in a chorus.   There the little mites sat, cross-legged upon the ground, holding upon their laps slabs upon which they wrote with a solution of water, gum and mimosa, which is a strong colouring liquid.

Schoolmasters combine teaching with public writing. They sell copies of the Koran in Arabic.   They write letters for illiterate merchants, friends and lovers.   They make amulets for the superstitious, and are, taking things all round, the busiest people in Timbuctu.   They frequently take advantage of the knowledge which they gain of people's business and secrets, and, perhaps, because of this are treated with deference by the population. Presents are given to these teachers by parents of pupils, and a slave will even be presented to the teacher whose pupil has been able to learn by heart the entire Koran.

The high priests, of whom every mosque possesses one, take great interest in the education of the young, and especially in the religious side of their training. Priests are generally chosen from the learned class, the *alfa*, and so are the *cadis*, the judges of criminal cases, who deliver judgment according to Mussulman law.

The French are sensible in the government of the natives, and although Timbuctu is under the high command of the military authorities, it also possesses a native *Emir*, or *Koyra-Koy*, a chief. Each secondary

quarter, such as the *Djingery-ber*, the *Badjindeh* ar
the *Sankore*, had subsidiary chiefs. Furthermore, tl
quarters of strangers, such as the *kimta*, the *Aal-sidi-A*
the *Kel-Nkunder*, claimed each its own chief; and tl
quarter of the Sansanding dyers was directly sel
governed.

A Moor (Timbuctu).

CHAPTER XXXI.

SUSPICIOUSNESS was one of the characteristics of the Timbuctu people, especially the better classes. Perhaps this distrust has been acquired by contact with the Tuareg.

When one entered a house, for instance, it was not customary—in fact, it would be deemed an insult—to be asked one's name or one's business by the slave or the servant at the door. All one did was to call out "*Salaamelek—Salaamelekku,*" and to wait in the first vestibule out of sight of the people in the street who might be interested in other people's affairs. Everybody was in Timbuctu. Beyond this vestibule was a covered court, in which the slaves and sometimes their master spent the greater part of the time. The caller was not supposed to enter this court until requested to do so, and it was in the vestibule that ordinary callers were received. There was generally a raised portion in the court, on which carpets and mats were spread. Pillars of palm-wood supported a heavy awning of skins. In the better houses, before one came to this inner court, a second vestibule was found, similar to the first. The covered court was surrounded by bedrooms for the women, while in the centre of the court slaves ground millet, others wove cotton, others supervised the cooking or entertained callers in lively conversation. Only

intimate friends were received in this particular portion
of the house.

Beyond the first court was an uncovered court with
dependencies, where the kitchen was situated, and all
the animals belonging to the family were kept. A stair-
case from the first or the second vestibule led to the
upper storey of the house.

The furniture of Timbuctu houses was not elaborate.
It had been greatly influenced by Moorish ideas. Carpets,
mats and richly-coloured blankets decorated the walls,
floors and odd corners, and cushions of various sizes
were laid upon the floor to sit upon, or rest one's back
against. Beds consisted of a mattress, sometimes a
wooden bedstead, or more often a *kara*, a kind of bedstead
of mud and wood. Blankets were used on these beds.
Wooden cases with heavy iron padlocks lined the walls
in the bedrooms, and in them clothes and valuables were
locked up. Outside the rooms on the upper floor there
was generally a balcony on which summer evenings
were spent.

It was on the balcony of Yacoma's house that I took
the photograph, reproduced in the illustration facing this
page, of handsome Madame Yacoma, her limbs much
ornamented with jewellery, and three balls of hair upon
her head.

I do not think that I have ever visited a town where
the varieties of headdress were so numerous and remarkable as in Timbuctu. When women were young, until
the age of thirteen or fourteen, they fastened their hair
into a plait which, with some additional black silk and
with plenty of jewels and ornaments attached to it, stuck
out behind and was called the *yellofoh*, or " one tress
only." From fourteen to fifteen they wore two or three

Soṅgoy woman, Tim ʃoctu.

queues, one behind and one in front, adding to them the fibre of the *kondji*, the plait behind being rolled up at the extremity and slightly lowered. This *coiffure*, which is called the *djnne-djnne*, or " in front-in front," is also much decorated with beads and silver triangles.

Unmarried women never showed balls of hair at the side of the head, but wore them on the top of the skull. Slaves, not married, had only one of these balls—a kind of pompom—on the right side. Most married women wore two of these pompoms, one over each ear. The two-ball arrangement for married women was a special *coiffure* fashionable in Djenne, the sister city to Timbuctu. When not in holiday dress, the girls also adorned themselves with these hair-balls, with an extra one behind the head.

Perhaps the most puzzling headdress to a male observer was the *korbo-tchirey*, words which, translated literally, mean " all sorts of rings, red "—words which require explanation. They mean that the top plait, stiffened, described curves in all directions, ending in a sort of spiral at the back of the head. A triangular ornament of red imitation coral, or stone, was placed at the end of the bigger loop upon the top of the head. In other instances, two plaits were substituted for the two side balls at the side of the face. A third circumscribed the forehead and turned over the right temple, where pendants were attached. The later *coiffure* was only worn when a girl lost her virginity. Curiously enough, old women displayed a similar headdress, but without the loop arrangement over the top of the head.

These are merely a few of the principal ways of wearing the hair. There were innumerable other styles according to the fancy, ingenuity or ambition of

individual ladies, but they were far too complicated for
me to comprehend how they were arranged. Less still
am I able to describe them.

The boys and men, too, had characteristic ways of
hair-cutting, according to class or caste. Sometimes
a line of hair from the front to the back of the head was
left upon the shaven head. This was called the *djorro-
marabu*. Then there was the *dahsi* worn by the *Sirfa*,
a broad line forming an angle, with the point at the back
of the head. The descendants of the Moors—the Arma
wore the hair in two different ways : either in one tuft
of hair over the right ear (the *manga*), worn by the people
originally from Fez, or else the *djokoti*, consisting of
five tufts at the corners of a square with a fifth in the
centre, adopted by the *Marakesh* people. Other people
occasionally wore three, four, or five lines or tufts, as
well as lines and tufts combined, upon the top of the
skull. The marabus had adopted the *tamali djokoti*,
a square tuft directly over the forehead. Slaves preferred the *djorro-nda-manga* headdress, a composition
of two ways above described, a line over the head and a
tuft on the right side of the forehead. Sometimes slaves
were seen with a small tuft and a pigtail.

The costumes in Timbuctu were like those all over
French Nigeria and the Senegal. The men wore the *tilbi*,
a long shirt open at the sides and sewn at the lower
extremity, with a deep pocket in front, and a large-sleeved
shirt underneath, the *messauria*, or else a similar garment,
the *farandja*. The richer people usually put on two
of these shirts one above the other, one being white and
one blue. Under this garment large pantaloons of white
or blue cotton were worn. The *semfiti*, a piece of stuff
with a long fringe, and the *disa*, a blue striped material,

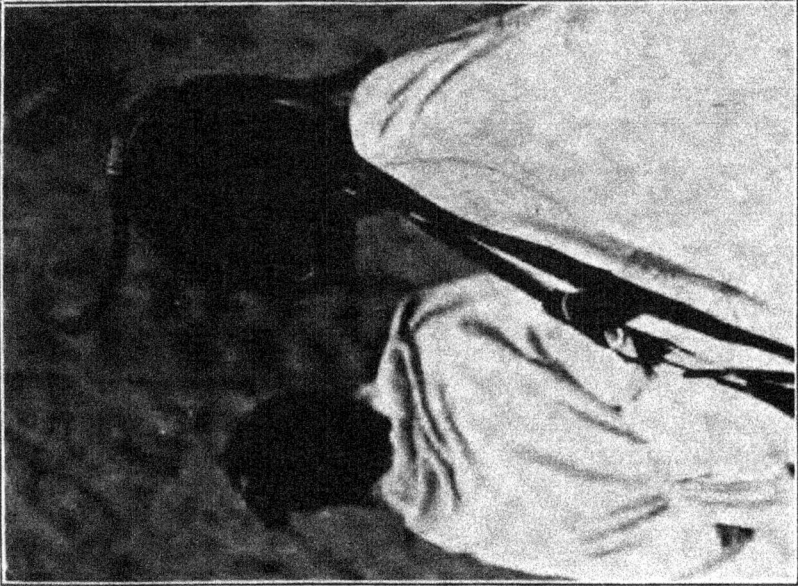

Curious head-dresses of Timbuctoo.

were used as scarves. A turban was donned over a cap, its long ends wound round the back of the head and over the mouth. The pointed white or blue cap was also worn alone. Women went about bareheaded in order to show their *coiffures*, or else with a black hood.

Timbuctu women wrap themselves in the *tafe*, which are of variable quality and of any colour according to taste, and also put on a *tilbi* similar to that of the men, but more ornamented with red, white, yellow and green silk. The *saya*, also a woman's garment, has long sleeves ending in a point.

Most people went about barefooted or in comfortable-looking sandals called the *tyelambu*. The better people protected their feet with slippers of a bilious yellow colour with the back part of the shoe folded inside. These were the *balga*. The women clad their feet in the *selba*, also a slipper, red instead of yellow, of Arab shape and certainly of a Moorish origin. Stylish top-boots for men are manufactured for the cold weather, as well as wooden clogs on which they toddle along during the rains. But yellow and red shoes are those most generally worn.

Until quite lately no one ever went out of the house unarmed, but things have changed owing to the trust which the natives feel in French protection. One seldom saw men carrying weapons in the streets, except old-fashioned chiefs, who would think it bad form to be seen out without their swords or spears. When going out of town, even for a short distance, however, all went armed.

Their spears, of various shapes, had evidently been copied from people of many nationalities who had found their way to Timbuctu. Some spears had plain broad heads, others narrow and pointed. One kind

had two barbs ; another a greater number. Some had
straight barbs, others barbs spirally curved and well
adapted to cause a rotatory movement during the
spear's flight. Like the Tuareg, the people of Timbuctu always carried a sword suspended to a sling over
the shoulder. Only the people from Mossi displayed a
bow and a quiver of poisoned arrows.

It was fashionable for men to go about the town
carrying a long stick ornamented with copper rings.

Prominent among the accessories of local dress were
amulets of all shapes in red or yellow leather. Numbers
of them, as with the Tuareg, were carried about the
person. In a town where men, women and children
smoked, it was but natural to see everybody provided
with a neat leather satchel, the *albeyti*, with numerous
little pockets containing tobacco, money, an earthenware pipe with mouthpiece of wood, or one made from
the tibia of a sheep, etc., etc.

Men and women of Timbuctu were not happy unless
highly ornamented. The men wore rings and stone or
else marble bracelets. Green, red, white and black
bracelets were made of coloured clay. Both sexes ornamented themselves with copper and silver anklets,
the *tche djenji* (or foot circlet), made in the shape of a
" C " and having two big spherical knobs.

The *cacao*, which was also fashionable, was a flattened silver plate (of a triangular form in section), the
back of which stuck out into a point.

The arms were much ornamented, the most notable
ornament being the *teybaraten djendji*, a porphyry ring
worn above the elbow on both arms by men and women.
Sometimes the gentler sex wore a *kamba iri* (or arm
pearls), a bracelet made of beads, instead of the ring of

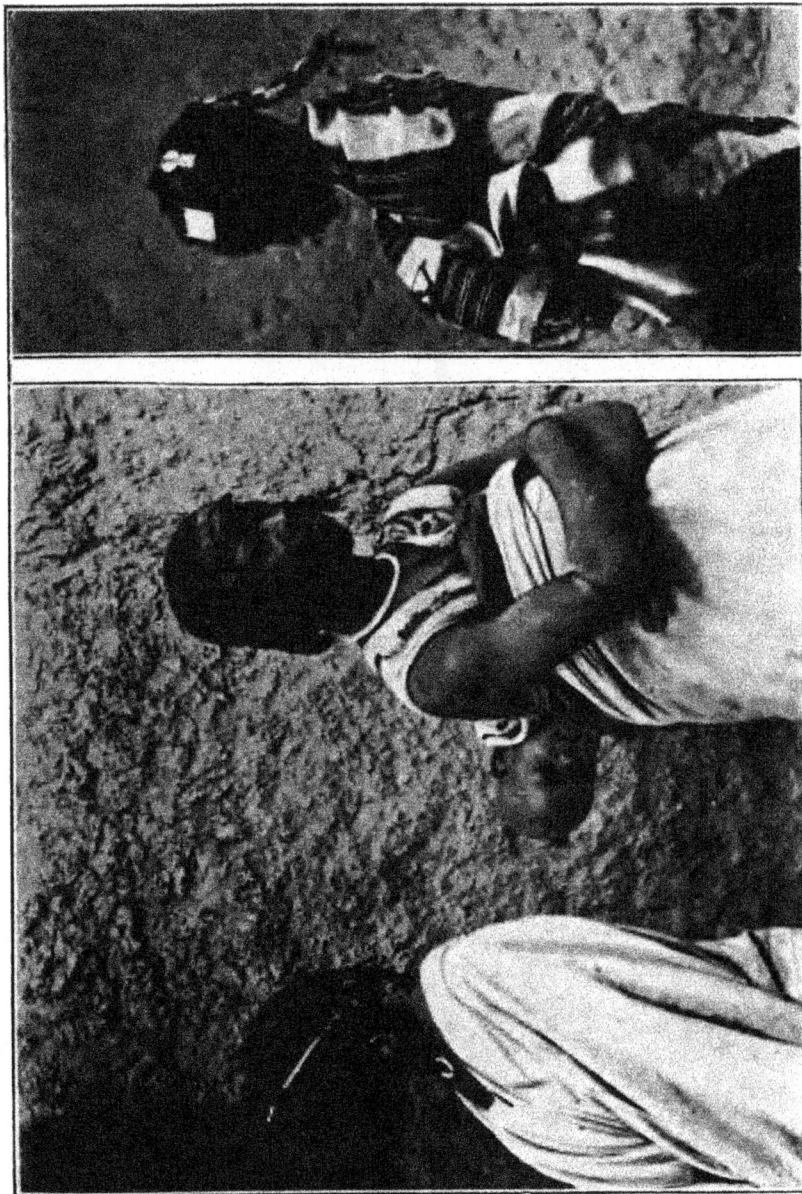

Head-dresses, Timbuctu : also Soṅgo · mode of carrying chi dren.

stone. Similar bracelets of a smaller kind were worn on the wrists, as well as the *sonko*, a silver bracelet with circular ornamentations upon it. Then more common was the *kullu*, a simple C-shaped ring of silver or iron, and the *sorboro*, of heavy brass with an outer edge of many points like the teeth of a cog-wheel.

The fingers and thumbs were decorated by the Timbuctu people with three distinct kinds of rings: the *kobe gani*, a thumb ring of silver (gold is never worn because their religion does not permit of a prayer being accepted when such a luxurious metal is worn upon the hand). A common form of this ring was a flat silver band, with small hemispheres in high relief all round it. Then there was the *mdama kofe*, or " chameleon nape," because the mitre-shaped projection on the flat band ring was covered with dots and a large bead on the summit of the mitre. The third kind, or *kugunni*, also in silver, was similar to the chameleon nape, except that it had an ovoid projection with spherical ornaments upon it, but without the bead. Coins were sometimes attached to rings, but this was not a characteristic feature of the Timbuctu jewellery.

There were only two special kinds of earrings. One was a silver crescent with a big ball of amber and a lower ball of coral (or imitation coral). This was called the *hanga-korbo*. The second, the *tolomi*, always made of gold, was a flat band shaped into a spiral and tapering to a point. Red silk was wound round it.

The nose did not escape ornamentation. The size of the nostrils certainly permitted such a luxury. The *nine-djere*, literally translated, " half nose," was a filigree ring with little bullets attached to it, and was worn through the right lobe. The *gabibi* (*gabibi* means " black body "), or serfs, wore it, while the Gakorei (the Moors, or " white body ") did not. All women wore the *baiya*, a small gold spiral ring in the central partition of the nose, to which it was attached without perforating the membrane.

Where women were most laden with jewellery was upon the hair and round the neck. Among the per-plexing quantity of gold head ornaments was the *kunna*, a sun-like circle of gold filigree, with gold bars radiating from the centre. The *yudon* was a circular gold plate with dots upon it in *repoussé* work. Then there was the *walatedje* (originally from Walate), a lozenge with hemi-spherical ornamentations all round. The *londuh*, a small spherical bell, was attached to the ends of the two tresses at the side of the face, or upon the neck. The *lader* (from the Arabic word which means " temple," from the position slightly in front of the ears where the ornament is worn) was formed of a square with triangles hanging from it at the lower end and with dotted ornamentations all round.

In silver we have many head ornaments : the *huttu*, a silver plate worn singly in the middle of the forehead, or in couples behind the head. Each possessed five small buttons. The *kantje*, another attractive minute silver ornament, was worn flat upon the head, usually in couples fastened with coloured silk threads. The *sahalia* was a triangle worn anyhow or anywhere upon the head ; while the *sorro*, a pear-shaped ornament, was always worn upon the forehead, where it replaced the *huttu* plate. The *tira* consisted merely of a silver amulet box, and was worn anywhere.

Now for the neck ornaments. The *kumna* is like the *lader*, only of much larger size, a square with triangular appendages in the lower part. The *betou* was very similar to the circular *kunna*, only it was made of a solid piece of gold instead of filigree work. Then there is the *soro fune*, also circular like the *betou*, with triangles in fretwork all round and a circle in the centre.

Perhaps one of the most characteristic ornaments was the *besaku*, a large rectangle with three pyramids in relief in the centre, surrounded by circular dots in relief, the longer and lower side of each triangle of this pyramid being decorated with sets of small hemispheres.

Unlike this class of work was the *finkoro*, a hemisphere in filigree with two hemispherical pendants underneath, also in filigree work, and two little bullets at the sides of the larger circle. The half-moon, or *handu djere*, was a mere pendant, the entire field of which was covered with lozenges of filigree, the points of each angle of these lozenges being decorated with small knobs.

I did not see any tattoos typical of the Timbuctu people, but their distinctive and favourite mark consisted of small vertical cicatrices at the outer angle of each eye. These marks, made when young, gradually disappeared. I have often seen young girls with cheeks and forehead disfigured by two or three deep incisions.

Women, besides the ornaments enumerated, were extremely fond of glass beads made of imitation amber and coral ; of small mirrors, and of blue, red and yellow silk decorations. Fabrics of all colours were appreciated by the women of Timbuctu.

CHAPTER XXXII.

In the way of languages Timbuctu could give points to the Tower of Babel. Every race of people which came to the sacred city for religious reasons, for warlike purposes, for trade or barter, as masters or as serfs or slaves, brought its own language. That most generally spoken is Soñgoy, which has become the language of the country, and is spoken as far as Agades in Aïr, and as far south as Djenne and Say, or, in other words, over the whole extent of the ancient empire of Askia. Of course, we find distinct dialects in Soñgoy, as in other languages. There is, for instance, the tongue spoken in Timbuctu itself, on the Niger north of the sixteenth degree of lat. N., and in all that section called by the French the " *boucle du Niger*," which goes by the name of the " town tongue," or *koyra-tijni*. Further south, between the thirteenth and sixteenth degrees of lat. N., we have the Djenne tongue, the *Djenne-tigni*, as it is locally pronounced. Elsewhere the *Soñgoy-tigni*, a purer type of the Soñgoy language, is spoken. There is no written Soñgoy language, and the variations in the form and pronunciation of words is not great in different localities. A good manual of the Soñgoy language has been written by two French missionaries of the White Fathers—Hacquard and Dupuis.

Curiously enough, one finds few legends of historical

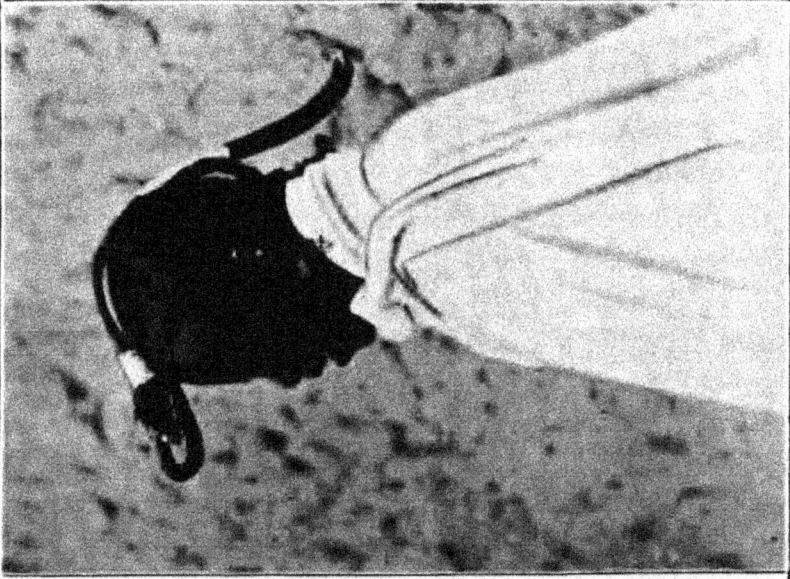

Soñgoy girl.

Timboctu children.

interest among the Soñgoy. A few of the legends speak
of fights between the fishermen of the east and those of
the south-east, the first personified in a man called Fono,
the second in a warrior called Faram.

Unlike the black tribes further south, which divide the
year into two seasons, the wet and the dry, we find that
the people in and round Timbuctu—who, of course, are
civilized as compared with the others—have four seasons
according to climatic phenomena at certain periods of
the year : the *fatafata*, from about January 20th, which
corresponds to our spring ; the *kuruh*, or hot season, from
the beginning of April ; the *keydia*, or rainy season, from
the beginning of June ; and the *kufu*, or cold season,
from about the middle of November.

The Soñgoy have subdivisions of seasons, the *kufu*,
for instance, being subdivided into " the white nights
and the black nights " The first part of the *keydia* is
the *tauré*, or " fever time." The *alhoua* runs from the
end of August to the 22nd of September ; and the
alojufur from September 22nd to November 13th.
The months are divided, as with the Arabs, into lunar
months of twenty-nine or thirty days.

The Timbuctu people are fond of holidays. The
tenth day of the second month, the *dedow*, is celebrated
with great feasting and exchange of presents, as being the
anniversary of Noah's exit from the ark ; but, curiously
enough, no holiday exists to celebrate the date of Noah's
departure on his great piece of navigation. Mahommed's
birthday is solemnly kept, and prayers are offered in
the mosques as well as in private houses with loud
rejoicings during the night. This is on the twelfth day
of the *almudu* month, and on the eighteenth of the
same month there is another holiday to celebrate the

anniversary of the prophet's circumcision. The first
of the tenth month, the *fer me*, marks the end of the
long fast.   The eighteenth day of the twelfth moon,
the *tfibsi*, is a great feast, during which all the people
adjourn to the east of the town near the tomb of Alfa-
Moya, where the *Imam* of the *Djingery-ber* mosque
sacrifices a sheep.   Then they all disperse and go to
their respective homes, each person who can afford it
immolating a ram in his own private house.

The *Djemãa*, or meeting day, falls, as with other
Mussulman people, on a Friday, which is the day of rest,
the week being divided as with us into seven days.

On going round the town with my learned friend,
Yacoma, I was shown the various ways of weighing and
measuring used by the Timbuctu people. Weights are
used for precious metals, such as gold and silver ; also for
silk. These weights are made of small pebbles, the
smallest of which is the *nustumun*, about one-sixteenth
of a French ounce, and the largest is the *arratel*, practically a French pound in weight. For gold the *bani*, a
pebble about the size of a pea, is used, and the *mutukal*,
or twenty-four *bani*, weighing about five grammes. Dry
goods are measured by the *mude*, about one litre (one
and three-quarter pints), the *sawal*, or four *mude*, and
the *tu-djere*, or ten *sawal*. For liquids the *sawal* is the
measure used. Woven materials are measured by the
length of the arm from the elbow to the tips of the
fingers, or by a corresponding measure on a stick called
the *kamba* or the *kala*. For greater lengths the *som-
burusu* of twenty-seven *kala* is used, as well as the *bahinsa*
of forty *kala*, the *ton* of sixty *kala*, and the *starura* of
sixty-five *kala*.

Fields, gardens and small pieces of land are measured

by the *somboy*, a stick the length of five *kala*. An easier way, but not so accurate, is the measure by paces. Long distances are computed by the number of days or months generally required to cover them on foot, on horseback or with camels.

The people in the region of Timbuctu have a fairly accurate idea of the four points of the compass, for which, however, they have no technical name. These points are in no way described in relation to the magnetic attraction of the Pole. "North," for instance, is *diaman*, which means nothing else than "seashore," by which they understand the Mediterranean Sea off the Morocco coast ; *djidji* is also another name. "South" is with them *isa*, which means "the river" (the Niger). The east happens to be in this case practically in the direction of Mecca, and is called the *altijibla*, and it is in that direction that the people face when they make their salaams in the morning and at night. As for the west, the *weyne-kamey*, it is the sunset, which, of course, does not correspond exactly with our west. As with all Mussulmans, the *altijibla*, the direction of Mecca, is for them the principal point of direction, and not the north as with us.

It was always of interest to me to note how all these people of uncivilized or semi-civilized countries can determine their bearings, with great accuracy, during the night and at times when the sky is cloudy and no bearings can be taken by the sun or stars. Even in difficult country, where nine hundred and ninety-nine out of a thousand Europeans would be absolutely at a loss to go in the right direction unless a constant watch were kept on the compass, I have noticed that these people, without instruments of any kind and apparently without any reflection, follow the exact direction for enormous distances over country they do not know and with no trails. In navigating canoes over hundreds of miles of inundated country, the same thing happens, and it is seldom that I have seen them make a mistake.

I know of a few cases of white people who are able to tell exactly where the magnetic north is. Personally, owing to constant practice, I have myself acquired that gift to a certain extent, but I believe that quite unconsciously the natives feel much more than we do the magnetic influence of the Pole, although they themselves are quite ignorant even of the existence of a magnetic Pole.

I noticed with my Somali servant that, although owing to the differences in latitude and longitude from those of Djibuti (in Somaliland), he was, when near the west coast of Africa, quite unable to gauge the exact time of the day or night by the sun in the first instance and the stars in the second ; and although he could no longer tell the exact direction of Mecca by the sun or the stars, still he could always tell quite accurately where the north was. He himself could not explain how he knew, but when I experimented on him, compass in hand, I noticed that he would turn his head round once or twice as though wavering for a few seconds, and, concentrating his ideas, remain in a sort of comatose state for some seconds ; then, as if led by some unknown influence, would suddenly point with his hand in the right direction of the magnetic Pole.

The hours of the day in Timbuctu, as everywhere in Africa where people have no watches, were measured entirely by the angle of the sun above the horizon.

" Tell me," I said one day to Yacoma, " what was the origin of Timbuctu ? "

" That is easy," replied my interlocutor, who was never at a loss in finding an accurate answer to anything regarding that region. " It was," said he, " originally a mere store established by the Tuareg and left under the care of an old slave called Timbuct."

Most places in this portion of Africa take the name of either the chief of the village or some notable person in connection with a site, so from Timbuct came the name of Timbuctu.

The people from the south and south-west, principally from Djenne, came to this place to exchange their goods with the Tuareg, and gradually it became an important market. The two mosques, the *Djingery-ber* and the *Sankore* were built. One of the Kings of Mali (to the south-west) conquered the place towards the end of the fourteenth century. Timbuctu had many vicissitudes from that time. It was taken and re-taken by the King of Mosi, by the Tuareg, by the Soñgoy King Gogo of Gao, and it was not until the fifteenth and sixteenth centuries that the town attained its greatest splendour. It was then that the Sultan of Morocco sent his army, which took possession of the place. Disputes arose among the Arma (Moors). The Tuareg, taking advantage of the discord among the Moors, attacked the town and reduced Timbuctu to servitude. It was not till 1827 that the Fulbeh arrived with Sheiku-Ahmadu and took possession of the sacred city. In 1861 El-Hadji Omar came with the Tukuler, a name of people we have already met.

Be this as it may, these Tukuler destroyed Ahmadu's empire, and Timbuctu again fell into the hands of the

Tuareg, who pillaged everything, and the town was reduced to wreck and ruin. The Kunta, who subsequently came to the help of the inhabitants, were unable to save the town from destruction.

"Come along with me," said Yacoma, "we will go for a stroll, and I will point out to you several houses which will interest you from an historical point of view."

Perhaps the first white man who came into Timbuctu was a Frenchman, Paul Imbert, a sailor, who was taken prisoner by the Arabs on the Atlantic coast and was taken in slavery to Timbuctu. He managed after some years to escape by way of Morocco, but, having no descriptive talent and no literary ability, he was only able to tell of his narrow escapes and adventures, but has left no valuable record of his remarkable journey and residence in Timbuctu. After that it was not till 1805-6 that the Scotchman, Mungo Park, came, *vid* the Sudan and the Niger; attacked by the natives, he died at Bussa, in the rapids.

"There—look!" said Yacoma. "That was Major Laing's house—the Englishman who came from Tripoli and arrived in Timbuctu in 1826. It was in that house that he put up during the several days he was in the sacred city, and, as you see, the French, in respect to his memory, have placed a little tablet on the wall of the mud house."

He was murdered by the Berabish on his return journey between Timbuctu and Arauan. The date of his death, as has been ascertained since, was September 24th, 1826.

I went inside the house, which was quite humble. An old man showed me a spot in the wall where, accord-

Fort Bonnier and Avenue, Timboctu.

Laing's house, Timboctu.

ing to an account which had been given to him by another
old man, Laing had hidden his money in a hole.

I heard from a French officer that fragments of
Laing's papers had been recovered in the desert among
the tribes, one piece containing a computation of
astronomical observations. It was rather curious that
nothing else had ever been traced of the belongings of
this adventurous traveller.

"Come along," said Yacoma to me, as he gently
pulled me by the sleeve. "Quite close to here is the
house of another famous traveller." A few minutes
later we stopped before a mud house, also very humble,
like all houses in Timbuctu. Yacoma pulled himself
together, stroked his moustache and beard, as he always
did when he was proud of something he was showing,
and beaming all over with joy, said: "Here, another
great traveller, this time a Frenchman . . . . you see,"
he modestly added, "the English are not the only people
who go and roam in distant countries—this time a
Frenchman of whom you have heard, René Caillé, came
the whole way across from Sierra Leone to Timbuctu in
1828, visiting Djenne *en route*. He lived in Timbuctu
some time and even returned alive to France, where he
gave an interesting description of his journey."

Then came the famous German, Barth, a magnificent
traveller, who lived in Timbuctu from September 27th,
1853, to May 8th, 1854. There are many people in
Timbuctu who remember him, and who speak highly of
his wonderful knowledge of everything. He had come
by way of Tripoli and Lake Tchad, had gone to Sokoto
on his way to Say upon the Niger, and had returned
home practically the same way.

In 1880 came Lenz, an Austrian, who lived in Timbuctu for three weeks. He had come from Morocco and went back *viâ* Sokoto, Medine and St. Louis.

Yacoma took me to the various houses where all these travellers had lived. Tablets had been placed on each door as a tribute to these brave pioneers.

It was not till 1887 that the trouble in Timbuctu began as far as the French were concerned. Monsieur Caron, from Kulikoro, went up the Niger on board the gunboat *Niger*, and was able to go as far as Kabara, which he reached on August 18th of the same year. Two years later, Lieutenant Jaime, on the gunboat *Mage*, and Ensign Hourst, on the *Niger*, arrived at Mopti on September 21st, 1889. Jaime came as far as Koryume, but both these officers were unable to enter into negotiations with the people of Timbuctu, and it was not until April 12th, 1893, when Colonel Archinaud took Djenne, that the inhabitants begged the sister city of Timbuctu to surrender. The chief of Timbuctu was then Yahia Alkaya of Arma descent. He declared that the people of Timbuctu would be happy to receive the French, but that the town was in possession of the Tuareg. Therefore a small party under Colonel Bonnier, and a flotilla, advanced by river towards Timbuctu, while Colonel Joffre proceeded towards Gundam. The Tuareg went *en masse* to near Kabara in order to fight the French, and, in fact, a small fight took place with Lieutenant Boiteux, who was proceeding on a barge. The Tuareg showed no signs of their proverbial bravery and beat a hasty retreat, so on December 15th of the same year—the inundation of the Niger being extraordinarily high that season—Lieutenant Boiteux was able to land from his barge at Timbuctu itself. He entered the town and signed a treaty of peace.

Not so lucky was Ensign Aube, who attempted to follow into the sacred city ten days later (December 25th). He and his party were massacred by the Tuareg between Kabara and Timbuctu; but the death of this officer was soon avenged by the plucky Lieutenant Boiteux, who, with a handful of men, immediately went out and inflicted severe punishment on the assassins. Later, on January 6th, 1894, Colonel Bonnier was able to instal himself in the city.

To make things clearer I will give the names of the various nomad tribes in the region of Timbuctu.

The local *Targui* or Tuareg tribes may be divided into five principal sections : (1) the *Tenguerighif*, whose camps are mostly on the right bank of the Niger. Their vassals, the *Inededren* live north of the Gundam stream; (2) the *Kel-temulaït*, also living on the right bank of the river, east of Timbuctu; (3) the *Irregenaten*, in the interior country of Aribinda and Gurma; (4) two groups of *Iguaddaren*—namely, the *Aribinda* on the right bank, and the Haussa on the left bank; (5) the *Oelimidden*, towards the east, near Gao (Gogo).

Then we have six distinct tribes of Arabs : (1) the *Berabish* (plural of the word *Berbush*), whom we have already met and who are the caravan men between Taodeni and Timbuctu; (2) the *Kunta*, found upon both banks of the Niger among the *Targui* tribes; (3) the *Tormoy*, a dissenting faction of *Berabish*, near Ras-el-Ma; (4) the *Allush*, between Sokolo and Basikuna; (5) the *Usra*, between Ras-el-Ma and Arauan; (6) the *Deyluba*, south of the route between Basikuna and Ras-el-Ma.

The *Iguellad* tribes are divided into three principal groups. East of Timbuctu and in the Faguibini country are the *Kel-antasar*; north of the stream Gundam are the *Kel-ncheria* and the *Kel-nkunder ;* while north of and round Lake Fati are the *Kel-Haussa.*

We also find other minor tribes in the country, such as the *Chêurfiga,* to the south-west of the Timbuctu region ; the *Kel-Essuk,* disseminated among other tribes; and the *Kel-Ulli,* mostly upon the Niger between Immelal and Ilua.

During Colonel Bonnier's occupation of Timbuctu, the *Tenguerighif-Kel-antasar* Tuareg caused annoyance by their constant raids around the town, until the French colonel went out with a company of *tirailleurs* and half a company of another regiment, attacked the raiders and dispersed them at Takubao. Unluckily, however, the following night the Tuareg returned in great force and pounced upon the French, who were massacred. Colonel Joffre, with his column, made a remarkable march overland, but encountered difficulty after difficulty upon the route, and did not arrive at Takubao until February 8th, reaching Timbuctu four days later and bringing in the remains of the murdered officers.

A fort was built on the south side of the town and named after the officer who had so bravely lost his life. Colonel Joffre began the work of organizing the town. Alfa-Seïdou, who had shown himself friendly toward the French, was appointed native chief of the town.

There were many subsequent fights with the Tuareg, and little by little several of the leading chiefs were brought to submission, while other groups, such as the *Tenguerighif,* the *Iguellad,* and the *Kel-temulaït,* came in of their own accord in order to fight against their rivals.

The subjection of the tribes around Timbuctu was not easy, and it is quite remarkable what the French officers have done in that difficult portion of the country,

Women and children of Timboctu.

especially as at a time when severe and salutary punishment should have been inflicted on the tribes once and for ever their hands were tied by politicians at home. Brigandage became rampant both on the Kabara and on the Gundam roads, and reached such a point that hostilities had to be begun again in order to establish peace in the region. The battle of Faraeh followed, then the fight of Amadia under Lieutenant (as he then was) Gouraud, and the *reconnaissances* of Tahakimt and Taaraiet, where brave Lieutenant Berar was killed in a hand-to-hand fight with the Tuareg.

It would take an entire volume to describe all these battles, which are interesting, and the extraordinary deeds of the French officers ; but in this volume I can merely enumerate these without going into details.

The Tuareg's mode of assault is generally to attack early in the morning, at about four o'clock, before sunlight, a time when people are asleep or sleepy.

It was found necessary to establish military posts, one at Lake Sumpi and one at Ras-el-Ma.

In 1895, partly owing to the severe punishment inflicted on the more fanatical tribes, partly to the good influence exercised by the French, the pacification of the country was proceeding quickly and firmly. Even Chebbun, the turbulent *amenukal* (or leader) of the *Tenguerighif*, came to submit, first at Gundam, and then travelled to Timbuctu in order to repeat his submission, much to the astonishment of the Timbuctu population, who witnessed this ancient oppressor turn into an humble subject of the French.

One can but admire the way in which the French proceeded at once to open up that country, and in 1896, no sooner had all the tribes quieted down than a hydrographic expedition under Lieutenant Hourst was despatched down the Niger.

The following year, 1897, the sphere of French influence was extended as far as the town of Basikuna in the desert, a few minutes south of the 16th degree of lat. N., 8° 30′ longitude W. of the Paris meridian.

Lieutenant Wirth, of the *Infanterie de Marine* succeeded, with a mere handful of men, and while pursuing a troop of *Allush*, in actually taking possession of the town of Basikuna after a violent assault upon that stronghold.

The pacification of the eastern portion of the country took three years, from 1896 to 1899, but even to this day those tribes are not to be absolutely relied upon, and it was only last winter, 1906, as we have seen, that we in British Nigeria had an open rebellion in Sokoto, and the French had one officer massacred upon the Niger and another officer killed in battle, while an extensive plot against the French was checked in time.

In the Ahaggar mountains the *Hoggar* tribe began to be troublesome, and, with the *Kunta* of the river banks were continually raiding. They were quickly beaten and dispersed at Akenken by the joint action of Captain Laperrine and Lieutenant Maillaud.

The riverine tribes of Tuareg, well recognizing their inferiority to the French on the battlefield, submitted to Captain Coleni; and even *Sakhawi*, chief of the *Iguaddaren* on the right bank of the Niger, handed over his sword in sign of submission to the French officer in 1896.

Although the *Hoggar* had been defeated it was not possible to leave a garrison in their country, and they again became troublesome, making incursions in the neighbouring country in the years 1896-7. On June 19th of the latter year a troop of some forty spahis who were reconnoitring the country were surrounded by the *Hoggar*, eight hundred strong, and were massacred, including the French officer, Lieutenant La Tour de St. Igest. A second detachment, under de Chevigné, which had come to assist the spahis, met with the same fate, the officer in charge being mortally wounded by several spears. Rescued just before death by " Maréchal de logis " de Libran, he died a few hours later. This was the disaster of Sereri. The *Hoggar*, elated at this victory, pillaged the country all round, and, becoming bold, advanced on the sacred town and demanded from the French the surrender of Timbuctu, a demand, however, which was not granted, and which the *Hoggar* were unable to enforce. Fearing the approach of French reinforcements, they eventually beat a hasty retreat.

We find many gallant fights in the reprisals which took place after the Sereri disaster ; for instance, the easily-won fight of Gurdjigay, and the battle of Zenka, in which Lieutenant Delestre, attacked by the enemy (*Kunta* of Abidni, *Iguaddaren* of Sakib and Sakhawi), was able with only forty Senegalese soldiers to put them to flight on June 24th, 1898.

Other glorious fights were fought, such as that of Dongoy, and minor ones. The post of Bamba, east of Timbuctu, was founded on November 28th of that same year, and the French, under Lieut.-Col. Klobb, established themselves at Gao further down the Niger on December 4th, 1898.

The *Kel-antasar*, tired of fighting, asked for terms of peace, and 'Gunna, their chief, begged to come and offer his submission, but prior to entering the French post he became frightened, and asked to see a French officer outside the town. Lieutenant Gressard went to meet him, and eventually was able to persuade the troublesome chief to follow him to Timbuctu. 'Gunna was, however, taken with such fear on approaching the town that he attempted to escape on his camel. The *tirailleurs* fired on him and he was killed.

Landah and Mohammed Ould N'Gunna, sent by their tribesmen, afterwards came to ascertain the conditions of peace, which was concluded. This practically ended hostilities in the Timbuctu region and the *boucle du Niger*.

That region was divided by the French into three *cercles* : Timbuctu, Gundam and Sumpi, which include the Kissu and Aribindi countries (or Gurma). The *cercle* of Gundam comprises the provinces of Ataram and Killi. The *cercle* of Sumpi extends as far as Lake Debo to the south-west, and is bounded by the Issa-ber on the east ; on the west, it extends as far as the region of Sahel, and on the north-west further than the Faguibini region. Beyond these two comes the *cercle* of Bamba, important on account of its position near to the Tuareg, on the east and north of the elbow of the Niger.

The vegetation in the neighbourhood of Timbuctu is not very attractive, and the flora is miserable. The principal and bigger trees are acacias, the *bisu*, the *albarkantegna*, the *bani*, the *aworwor-kasan*, and the *kardji-korey*.

The *hore* and the *kabegna* produce scented flowers.

Then we have the *kasu*, the *tendja-bundu*, the *dareygna* (jujube-tree) and the *kiraw* (*salvadora persica*), a useful plant in these regions, its roots being much used by the natives for making tooth-brushes, as the fibres easily divide on being pressed against the teeth. The wood, too, possesses cleansing qualities, and the juice of the fruit has quite a refreshing, slightly caustic sting.

A few large *baransam* are to be found, similar to those we found on the right side of the Kabara-Timbuctu channel.

A few date palms, the *gorboy-musukuru*, the *gorboy-homo*, with long green thorns and a bitter fruit much enjoyed by the children, and a number of dwarf palms are to be found, as well as the forked palm, *thebaïde*.

Among the most useful shrubs is the *asclepia gigantea* (*turdjia*), the wood of which, made into charcoal and ground, is much used by the natives for the manufacture of gunpowder. There are, besides, among the most common shrubs, the *assanna*, the *turituri*, the *berre*, the *turi-ferre*, and the *bubere*.

Grassy plants are plentiful, growing all over the country. The most abundant as well as the most diabolical is the *daney* (*Pennisetum distychum*), usually called the *kram-kram*, a small grain in a spiked envelope. As we have already experienced, it is enough to walk a few yards anywhere in the desert to find oneself covered with these *kram-kram*. They attach themselves so firmly to one's clothes or one's skin, that it takes some patience to remove them. They cause discomfort to men and animals. The grain of the *daney* is used as food by poor people, and they say that it makes excellent eating, although the trouble and pain which one has in removing it from its envelope take away a great deal of the pleasure of eating it.

It is curious to find how little fruit there is of an edible character. Experiments on some of the pretty wild fruit one occasionally finds might prove deadly.

Even the sting of some of the plants—and nearly all the plants one sees have thorns or spikes—is dangerous. They say that the sting of the thistle, *alladjerkardji*, is fatal.

The *gandataso* produces a fruit ejecting a white latex that tastes like hazel-nut, and among the creepers the *hanum* produces a bitter fruit named the *gao*. Prominent among the climbing plants we have the *lumba-lumba*, the *lilidji* and the *hauatuh*.

Where the vegetation is most luxurious is in the water. We find the white water-lilies, as well as whole miles in the inundated country of that excellent forage plant, the *borgu*, which the natives use both in the manufacture of a refreshing drink and in making their sweets.

In the Kissu and Killi provinces the vegetation is richer, and there are plenty of *baobab* trees, the *doney*, the rubber vine (the *lindjigna*), and palm-trees, such as the *phœnix dactylifera* in the northern part of the desert, most useful in more ways than one. The date, with its abundance of sugar and farinaceous qualities, supplies an excellent food. The leaf is of great use in the construction of huts, and, from its fibre baskets, ropes, nets, etc., are made. The inner fibre is used for filling saddles, cushions, etc., and the stones of the dates when ground are good food for animals. The latex in its normal state is a refreshing drink, and when fermented becomes a powerful liquor. The flower possesses, they say, aphrodisiacal qualities much valued by the natives, and the envelope of the flowers before blooming is medicinal.

The trunk of the *phœnix dactylifera* is about the most suitable in that region for making the columns and rafters supporting the heavy flat roofs. Boxes and other

articles of furniture are manufactured from this most
excellent wood. It is one of the few woods which is not
attacked by white ants, and the moisture of the rainy
season does not affect it as much as other woods. A few
male plants are sufficient to fructify a whole oasis of
female palms. I have often noticed how female palms
were found in quantities in a stunted, dwarf-like condition ; this was only when no male plants were to be
found in the neighbourhood.

The *cucifera thebaïca*, the *dum* palm of the Sudan,
which we find nearly the whole way across Africa, is also
to be found here, but is not common.

We occasionally find tamarind trees in the desert,
and the fruit of the *tamarix articulata* has most astringent
qualities. It is used mostly for tanning. The Arabs
call it *ethel*.

The *salvadora persica*, the *tegui* or *tigfat* of the Timbuctu people, is very common on the banks of the Niger.
Its fruit is good to eat, and the natives say that it
possesses medicinal qualities. The bark is supposed to
have beneficial effects when people are bitten by veno-
mous animals, and the wood, very fibrous and with a
pleasant odour, makes good toothpicks. So does also the
artiphix halimus (the *guetof* of the Arabs and *aramas* of
the Temahaq), a plant whose wood has a salty taste and
which is said by the natives to be anti-scorbutic.

Another plant which is much used in powdered form
by Arab and also by Soñgoy women upon certain organs
is the *nicotiana rustica*, a kind of tobacco imported mostly
from the north, where it is much in use among the
Arabs of the south-easterly region of the Algerian Sahara.
It possesses, they say, aphrodisiac qualities like those
of the flower of the *phœnix dactylifera*.

CHAPTER XXXIII.

I LEFT Timbuctu on November 29th. The Niger flows at low water fifteen kilometres south of the city. With the beginning of the floods an arm leaves the river at Koroyume (Hyena's Mouth), and, flowing at first parallel to the Niger, and then in an east-south-easterly direction, reaches a place called Day, about ten kilometres from Timbuctu.

The Soñgoy king of Gao, who was a practical man, dug a canal, which was afterwards straightened, enlarged, and deepened by Ahmadu-Sheïku, and which prolonged this watercourse for three kilometres beyond Day towards Kabara. The latter place, as we have already seen, is only seven kilometres from Timbuctu.

At high water the entire country between Sumpi and Gundam is flooded, and only the villages on the tops of dunes are visible. About every three years, when the water is abnormally high during the months of January and February, one can go by boat to within three hundred yards of Timbuctu. Kabara can be approached by water between November and April, Koroyume from May to September, and Day from September to November.

Between Timbuctu and Niafunké the country was flat and uninteresting. The latter village had large avenues with shabby domed huts of thatch or matting.

The inhabitants of Niafunké village were Fulbeh and Burdam. In this particular region the Fulbeh

Musician and dancer on the Upper Niger.

had given up their nomadic habits and had become sedentary.

The population of the *cercle* consisted of Fulbeh and Bambara on the left bank of the stream, people who spoke impure Bambara and closely resembled the Fulbeh, as they had intermarried with these people and had settled in this region among them for a considerable length of time.

The Gabibi, pure blacks, were to be found on both banks of the river, and were numerous also along the tributaries. There were only a few at Marka.

On the west frontier of the Niafunké province there were four villages of Moors and a few Tuareg.

We had now seen the last of the military territory and were in a portion of the country considered civilized enough to have civil administration. The town of Niafunké itself had 1,800 inhabitants. South-east, upon the Bara-issa, we found Saraferé (2,955 inhabitants), a great market in constant communication with Niafunké. Also there was another great village, Koli-Koli, on an arm of the Niger. Korienza, with 3,127 inhabitants, was a great market for oxen, sheep, millet and rice. The natives in that region purchased cotton goods, white and blue. Real and imitation amber were also valued, and found a ready sale.

These people were Mahommedans. At Niafunké was to be seen a big mosque with a long arcade on its eastern side and a high enclosure of mud.

Indigo was produced in small quantities. Cotton-cloth was woven by the natives, who also produced a woollen material. They dyed their fabrics with indigo. They also used another colouring plant called the *karandafa*, which imparted a fast red colour.

Slabs of salt from the Taodeni mines sold here ε an average of sixteen francs each. Salt, longclotl and *cori* shells were the currency, the natives bein reluctant in accepting money in payment.

For about twenty-five or thirty kilometres along tl frontier of the *cercle*, and near the villages of Tondida Diarto and Dyanke, on the same line, and also upon tl mounts of Tolidaro, some interesting stone implemen were to be found. The natives interred these stone ax and hammers with their dead, as they believed them be portions of shooting stars which fell upon the earl and brought luck to those who possessed them.

These implements seemed more recent than tho found near Tchekna and on the Wadaian frontier. Tl small scrapers were beautifully finished, some of a mo elongated shape than others. Pestles of red or blac stone about three-quarters of an inch in diameter we frequently found. It is amazing what a fine polish the people could impart to the sides of these implement which were either cylindrical or quadrangular. Larξ axes, from two to three inches long, and stone hammeι of a similar length, were met with, and were somewhε thicker and better made than those on the Wadaia frontier. Both the hammers and the axes were use with a forked stick, side grooves being easily discernibl on these implements. Many, however, were held in th hollow of the hand without a stick. Peculiar sma triangular scrapers were also found, which were evidentl used for shaping stone implements, and these had sharp edge on both sides. There were axes of hard re stone, four inches long and two inches wide at the wides part ; these were flat on both sides, almost triangulaι with a curved blade ; and also some smaller ones, tw and a half inches long and almost rectangular in shape. Red stone polishers of an almost conical shape were common enough, and also a pyramidal polisher.

Monsieur Descemet, *administrateur* in charge of the *Cercle de l'Issa-Ber*, had made a great collection of these implements, which he proposed to present to the museum in Paris.

The Fulbeh were seldom to be seen in the streets, especially the women. They were of retiring habits and spent most of their time inside their huts.

I left Niafunké at night, and in the morning went across Lake Debo, a village standing at the mouth of the lake, with a rock upon a fairly high mound on the right of us. The channel of the river was narrow, not more than fifteen to twenty yards wide. The natives had made *barrages* across these places in order to catch fish. One of these *barrages* which we met with—a regular matting of reeds—caught our rudder. The small steamer was swung round and nearly grounded. It was fully an hour before we could extricate ourselves. Three or four more of these obstacles were encountered. During the night we had an exciting chase after several canoes full of men, as the Government had forbidden the natives to put up these obstacles, which were dangerous to the navigation of the river.

We arrived at Mopti, one of the prettiest stations upon the Upper Niger, with fine Government buildings, offices and an interesting village. I saw here for the first time on my journey rude baked cylindrical pipes used for draining the water from flat roofs. All the houses were flat-roofed, in the Moorish or Arab style. The population of Mopti was entirely composed of fishermen and a few shepherds ; the cattle, which are abundant in this region, being kept at a great distance from t town during the inundations.

A French merchant had built himself a fine house this place, and I was told that he was doing excelle business, wool of fair quality being obtainable he and fetching good prices. It was the chief article export.

The natives of this place had long faces, and son what slanting eyes.

The river at this point described a big elbow. Mo] was situated at the junction of the Mayel-Balevel a the Niger. Djenne was situated on the Bami riv which further on takes the name of Mayel-Balevel.

At night we reached Quakuru, a quaint village wi curious structures—clubs for young men and girls meet in at night. These clubs seemed to be great instit tions in this part of the country. One of these hou: was decorated with peculiar ornamentations represei ing some animal, but I could not well distinguish wh animal. There were also curious arrangements of i verted symbolical triangles upon an upright line. Snak ornamented each side of the door, and flat columns form the façade of the building, which had on the roof seve: pyramids of mud.

The interior was in three sections, extremely simj and dirty, with suggestive mats, much worn, strev upon the floor, and also some layers of straw.

The double cross, such as we have on the Briti flag, formed one of the peculiar designs upon the w inside. A semicircular cavity was used as a recepta: for a light.

There were other such houses in the village, t smaller.

Another feature in the streets of Quakuru were the many weaving-looms stretched out at great length in the larger spaces in the village. The natives constructed small, neat portable weaving-looms, quickly erected, the comb being worked with the left hand, while the sets of threads were lowered and raised by two alternate frames of heddles worked by treadles. The cloth was narrow.

From Quakuru I visited the town of Djenne, the journey, in a canoe belonging to Mr. Elliott, of the African Association, taking the best part of the evening and night.

Djenne was the sister city of Timbuctu, the trade from south and north collecting at these two principal markets of exchange.

Quite unlike Timbuctu, which had a Moorish character, Djenne possessed marked characteristics, especially in her architecture, which reminded me forcibly of Egypt. Perhaps this architecture came with the Fulbeh. The high doorways with projecting columns right up to the top of the house, the small *musharabeah* windows between these two columns, the waterspouts from the roof, the two quadrangles at the summit of the house between square columns, and the small pyramids one above the other ornamenting the roof, were quite unlike anything I had so far met in this zone of Africa.

The streets were winding and beautifully clean. The whole place was entrancingly interesting and picturesque —infinitely more so than Timbuctu.

I was fortunate in taking several good photographs, reproductions of which will be found in this book, and which will give a better idea of the architecture than a description.

Djenne is situated in a delightful spot. Its pretty harbour for fishing boats and for canoes carrying merchandise; the charming little market-place where business is brisk; the dense population of well-to-do and well-dressed people—all contributed to making it attractive to me who had been for a year among most inartistic natives and unpicturesque country.

The local industries consisted chiefly of leather-tanning, cotton and wool weaving, and pottery, in making which the women were adepts. They turned the huge jars on a revolving platform, primitively made, but which answered the purpose to perfection. The ornamentations on these pots were drawn with some regularity and dexterity with rudimentary tools, some-times merely with a short stick. As a rule, most of the work was done either with the palm of the hand or with the fingers and nails.

The population of Djenne was mixed, and consisted chiefly of Soñgoy, Fulbeh (who came next in number), Bambara and Bozo. The latter were the river people, the navigators of the stream. The few Marka (or Sara-kollé) in the place entirely monopolized the construction of sewn canoes. The Marka had remained Mussulmans. All the people of Djenne spoke four languages fluently: Bambara, Soñgoy, Fulbeh and Bozo.

The Bambara were fetishists, and they seemed to attribute their origin to any animal they happened at some time or other to have selected as their protector.

There were few dogs in Djenne, as the Bambara ate them when they could get them. They had a perfect craving for dogs' flesh.

Near Djenne was, in fact, a small enclosed house

where people went to sacrifice chickens and dogs. There a *gna* (a fetish) was displayed. The manner in which the chicken or other sacrificed animal fell was an indication of whether good luck was forthcoming to the man who had paid for the sacrifice. If the chicken dropped dead on its back it meant good luck.

There was formerly at Djenne a mosque of great proportions, with a hundred quadrangular columns. That mosque had collapsed, and was in ruins. The French are to be praised for their consideration towards the natives in reconstructing this place of worship for them. I think the population of Djenne appreciated the compliment. Hundreds of workmen could be seen carrying mud bricks. Many of the columns had already been reconstructed ; while drummers and flute-players stood gracefully under the shade of a tree, making the greatest possible noise in order to keep the workmen in good temper. One of the illustrations in this work reproduces that scene.

Schools under Algerian teachers were established by the French at Djenne, and several French merchants had opened commerical establishments.

The *administrateur*, a most considerate and alert official, seemed to keep both white men and natives in the place quite happy.

Remains of the Moorish invasion could be perceived in Djenne, a Moorish house of an irregular quadrangular shape being still to be found. An ante-room occupied all one side of the front, and another long room stretched along the right-hand wall, as you entered, for one-third across the remaining space. On the left side a smaller elevated room could be reached by a flight of steps, the house possessing two floors. In this particular room was a heavy wooden Moorish press in good preservation. In the court was a well—also of Moorish origin—most beautifully made, twenty-four or twenty-five feet deep, and lined with glazed earthenware cylinders, the mouth of the well being formed by a *canari*, the bottom of which had been cut.

The trade of Djenne consisted of ostrich feathers, skins, cotton, egrets and grain, the latter mostly for local bartering. Salt, which came from the north, was distributed from this point south and east among the people of the loop of the Niger.

The elevation of Djenne was 1,050 feet.

Having returned to Quakuru I proceeded up the main stream to Diafarabé, the country all round being flat and sandy, and almost treeless. From Diafarabé the banks were slightly higher, with a good many trees upon them. The river was getting low. In a few days it had gone down three feet below its former level.

The villages as we went along the Niger had flat roofs. Numerous flocks of sheep were to be seen. Sansanding, another important trading centre (1,100 feet) was principally known for its trade in valuable egrets, formerly plentiful in this region, but now scarce. Thousands of false egrets lined the stream, but during the whole journey I only noticed four or five of the rarer birds. Hippopotami, too, were getting scarce, and I only saw one on the whole journey between Kabara and Sansanding. The river was altogether uninteresting, with only now and then an occasional island dividing the Niger into one or more arms.

On December 5th we had a heavy mist. The heat during the day was stifling, while the nights were damp and cold. Mosquitoes abounded.

Only a few forked palm-trees were to be seen near Sansanding and along the stream. The only thing that attracted my attention was a number of long canoes, twenty-three feet from bow to stern, sewn up in the middle. Plenty of *fromagers*, conical-shaped trees, with a few leaves on the summit and most vigorous roots, were to be seen, as well as *eriodendron anfractuosum*.

The market of Segu, which I next visited upon the Niger, was also important enough. The market-place, under the shade of numerous trees, was picturesque. Many natives squatted about selling powdered tobacco, manioc, potatoes, tomatoes, lemons, square lumps of salt, cheap cotton goods, amber, coral beads and blankets.

There was a mosque at this place walled all around with a colonnade of rectangular columns and having pointed pyramids upon the roof on the east side. A triangular-shaped minaret of the mosque and the fine Government buildings, especially the school, were the only things of interest at Segu.

Nyanina village, which I visited the following day, possessed flat-roofed houses along the high river-bank. Crooked doors gave entrance to a hall in these homes. Then a filthy courtyard and several rooms irregularly built were found within the enclosing wall. Here were women having their hair done by servants ; children screaming at the sight of a foreigner ; a tumbling-down loom or two ; but that was all.

The locks on the doors were ingenious enough in these homes, the keyhole, which was not in the door but in the wall, being large enough for a man's arm to go easily through. A wooden key one foot long and with vertical iron points, not unlike a gigantic toothbrush, was inserted in the wooden lock, wherein loose points, formed by two heavy pieces of wood kept in position between two vertical pillars, were found in the upper part ; when the loose points were removed from their position the lock could be easily unfastened.

The architecture of villages along the Upper Niger did not resemble in the slightest degree that of Djenne.

Dried fish was sold in quantities. Indigo cones were stored in great numbers inside houses and were much used for dyeing purposes, the cloth soaked in indigo solution being struck hard with big wooden mallets in order to beat the colour well into the fabric.

Deep natural *cuvettes* filled with water were to be found in the village.

In the evening, climbing up the steep bank of the river, we entered the town by a narrow gateway. A native dance was in progress, a few boys beating tam-tams which they held between their bent knees and on which they tapped with the fingers of both hands ; others had small drums slung from the right shoulder and tapped them with sticks. Other boys danced, two at a time, lifting first one arm with a swing, then the other, a simultaneous movement of the legs taking place, quite graceful, and which, curiously enough, was identical with a Shoka dance I had seen in Central Asia upon the heights of the Himahlyas. This dance was calculated to render the arms and legs supple and the movements graceful. To a quicker time of the drums a jumping dance, in which the dancers kicked their own backs, took place. Girls came and joined in this dance. Then a squatting dance, similar to the Cossack dance, but without the final split, was performed.

Beyond Nyamina the river banks were a little more

clothed with verdant trees. A great many false egrets were to be seen all along, and a flat-topped hill stood before us as we approached Kulikoro, among a lot of sandbanks, which were now beginning to show well above the surface of the water.

CHAPTER XXXIV.

WE find that in the Upper Niger valley import: river courses have their birth upon soil of primary forn tion and flow between " walls of sandstone," often cascades, forcing a passage between rocks and alo tortuous channels. When at the last stage of this natu stairway they form immense valleys.

Rocks of igneous origin, such as gneiss-quartzi diabase, porphyrys, granites, etc., are visible on t surface in certain points of the colony. Round the the greater part of the upper soil is formed of sandsto of undetermined age. Towards the summits and up the slopes of sandstone undulations, there was lateri varied in consistence and appearance.

The mountainous country constitutes a forest zo rich enough in rubber (the *landolphia heudeloti karité*, fairly valuable woods, and a variety of spices.

In the way of mineral wealth, we have iron, go and lime. The mineral and forestal resources of t mountainous region are not to be compared with the which might be brought about by agricultural develo ment, and the breeding of cattle and sheep between t forest zone and the semi-desert zone in the northe part of the French colony.

From Kangala to Sansanding the Niger flows in well-traced bed as much as a thousand yards wide certain places. At high water the river floods the surrounding country, but seldom for a breadth of more than half a mile. In this section of the Niger valley the level of low and high water varies from fifty to ninety centimetres (twenty to thirty-six inches). The rainy season begins at the end of May and ends in October. Last year, 1906, however, the last rains were registered on the 2nd of November.

A dry north-north-easterly wind, "the harnattan," blows during November, causing a distinct lowering in the temperature.

The soil in that region is formed mostly of sand and clay, but has no great depth, and is not calcareous enough—a common fault of many a tropical soil. In some districts we find a clay mud fairly fertile, but not porous enough—in fact, quite waterproof—and difficult to work. These are the regions most often inundated during part of the rainy season, and generally used by the natives for the cultivation of rice.

As far as Nyamina the river valley is narrow ; further on it widens considerably, and what the French so well define as " *affleurements grèseux,*" between which the valley is encased, altogether disappear. From this point the Niger flows across a country fairly well populated and fertile.

Between Sansanding and Diafarabé the Niger divides itself into numerous arms. On the left bank it receives the tributary Bani. These arms converge towards a great basin, the Debo lake, at the entrance of which are found four islets of sandstone ; they are the spurs of the mountain mass of Bandiagara.

The aspect of this region changes with the seasons. During low water a succession of plains is found, on

which can be seen grazing numerous herds of *jebu* ox
and flocks of sheep, the fleeces of which furnish go
wool.

The French are now beginning the exportation
wool with success, I am told. When the colony is furth
developed there will probably also be a demand f
meat and milk.

The Bani and the principal arms of the Niger tr
versing the above plain are navigable all the year roun
for small boats and barges from Djenne, from San
Mopti (*vià* Sofara), and from Mopti to Kulikoro, tl
terminus of the railway from Kayes to the Niger.

During flood-time the plain is transformed into
huge green lake—green because of the immense quantit
of *borgu* (the *panicum*), a wild water-plant of gre:
utility in those regions. The *borgu* is a forage pla:
containing much nourishment, being rich in sugar.

Monsieur Vuillet (of the agricultural station
Kulikoro) tells me that there are two to three millic
sheep and goats in the middle valley of the Niger betwee
the 14th and 17th degrees of lat. N.

This region, when flooded, has immense padd'
fields between a regular network of channels. Villag:
and plantations of millet can be seen scattered upc
islands in the lake formed by the inundation.

Lake Debo has two outlets, which later join again-
the Issa-Ber on the left and the Bara-Issa on the righ
At Sarafere the Bara-Issa receives another ramificatic
of the river, the Koli-Koli, a narrow and tortuous channe
which forms east of Lake Debo another lake, the Lal
of Korienza.

In this part the waters of the Niger flow across lo
plains which are inundated at high water, and the cha:

nels of the river, which are ill-defined, are bordered
here and there by sand dunes with hardly any vegetation
upon them, or with a few *dum* palms. Further on, the
Niger skirts small mountainous masses with no well-
defined connection. During flood-time the water fills
great natural reservoirs, at different elevations, from
which the water gradually flows on the actual river
bed where this is choked, as, for instance, between Bamba
and Gao in the narrow *défilé* of Tossaye.

The climate in this part of the Nigerian valley is
dry. The difference between the higher and lower
levels of the water does not exceed thirty centimetres
(twelve inches) in the region of Timbuctu during the
rainy season. The natives utilize the bed of the lake
when dry and the various marshes enriched by the
inundation for agricultural purposes. Rice is cultivated
during the ascending period of the flood, and millet and
corn are grown during the decreasing period.

In what the French call " *la boucle du Niger,*" the
curve or elbow north of the fifteenth degree of latitude,
the agricultural resources cannot attain any serious
development until some method has been devised for
obtaining a more systematic irrigation from the vast
reservoirs. The agricultural possibilities of the High
Senegal and Niger are somewhat limited by the scanti-
ness of the population, but this portion of the country
is good, I think, for breeding purposes, the grazing being
of excellent quality for oxen and sheep.

From the last census made by the French the total
population of the twenty-one civil *cercles* of the High
Senegal and Niger is 3,935,724 inhabitants. This population is subdivided as follows :—

(1) On the railway from Kayes to the Niger :

Cercle de Kayes ..	.. .. ..	60,070	inhabitant
„ „ Médine	.. .. ..	5,065	„
„ „ Bafoulabé	.. .. ..	65,273	
„ „ Kita ..	.. .. ..	65,865	
„ „ Bamako	.. .. ..	160,878	

(2) On the Niger and its tributary, the Bani :

Cercle de Ségou ..	.. .. ..	168,785	inhabitant
„ „ Djenne	.. .. ..	69,635	„
„ „ Koutiala	.. .. ..	223,403	
„ „ Bandiagara ..	.. .. ..	171,119	
„ „ l'Issa-Ber	.. .. ..	59,597	

(3) In the Sahel ·

Cercle de Nioro ..	.. .. ..	114,228	inhabitant
„ „ Goumbou	.. .. ..	67,950	„
„ „ Sokolo	.. .. ..	34,770	

(4) In other regions :

Cercle de Satadougou ..	.. ..	34,194	inhabitant
„ „ Bougouni	.. .. ..	101,492	„
„ „ Sikasso	.. ..	164,410	
„ „ Bobo-Dioulasso		230,000	
„ du Lobi ..	.. .. ..	188,900	
de Koury ..	.. .. ..	224,266	
„ „ Ouahigouya ..		249,742	
„ „ Ouagadougou..		1,467,082	

These are the races in their approximate proportion

Bambara, mostly agriculturists	1,287,0
Sarracole, or Maraka, agriculturists, cattle breeders and traders	414,1
Khassonké, agriculturists	73,2
Diula, traders	110,6
Fulbeh and Tukuler, shepherds and occasionally agriculturists	336,0
Gurmantché, agriculturists and cattle breeders	15,7
Bariba, cattle breeders..	3,0
Mossi, agriculturists and cattle breeders	524,1
Moors, shepherds and camelmen	10,8
Uolof, traders and workmen	3,2
Various races	1,156,7

The colony of the High Senegal and Niger possesses two agricultural stations, situated, one in Kulikoro (*cercle* of Bamako), the other at Bamfora (*cercle* of Bobo-Dioulasso).

I inspected the agricultural station installed by the French Government at Kulikoro in 1902, which is under the able direction of Monsieur Jean Vuillet, an enthusiastic and hard-working gentleman, whose serious study of the agricultural resources of the country should lead to valuable results in the future development of that interesting French colony.

The station includes a farming school, model agricultural villages and a botanical garden where innumerable experiments are made with indigenous and imported plants. It is situated on the left bank of the Niger, about six kilometres from the railway station. It spreads over 400 hectares of ground (1,000 acres), of which 75 hectares (187 acres 2 rods) are preserved for the farming school and gardens. Three hundred hectares (750 acres) are divided among the people of the model agricultural villages. The agricultural station lies between the river and a sandstone mass of undetermined age ; a small stream which only flows during the rainy season runs a snaky course through the station under a beautiful arcade of verdure.

Monsieur Vuillet, to whom I am indebted for much information about the agriculture of that region, told me that in the Kulikoro district seasons are clearly defined. First, the rainy season, from June to October ; second, the dry season, relatively cold, from October to March ; third, the dry season, quite torrid, from March to June.

In a climate of this kind the richer equatorial crops,

such as coffee, cocoa, nutmeg, pepper and quinquin
cannot possibly succeed. The experiments made wi
these have generally not been successful. The coff
plant, the quinquina, the anise (the starred anise), t
hevea (or rubber tree of the Amazon), even when o
tained from the nursery during the wet season, ha
invariably been killed towards the month of Janua
by the great dryness of the air and by the chilliness
the temperature at night.

One can form a fairly accurate idea of the agricultu
future of the Kulikoro region by studying the indigeno
crops and acclimatized plants grown at the agricultu
station of Kulikoro.

In the Higher Niger the distance from the sea a
the proximity of the desert have serious effects
climatic conditions. One might almost say that in th
part of the French Sudan the climate is tropical duri
four months of the year, and semi-Saharian during t
other eight months.

Therefore, the experiments made at the agricultu
station of Kulikoro have shown that vegetables capab
of bearing great dryness and annual tropical crops a
the most suitable for the locality. In the first catego
are plants which are successful on the Mediterrane
side of Africa ; in the second group are tropical annual
These can be greatly improved by rational processes
cultivation different from those at present adopted b
the natives.

The efforts of the managers of the agricultur
station have been greatly directed towards the improv
ment of the local cotton-growing industry, which ma
have a future in the country, and to the creation
hybrids. Parasitic diseases have been carefully studie

and so have the effects of climatic conditions upon local and foreign plants and their hybrids.

Experiments with American cotton from Upland, Louisiana, Mississippi, and the river Benders, and with the cotton called the " Excelsior Prolific," have shown that it is possible to produce cotton upon the Niger that will fulfil the exacting requirements of French looms. American cottons have drawbacks, as they are very sensitive to parasitic and climatic influences, and need a soil of unusual fertility. Artificial fertilization is also sometimes necessary. The fibre obtained is somewhat shorter and lacking in regularity.

Among the more dangerous parasites are the *sylepta derogata fab*, or green twister caterpillar ; the *earias insulana boisd ;* the dangerous little coleoptera of the *buprestides* family ; the *sphenoptera*, whose larva with its powerful mandibles pierces the root and bores grooves in the trunk, causing great damage to the plants.

No efficacious method of fighting these parasites has yet been found ; but by planting every year, and by taking care not to grow crops of cotton more than one year in the same ground, one might, to a great extent, thwart the development of many of these parasites. Selection and crossing of local and foreign cotton-plants might produce varieties of cotton which would resist their most dangerous enemies.

Monsieur Vuillet says that the hybrids obtained up to the present time at Kulikoro have given variable results, and they may not have an important commercial future ; whereas careful selection of indigenous cotton with improved methods of cultivation has produced satisfactory and promising results.

By the employment of early varieties and by planting late, it is probable that the ravages of insects and of cryptogamous parasites, which swarm during the wet season, might be escaped.

Local cotton is grown by the native as an accessory to his millet and maize plantations, and the same method could, I think, be applied to American cotton if a variety could be found able to stand local conditions.

In the year 1906 a *consortium* formed by the Colonial Cotton Association bought cotton from American seeds distributed to the indigenous cultivators in 1905, and paid fifteen centimes a kilo. (1½d.) husked. This was the price (in 1905) of cotton at Baramandugu, the important market between San and Djenne.

It has been shown that thirty-four per cent. net of cotton was obtained from this crop.

The Colonial Cotton Association is putting up two husking machines at Segu, of sixty saws each, and two English husking machines, of forty-five saws, were there previously, one with a hydraulic press, the other with an articulated Décauville system.

In 1905 the crop of the Sansanding territory, amounting to 8,039 kilos., grown from Mississippi R.B. seeds, and 2,686 kilos., from Excelsior Prolific seeds, were husked at Sansanding by Chief Fama Mademba. This black chief possesses a husking machine, and he obtained 121 bales of raw cotton of a similar quality to the 165 bales produced by the *consortium*, the weight of the latter being 7,405 kilos.

In the year 1906–7 Monsieur Vuillet tells me that the total crop of the High Senegal and Niger colony will not be less than two thousand tons. With some care, especially in the selection of seeds and of suitable soil for the plantations, I think the culture of cotton upon the Niger is susceptible of considerable extension.

Besides cotton, there are other indigenous crops which may have a future, in particular the arachide (peanut), sesame, rice and tobacco.

Following the sound advice given by the Administration for the last few years, the native has taken to the production of large quantities of arachide, and in the year 1906 over six thousand tons of that oleaginous nut were sold by the natives.

In the valley of the Niger this plant which has given the Senegal a great portion of its prosperity finds conditions particularly adapted for its growth. Unhappily, the arachide in its shell is somewhat cumbersome to transport ; on the other hand, it would not be advantageous to strip the nut of its envelope, as is done in the Mozambique and Coromandel, as the arachide in that condition is not so easily preserved. Therefore the extent of the zone capable of furnishing arachide to exporters is limited by the difficulties of transport.

It is in consideration of this state of affairs that the local government has asked the *Administrateurs* to employ their influence over the natives to develop the culture of sesame jointly with the culture of the arachide. The value of sesame is higher than that of the arachide in its shell; but the interest in the first of these two oleaginous products lies mostly in its much greater density, a precious quality from the point of view of facility and cost of packing for transport.

Two other local plants which offer alimentary articles of commercial value are the *karité* (or butter tree), and the rubber vine, locally known under the name of *gohine,* the *landolphia heudelotii.* The traders established in the region of Bamako are seriously beginning to export the butter as well as the *karité* nuts. This movement is encouraged by certain manufacturers and chemists in Europe, who are now studying practical ways of utilizing these valuable products. *Karité* butter is already on the market in France under various names, *végétaline* being the most usual.

The *karité* is a tree extremely common in the High Senegal and Niger, and in certain places forms actual forests. It is respected by the blacks, and seems to resist the frequent grass fires. A decree dated July 29th, 1906, by Governor Ponty, of the High Senegal, forbids the destruction of the *karité* trees.

In the High Senegal and Niger, between the parallel of San and the southern frontier, one finds the vine, *gohine,* or *landolphia heudelotii,* which produces the entire quantity of rubber exported from the colony. The *landolphia heudelotii* is chiefly abundant up to the tenth degree of latitude north, fairly common as far as the twelfth degree, and scarce further north. Beyond lat. 13° 4' (or 5') N. the vine is not found at all. Its dissemination is irregular. Even in regions where trees are dense one may sometimes go ten or fifteen miles without seeing one of these vines, and may then come upon localities where hundreds of clusters are found in a limited space.

The principal markets for rubber are Sikasso, Bamako, Buguni and Bobo-Dioulasso. The exportation of rubber, which practically only began in 1899, is to-day one of the most important of local trades. In 1902 two hundred and fifty thousand kilos. were exported. Seven hundred and fifty thousand kilos. were exported in 1904, and seven hundred thousand kilos. during the first eleven months of the year 1906. The preservation of this considerable source of wealth needs safeguarding by a rational exploitation of the country—a difficult problem when you think of the ignorance of the natives and the impatient activity of improvident commercial agents.

The Administration does all in its power to persuade the natives to extend the multiplication of the precious rubber vine artificially. It teaches the best processes of extracting the latex without injuring the plants. Special and strict regulations have been established to prevent fraud or abuses.

Since the year 1902 a practical school has been established at Bobo-Dioulasso in order to teach the natives how they can make a profit by bringing in rubber for sale, as they were previously ignorant of the value of the rubber. This school has been fairly successful notwithstanding the primitive state of the population from which the students are recruited. There were 150 students in 1902, 214 in 1903, and only 150 in 1905. These students, under the direction of a teacher, were sent out into the forest, where practical demonstrations were given to them of how to extract and coagulate the latex. In their turn students have been able to teach what they had learnt to inhabitants of other villages.

Governor Ponty has long had in mind a project of multiplying schools of this kind, and of teaching the natives the cultivation of the rubber vine. Plantations have, in fact, been started at Bobo-Dioulasso, Kulikoro, Bamfora, Sikasso and Buguni. At Bamfora an agricultural station was started in 1904.

Here are some figures from the technical schools

teaching the management of rubber plants, especial
of the *gohine* :

Schools.	Number of Pupils.	Seeds of the *lan dolphia heudelot i*
Principal School of Bamfora......	69	1,800,000
Branch School of Bobo-Dioulasso	150	5,000
Branch School of Sikasso	294	150,000
Branch School of Buguni	200 regular, 1,000 temporary	115,420
Branch School of Kutiala	88	1,200,000

In the neighbourhood of San seventy thousand see
were planted in the *cercle* of Ségu. One hundred a
twenty thousand seeds were planted in the Banin
district.

It was pleasant to find at the school of Bamfora t
students sent over from British Nigeria to study Fren
methods.

The following table shows the progress which h
been made in 1906 :

Schools.	Number of Pupils.	Seeds planted.		Percentage of successfully-grown *Gohin* Vines.
		Gohine.	*Manihot Glaziovii.*	
Principal School of Bamfora	366	220,000	20,000	80 p. 100
Branch School of Bobo-Dioulasso..	940	1,000,000	20,000	70 p. 100
Branch School of Sikasso	324	2,875,000	none	58 p. 100
Branch School of Buguni	{ 400 regular, 2,500 others }	4,800,000	none	63 p. 100
Branch School of Kutiala	47	1,000,000	none	60 p. 100

NOTE.—The number of pupils in this table represents merely the actual num
who assisted in the plantations, and does not represent the total number (about dou
the above figures) who followed the classes in each school.

The *gohine* vine is ready for use when eight or t

years old, and at that age will give an average of about fifty ounces of dry rubber annually.

Experiments have been made at Kulikoro with fifty plants of the *ficus elastica* of a variety from the far east. Up to the present time these plants have done well. From the *Jardin de Nogent,* on the Seine, a collection of plants of *sisal (agave rigida var-sisalana)* and of *furcroya* have been sent to Kulikoro, and Monsieur Vuillet showed me how remarkably vigorous was their growth. Both produce textile fibres much in demand in commerce, and the commercial side of their cultivation is being studied at Kulikoro.

Another plant under observation at Kulikoro—a plant which may become of great importance in the exports of the colony—is the indigenous *bagana* (Bambara name), an acacia described by Guillemin and Perrottet in their *Flore de la Sénégambie,* and named by these authors *Acacia Adamsonii,* in honour of Adamson, the first botanist who explored the Senegal. It is a variety of the *Acacia Arabica* of Wildenow. Under normal conditions a tree from three to four years old gives several kilos. of pods, which, according to the *Laboratoire de recherches cliniques* of the *Jardin de Nogent,* contain as much as forty-five per cent. of an excellent tannin, which, dissolved in water, produces a light yellow dye, and, when mixed with salts of iron, a bluish-black precipitate.

Besides the agricultural school at Kulikoro, the French have established a station for breeding horses and improving the local breeds of cattle, sheep and goats. There are also ostrich and dairy farms and a botanical garden possessing a rich collection of useful indigenous and exotic plants.

Natives interested in any branch of cultivation ca
obtain seeds and plants free from the station, and tuitio
is given them gratis.

With a practical man at the head of the station lik
Monsieur Vuillet, whose devotion to his work know
no bounds, the station will, I think, in a few years, be o
great use in the colony of the High Senegal and Niger.

The Governor's palace in the new capital of Bamako (Upper Senegal-Niger Province).

CHAPTER XXXV.

FROM the Upper Niger to the Upper Senegal, the French have built an excellent railway, without exception the most perfectly engineered and constructed colonial railway I have seen. The line was so well laid that no vibration was felt in the carriages. The station buildings were built in a sensible, practical manner, and at the principal stations the government had put up small but comfortable hotels. At Kulikoro, the terminus of the railway, was a spacious, almost luxurious, hotel (932 feet above sea-level by hypsometrical apparatus).

The distance between Kulikoro and Kayes was 553 kilometres. Well-appointed workshops had been constructed at several points where any repairs could be made to engines and carriages.

Splendid iron bridges had been built over the principal streams. There is no doubt that for work of this kind the French surpass most nations.

The French had two small steam *vedettes* upon the Niger, with accommodation for two passengers each, and they possessed a new vessel, the *Mage*, somewhat larger, with accommodation for some twelve or fourteen first-class passengers, but which often carried as many as fifty or sixty, without counting native passengers.

Although travelling by steamer sounds grander than

travelling by canoe, it was not nearly so pleasant. One gained speed, of course, the *Mage* possessing excellent engines, and for two or three months during high water she could make good runs up the river as far as Kabara. With a few alterations in the river bed and the blasting of a few rocks, she will some day be able to travel at high water as far as Gao, and even further.

I understand that another steamer is being built to be sent out to the Upper Niger. This one, I am told, will have many improvements which will make navigation more comfortable than at present. Commandant Le Blevec, who has been entrusted with the navigation of the Niger, is an able officer, and no doubt will succeed in doing all that is right and practicable in order to establish an easier and faster communication between the coast and Timbuctu in connection with the railway.

With a considerable amount of luck, and if one has special steamers and trains waiting, it is possible to reach Timbuctu from Paris in thirty days, or perhaps even less. But, since when the water was high in the Niger, it was low in the Senegal, it was generally imperative to travel by canoe or barge either up the Niger, or at least for a portion of the Senegal. This made the journey that way from Europe occupy nearer two months than one in most cases.

The Senegal is so well known that it is not worth my while to go into a description of the country.

I left Kulikoro on December 10th and visited Bamako, the future capital of the Upper Niger and Senegal, for the capital is to be shifted from Kayes, where it is now located.

Yellow fever had been so bad in all that region that there seemed to be great uncertainty about trains being

Baobab tree.

despatched to the Senegal. Passenger trains only ran twice a week under ordinary circumstances, but did not run at all when yellow fever prevailed, so passengers, French officers and soldiers returning to their own country, had accumulated along the line for some months, waiting to be conveyed to the coast.

On December 11th, partly, I think, to oblige Mr. Elliot, of the African Association, and myself, a quarantine train was run through. We started off, dozens of people crammed into each carriage, and the carriages screened all round with gauze, so that we should not be stung by mosquitoes, the consequence being that we were suffocated instead by precautionary methods. We were roasted alive during the day with the hot sun striking on the carriage, and no air penetrating through the thick mosquito-netting in which we were enveloped. We travelled through uninteresting, barren country.

We were not allowed to get out of the train at any of the intermediate stations. At Kati, for instance, we stopped a long way from the station, as yellow fever had not subsided. Later, beyond a further station called Kita, where the railway described a great loop, the scenery got a little better. High rocks in horizontal strata were to be seen upon the surrounding mountains. In one place a commotion must have been experienced, at least judging by the huge boulders which were strewn all over the landscape in places where they did not belong.

The train ran in the daytime, but always halted for the night. We left Tokoto the next morning. There were beautiful workshops at that place ; also up-to-date presses for extracting arachide oil, an ice machine and well-appointed warehouses. Any portion of damaged

engines could be replaced here. In fact, one e
which had been damaged in a bridge accident had
practically rebuilt at this place. There were four
buildings, which were supposed to accommodate
people.

Many *baobab* trees (the *Adamsonia digitata*) were
to be seen all over the landscape. From Bag
began a most interesting series of huge rocks ;
rently eroded by the action of water into all sor
fantastic shapes, some like gigantic towers upon a cc
base. On one side of us as we steamed on were
pressive masses of red and black rock. There w
fine steel bridge at Mahina.

In the first-class compartment, which was just
enough to hold six, there were no less than fou
passengers, all very jolly and pleasant. One of
officers had purchased a lot of bananas and other
of which he ate more than he should. A bottl
cherries in rum was then opened and handed roun
all the passengers. We all took some, and as I am
accustomed to alcohol, I fell fast asleep. Half an
later I awoke on hearing moans. The French o
who had eaten the fruit was lying in front of me
face almost unrecognizable. It had become a gh
greenish-yellow, with livid eyes and lips. He was (
plaining of suffocation. He had torn his collar.
neck had become much swollen, and his stomach
visibly swelling. The skin of his body had become
bilious lemon yellow. We all knew what it meant.
was seized with sickness and ejected deadly-looking b
matter. There was no excitement in the carriage.
heat was stifling, and the stench from the sick man
bearable. We travelled eight hours longer, until

St. Louis, Senegal.

night we fortunately reached Kayes (113 feet above
sea-level by hypsometrical apparatus), the present
capital of the Upper Senegal, where another surprise
awaited us.

DISTANCES ON THE KAYES–KULIKORO RAILROAD.

Kayes	to	Medine	..	..	..	..	12 kilometres
,,	,,	Malima	..	..	..	..	116
	,,	Tokoto	..	..	..	..	239
	,,	Kita	..	..	..	..	310
	,,	Nafadie	..	..	..	..	404
	,,	Kati	..	..	..	..	481
	,,	Bamako	..	..	..	..	496
,,	,,	Kulikoro	..	..	..	..	553 ,,

The yellow fever patient was at once removed in a
dying condition to the hospital, and all the other passengers were informed that they would be kept under
observation for thirteen days, it having been calculated
that thirteen days before a mosquito should have—if it
had not—stung this man. It so happened that where
we were thirteen days before we never saw any mosquitoes, but whether there were mosquitoes or not, science
said that he had been stung by one which had given
him yellow fever, and we all had to go and show our
tongues and have our pulses felt twice a day to make
sure that we should not develop the disease.

Dr. Gouzien, a magnificent physician, the discoverer
of the only safe cure for black-water fever by subcutaneous injections of salt, was extremely kind and
certainly made the quarantine days quite delightful
with his charming and interesting hospitality during the
time I was at Kayes.

In the Grand Hotel—for Kayes possessed a Grand
Hotel—we found a thoughtful proprietor and really
excellent food. I tried to pass the days as pleasantly as

possible, the younger French officials and officers be:
extraordinarily lively and amusing. Grand opera a
concerts, with but a single musical instrument in 1
place, were heard every night in the hotel, some of 1
improvised parodies of operas performed by the youn;
officials being extremely witty and amusing.

There were many merchants at Kayes—Dutch a
French, and French firms with English capital. Gove
ment tramways had been laid between the hig
plateau, on which the Government buildings and offi
had been erected, and the commercial town. Th
was a long drive along the Senegal, but my first
perience of walking along this drive was not a ha]
one. A man, having discovered a snake in his hou
fired several shots with a Lebel rifle in our directior
I was strolling with a friend. The reptile and we
narrow escapes.

I took an opportunity of visiting the Felu Fi
about eight hundred feet wide and forty-five to fifty
high among the giant rocks of an extensive rocky plate
The upper and larger fall was in two tiers, with
immense stretch of innumerable perforations in the ro
and natural stone bridges with blackened walls. Th
perforations appeared to have been caused by volca
action and increased by erosion of water. Bei
reaching the falls was an immense stretch of c
glomerate rock for several miles, especially on the no
side of the river.

The delay owing to the quarantine had evil c
sequences. The Senegal river was getting lower a
lower, and the small *monoroue* steamers (why cal
monoroue I do not know, as they possess two st
wheels) were now unable to come up as far as Ka\

It was a question for speculation whether they could even reach Bakel, further down-stream. This would involve going down the river at least for some distance in a barge.

This portion of the country was civilized. My provisions and clothes had come to an end, and there remained no more work for me. I was, therefore, anxious to reach the coast as soon as possible.

When the quarantine was over, I left Kayes by barge, a convoy of French officers and three missionaries also coming down the river. There was nothing of interest along the stream. Many of the villages had been washed away by the heavy flood which had also swamped the commercial portion of the town of Kayes and destroyed thousands of pounds of merchandise.

Bakel, with its fort and block-houses, built in 1861, was interesting historically. Obsolete but serviceable Creuzot guns stood at the entrance of the *Administrateur's* house. The village was partly on a hill, where the former residency stood, partly along the bank of the Senegal. The inhabitants were Bambara, Saracolle and Tukuler.

It was amusing to see at this place, where we fortunately found the *monoroue* waiting for us, black men carrying coal to the ship, each block wrapped up in a piece of paper so as not to get their hands and clothes dirty. Needless to say, coaling on such principles took endless time.

We eventually steamed down on the little *monoroue*, with accommodation for four or six passengers, one cabin only, but no washstands and most primitive sanitary arrangements. She carried some eighty passengers, with mountains of baggage, several hundred sacks of grain and some tons of rubber, which filled all the lower deck.

There was no room to turn round. Worse luck, two much-exhausted Sisters of Mercy were also travelling on the boat, and one of them was seized with yellow fever.

At Matam there were square mud huts with thatched roofs and stockades of wood and thorns in which the natives kept their cattle. The filthy streets were not even straight, and the greatest disorder prevailed in the place.

At Gueal further down we saw, in a picturesque spot upon a height, what had been formerly a British fort, with big rocks of burnt-sienna colour behind it, and a plateau. The fort covered the elbow of the river where it was extremely tortuous, some miles before arriving at Kaiddi. When we first perceived Kaiddi the white fort was prominent against the greyish haze on the distant horizon-line.

Kaiddi was strongly protected, as there was a main route from there to Mauritania. Considerable trouble was being given to the French by the natives at the time of my visit, and a Moorish attack was feared. The post stood on a height. On the river bank was to be seen the wreck of a steamer. Big steamers can travel up the Senegal as far as Kayes during the high flood.

The river was tortuous and narrow between Kaiddi and Salde, and not more than seventy to eighty yards wide. Tobacco, cotton and maize were raised in quantities. Villages were scattered here and there, and as we went along boys ran along the banks calling out for empty bottles, which were in great demand in this country.

The climate was damp and the days gloomy, with dark, heavy, grey clouds overhead as we were going towards the sea.

The poor Sister of Mercy was by now in a dying condition. It was tragic to see this little thing, only twenty-two or twenty-three years of age, a martyr to her work, suffering courageously, while the military doctor made injections of salt under her skin, a process causing considerable pain to the patient. She behaved bravely. Never a murmur of complaint was heard from her lips. I have seen few men who could stand pain unflinchingly like this poor little woman. Her nun companion was preparing her for the other world and often knelt by her side praying. The patient, when not delirious, said, in a faint voice, that she was quite resigned, happy, very happy, to pass away and be with God. She remained thus between life and death.

Our next excitement was when we ran down a canoe during the night.

The cold seemed intense to us as we were approaching the coast, a piercing wind making the French shiver all over. It was amusing to see them wrapped in heavy overcoats with collars turned up.

At Podor, where we arrived on December 22nd, I changed from the *monoroue Sikasso* to a larger steamer, the *Borgnis Désordès*, an excellently-managed boat, extremely comfortable—almost luxurious. In this boat, travelling at a good speed, I arrived at St. Louis at the mouth of the Senegal, on the 16th degree of lat. N., two days later.

St. Louis, like all the larger stations upon the Senegal, had a strong Spanish look about it. It was a charming little town, with neat streets lined with houses and verandahs in regular Spanish colonial style.

Beautiful waterworks had been made near the city, at Khor, three kilometres away, where two engines worked intermittently under a well-constructed stone shed. There were four filters and two reservoirs, the water being conveyed by an iron tube from Makhana, eighteen kilometres from St. Louis. Fresh water filled a channel during the rainy season, and when at its highest the outlet was closed so as to prevent sea-water coming in. It then formed a capacious reservoir, although the evaporation, owing to the heat of the sun and the easterly winds, was considerable, not less than seven millimetres during the dry season.

Governor Guy, of the Senegal, and Monsieur Ponty, the Governor of the High Senegal and Niger, whom I had the pleasure of meeting here, as well as Monsieur Repiquet, showed me unbounded civility and furnished me with valuable information about that colony, which I propose to use in a separate work. It was a pleasure to see on what sensible lines the colony was conducted, and how well the natives were kept in hand.

Perhaps the civilized natives were not so attractive to me as the uncivilized ones. With few exceptions, the half-castes were less attractive still.

I was in St. Louis at Christmas and on New Year's Day. The whole native town (including half-castes), all christianized in that region, were parading the streets from early morning till late at night, dragging paper ships, towers and fantastic lanterns. Dressed up in their best clothes, they strolled about lazily, dragging their feet, and chanting. Those who were not pulling the cart on which paper transparencies were displayed

Governor Guy
of the
Senegal.

Governor Ponty
of the
High Senegal-Niger.

carried a lantern or a lighted candle in their hands. Days and days were thus occupied.

The natives and half-castes were conceited, even supercilious. I remember asking a man whether he was a French "subject," or a British subject from Sierra Leone. His offended answer was : "*Moi, pas 'sujet,' moi ' citoyen,' la même chose que blanc* " Some of these men were impudent, and even when walking on the pavement I have seen white ladies obliged to step into the street to let these fellows go by. The French have been too good to these blacks in allowing them to have the same privileges as white people, for which they showed little gratitude.

As St. Louis was not absolutely the most westerly point of Africa, I continued my journey to Cape Verde by the excellent little coast railway between St. Louis and Dakar. Dakar is a most important point, being the capital of the entire French Sudan. A magnificent palace is being built for the Governor at the cost of a great many millions. Perhaps to a man coming from Central Africa it appeared outwardly more like a magnificent opera-house than a suitable colonial residence, but on visiting the inside one could not help being impressed by the princely arrangements which had been made in the future home of the Governor.

More important than this, however, were the beautiful harbour works which were made at that place by the French and which rendered Dakar a safe and deep anchorage. Long artificial piers projected into the sea, and elaborate docks on the latest and most scientific principles were being constructed.

When I visited Dakar it appeared like a gigantic workshop, as all the works were progressing well, but were not finished. In a few years, undoubtedly, Dakar will be the finest city on the west coast of Africa. A railway will branch off from Thies, near Dakar, towards the interior, and I understand that there is a project of building a line between Thies and Kayes. This would avoid the uncertain navigation of the Senegal river, and would shorten the distance to Timbuctu by many days, besides opening up the rich country between.

TELEGRAPHIC LINES IN USE IN WEST AFRICAN FRENCH POSSESSIONS.

1. Saint Louis—Dakar.
2. Dakar—Ambidédi, via Joal, Kaolakh, Maka—Kolibentan.
3. Tivaonane—Foundiougne.
4. Dakar—Carabone, via Kaolakh, Maka—Kolibentan and Sedhian.
5. Dakar—Konakry, via Konakry Maka—Kolibentan—Boké—Boffa and Dubréka.
6. Dakar—Timbuctu, via Kayes—Bamako—Sokoto and Niafunké.
7. Badoumbé to Sokoto, via Nioro and Goumbou.
8. Ségu—Niamey, via San—Bandiagara and Dori.
9. San—Driapaga, via Koury—Anagadougou and Fada—N'Gourna.
10. Sikasso and Bobo—Dioudassou.
11. Sikasso—Koroko.
12. Konakry—Kita, via Kindia—Timbo—Kouroussa—Kam-Kan and Sigouri.
13. Dubréka—Farmoréa.
14. Timbo—Labé.
15. Konakry—Beyla, via Kindra Farama and Kissidougou.
16. Bingerville—Tabu.
17. Bingerville—Bobo—Diubasso, via Koniadiokofi or Boudoukou.
18. Bingerville—Aboisso.
19. Porto-Novo—Niamey, via Zagnadado—Savalou—Djougou and Say.
20. Porto-Novo—Say, via Zagnado—Savadou—Sarakou—Kandi.
21. Zagnado—Abomey.
22. Porto-Novo—Agaone.
23. Carnorville—Djugu.

A projected line from Niamey to Zinder is under consideration.

The Governor's new palace at Dakar.

The Congo net comprises :

1. A line from Libreville to Brazzaville, *viâ* Cap Lopez Serté—Cama—Mayoumba—Loango—Loudima—Madingou and Comba.
2. Libreville to N'Djoé.
3. Loango to Massabé.
4. Sub-fluvial cable from Brazzaville to Kuichassa.
5. A line from Liranga to Desbordeville, which will eventually extend from Brazzaville to Fort Archambault, *viâ* Bangui—Fort Possel and Fort Crampel.

I have not sufficient space in this work to deal with the commerce and general development of this region. I will merely take the reader the few kilometres which separate Dakar from Cape Verde, where, in the company of Monsieur Belondrade, who was in charge, I inspected the " Phare des Mamelles," the light being three hundred and forty feet above the sea and visible thirty-two geographical miles at sea. The lighthouse was provided with two French keepers and two natives, and had a semaphoric signalling station. It gave flashes every thirty seconds. The Mamelles were ten kilometres west of Dakar.

Five kilometres further towards the most westerly angle forming the last point of Africa in the Atlantic Ocean was the *phare* of the Almadies, a small lighthouse with a fixed light, seventy-two feet above the sea, showing red flashes every thirty seconds, and only visible nine miles at sea.

The rocks beyond Cape Verde extended for two miles and a half just under the surface of the water. I climbed on to the very last rock of Cape Verde—and nearly slipped into the sea—so that there should be no mistake about my having reached the most westerly point of Africa. Thus ended at this place, on January 5th, 1907, the longest trans-African journey which has ever been taken from east to west.

At this point—I might as well tell what a sober man I had been—I drank in the company of the French gentleman who accompanied me the only two bottles of champagne which I had carried the entire way across Africa. Except the cherries in rum, with our friend with yellow fever in the train, this was the only stimulant I had taken during the last twelve months, and it was done to drink the success of the journey, and not because I needed it.

The entire journey from Djibuti, where I had started on January 6th, 1906, to this place had taken 364 days, the distance covered being no less than 8,500 miles. I had arrived in flourishing health, and although glad to return to Europe and to my friends, I was indeed sorry that so delightful a journey had ended.

FINIS.

Cape Verde, where Author ended his journey.
The rocks represented in this photograph are the most westerly of the African Continent).

INDEX

INDEX

ABESHER, ii. 272.
Abigar tribe, the, i. 255, 256, 257, 261.
Ablutions, i. 100.
Abu Bakir Basha, i. 34.
Abuk tribe, the, i. 341.
Abuna, the, i. 75, 105.
Abu Shakka, i. 344, 349.
Abwong, i. 273, 289, 290.
Abyssinia, Administration of, i. 77 ; the climate of, i. 126 ; the bank of, i. 26, 130–135 ; politically, i. 76–84, 118–125.
Abyssinia, Western, commercial possibilities of, i. 20.
Abyssinian custom-houses, i. 57, 64, 155, 161, 206 ; exports and imports, i. 4, 27, 218 ; justice, i. 78, 134 ; marriages, i. 110 ; priests, i. 74, 116 ; soldiers, i. 15, 34, 38, 41, 45, 54, 60, 73, 82, 99, 137, 156, 163, 186, 205 ; weather, i. 134.
Abyssinians, i. 27, 56, 59, 123, 151, 169, 171, 191, 277, 290.
Adde Galla, i. 10, 14.
Addis-Jebbo, i. 170.
Adis-Ababa, i. 47, 70, 71 ; British Legation, i. 71 ; hotel in, i. 71 ; imperial palace, i. 91 ; official buildings in, i. 91, Russian Legation, i. 71.
Adis-Alem, i. 105, 137.
Adjira tribe, the, i. 268.
Afuk tribe, the, i. 341.
Agafars Indeilalo (Vice-Governor of Gori), i. 193.
Agricultural stations, ii. 471, 477.

Agriculture, i. 62, 112, 134, 141, 159, 182, 189, 313, 315, 356 ; ii. 177, 134, 185, 213, 275, 276, 303, 323, 386, 388, 392, 413, 466–480, 488.
Aguok tribe, the, i. 341.
Ahmadu's empire, ii. 441.
Aiuti, Capt., ii. 133.
Aiwal tribe, the, i. 273, 276, 280.
Ajah tribe, the, i. 374, 383, 385.
Albinoes, ii. 122.
Algeria, ii. 303, 314.
Ali Effendi Wahbi, i. 372, 376.
Ali Sabieh, i. 14.
Ali Zaki Yonobashi, i. 289.
Allush tribe, the, ii. 445.
Ambatch wood, i. 292, 306, 314, 319 ; ii. 218, 229, 279.
America, i. 124.
Amien, i. 325.
Ancestral worship, i. 310.
Anchorages, i. 6.
Aniar tribe, the, i. 341.
Annamites, ii. 63.
Antelopes, ii. 20, 23, 31.
Anthills, i. 301.
Anuak tribe, the, i. 247, 276, 302, 308.
Arab influence, ii. 187, 193, 208.
Arabs, i. 8, 17, 24, 27 ; ii. 4, 26, 29, 50, 58, 61, 82, 129, 158, 216, 256, 262, 273, 315, 318, 394, 409.
Argaga, i. 47.
Arma tribe, the, ii. 394, 409, 441.
Armanxopoulo, Mr. Timoleon, i. 191.
Armenians, i. 17.

Dunzo, ii. 383.
Duveyrier, ii. 267, 270, 329, 345.

Eagles, i. 316.
Ebback tribe, the, ii. 391.
Eclipses, ii. 346.
Egypt, i. 120 ; ii. 262, 271, 376, 388, 459 ; irrigation of, i. 298.
Egyptian influence, i. 69, 113.
Electricity, i. 361.
Elephantiasis, i. 108.
Elephants, i. 216, 229, 258 ; ii. 10, 13, 20, 62, 76, 191.
Elevations, i. 11, 16, 20, 21, 22, 27, 40, 44, 45, 47, 49, 52, 54, 56, 58, 62, 63, 66, 69, 70, 116, 139, 141, 142, 146, 147, 149, 153, 155, 156, 158, 159, 160, 162, 163, 167, 169, 172, 174, 178, 179, 180, 181, 182, 183, 184, 189, 190, 191, 196, 197, 206, 215, 241, 290, 339, 355, 358, 362, 363, 364, 365, 366, 367, 372 ; ii. 3, 4, 7, 8, 10, 11, 16, 24, 25, 27, 28, 33, 35, 36, 37, 51, 52, 54, 83, 111, 117, 132, 150, 165, 167, 168, 169, 173, 175, 185, 186, 190, 201, 250, 251, 255, 258, 280, 285, 296, 298, 299, 304, 314, 322, 324, 363, 364, 367, 370, 372, 373, 381, 404, 421, 422, 462, 481.
Ella Balla, i. 43.
Elliott, Mr., of the African Association, ii. 459, 483.
Emaka tribe, the, ii. 391.
Emdoco (or Endogo) tribe, the, i. 355, 373, 378.
Ennedi tribe, the, ii. 270.
Epiphany, the, i. 100.
Erroneous ideas of Europeans, i. 116.
Escarpments, i. 49, 62, 200, 207.
Espionage, ii. 25, 65.
Es-Souk, ii. 328.
Ethiopian railway, i. 8, 12–16, 80, 118.
Euphorbia candelabrum, the, i. 20, 139, 183, 320.

Evil eye, the, i. 103, 105, 311 ; ii. 263.
Excavations, i. 67.

Fabre, Lieut., ii. 376.
Fallanghes, the, i. 272.
Falli tribe, the, i. 341.
Family affection, i. 112.
Fellah, the, i. 306.
Felu falls, the, ii. 486.
Ferogheh tribe, the, i. 373, 375, 383.
Ferruginous rock, i. 325, 351, 361 ; ii. 308.
Fetishes, ii. 230.
Finda, ii. 183.
Firearms, i. 4.
Fire cure, i. 285 ; ii. 128.
Fire lighting by friction, i. 284 ; ii. 54.
Fishing, i. 248, 253, 314 ; ii. 117, 150.
Fishing harpoons, i. 257, 269, 307.
Fitaurari Apti Gorghis, i. 113.
Forest, i. 139, 141, 147, 190.
Fort Archambault, ii. 158, 186, 187, 188, 190.
Fort Bonnier, ii. 404.
Fort Bretonnet. See Busso.
Fort Crampel (Grebanghi), ii. 157, 176, 177, 182.
Fort Kusseri, ii., 210, 211.
Fort Lamy, ii. 205, 208, 210.
Fort Possel, ii. 155, 165.
Fort Sibut (or Krebadje), ii. 157, 166, 169, 171.
Fortifications, i. 135, 353.
Forts, ii. 207, 255 : British, i. 23 ; French, i. 14.
Fossils, ii. 307, 423.
Four tribe, the, i. 374.
Fourcade, Lieut., ii. 372.
Foureau, ii. 314.
France, i. 119, 124.
Franco-German Delimitation Commission, ii. 194.
French, the, i. 17, 76, 340, 372 ; ii. 192, 411, 425.
French Congo, i. 288 ; ii. 1.

French Congo boundary, the, i.
373 ; able-bodied men and
rifles possessed by sultans on
the, i. 378–379.
Frenchmen, i. 53.
French Somaliland, i. 5, 119.
Freydenberg, Lieut., ii. 221, 241,
245.
Fulbe tribe, the, ii. 376, 394, 395,
398, 409, 441, 454, 459, 460.
Fulconis, Dr., ii. 82, 86.
Funclunia elastica, the, ii. 122,
151.
Funerals, i. 101, 226, 282, 381,
388 ; ii. 129, 147, 159, 227,
264–265, 352.
Furumeh tribe, the, i. 341.

GABIBI tribe, the, ii. 455.
Gabu tribe, the, ii. 27, 39, 42.
Gaden, Commandant, ii. 207, 315,
319.
Gaetani, Don Livio, i. 128.
Gaji, i. 183.
Galla, the, i. 8, 11, 19, 22, 27,
47, 56, 66, 70, 76, 112, 120,
122, 138, 140, 142, 148, 154,
159, 164, 181, 188, 197, 208,
263, 320.
Gambela, i. 200, 215, 217, 221.
Gambu, ii. 101.
Ganapia, ii. 101.
Gao, ii. 375, 389, 391, 449.
Garstin, Sir William, i. 298.
Gauckler, Lieut., ii. 252, 259,
274, 282.
Gazelles, i. 43.
Gentil, Monsieur, ii. 177, 205, 208,
315.
German Cameroon, ii. 165, 194,
201–216 ; Sultans in, ii. 213.
German commercial travellers, i.
13.
German machinery, i. 134.
Germans, i. 16, 20, 32, 206 ; ii.
199, 244, 271.
Germany, i. 124.
Gerolimato, Mr. John, i. 24, 28,
121, 201.
Ghedebursi (or Gadabursi) tribe,
the, i. 7, 46.

Gherar trees, i. 146, 154, 180,
185, 270, 277, 299, 331.
Ghosts and evil spirits, i. 104,
282 ; ii. 70, 160, 180.
Giants, ii. 330.
Giraffes, i. 216, 229, 275, 329,
334 ; ii. 9.
Goba, monastery of, i. 66.
Godart, Lieut., ii. 255.
Godjam district, the, i. 70, 111,
220.
Godoburkha, i. 62.
Gogognar, i. 271.
Gold, i. 122, 134, 208, 297 ; ii.
396.
Goldie, Mr. H. M., i. 27.
Golo characteristics, i. 348 ; hair
dresses, i. 345 ; huts, i. 345 ;
tribe, the, i. 344, 355, 356,
373 ; ii. 39.
Golu tribe, the, ii. 157.
Gombi tribe, the, ii. 134.
Gomma, i. 206.
Gourselik, ii. 302.
Gonda, the, i. 111.
Gondokoro, i. 298.
Gongufema, ii. 266.
Good Hope, Cape of, ii. 62.
Goraki language, the, i. 113 ;
marriages, i. 113.
Goraki (or Guraghi) tribe, the, i.
70, 112.
Gori, i. 140, 187, 191, 201.
Gouraud, Colonel, ii. 206, 272,
319, 447.
Gouri, ii. 300, 301, 302, 304,
309.
Gouzien, Dr. ii. 485.
Governors, i. 16, 24, 25, 192 ; ii.
477, 490.
Gozobanghi, ii. 114.
Gras cartridges, i. 5, 59, 149, 185 ;
rifles, i. 25, 38, 73 ; ii. 26,
27, 95.
Graves, i. 56, 58, 69, 154, 162,
181, 197, 345 ; ii. 231 ; General
Gatacre's, i. 227.
Great Britain, i. 119, 124.
Grebangui, ii. 183.
Greeks, i. 16, 24, 65, 191, 200,
218, 220, 227, 323, 339.

Gubbera, Chief, ii. 37.
Guidam Bado, ii. 361.
Guinea-fowl, i. 315.
Guinea-worm, ii. 351.
Gulfei, ii. 214.
Gurgura tribe, the, i. 35, 46.
Guy, Governor, of the Senegal, ii. 490.

HABEREUAL tribe, the, i. 7, 46.
Habitations, architecture of, i. 144, 237, 238, 259, 263, 266, 270, 274, 318, 327, 345, 352, 386, 387 ; ii. 71, 74, 95, 202, 252, 368, 379, 428, 459, 464.
Haddad tribe, the, ii. 221, 227, 235.
Hair-dresses, i. 22, 25, 101, 117, 140, 155, 165, 167, 186, 198, 233, 235, 242, 245, 248, 308, 326, 345, 348, 385 ; ii. 34, 119, 130, 144, 168, 353, 428.
Hallucinations, ii. 345.
Hamdan Effendi, i. 264.
Hardellet, Lieut., i. 221.
Harem, Sultan of Bongasso's, ii. 94.
Harnattan (wind), ii. 241, 243.
Harrar, i. 10, 19, 47, 133.
Harrington, Sir John, i. 72, 74, 85, 87, 89, 127, 128, 130, 133.
Hartebeest, ii. 20.
Haussa saddles, ii. 323 ; tribe, ii. 196, 224, 285, 315, 321, 324, 365, 370, 388.
Hawks, i. 21.
Hawuya tribe, the, i. 39, 44, 46.
Headgears, i. 36, 98, 117, 173, 199.
Heredity, ii. 41, 234, 235.
Hermits, i. 70.
Herons, i. 258.
Herrer, i. 121.
Hides, i. 201.
High Senegal and Niger, ii. 469 ; population of, ii. 470.
High Ubanghi, ii. 1, 64.
Higlig, i. 333.
Hindu, i. 8, 17, 25, 27, 31.
Hippopotami, i. 161, 209, 215, 259, 265, 314 ; ii. 31, 77, 185, 201.

Hofrat-el-Nahas, i. 373.
Hoggar tribe, the, ii. 448, 449.
Honko, ii. 202.
Hotels, i. 5.
Hot springs, i. 139 ; ii. 272.
Hourst, Lieut., ii. 448.
Hunger, relief from, i. 285.
Hunting expeditions, i. 286, 292 ; ii. 71, 181.
Hydromel, i. 29.
Hyenas, i. 40, 53, 216.
Hypnotism, ii. 144.

ICE factories, i. 7.
Ideni, i. 227, 234.
Idols, ii. 148.
Iguaddaren tribe, the, ii. 398, 445, 449.
Iguellad tribes, the, ii. 445
Ilg, Mr. (Councillor of State), i. 74, 126.
Ilimidden tribe, the, ii. 445.
Illnesses, i. 104, 108, 148, 162, 176, 180, 184, 198, 229, 238, 277, 278, 284, 285, 295 ; ii. 141, 160, 189, 263, 337, 348, 349, 376, 389, 482, 488.
Imbert, M. Paul, ii. 442.
Implements, i. 7, 274, 344 ; stone and flint, ii. 390, 395, 456.
Inedreden tribe, the, ii. 445.
Inkari tribe, the, ii. 391.
Intoxicants, i. 37, 95, 193, 283 ; ii. 75, 85.
Inuellen tribe, the, ii. 391.
Inundations, ii. 403, 413, 454.
Invasions, ii. 394.
Irena, ii. 184.
Irikassa, ii. 112.
Irregenaten tribe, the, ii. 398, 445.
Islamic movement, ii. 207.
Islands, floating, i. 300.
Issa, the, i. 7, 27, 46.
Italians, i. 128, 340 ; ii. 132, 133, 134, 135.
Italy, i. 119.
Itang, i. 216.
Ito tribe, the, i. 46.
Ivory, i. 114, 134, 135, 216, 220, 245, 323, 372, 375 ; ii. 3, 29, 65, 115, 139, 151.

Printed at The Chapel River Press, Kingston, Surrey.

In 1 vol., royal 8vo, with numerous Illustrations from Photographs taken especially for this book. Price 21s. net.

Porfirio Diaz,
Seven Times President of Mexico.

By Mrs. ALEC TWEEDIE, Author of "Mexico, as I Saw It," &c.

Folk Tales from Tibet.

By CAPTAIN W. F. T. O'CONNOR, Secretary and Interpreter to the Tibet Expedition. In one vol., 4to, with twelve Illustrations in colour, reproduced from Paintings by a native Tibetan Artist. Price 6s. net.

"Here is a delightful new picture story-book to give to a girl or boy at Christmas."
—*The Spectator.*

Second Edition, in 1 vol., crown 8vo, with numerous Illustrations. Price 6s. net.

Six Years at the Russian Court.

Personal Experiences. By M. EAGAR.

Tales of Old Sicily.

By the HON. ALEXANDER NELSON HOOD, Author of "Adria: A Tale of Venice," &c. One vol. Price 6s.

"The originality of this book is not its least charm ; it is a scholarly mingling of history and fiction in which fiction is subordinated to the historical fact."—*Morning Post.*
"A book which, in its balanced dignity, its lack of all vulgar sensationalism, its real feeling, and its occasional sober beauty, is a refreshing contrast to the hasty and gaudy efforts which so often in these days tout for the applause of the crowd." *Westminster Gazette.*

Celebrated Crimes of the Russian Court.

By ALEXANDRE DUMAS. With numerous Portraits. Demy 8vo, cloth, gilt top. Price 6s. net.

"Nobody would look to Dumas for strictly accurate history, but as a series of powerful moving tales founded on the crimes and cruelties of the Russian Court the book is well worth reading."—*Truth.*
"There will doubtless be found even at the present day plenty of readers for these entertaining Russian romances in their English version."—*Daily Telegraph.*

CPSIA information can be obtained at www.ICGtesting.com
Printed in the USA
BVOW06s2155090815

412549BV00020B/460/P